The Politics of the Pill

The Politics of the Pill

*Gender, Framing, and Policymaking
in the Battle over Birth Control*

RACHEL VANSICKLE-WARD
and
KEVIN WALLSTEN

OXFORD
UNIVERSITY PRESS

OXFORD
UNIVERSITY PRESS

Oxford University Press is a department of the University of Oxford. It furthers
the University's objective of excellence in research, scholarship, and education
by publishing worldwide. Oxford is a registered trade mark of Oxford University
Press in the UK and certain other countries.

Published in the United States of America by Oxford University Press
198 Madison Avenue, New York, NY 10016, United States of America.

© Oxford University Press 2019

All rights reserved. No part of this publication may be reproduced, stored in
a retrieval system, or transmitted, in any form or by any means, without the
prior permission in writing of Oxford University Press, or as expressly permitted
by law, by license, or under terms agreed with the appropriate reproduction
rights organization. Inquiries concerning reproduction outside the scope of the
above should be sent to the Rights Department, Oxford University Press, at the
address above.

You must not circulate this work in any other form
and you must impose this same condition on any acquirer.

Library of Congress Cataloging-in-Publication Data
Names: VanSickle-Ward, Rachel, 1977– author | Wallsten, Kevin, author.
Title: The politics of the pill : gender, framing and policymaking in the
battle over birth control / Rachel VanSickle-Ward, Professor of Political
Studies, Pitzer College, Kevin Wallsten, Associate Professor of Political
Science California State University, Long Beach.
Description: New York, NY : Oxford University Press, [2019]
Identifiers: LCCN 2019017401 | ISBN 9780190675349 (hardback) |
ISBN 9780190675356 (pbk.) | ISBN 9780190675363 (pdf) |
ISBN 9780190675370 (epub) | ISBN 9780190909536 (online)
Subjects: LCSH: Birth control—Government policy—United States. |
Birth control—Law and legislation—United States. |
Reproductive rights—Political aspects—United States.
Classification: LCC HQ766.5.U5 V32 2019 | DDC 363.9/60973—dc23
LC record available at https://lccn.loc.gov/2019017401

1 3 5 7 9 8 6 4 2

Paperback printed by Marquis, Canada
Hardback printed by Bridgeport National Bindery, Inc., United States of America

For Neil, Gabriel and Rebecca

—RVW

For Kate and Emma

—KW

CONTENTS

Acknowledgments ix

1. Introduction: Where are the Women? 1

PART I POLICY

2. The History of the Pill 25
3. Contraception Coverage Policy in the States 39
4. Contraception Coverage Policy in Congress 62
5. Contraception Coverage in the Courts 84

PART II MEDIA AND PUBLIC OPINION

6. Media Sourcing 105
7. Media Frames 129
8. Public Opinion 150
9. Experiment: Frames and Public Opinion 182
10. The Politics of the Pill: Looking Forward 213

Appendices 229
Notes 241
Works Cited 249
Index 279

ACKNOWLEDGMENTS

We are deeply grateful for the many people who made this book possible. Special thanks to the students of the Fall 2012 Battle over Birth Control scholar in residence seminar, where we first developed some of the key ideas for this book: Shiyana Gunasekara. Jared Calvert, Claire Courtney, Lisi Kent-Isaac, Rachel Kipnes, Maria Krol-Sinclair, Aidan Lukomnik, Leora Paradise, Ruth Sampson, Mayte Sanchez, Jenna Florio, Jenna Slate, Gabriel Villarreal, Nicholas Weinmeister, and Michael Miller. Many other talented students have contributed as research assistants and/or seminar participants over the years, including Taliah Mancini, Rachel Bolton, Miriam Stiefel, Alison Lipman, and Anna Nichols. Their insights and assistance made this book stronger, and are sincerely appreciated.

Two students in particular bookended this volume and deserve special mention. Shiyana Gunasekara helped launch this project including co-authoring a conference paper that served as the springboard for chapter 7. Dana Nothnagel saw the book through to completion, doing heavy lifting on the coding for chapters 4 and 5 and on citations. Both students helped develop the coding schemes, steeped themselves in the literature on the topic, performed countless hours on data collection and content analysis, and asked important questions and offered feedback that sharpened our thinking and improved the work overall. Throughout they were curious, meticulous, positive, and passionate about the project. Their contributions cannot be overstated. We can't imagine writing this book without them, and we are profoundly thankful for their brilliance and dedication.

We are also indebted to a number of our colleagues, and to the anonymous reviewers of the manuscript. Amanda Hollis-Brusky gave thoughtful feedback on chapter 5 and also generously allowed for brief excerpts of an earlier co-authored paper to be included in this work (VanSickle-Ward and Hollis-Brusky 2013). Josh Wilson and Megan Mullin were shrewd sounding boards as the project developed, Lisa Marley recommended helpful sources, Jenn Merolla and Chuck Shipan offered excellent counsel on the book prospectus, and Leanne Powner provided helpful comments on an early draft. Tatishe Nteta, Cora Goldstein, Kathy Yep, Brinda Sarathy, Emma Stephens, and Adrian Pantoja provided intellectual and moral support. Jill Greenlee and Erin Cassese provided extensive, detailed, and astute suggestions on the manuscript as a whole and the final product was considerably improved by their advice. Any errors that remain are of course ours alone.

We have been fortunate to present sections of this work at a number of conferences and invited talks hosted by the Western Political Science Association, the Midwest Political Science Association, the State Politics and Policy Section, The Southern California Law and Social Science forum, Resisting Women's Political Leadership: Theory Data and Solutions, and The National Women's Political Caucus. We are grateful for comments and suggestions from discussants and audience members at these events, and to the conference organizers who made them possible. A number of thoughtful interview subjects took time out of their busy schedules to speak with us for this project, and their reflections were truly invaluable. We want to particularly thank Susan Wood and Mona Shah whose early guidance was of great help.

Our thanks also go to our editorial team at Oxford University Press. Dave McBride's early enthusiasm for the project never wavered, and Emily Mackenzie graciously shepherded us through the production process (along with Asish Krishna and Leslie Johnson). We are further grateful to institutional support provided by Pitzer College and Cal State Long Beach.

Finally, and most importantly, we are tremendously grateful to our families for their support and encouragement. Of special note, Rachel is deeply grateful to Gabriel and Rebecca, who bring joy, love, and laughter to each day, and to Neil, who supports and inspires her in every possible way, and who wisely didn't believe her when she said her previous book was her last. And Kevin is eternally grateful to Kate, whose warmth, wisdom, and wit have carried him through the challenges of this book (as well as much else) and to Emma, whose arrival finally made him realize that he was doing something right after all.

1

Introduction: Where Are the Women?

On August 1, 2011, the Department of Health and Human Services (HHS) announced a new set of guidelines for implementing the preventative care portions of the 2010 Affordable Care Act (ACA). Given what was to come, there was surprisingly little public controversy in the immediate wake of this announcement. Women's health advocates across the country lauded the new policy. Prominent organizations such as the American Civil Liberties Union (ACLU) and Planned Parenthood, for example, issued press releases calling the rule "monumental for millions of women" and "a historic victory for women's health." Republican lawmakers and religious leaders, of course, did not share this enthusiasm. Signaling their opposition to HHS's decision, congressional Republicans organized First Amendment–themed hearings (such as the House Judiciary Committee Subcommittee on the Constitution's "State of Religious Liberty" panel) and introduced symbolic bills implying government overreach (such as the August 2011 "Respect for Conscience Act of 2011").

Not to be outdone, clergy members took to the pulpits and to the administrative commenting process to voice their objections to the rule (Lipton-Lubet 2014). Despite these repeated attempts to engage the country, very few people were listening. The media apparently had little interest in covering what appeared to be just another elite-level squabble, and predictably, the public remained largely uninterested in the question of who should pay for contraception coverage.

On January 20, 2012, however, the Obama administration reaffirmed its commitment to implementing the HHS rule of August 2011, with a new, one-year grace period for organizations with religious objections. Congressional Republicans once again mobilized opposition to the administration's decision to stay the course by invoking arguments about religious freedom and by organizing a new round of oversight hearings—with not-so-subtle titles such as "Executive Overreach: The HHS Mandate versus Religious Liberty" (Lipton-Lubet 2014).

The Politics of the Pill: Gender, Framing, and Policymaking in the Battle over Birth Control. Rachel VanSickle-Ward, Kevin Wallsten, Oxford University Press (2019). © Oxford University Press.
DOI: 10.1093/oso/9780190675349.001.0001

Most famously, on February 16, 2012, Republican representative Darrell Issa, chair of the House Oversight Committee, assembled a panel of clergy members and theologians titled "Lines Crossed: Separation of Church and State—Has the Obama Administration Trampled on Freedom of Religion and Freedom of Conscience?" In the process of inviting speakers to the panel, Issa turned down a special request from House Democrats to allow Georgetown law student Sandra Fluke to testify about the importance of contraception coverage for university students. Issa explained his decision to exclude Fluke by claiming the hearing was exclusively focused on "religious freedom" and Fluke was not "appropriate" or "qualified."

The political backlash to the exclusion of Fluke and the ensuing all-male hearing was fast and furious. Planned Parenthood tweeted a picture of the womanless panel with the message "What's wrong with this picture?" and the hashtag #WhereAreTheWomen? Before walking out of the hearing in protest with two other Democratic members of the House, Representative Carolyn Maloney asked,

> What I want to know is, where are the women? I look at this panel, and I don't see one single individual representing the tens of millions of women across the country who want and need insurance coverage for basic preventative health care services, including family planning. Where are the women?

Maloney's "where are the women" refrain became a rallying cry for defenders of the mandate who were outraged that women were not given a greater voice in the development of policy that so dramatically affected them.

More than two years later, on June 30, 2014, the U.S. Supreme Court ruled in *Burwell v. Hobby Lobby Stores Inc.*[1] (hereafter, *Hobby Lobby*) that closely held companies could not be required to provide insurance coverage for contraception if such coverage violated the owner's sincerely held religious beliefs. In a lengthy and vigorous dissent, Justice Ruth Bader Ginsburg argued that the decision's "startling breadth" evidenced a court that had "ventured into a minefield." Shortly thereafter, Katie Couric interviewed Ginsburg about the case. "Contraceptive protection is something that every woman must have access to, to control her own destiny," Ginsburg maintained. Couric asked Ginsburg if she believed "that the five male justices truly understood the ramifications of their decision." Ginsberg replied, "I would have to say no" ("Exclusive: Ruth Bader Ginsburg on Hobby Lobby Dissent" 2015).

Underpinning Planned Parenthood's, Maloney's, and Ginsburg's objections is the belief that women's voices are vital in policy discussions about reproductive rights. Our purpose in this book is to probe this claim in more depth, exploring how and why women's voices and actions shape the contemporary politics of birth control in the United States. While situating this exploration in the appropriate historical context, we focus most of our attention on the controversy surrounding insurance coverage of contraception between Congress's 2009 deliberations over the ACA and the Supreme Court's 2016 ruling in *Zubik v. Burwell*. Specifically, we ask three questions about the politics of the pill during this often contentious seven-year period: Who spoke? What did they say? Did it matter?

In setting out to answer these questions, we cast a wide net, examining legislative floor debates, committee hearings, statutory wording, regulations, amicus briefs, media coverage, Supreme Court oral arguments, Supreme Court rulings, and public opinion polls. More concretely, our book comprises two parts: Part I (chapters 2–5) considers how birth control policy unfolded; Part II (chapters 6–9) considers how it was framed by the media and viewed by the public. Throughout this examination, we emphasize the ways in which contraception policy fits into a broader conversation about women's agency and reproductive health, and we consider how gender intersected with other identities, namely religion and partisanship, in driving policy frames, narratives and attitudes. Along the way, we address perennial questions in the study of American democracy about the link between descriptive and substantive representation, identity and ideology, and personal and political priorities.

Our central argument is that representation matters: who has a voice significantly impacts policy attitudes, deliberation, and outcomes. While women's participation in the debate over birth control was limited by a lack of gender parity in the legislatures, the courts, and the media, women nevertheless shaped policymaking on birth control in myriad and interconnected ways. Scholars often think of gender as influential in relatively modest ways, constrained by party, ideology, and institutional or professional norms. The findings presented in this book illustrate that while the impact of women's voices is, in fact, sometimes subtle, it is nonetheless significant. A few phrases in a bill that would have been left out but for women in key roles become the basis for dramatic expansion of the coverage of birth control. A female journalist assigned to cover contraception chooses to interview an additional woman for her reporting, leading to a greater overall emphasis on women's health considerations in news coverage. A news story framed around women's reproductive rights rather than religious liberty concerns produces a slightly different overall distribution of public opinion for mandated insurance coverage of birth control. We find, in other words, that Maloney's and Ginsburg's complaints are worth taking seriously: the inclusion and exclusion of women has, indeed, had an important impact on the tenor, quantity, and quality of contraception debate across time, place, and venue.

We premise this book on the belief that understanding the dynamics of birth control policy is hugely important in its own right. With that said, the evidence presented here communicates three more general lessons about gender and American politics. First, descriptive representation (i.e., the numbers of women in positions of power) impacts how issues are framed in policymaking debates, news coverage, and the public. Second, studying descriptive representation on a single issue across multiple venues unearths impacts that may otherwise go unnoticed. And finally, while women might be denied a voice in some contexts and in some moments, women are often politically resourceful and can still manage to influence how policy debates unfold—with a few women in a few key places able to change the trajectory of an issue. In other words, while women's voices are often not visible enough, they can, even in the minority, be consequential.

Explaining Our Approach

This book tells the story of contemporary birth control policy and the role that women played in it. Our principal contributions are twofold. First, we chart the twists and turns of a fascinating, controversial, and consequential policy debate. How did a medication used by millions of American women on a regular basis become such a fraught political issue? How did a few lines in a one-thousand-page law[2] become the foundation for heated committee hearings, a landmark Supreme Court ruling (*Burwell v. Hobby Lobby Stores, Inc.*, 134 S. Ct. 2751), and hundreds of other lower court cases ("HHS Mandate Information Central" 2015)? How did an issue most major news outlets ignored for a decade become one of the most widely covered controversies of the 2012 election campaign? Second, we use our analysis of contraception politics as a vehicle for identifying more generally the position of women in the public sphere and the influence that gender exerts across policymaking and media venues.

In the remainder of this chapter we argue for the necessity of an in-depth analysis of contemporary birth control politics in the United States. First, we detail the ways in which contraception issues are uniquely significant for the quality of women's lives. Among many other things, expanding access to and insurance coverage of contraception is directly linked to women's economic prosperity, political empowerment, and personal well-being. Debates about contraception are, therefore, an essential area of academic inquiry. Second, we situate the project in the existing literature on gender, framing, representation, policymaking, and political communication. Specifically, in arguing for a link between descriptive representation and policy framing, we make the case that birth control provides a high-leverage litmus test for evaluating women's influence in the political process. Finally, we describe the contours of the book, summarize our methodological approach, and explain why a cross-venue, over-time assessment of framing choices is the most fruitful approach for identifying gender's role in controversies over contraception.

Why Birth Control Matters: Contraception and Women's Health

Justice Sandra Day O'Connor stated in *Planned Parenthood of Southeastern Pa. v. Casey* (505 U.S. 833, 1992), that "The ability of women to participate equally in the economic and social life of the Nation has been facilitated by their ability to control their reproductive lives." As the next chapter illustrates in more detail, women's freedom to exert this control has never come without controversy. The widespread availability of pornography during the Civil War spawned a movement to ban materials and items that were "obscene, lewd, or lascivious" (Buchanan 2009, 75). In the late nineteenth century, this movement culminated in the passage of "Comstock" laws that, among other things, heavily proscribed the sale of contraceptive devices and birth control information (Conway et al. 2004). While there were some variations across the states, most of these laws remained in effect throughout the early and mid-1900s. In 1965 the Supreme Court invalidated a Connecticut Comstock law that prohibited the use of "any drug, medicinal article or instrument for the purpose of preventing conception" on the grounds that it violated the "right to marital privacy" (*Griswold v. Connecticut*). A few years later, the Court struck down restrictions on contraception for unmarried persons as well (*Eisenstadt v. Baird*, 1972).

In response to these legal changes, contraception use jumped dramatically among young single women in the 1970s and has remained high ever since (Asbell 1995). According to recent estimates, approximately 63 million women in the United States are now between ages 15 and 44, the years generally considered to be "reproductive age." On average, these women spend 90% of this period of their lives trying *not* to get pregnant (King and Meyer 1997) and nearly two-thirds (62%) will use some form of birth control to prevent conception (Guttmacher Institute 2015). Importantly, 58% of oral contraception users report using the pill for its entirely noncontraceptive health benefits as well (Guttmacher Institute 2015).

Despite widespread use of contraceptives, however, the National Institute of Health reports that almost half of all pregnancies in the United States are unintentional (Finer and Zolna 2011). Perhaps more importantly, unintentional pregnancies are not evenly distributed across the socioeconomic spectrum—with the rate of unplanned deliveries for poor women being nearly five times as high as that for wealthier women (Reeves and Venator 2015). What explains this class-based disparity? Lack of access to affordable contraception is an essential part of the story (Postlethwaite et al. 2007). The most common form of birth control ("the pill") typically requires a prescription and costs up to eight hundred dollars a year (Snider 2019. Longer-lasting methods, including IUDs, are more expensive still, and costs can run into the thousands (Brooker 2012). Historically, health insurance has not provided much help for women seeking access to contraception. In addition to the relatively large percentage of women who have not had health coverage at all, many insurance plans did not pay for birth control until state laws began mandating it in the mid-1990s (VanSickle-Ward and Hollis-Brusky 2013).

Laws mandating contraception coverage are premised on the assumption that decisions about when or whether to conceive is essential to women's agency, equality, and personhood. Extensive evidence shows, for example, that unplanned pregnancies pose serious risks to women's health and economic security. Relatedly, diffusion of the pill has been linked to increases in women's college attendance and graduation rates (Hock 2007), increases in the representation of women in professional occupations (Goldin and Katz 2002), and increases in female earnings (Bailey et al. 2012). According to King and Meyer, scholars "repeatedly identify the limiting and spacing of births as the single greatest factor in improving physical and economic well-being among women" (1997, 3).

The significance of contraception for women's lives makes the issue of birth control a "critical" (Yin 1989) or "crucial" (Eckstein 1975) case for assessing women's role in the political process. Historically, women have been marginalized in political discourse through an interlocking and self-reinforcing combination of economic, religious, social, cultural, and legal practices. The extent and nature of women's citizenship in the United States remains, therefore, a fundamental question for observers of American politics. If women are sidelined in debates over contraception, we should be deeply skeptical about whether their voices are being included in debates over less salient questions. Indeed, as Feree, Gamson, Gerhards, and Rucht (2002) write about the related issue of abortion, "How women are spoken about, as well as how women as actors speak on this issue provides clues to women's position in the public sphere more generally" (6).

While this book is the first to focus comprehensively on the expansion of birth control access leading up to and during the Obama years, our work is nonetheless informed by a rich conversation about representation and reproductive policy. In addition to works on abortion and fetal harm policy (Luker 1984; Wilson 2013; Schroedel 2000), there are numerous studies of the historical development and popularization of birth control (Schoen 2005; Watkins 2001; Eig 2016; McCann 1999; Reed 2014; May 2011), the FDA approval process for reproductive drugs (Haussman 2013), and state-level fertility policies in the

1970s, 1980s, and 1990s (McFarlane and Meier 2001). Other books on gender and politics, reproductive rights, and women's issues also touch on the question of contraceptives (Swers 2013; Conway, Ahern, and Steuernagel 2005; Rhode 2014; Roberts 1999; Davis 2011; Solinger 2013).

Also germane to our purposes here, a compelling legal literature examines so-called conscience clause exemptions to state-level birth control mandates. Some scholarship on these conscience clauses has focused on constitutional questions, highlighting how variations in wording can affect the delicate balance between the free exercise and establishment clauses (Stabile 2004; Bailey 2004; Gilbert 2006; Miller 2006; Kubasek, Tagliarina, and Staggs 2007). Advocacy organizations have joined this academic debate by examining the phrasing, constitutionality, and impact of conscience clause exemptions on women's reproductive health (ACLU 2002; Guttmacher Institute 2012a; Center for Reproductive Rights 2012). Other scholarship has directed attention toward the political factors promoting the adoption of contraception insurance mandates (Tolbert and Steuernagel 2001). Recent work by VanSickle-Ward and Hollis-Brusky (2013) assesses the level of precision in state contraception laws as a function of political and institutional fragmentation, and considers the consequences of statutory specificity in court decisions.

This literature provides invaluable historical, economic, legal, and cultural context, and engages themes of gender, health, morality, and politics in ways that help inform the analytical framework we employ here. Building on this work, our book's goal is to comprehensively describe and explain recent debates over birth control across multiple policymaking and media forums, and to examine what these debates tell us about contemporary gender politics in the United States. In other words, we offer a 360-degree perspective—covering policy construction, implementation, interpretation, media coverage, public opinion, and the intersections therein.

Why Representation Matters: Gender, Representation, and Policy

Few topics are more central to gender and politics in the United States than issues of representation. In the chapters that follow, we probe the research on representation in far more depth. Here, however, we present an overview of some of the major ideas in the academic study of representation. In her foundational work on the subject, Hannah Pitkin (1972) distinguished between *descriptive representation*, in which a representative "stands for" a group because of a shared demographic characteristic, and *substantive representation*, in which a representative promotes the interests or policy preferences of a group. Gender and politics scholars are engaged in a rich and active dialogue regarding how and when these descriptors are and are not linked. Do women in office produce different policies than their male counterparts? On balance, the answer appears to be a qualified and conditional yes, with a bevy of what Beth Reingold refers to as "ifs, ands, and buts" (Reingold in Wolbrecht, Beckwith, and Baldez 2008, 129).

Underneath this question, and contributing to the varied and sometimes conflicting empirical findings, is a series of important and potentially confounding subquestions about representation: What, exactly, is a "women's" issue? Is it an issue to which women pay more attention? Is it an issue that affects women, on balance, more than men? Is it an issue that affects an equal number of men and women but exerts a different impact on women than men? Perhaps it has less to do with the scope and size of consequences and more to do with which women are affected. What about substantive representation? How might this concept be measured? Roll call votes? Public statements of support? Success in securing passage of important bills?

Empirical investigations into questions of this kind most commonly focus on Congress (Carroll 2002; Dodson 2006; Dolan 1997; Frederick 2011; Swers 2002, 2013), although work comparing women in state legislatures has also been prevalent (Poggione 2004; Reingold and Smith 2012; Osborn 2012; Carroll 2001). Numerous studies show that women legislators take distinct policy stances, introduce more bills on women's issues, employ different rhetoric in floor speeches, and bring new perspectives to existing policy discussions (Karpowitz and Mendelberg 2014; Pearson and Dancey 2011a; 2011b; Reingold 2008; Swers 2002; 2013; Mansbridge 1999). The existing research also consistently shows that (partly reflecting the gender gap in the attitudes found in the mass public) women legislators have more liberal voting records than their male counterparts (Frederick 2011; Boles and Scheurer 2007). Importantly, however, the literature's findings on female legislative behavior have not been uniform. Several studies identify limited or no impact for gender on legislator policy goals (Barnello 1999; Wolbrecht 2002; Frederick 2009). Additionally, some work that finds evidence of gender differences in behavior also notes that the differences between men and women are small, less important than partisanship, and heavily contextualized by time period and issue type.

While far less prevalent than the legislative studies, scholarship on decision making in the courts has also considered the impact of gender, with decidedly mixed results. Recent research has found that women influence outcomes on appellate courts even when they are in the minority (Farhang and Wawro 2004) and that women serving as district court judges reach settlement in their cases with greater frequency and alacrity than male judges (Boyd, Epstein, and Martin 2010). Studies such as these often emphasize the effects of judge gender on highly gendered areas of law, such as sexual discrimination and sexual harassment (Boyd, Epstein, and Martin 2010; Peresie 2005). But, once again, a sufficiently large literature in judicial politics finds limited or no impact for gender (Ashenfelter, Eisenberg, and Schwab 1995; Sisk, Heise, and Morriss 1998; Kulik, Perry, and Pepper 2003; Walker and Barrow 1985; Segal 2000).

In recent years, attention to women in the bureaucracy has grown alongside studies of the legislative and judicial branches (Keiser et al. 2002; Wilkins 2007; Meier and Nicholson-Crotty 2006). These investigations' articulation of passive and active representation echo the categories of descriptive and substantive representation coined by Pitkin and more typically used in research on the legislature. On balance, these studies tend to uncover evidence linking gender and "active representation." Saidel and Loscocco (2005), for example, demonstrate that working in a "gendered institution" influences whether a leader pursues a women-centered policy agenda, regardless of the leader's gender. Other work has looked beyond state and federal governments to identify the impact that women working in American cities have on policy at the local level (Holman 2014; Smith, Reingold, and Owens 2012).

As this brief review makes clear, work on the impact of representation, and the contributions of women in driving policy, is very often siloed off by fairly artificial institutional boundaries—with many studies addressing only the legislature, only the courts, or only the bureaucracy. This segregation of intellectual concerns has undoubtedly (and unfortunately) inhibited the development of a comprehensive understanding of gender's impact on lawmaking and policy implementation. The solution to this problem, as we see it, is to carefully trace the influence of gender on a single policy issue across multiple venues and across time—dwelling where necessary on the connections between the public, the three branches of government, and the fourth estate. We believe that a cross-venue, over-time approach helps us avoid the pitfalls that have trapped so many previous attempts at assessing gender's influence—namely, missing the way that relatively small (though not insignificant) gender effects accumulate throughout the multiple stages of the policymaking process.

Why Framing Matters: Framing throughout the Policymaking Process

The research described up to this point offers much to draw from in terms of theoretical foundations and empirical analyses of the impact of women in public office. Work on the impact of gender on one policy across multiple venues, however, is more limited. We know a great deal about how women act as legislators and are learning more about how they act as judges, civil servants, and agency heads. There are important studies on how gender affects deliberation (Karpowitz and Mendelberg 2014), rhetoric in and frequency of floor speeches (Pearson and Dancey 2011a; 2011b), public opinion (Greenlee 2014; Huddy,

Cassese, and Lizotte 2008; Wolbrecht, Beckwith, and Baldez 2008), reporting (Armstrong 2004; Zoch and Turk 1998; Liebler and Smith 1997; Piper-Aiken 1999; Rodgers and Thorson 2000 Weaver and Wilhoit 1992), and venue-specific policy adoption. Few studies explore these in relationship to one another. Thus, in addition to explaining the evolution of birth control policy, our book offers a unique analysis of the impact of gender across venues.

Our cross-venue, over-time analytic approach centers on the importance of framing. To frame an issue is to situate it within a broader policy conversation. Analyses of framing in studies of public policy often begin with the assumption that all issues are inherently complex and multidimensional. There are many ways, in other words, to understand and define the same problem. As Entman (1993) writes, framing is the process of selecting "some aspects of a perceived reality to make them more salient, thus promoting a particular problem definition, causal interpretation, moral evaluation, and/or treatment recommendation" (52). In their work on social movement mobilizations, Snow and Benford (1988) identify three core elements of the framing process: (1) diagnostic framing (which both defines the nature of a political problem and assigns blame for it), (2) prognostic framing (which suggests solutions for solving the problem defined by the diagnostic frame), and (3) motivational framing (which provides a call to arms and a rationale for taking political action.[3]

Throughout the policymaking process, various stakeholders compete to promote their diagnostic, prognostic, and motivational frames at the expense of others by strategically deploying resources and communication strategies (such as a selective presentation of the relevant facts or appeals based on emotion). Success or failure in this iterative contest is dependent, in part, on the proffered frame's resonance with existing values, ideals, and principles. In the United States, the preeminent values, ideals, and principles are equality, efficiency, security, and liberty (Stone 1997). Progress, participation, patriotism, fairness, and economic growth are also important (Baumgartner and Jones 1993, 7). Frames that resonate with American policymakers, the American media, and the American public often connect to at least one of these themes.

With this background in mind, there are at least four primary ways that framing contests matter in determining political outcomes: policy formation, privileging of expertise, support mobilization, and opinion persuasion. We address each of these briefly in turn. As Deborah Stone (1997) explains, the diagnostic and prognostic frames (or, in her terminology, "stories") adopted by policymakers clearly denote winners and losers, good guys and bad guys, and allies and adversaries. Once adopted, diagnostic and prognostic frames exert a series of direct and indirect influences on statutory construction and implementation (Stone 1997; Schon and Rein 1994; McFarlane and Meier 2001).

Indeed, the outcome of early struggles over diagnostic and prognostic frames invariably sets off a chain reaction of path-dependent events that heavily structure how subsequent policy debates play out. According to Stone, "Policy stories use many literary and rhetorical divides to lead the audience ineluctable to a course of action" (1997, 144).[4]

Framing has concrete consequences for statutory construction and implementation (Stone, Schon, and Rein 1994; MacFarlane and Meier 2001). How an issue is framed affects how a newly introduced piece of legislation is worded, which committee it gets assigned to, and which section of the code it is written into if enacted. These decisions in turn affect which agencies are charged with implementing a given policy, and which areas of jurisprudence are most relevant if the policy encounters legal challenges. We know these dynamics to be significant for the evolution of reproductive rights. As MacFarlane and Meier (2001) explain, "By assigning family planning to a health bureaucracy fertility becomes a health problem, not an education problem" (14). Notably, this process is path-dependent; as we show throughout the book, early policy framing sets a course of action that can dramatically shape later outcomes.

It is important to point out here, however, that diagnostic and prognostic frames are never permanent, and attempts at reframing are numerous. Opponents of a policy premised on a dominant frame, for example, have strong incentives to promote new understandings of the policy problem in question and characterize old understandings in a less compelling way (Haynes, Merolla, and Ramakrishnan 2016). Similarly, all political actors aim to strategically redefine who is to blame and what appropriate solutions might look like in order to secure the most sympathetic legislative committee, or hitch to a legal bailiwick where precedent is more likely to produce a desired outcome.

In addition to influencing policy formation, the outcomes of struggles over diagnostic and prognostic framing also dictate what topics are open for debate, who is called on to speak, and how that speech is received. Prognostic and diagnostic frames can make an issue appear technical, complicated, and relevant only to a narrowly defined group of policy experts. Alternatively, problems can be defined and solutions proposed in ways that are nontechnical, comprehensible, and accessible to average members of the public (Rochefort and Cobb 1994, 5). In a very significant sense, therefore, who is considered an expert in witness testimony before legislative committees, in judicial opinions, and in press accounts are all determined by the winners and losers of the diagnostic and prognostic framing contests. In short, there is a clear connection is present between frame selection and the privileging of certain types of expertise in political debates. Throughout the rest of this book, we see how the question of "Who speaks?" is intimately related to the questions "What is the problem?" and "What should be done?"

Diagnostic and prognostic frames are not the only part of the framing process that matters for policy outcomes. As mentioned above, motivational frames that serve as a call to action are also important. In her study of reproductive justice activists, for example, Price notes that "stories can serve as consciousness-raising tools for grassroots, political organizing. Reproductive justice activists consciously use storytelling as a form of activism" (Price 2010, 49). Similarly, in their work on immigration policy, Merolla, Ramakrishnan, and Haynes (2016) describe the ways in which motivational frames help build coalitions in support of policy change. In addition, Cindy Simon Rosenthal documents the strategic use of framing by interest groups in public discourse over Title IX enforcement (Rosenthal 2008). In the chapters that follow, we show how advocacy groups framed their calls to action in the debate over birth control.

Collectively, the diagnostic, prognostic, and motivational frames employed in political debates have the potential to shape public preferences. Indeed, the interplay over framing between advocacy groups, elites, media coverage, and public opinion has long been of interest to policy scholars (Arnold 1990; Baumgartner and Jones 1993; Schattschneider 1975). More recent work has emphasized the particular significance of framing effects in the context of support for funding levels for women's health programs (Cassese and Hannagan 2014), and the power of frames to elicit emotional response (Merolla and Zechmeister 2009). In the second half of this book, the impact of frames on public perceptions takes center stage.

Frames in the Debate over Contraception

Comparing the framing of birth control across different policy venues and media domains over different periods of time provides a unique opportunity to observe how fundamental values can be repackaged, repurposed, and reordered in response to political imperatives. The question of access to and insurance coverage of contraception reveals and invokes deep cultural divides in the United States about gender roles, economic equality, government spending, religious liberty, sexual morality, health care, and the right to privacy. While this is the first book on the subject, ours is not the only investigation into the competing frames (or "narratives") used in debates about birth control coverage. Amy Rasmussen (2011), for example, examines the framing contests surrounding Maryland's 1998 contraceptive mandate, finding that supporters of mandated birth control coverage employed two primary issue frames in an effort to expand the category of "health care" to include contraception: a "medical frame" and an "equity frame." Opponents of contraceptive mandates, by contrast, rejected these "inclusive" frames and relied on "market-based," religious, and morality frames to justify the exclusion of birth control from the "health care" category. In a more recent investigation, Lipton-Lubet (2014) argues that there were "dueling narratives" in the 2011 debate over the ACA's contraception mandate: a "war on women" frame and a "war on religion" frame. Lipton-Lubet defines the "war on women" frame as emphasizing "women's equality and basic fairness." It also strategically positioned opponents of the contraceptive mandate as wanting to "turn back the clock on women's rights and autonomy." By contrast, the "war on religion" frame suggested that the contraceptive mandate was an "infringement on the freedom of institutions and individuals to order their lives in accordance with their religious beliefs" (361). These studies provide an invaluable starting point for our examination of the politics of contraception in the United States.

What is novel about the research presented in this book is not just the broader scope of its analysis but also the focus on representation in driving frames. We know from the literature on representation that having women in positions of power influences policymaking, though as we noted, we know little about how that influence transcends venue. And we know that framing influences policymaking. We know much less, however, about how representation influences framing throughout the policymaking process. This volume tells that story.

The bulk of this book's empirical chapters track the relative importance of competing frames about the ACA's contraceptive mandate across multiple venues of political debate. Specifically, we derived six distinct, though interconnected, frames from content analysis of media coverage and legislative debates between August 1, 2011, and August 1, 2012:

> *Religious freedom:* This frame highlights the effect of the mandate on religious liberty and frequently focused on the appropriateness and breadth of an exemption of contraceptive coverage for religious entities, particularly those administered by or affiliated with the Catholic Church.
>
> *Health:* This frame includes women's health (including the importance of birth control to women's overall health), public health (such as discussions of population control and teen pregnancy), and discussion of how birth control coverage connects to health-care reform and preventative care more generally.
>
> *Women's/reproductive rights:* This frame addresses women's agency, gender equality, women's bodily autonomy and self-determination, reproductive rights, and discussions of inclusion and exclusion of women from the birth control debate.
>
> *Economics:* This frame focuses on what fees, taxes, or externalities would be bestowed upon the public, insurance companies, and employers by mandated coverage of contraception.

Morality: This category encompasses frames that deal with appropriate moral or sexual behavior, including premarital sex and perceived sexual promiscuity.

Partisan/strategic game: This frame emphasizes the contraception issue primarily in terms of how it will affect the two major parties, including discussion of "horserace" (who is ahead and who is behind and what strategies are being deployed), polling, public support, legislative debates, and the 2012 presidential candidates (Barack Obama and Mitt Romney).

In addition to expanding the number of framing categories, the data presented in the following chapters build on the framing analyses of previous work in a number of important ways. First, we show that the dominant frames employed in debates over the ACA's contraceptive mandate shifted quickly over time and across venues. Most notably, we find that the prominence of the religious freedom and reproductive rights frames ebbed and flowed significantly between 2011 and 2012—with reproductive rights receiving more attention early in the debate and religious freedom receiving more attention later. Neither of these frames was able to achieve sustained dominance in the public's, the media's, Congress's, or the judiciary's understanding of the mandate.

Second, we demonstrate that electoral considerations framed the debate over contraception in ways that have been (but should not be) ignored in favor of a strictly substantive focus on women's health, reproductive rights, morality, economics, and religious freedom. Our data show that a nontrivial proportion of the overall debate about the ACA's contraceptive mandate focused on questions of who was winning and losing at any given moment or the strategies and tactics being employed by politicians, parties, and interest groups. What's more, exposure to this strategic game frame had a significant effect on the public's engagement with the issue. Grappling with the role played by the strategic game elements of political discourse around the contraceptive mandate—and specifically the fact that men in the media were more likely to promote this frame—is a central strength of our work.

Third, we illustrate a clear connection between frame selection and the privileging of certain types of expertise in the debate over contraceptive coverage. As we show in the following chapters, emphasizing health considerations related to contraception promotes the expertise of medical professionals and, in some cases, the voices of average women themselves. A women's rights framing of contraception also positions women as legitimate participants in public discourse. Framing birth control mandates as an issue of religious liberty, however, elevates the voices of clergy, theologians, and other spokespersons for religious institutions. Importantly, these voices are also likely to be predominantly male.

The outcome of the struggle to frame the contraceptive mandate, in short, dictated the answer to the question of "Who speaks?"

Finally, our data show that female voices played a central role in elevating the prominence of the gendered frames (i.e., health, women's rights, and morality) and deemphasizing the religion frame. While previous studies do a commendable job inventorying the frames used in public discourse around birth control, they are less concerned with the relationship those frames have to the gender identities of proponents and opponents of contraceptive mandates. In this book we make a strong causal claim about the influence of gender on framing choices across venues and across time. Put simply, we show that when women spoke on birth control in state legislatures, the Congress, the Supreme Court, or the media, or to public opinion pollsters, they said fundamentally different things than men.

How the Book Is Organized

In the previous section we highlighted the book's central findings: that women's presence or absence at various points in the development, implementation, and enforcement of policies governing access to birth control mattered in tangible ways, including which laws were adopted, how they were worded, how they were reported on, how they were perceived by the public, and how they were interpreted. From editorial pages to floor votes to judicial rulings to public opinion polls, women are, on balance, more supportive of birth control coverage, more opposed to barriers based on religious objections, and more likely than their male counterparts to view the issue in terms of health care and women's rights.

A Note on Methodology: Operationalizing Gender

In this book we make the case that reproductive rights policies generally, and birth control specifically, affect women in immediate, concrete, and personal ways. Moreover, we present unambiguous evidence that women—across different periods of time and across different institutional contexts—viewed, framed, and advocated for this issue in ways that were, on balance, distinct from that of men. It is important to point out here, however, that these findings should *not* be interpreted to mean that women speak with a singular voice on contraception. Throughout the analyses that follow, we make a concerted effort to avoid essentializing gender and attempt to tell (where the data allow) a nuanced story about the variation among women that inevitably grows from their distinct racial, partisan, and religious identities. We are cognizant, though, that there are fundamental limits to our approach, particularly around diversity within gender.

While we look broadly across domains, we generally consider gender in two ways: the gender of the actor involved—policymakers, reporters, survey respondents—and the gendered nature of the discussion—that is, the frames employed in policy deliberation and media coverage. While on the one hand the discussion of gender is quite expansive, in that we consider the gender of actors from a range of milieus, on the other it is admittedly limited, particularly in that it is captured in a binary fashion.[5]

Conceptually, we treated gender as though it contained only two distinct, mutually exclusive categories. Operationally, we placed survey respondents, policymakers, journalists, and news sources into one of these two gender-based categories on the basis of either self-reporting or on how stereotypically male or stereotypically female their name was. The strength of this approach was that it allowed us to measure a large number of political actors across a wide array of venues without essentializing based on appearance or biological traits. This point is important: we endeavor to report gender as the actors in our study report it. There are, however, drawbacks to this method—namely, the possibility of measurement error (i.e., misgendering a policymaker, journalist, or news source), and the inability to identify non-binary individuals.[6]

On one level, this conceptualization and measurement scheme reflects the data we had at our disposal. Survey data report gender in this manner; people who identify outside of the binary are numerically small and not accurately categorized or counted. Legislative debates, committee hearings, court arguments, and news reports implicitly adopted the same binary approach to gender that we used here. The legislators and judicial actors included self-identified as either male or female. Indeed, there was no evidence in any of our data that these actors were problematizing the idea of gender or acknowledging the complexity of gender identity. Even still, existing categories are limited, and the limits of our methodology should be laid bare. Future work on reproductive rights policy debates would do well to adopt a more expansive and nuanced definition of gender.

Chapter Overview

This book is organized into two main sections. Part I (chapters 2–5) focuses on explaining the historical context and contemporary dynamics driving policymaking on birth control, with a particular focus on how contraception has been framed during legislative and judicial deliberations. Part II (chapters 6–9) considers the causes and consequences of those frames for news coverage and public opinion on birth control issues. While the bulk of the book focuses on the ins and outs of recent policymaking, chapter 2 takes a step back and places current debates about contraception in a broader historical context. To be more precise, in the next chapter, we explore the evolution of contraception policy in the United States since the early twentieth century. We focus on the advocacy of Margaret Sanger and Katherine McCormick; the development of the first hormonal birth control pill by John Rock and Gregory Pincus; the role of race, gender, and religion in the evolving debate over contraception use; and legal struggles over securing access to and regulation of hormonal birth control.

In chapter 3 we begin our discussion of contemporary contraceptive coverage policy by investigating birth control mandates at the state level. Long before the 2011 announcement of the HHS rule requiring providers of group health insurance to cover the costs of birth control as part of the ACA, twenty-eight states adopted their own policies mandating coverage of prescription contraceptives for women (VanSickle-Ward and Hollis-Brusky 2013). Chapter 3 presents the political, ideological, and religious factors that led states to adopt these policies, with a particular focus on the role that female legislators played in their passage. Our analyses show that, even after controlling for ideology and partisanship, states with more women in the legislature were more likely to adopt birth control coverage laws than states with fewer women in the legislature. These findings provide us with a useful springboard for leaping into a discussion about the ways in which state-level contraceptive mandates, along with their widely varying conscience clause exemptions, set the stage for the national debate around the ACA in 2011 and 2012.

In chapter 4 we offer a detailed examination of contraceptive coverage under the ACA. Although the ACA was not the first attempt to ensure coverage of contraception, it was easily the most visible, sweeping, and significant. The ACA added language to the existing Public Health Service Act (also incorporated under the Employee Retirement Income Security Act and the Internal Revenue Code) that required health plans to cover preventative care services with no cost-sharing imposition on the insured individual (Brougher 2012). Designated the "Women's Health Amendment," the provision was the first significant Senate amendment to the ACA, and was approved by a 61-39 vote margin on December 3, 2009 (Brooker 2012). Building on related sections that covered preventative care more generally, the amendment focused on preventative care specifically relevant to women, stating "with respect to women, such additional preventative care and screenings ... as provided for in comprehensive guidelines supported by the Health Resources and Services Administration" (42 USC 300gg-13(a)(4)) (Brougher 2012).[7] An explicitly gendered framing "with respect to women" was thus explicit from the start.

Utilizing content analysis and in-depth interviews of policy elites, we detail in chapter 4 the evolution of this policy, from the struggle to ensure its inclusion in the ACA to the controversy over rules that emerged defining preventative care as including contraception. We trace the trajectory of policy frames across congressional debate, committee hearings, and announcements of federal rules. We consider how these frames were marshaled and by whom. In so doing, we explain the impact of gender in selecting frames, explore how the frames were transmitted and amplified, and discuss how frame selection shaped policy outcomes. We show that the debate over contraception in the ACA shifted course over time—from being predominantly about health care initially to being predominantly about religious freedom after the law's passage. We also show that framing choices were more dependent on the gender of the speaker than on the speaker's partisanship. Together, these findings reveal the extent to which the debate of the ACA's contraception requirements were dynamic (rather than static) and shaped by gender considerations.

In chapter 5 we turn to contraceptive coverage in the courts. The controversy over contraception care prompted the ACA's second trip to the Supreme Court.[8] At issue in the case was whether the ACA's contraceptive mandate violated the federal Religious Freedom Restoration Act (RFRA). According to the RFRA, "Government shall not substantially burden a person's exercise of religion even if the burden results from a rule of general applicability, except when furthering a "compelling government interest" in the "least restrictive means" available (42 U.S. Code § 2000bb–1). Families owning Hobby Lobby and Conestega Wood Specialties claimed a religious objection to covering four types of birth control out of the twenty-four approved by the FDA (specifically, intrauterine devices [IUDs] and morning-after pills). The court's majority, citing the Dictionary Act, concluded that these for-profit companies could be viewed as "persons" and were thus eligible for protection under RFRA. The majority further found that the requirement to cover all forms of FDA-approved birth control constituted a substantial burden on the ability of the corporations to freely exercise their religion, particularly in terms of the financial cost.

In chapter 5 we use content analysis to analyze the frames employed in oral and written arguments, amici curiae briefs, and the opinion and dissent. Here again we find that the debate evolved over time and that gender matters in terms of how the issue of birth control coverage is framed. To be more precise, our statistical analyses demonstrate that (1) religious freedom frames were almost entirely absent in the initial debates over the ACA but became dominant in the process of litigation (with health care having a low profile but making a noticeable comeback in later court rulings), and (2) gender shaped framing in persistent ways that transcended both issue position (for or against) and venue.

In chapters 6 and 7 we examine contraception coverage in the press. We look specifically in chapter 6 at who was quoted in news coverage about the contraceptive mandate. Academic researchers have conducted numerous studies of sourcing patterns in an attempt to identify the kinds of actors who are most influential in shaping the media's agenda. One particularly lively area of inquiry centers on whether a reporter's gender influences the sourcing decisions made in news coverage. Some studies of sourcing patterns show that male and female reporters differ in their propensity to cite male and female sources and in the prominence of those sources (Armstrong 2004; Zoch and Turk 1998; Piper-Aiken 1999; Rodgers and Thorson 2003; Weaver and Wilhoit 1992). Other studies show little role for gender (Liebler and Smith 1997).

To provide more clarity about how gender influenced reporting about birth control policy, we examine media coverage of the debate surrounding contraception from August 1, 2011—the date the definition of women's health care was expanded to include contraceptives—until August 1, 2012—the date a modified mandate was enacted. We find that the media's general tendency to rely on male sources was less pronounced in articles on the contraceptive mandate published by female authors and in reports appearing in newspapers with more gender-balanced staffs. These findings legitimize the concerns of media watchdog organizations that push for newsroom diversification and answer the more substantively direct question of whether having more female reporters leads to a qualitatively different kind of reporting on issues directly impacting women.

In chapter 7 we consider the ways in which birth control policy was framed in political news coverage. Did women report on the mandate differently than men? Using the same data from our study of sourcing patterns in chapter 6, we tracked the frames used in every print media article between August 1, 2011, and August 1, 2012, that mentioned the terms "birth control" or "contraceptives" in the title or lead paragraph. After demonstrating that news reports framed the birth control mandate as a religious issue more frequently than an economic, women's rights, or health issue, we assess the impact that an author's gender and the gender of quoted sources had on an article's dominant frame. Mimicking our findings in chapter 6 about sourcing decisions, we demonstrate that female journalists employed gendered frames (i.e., women's health, reproductive rights, and morality) in their reporting far more often than male journalists. Additionally, we present evidence in chapter 7 showing that female reporting exerted an indirect influence on news frames by increasing the proportion of women quoted in articles about the contraception mandate. Put simply, allowing women to write and speak made a profound difference in how the media covered contraception policy.

We turn our attention in chapter 8 to the public's views on birth control. Most public opinion scholarship on reproductive rights policy has focused narrowly on the issue of abortion and has largely ignored attitudes toward contraception. In chapter 8 we describe the contours of public support for access to birth control over the last sixty years and for the contraceptive mandate of the ACA between 2011 and 2014. Drawing on data from numerous polling organizations, we show that majorities of both political parties, both genders, and all races and religious affiliations have had stable and supportive opinions since at least the 1950s on whether women should have access to birth control and whether contraceptives are "morally acceptable." Our analysis also reveals, however, that large partisan, gender, and "God-based" gaps in public support for requiring health insurance coverage of contraceptives developed as a result of the 2012 debate over the ACA's birth control mandate. The divisions in public opinion driven by the competing accusations of a "war on women" and a "war on religion" still persist today.

Building on our findings in chapter 7 that male and female reporters emphasized very different elements in their coverage of birth control policy, in chapter 9 we assess whether exposure to different author bylines and frames in news coverage matters for how members of the public feel about birth control policy. Using a series of survey experiments administered through Amazon's Mechanical Turk, we measure how exposure to the kinds of articles typically produced by male and female reporters influences media trust, political cynicism, and opinions about birth control policy. The results of our experimental manipulations show that women asked to read articles on the contraceptive mandate written by other women viewed the media as more credible than women asked to read articles written by men. In addition, we demonstrate that strategic game coverage, which was the most common type of contraceptive mandate story authored by male journalists, significantly decreased perceptions of media credibility, enhanced feelings of political cynicism, reduced issue-specific information retention, and encouraged more frequent expressions of negativity among *all* experimental participants. In line with previous research, our experiments also show that news frames shape policy opinions. Specifically, our data reveal that support for the contraceptive mandate increased after reading an article framed around women's health, reproductive rights, and sexual morality. These findings demonstrate the substantively large consequences that marginalizing female voices in media discussions of contraceptive policy have for political discourse in the United States. Table 1.1 illustrates our key findings from each chapter.

Table 1.1 **Summary of Key Empirical Findings**

Chapter	Venue	How gender is measured	Effect
2	Historical overview	Consideration of activists, policymakers, and nonelites	Development and political advocacy around birth control
3	State legislatures	Percentage of women in legislature	Adoption of birth control coverage laws
4	Congress	Gender of legislator/witness	Adoption of birth control coverage Frames employed
5	Supreme Court	Gender of attorneys, justices, and amici brief authors	Rulings on birth control coverage Frames employed
6	Media coverage (sources)	Gender of reporter ("byline diversity") Gender of newsroom ("newsroom diversity")	Gender of sources ("source diversity")
7	Media coverage (frames)	Gender of sources ("source diversity") Gender of reporter ("byline diversity") Gender of newsroom ("newsroom diversity")	Frames employed ("content diversity")
8	Public opinion (cross-sectional)	Gender of survey respondents	Attitudes toward birth control
9	Public opinion (experimental)	Frame of news article ("gendered" vs. "nongendered") Gender of reporter	Attitudes toward birth control Perceptions of media credibility

In the concluding chapter of the book (chapter 10), we synthesize the lessons learned from our various analyses and explain the implications of our findings for the significance of women's voices in political debate more broadly. We marshal the evidence gathered to answer the three central questions posed in the beginning book: Who speaks? What do they say? Does it matter? We argue that the presence or absence of female politicians, reporters, activists, and judges has dramatic consequences for the timing, tone, and trajectory of public debates and policy outcomes on birth control. Additionally, we consider how lingering debates over contraception coverage, and the persistent disparities in who speaks and who is heard, inform our expectations about gender and politics in the years to come.

PART I

POLICY

2

The History of the Pill

This book is an examination of a fairly recent set of controversies related to contraception. Understanding contemporary debates about birth control requires, however, a brief excursion into the history of reproductive rights. The history of birth control, broadly defined, is essentially as old as the history of birth itself. As Jonathan Eig (2014, 7) put it in his compelling account of the development of hormonal birth control, "For as long as men and women have been making babies, they've been trying not to." We should be clear from the outset, therefore, that this chapter does not endeavor to cover every aspect of the history of birth control. Instead, we limit this chapter's analysis almost exclusively to the United States and, more directly, to the actors and events that exerted the largest influence on the unique evolution of American debates over contraception.

Drawing on a number of excellent historical accounts, in the sections that follow we show that the primary themes explored in this book—religion, economics, politics, health, morality, and women's autonomy—have been present, and in some cases in tension with one another, since the start of our long national conversation about contraception. Notably, the voices present in the conversation are afforded differing levels of status and validity. Throughout this chapter we highlight the ways in which regulation of reproduction is rooted in struggles over equality, whose expertise is valued, and whose voice is heard. The quote above might be better restated, "For as long as men and women have been making babies, there has been a struggle over who gets to decide if they have to." Our overview illustrates that women and men have often had different perspectives on access to legal and affordable birth control, even in situations where they were nominally on the same side of the issue, born of the lived experience and access to power. Race also has played a critical role in shaping outlook and influence. The policies and practices that emerge are the product of who was participating in these debates. In short, this chapter lays a foundation that animates the rest of the book: Who speaks? What do they say? Does it matter?

The Politics of the Pill: Gender, Framing, and Policymaking in the Battle over Birth Control. Rachel VanSickle-Ward, Kevin Wallsten, Oxford University Press (2019). © Oxford University Press.
DOI: 10.1093/oso/9780190675349.001.0001

Birth Control Advocacy

Long before hormonal birth control was invented, humans were experimenting with ways to prevent or delay pregnancy. Not surprisingly, some methods were more effective than others. The earliest "condoms" were fashioned during the third millennium BCE from animal intestines, fish bladder, and linen. Later came the first chemical spermicides and pessaries (vaginal plugs) (Thompson 2013). Ancient Egyptian texts provide accounts of some pessaries made from fermented dough and crocodile dung, and others from tree bark, honey, and gum (Speroff and Darney 1996). Women also ingested a variety of plants and herbs believed to have prophylactic effects. A number of these early practices, often passed from woman to woman, had some success (silphuim, for instance, apparently worked so well that it was consumed to the point of extinction), and a handful are even used to this day (Speroff and Darney 1996). But many failed, and women frequently fell ill or died as a result of their use (Grimes et al. 2000). The vulcanization of rubber in 1838 set the stage for pivotal development in birth control options—rubber condoms and diaphragms (Gibson 2015). And of course, throughout history, men and women have used "natural methods"—chiefly withdrawal and timed abstinence.

The most significant historical period for our purposes here is the expansion of legal access to and the development of hormonal birth control in the 20th century. The most commonly employed forms of pregnancy prevention prior to the advent of hormonal methods—withdrawal and condoms—relied on *both* the consent and active participation of men. Numerous firsthand accounts and countless unwanted pregnancies illustrate that men often did not comply with attempts to avoid conception or did not do so effectively. One woman with syphilis described life with very sick children and an unsympathetic husband in a heart-wrenching letter to early birth control activist, sex educator, writer, and nurse Margaret Sanger: "I have tried to keep myself away from my husband since my last baby was born, but it causes quarrels, and once he left me, saying I wasn't doing my duty as a wife" (Eig 2014, 49). Scientists who conducted early research on hormonal birth control received personal accounts as well, such as this account to Gregory Pincus (Marks 2010, 7):

> I am about 30 years old have 6 children, oldest little over 7, youngest a few days. My health don't seem to make it possible to go on this way. We have tried to be careful and tried this and that, but I get pregnant anyway. When I read this article [in *Science Digest* (Sept. 1957)] I couldn't help but cry, for I thought there is my ray of hope.

Options beyond condoms, withdrawal, and abstinence existed—namely sponges, diaphragm, pessaries, surgical sterilization, and abortion—but information about and access to these devices was extremely limited (May 2011, 4). This is not to imply, of course, that women gave up on the hopes of preventing conception. Women were, and are, endlessly creative regarding contraception. They bought products supposedly designed for regulation of the menstrual cycle, with warnings of "side effects" of causing miscarriage and preventing pregnancy. But unwanted pregnancy and the resulting suffering persisted. Parents of large families struggled to provide for their children, and children frequently died or went to live on the street (Eig 2014, 48). Women frequently died in childbirth.[1]

As Elaine May explains in her excellent history of the pill in the United States, "Birth control advocates promoted contraception as a radical idea linked to political change as well as personal emancipation" (2011, 17). Margaret Sanger, the most prominent champion of birth control access and founder of what would eventually become Planned Parenthood, was the daughter of Irish Catholic immigrants and the sister of ten siblings. Her mother's health deteriorated and she passed away at 50—the result, Sanger believed, of near constant pregnancy (May 2011, 17). Also formative for Sanger were her experiences as a nurse where she witnessed firsthand the misery wrought by women's lack of control over their reproduction:

> She watched women die because their bodies could not hold up against the strain of producing so many babies in such poor conditions, or because they used primitive birth control devices that caused infection, or because butchers posing as [abortion providers] botched their jobs. (Eig 2014, 35)

Her political activism was shaped by socialist Eugene Debs and anarchist Emma Goldman; early on, her beliefs about gender equality were linked to class. In 1914 she wrote in her self-published paper, *The Woman Rebel*, that "the working class can use direct action by refusing to supply the market with children to be exploited, by refusing to populate the earth with slaves" (May 2011, 17). The term "birth control" was first coined by Sanger in the same publication.

For 20th-century birth control activists like Sanger, contraceptive development and access were inextricably linked to women's liberation. They believed that "voluntary motherhood" was essential to women's ability to fully exercise their rights (May 2011, 15). Further, Sanger and her allies believed that decoupling sex and motherhood, giving women the right to have sex for pleasure, was essential for a just society. As Eig writes (2014, 55),

For the women of Sanger's age, reproduction was the sole purpose of living. Motherhood was the only job that counted. Rare was the woman whose identity extended beyond that of her husband.... In attempting to give women the power to rule their own bodies, Sanger was in fact launching a human rights campaign that would have world-changing impact, reshaping everything including family, politics, and the economy. Once they gained control of their reproductive systems, they would go the next step; they would declare their identities. Womanhood would no longer mean the same thing as motherhood.

Not surprisingly, decoupling womanhood from motherhood and sex from reproduction faced tremendous opposition, particularly from religious institutions. Historically, there has been tremendous variation in how adherents of different religious faiths view artificial contraception. According to Flann Campbell (1960), use of birth control was officially prohibited by most Christian denominations until 1930 when the Anglican Communion shifted course on the question of contraception. Quickly following the Anglican Communion's lead, most Protestant churches came to accept birth control as a matter of freedom of conscience (though many raised concerns about contraception's encouragement of promiscuity). Many branches of Judaism have also been supportive of birth control access.

From the outset, birth control advocates faced staunch resistance from the Roman Catholic Church. The Catholic Church's opposition to birth control (and endorsement of abstinence) is longstanding, at least according to formal pronouncements. In 1997, for example, the Vatican released a strongly worded document titled *Vademecum for Confessors* (2:4) that stated, "The Church has always taught the intrinsic evil of contraception." The most important modern articulation of the Catholic Church's perspective on birth control came with Pope Paul VI's 1968 *Humanae Vitae* encyclical. As the encyclical stated,

> Equally to be condemned, as the magisterium of the Church has affirmed on many occasions, is direct sterilization, whether of the man or of the woman, whether permanent or temporary. Similarly excluded is any action which either before, at the moment of, or after sexual intercourse, is specifically intended to prevent procreation—whether as an end or as a means.

There were, of course, individual priests who supported access to contraceptives in direct defiance of official church doctrine, particularly after Vatican II allowed for more dissent generally (May 2011, 125). Overall, however, the Catholic Church has been fairly consistent and persistent in its staunch opposition to contraception.

Since the pill became popularized, however, a striking disconnect has arisen between the Catholic Church as an institution and rank-and-file Catholics. Eig notes that "when a *Catholic Digest* survey in 1952 found that more than half of all Catholics did not regard 'mechanical birth control' as inherently sinful, Paul Byssard, the priest who ran the magazine, was so disturbed he decided not to publish the results" (Eig 2014, 226). A few years later nearly a third of Catholic women reported using contraception other than rhythm or abstinence (Eig 2014, 226). By 1965, 75% of U.S. Catholics supported widespread access to contraception, and a significant number of priests shared this view (May 2011, 125). More recent surveys suggest that as many as three-quarters (78%) of American Catholics believe the church should change its stance on contraception and allow Catholics to use birth control (Lipka 2013).

Notably, several key players in the development and promotion of the pill were Catholic: Sanger was a lapsed Catholic; John Rock, the gynecologist who first tested the hormone on human subjects, was a practicing Catholic who took on the church's teaching directly. Some even argue that Rock designed the pill in part to comply with the Catholic view of reproduction—including the placebo week to approximate the "natural" menstrual cycle (Andrist et al. 2004; Gladwell 2000). The FDA administrator who approved the pill, Dr. Pasquale DeFelice, was Catholic, as was, of course, President John F. Kennedy, who publicly supported family planning (Marks 2010; May 2011). But official church doctrine remained steadfastly opposed, and as we see in later chapters, Catholic organizations proved to be one of the most outspoken voices against providing insurance coverage for contraception.

Legal Context

In 1916 Sanger founded a family planning clinic in Brownsville, in Brooklyn, New York, the first of its kind in the United States. Staffed largely by nurses, the clinic provided pessaries and condoms to the surrounding community. The pamphlets promoting the clinic highlighted economic considerations, contraception as an alternative to abortion, and the explicit outreach to women who already had children (Eig 2014 47):[2]

> MOTHERS! Can you afford to have a large family? Do you want any more children? If not, why do you have them? DO NOT KILL, DO NOT TAKE LIFE, BUT PREVENT. Safe, harmless information can be obtained at 46 Amboy Street.

Interest was immediate and intense; so was the backlash. Advertising was done clandestinely, and the clinic was run in secret. Nevertheless, it provided services to more than 100 women on its first day of operation, and nearly four times that many over the first 10 days it was open.[3] Authorities promptly closed the clinic for violating Comstock laws.

Contrary to conventional wisdom, birth control and abortion were not always taboo and forbidden; the history is much more complicated (Luker 1985). In the United States, restrictive policies emerged in the late 1800s and were "promoted largely by the emerging medical profession, whose mostly male practitioners sought to take control over the process of pregnancy and birth from midwives and lay healers" (May 2011, 16). As we noted in this chapter's introduction, regulating reproduction is rooted in struggles over equality, whose expertise is deemed worthy, and whose voice is amplified. It is not surprising, then, that efforts to restrict access to birth control were tied to larger struggles regulating sexuality and morality. U.S. postal inspector Anthony Comstock campaigned vociferously against birth control and other forms of "obscenity," resulting in the adoption of the Comstock Act of 1873, which banned distribution and advertisement of obscene material. Specifically, the statute prohibited (18 U.S. Code § 1461):

> Every obscene, lewd, lascivious, indecent, filthy or vile article, matter, thing, device, or substance; and—
> Every article or thing designed, adapted, or intended for producing abortion, or for any indecent or immoral use; and
> Every article, instrument, substance, drug, medicine, or thing which is advertised or described in a manner calculated to lead another to use or apply it for producing abortion, or for any indecent or immoral purpose.[4]

The law largely targeted birth control, sex toys, and pornography as "indecent and immoral." It was much more than symbolic; Comstock himself led the charge—arresting hundreds of violators and confiscating tens of thousands of pieces of obscene material, including contraceptive devices. Some women took their own life rather than face charges of immorality (Eig 2014, 44). The federal law was also quite successful in spurring state-level copycat statutes—by 1920, 45 states had enacted related antiobscenity laws (Bailey 2010).

The commitment that Comstock and his allies demonstrated in cracking down on birth control usage was matched by Sanger and her allies in fighting back to expand access. Sanger had a long history of civil disobedience. Her first arrest preceded the clinic opening; it occurred in 1914 for championing contraceptives in the *Woman Rebel* (May 2011, 18). While she was in Europe to evade imprisonment, Sanger's husband was arrested for distributing her pamphlets and convicted on obscenity charges. Highlighting the ever-present religious themes attendant to reproductive discussion, the presiding judge stated that he had run afoul not just of "the laws of man, but the law of God as well, in your scheme to prevent motherhood" (Eig 2014, 45). After she was arrested for opening the clinic, she was sentenced to a month in jail for civil disobedience and violation of Comstock laws. Thus began a series of arrests and releases, clinic closings and reopenings, all with the goal of changing the law. While she was the most prominent activist, she was not alone; about 20 other birth control advocates were imprisoned during this period (May 2011, 18).

Their efforts were ultimately, albeit incrementally, successful. Civil liberty attorneys and activists, including Sanger herself, strategically challenged Comstock laws and their progeny in court. An early appeal resulted in Sanger's conviction being upheld but an exception for physicians prescribing contraception for the "cure and prevention of a disease" (May 2011, 19). In 1936 *United States v. One Package of Japanese Pessaries* was decided by the U.S. Court of Appeals for the Second Circuit, removing restrictions on doctors sending birth control via the mail. Shortly after, the American Medical Association (AMA) formally recognized the medical legitimacy of contraception. The AMA-commissioned Committee to Study Contraceptive Practice stated, "The intelligent voluntary spacing of pregnancies may be desirable for the health and general well-being of mother and children" (Engelman 2011, 169). These victories were noteworthy, but also set the stage for ongoing conversations about legitimate and illegitimate uses of birth control, debates that were often policed by mostly male doctors rather than the women in need of the devices. Moreover, neither the *One Package* ruling nor AMA approval translated into automatic legal access; rather, significant state variations continued. In the years after *One Package* was decided, state-level restrictions, or "little Comstock laws," persisted: a number of states continued to restrict the advertising of contraception, and three states—Connecticut, Massachusetts, and Mississippi—prohibited contraception outright (Bailey 2010; Engelman 2011; Eig 2014a).

It would be several decades before U.S. Supreme Court cases established nationwide legal protections for contraceptive use. In 1965's *Griswold v. Connecticut* (381 U.S. 479), the court's majority held that the state's ban on contraceptive use constituted an unconstitutional violation of a fundamental right to privacy in the context of marriage.[5] Virtually all states repealed or modified contraceptive bans pertaining to married couples in compliance (Bailey 2010). Seven years after Griswold, *Eisenstadt v. Baird* (1972) struck down a Massachusetts law barring the distribution of contraceptive devices to unmarried individuals, thereby extending legal access regardless of marital status. Thus by the mid-seventies, the most stringent legal barriers to contraceptive use had fallen, but as we explore later in this chapter, other significant barriers remained.

The Role of Race

As with all notable social movements in the United States, race played a central role in shaping perspectives on birth control promotion and access. While Sanger's activism for birth control was initially forged in feminism and focused on the autonomy and the liberation of women, she struck strategic alliances with eugenics advocates and proponents of population control. In part this was because the mainstream women's movement of the time was largely focused on glorifying motherhood, which made for an uneasy alliance with birth control advocacy. As Dorothy Roberts, legal scholar and expert on race and reproductive health, explains (1997, 72),

> By framing her campaign in eugenics, Sanger could demonstrate that birth control served the nation's interest.... The language of eugenics gave scientific evidence to the movement's claim that birth control was an aspect of public health.... It helped to contest religious objections to birth control as interfering with God's will.

While eugenics has lost the celebrated scientific status it enjoyed in the twenties, the ugly legacy of this alliance persists, particularly when considering birth control in the context of forced sterilization.

The racial dimensions of this legacy are complicated. There is no question that eugenics was linked to racism, even if Sanger herself did not promote a racialized eugenics (Roberts 1997). Again, Roberts is instructive here (1997, 81):

> It appears that Sanger was motivated by a genuine concern to improve the health of the poor mothers she served, rather than eliminate their stock [but] in a society marked by racial hierarchy, [eugenic] principles inevitably produced policies designed to reduce black women's fertility.

In other words, given how deeply racism was (and is) ingrained into American culture, it is impossible to fully disentangle efforts to expand birth control from white supremacy. It is also clear that black civil rights activists themselves, most prominently W. E. B. Du Bois, pushed for greater access to contraceptives in predominantly black communities. Du Bois and Sanger teamed up to form the Negro Project to counter segregation-era policies that restricted birth control clinics to white women only, and open clinics staffed by African American nurses and doctors (Gandy 2015). Sanger also spoke out against racism in other contexts: "Discrimination is a world-wide thing. It has to be opposed everywhere. That is why I feel the Negro's plight here is linked with that of the oppressed around the globe" (*Chicago Defender* 1945, quoted in Gandy 2015). Nevertheless, the linked history between racism and birth control promotion, population control and eugenics remains relevant. Race and gender scholar Angela Davis explains the tension between what she views as the liberating potential of birth control access, and the limitations of the movements to expand it (1983, 202):

> Birth control—individual choice, safe contraceptive methods, as well as abortions when necessary—is a fundamental prerequisite for the emancipation of women. ... The progressive potential of birth control remains indisputable. But in actuality the historical record of this movement leaves much to be desired in the realm of challenges to racism and class exploitation.

Racist practices linked to coercive birth control targeted toward women of color have persisted throughout the 20th century. Forced sterilization programs targeting black women were particularly common in southern states; Asians and Latinos, were particularly targeted in California (Ko 2016, No Más Bebés 2015). Evidence of widespread sterilization of Native American women exists through the 1970s and 1980s (Ko 2016)[6]. Moreover, more subtle—or, in some cases, not subtle at all—forms of racism are evident in rhetoric and policies surrounding birth control promotion, discussions of fertility, and welfare policy. These have included stigmatization of black women throughout welfare reform debates as hyperfertile and hypersexualized (Hancock 2004); legislation such as the bill introduced in 1958 by Mississippi state representative David H. Glass titled "An Act to Discourage Immorality of Unmarried Females by Providing for Sterilization of the Unwed Mother Under Conditions of the Act; and for Related Purposes," which explicitly targeted black women (Solinger 1992); and numerous policies that either paid welfare recipients for using hormonal birth control or threatened to withhold benefits if they did not (Brown and Eisenberg 1995; Harting et al. 1969; Morrison 1965; Shepherd 1964; Rosenfield et al. 1991; Lewin 1991).

It is further important to consider the gendered divides within racial equality activists. Feminists of color frequently played a dual role in pressuring groups dominated by white women to take the concerns of women of color more seriously, while simultaneously pressuring men of color to more fully embrace gender equality. In the 1970s, for example, black feminists were outspoken not just in promoting health access to birth control for women of color, but in resisting efforts by the Black Panthers and the Nation of Islam to equate birth control access with racial genocide, even if they were sympathetic to the distrust that gave rise to that concern (Nelson 2003, 87). Some policymakers were pointed in presenting this perspective. Shirley Chisholm, the first black woman elected to the U.S. Congress and the first black candidate to run at the top of a major party presidential ticket, put it thusly: "To label family planning and legal abortion programs 'genocide' is male rhetoric, for male ears. It falls flat to female listeners and to thoughtful male ones" (Chisholm 2010, 130).

As we revisit in chapter 8 on public opinion, this history has shaped racial divisions in attitudes over time, but differences in white and black attitudes on the current debate are relatively minor. Moreover, advocacy groups that work specifically on the concerns of reproductive justice for women of color were uniform in supporting expanding access to contraception under the ACA. But it is nevertheless the case that white voices, those of elected officials and media sources, dominated the public conversation around birth control, and therefore also constitute much of our analysis. It is worth thinking critically about which voices were not being heard.

Scientific Context

Legal barriers were not the only obstacles to reliable birth control. Advocates still believed that existing methods were too reliant on men's compliance, and dreamed of a simpler approach. More broadly, raised awareness of venereal disease during World War I invited an era where "Americans began to think of sex as a matter of public health worthy of scientific and social research" (Eig 2014, 49). By midcentury, technological solutions to social problems were very much in vogue, and physicians enjoyed a newfound level of admiration and respect for their expertise (Watkins 2001).

In 1950 Katherine McCormick, a wealthy feminist activist and MIT graduate, reached out to Sanger about funding nascent birth control research (May 2011, 22). The two met years earlier, at a talk of Sanger's, and their collaboration would prove to be a deeply fruitful one. The women teamed up with biologist Gregory Pincus, who pioneered the use of progesterone to inhibit ovulation, and later John Rock, the gynecologist who first tested the hormone on human subjects and served as a prominent advocate for its use in the United States (May 2011, 14). Other key players in the scientific development of hormonal birth control include Carl Djerassi and Russell Marker, chemists who synthesized progesterone from Mexican yams, and Min Chueh Chang, a biologist who collaborated with Pincus and performed many of the their early tests, including the first animal experiments.

While the contributions of these scientists are clearly significant, scholars of the development and history of the pill are careful to steer readers away from oversimplified narratives with just a few instrumental heroes. Specifically, as historian of medicine Lara Marks explains, many of the most important contributions were marginalized at the time (2010, 11–12):

> The making of the pill was dependent on the expertise and knowledge of a variety of people—men and women—from a multitude of disciplines and backgrounds. One of the most interesting features of these individuals was that many of them remained on the periphery of society and their work was often viewed with great suspicion, reflecting the sensitive nature of contraceptive research in the first half of the twentieth century. Only once the pill had become an accepted part of life were they celebrated.

The gendered patterns were stark. Women championed the pill's development and bore the risks of early testing, while "men responded to the pill primarily through media spokesmen, who took up the social, sexual and moral implications of oral contraceptives" (May 2011, 6). From the inception of hormonal birth control, the disconnect between women's private lives and men's public commentary is evident.

After smaller-scale tests in Boston under the pretense of infertility treatment,[7] the first large-scale clinical trials took place in Puerto Rico, beginning in 1956 under the supervision of two female physicians, Drs. Edris Rice-Wray and Adaline Satterthwaite (Marks 2010; May 2011). Birth control was legal in Puerto Rico, and birth control clinics were prevalent. Poverty was rampant. Consent in these trials was troublingly limited. There is evidence that the women who participated were desperate for more reliable birth control and signed up for the testing willingly, and their health was monitored. They were informed, to some degree, of the nature of the research, but while the process was relatively standard for the time, it falls far short of what we would consider informed consent today (Marks 2010, 102–3). Specifically, language and literacy limitations call into question their ability to fully consent. Moreover, the women who participated were not made completely aware of the risks, and serious side effects, including dizziness, headaches, and nausea, were common. While Rice-Wray was troubled enough that she sought to end the study, Rock and Pincus were dismissive; the latter even wrote off the women's complaints as psychosomatic (May 2011, 31). Concerns about side effects, racist coercion, and the attendant gendered dimensions of male doctors seemingly unconcerned with women's consent or suffering would remerge in feminist critiques of the pill in the 1970s and beyond.

The Food and Drug Administration approved Envoid, the first U.S. oral hormonal contraceptive, for contraceptive use in 1960 (use for treating menstrual disorder had been approved a few years earlier, prompting an "unusually large number of women [to] report severe menstrual disorders" [Nikolchev 2010]). Five years later, nearly 6.5 million American women were taking oral birth control (Gibson 2015). Worldwide, roughly 200 million women have taken the pill; around 70 million used it daily at the start of the 21st century (Marks 2010, 3). In the mid-2010s, roughly 10 million persons in the United States used the pill, and a few million used other hormonal methods (Guttmacher Institute 2018).

Unlike barrier methods, hormonal birth control uses synthetic forms of hormones, usually progesterone and estrogen, to inhibit ovulation. In the decades that followed, other devices were developed: intrauterine devices (IUDs) in the 1960s; low-dose pills and the copper IUD in the 1980s; Norplant, implants, injectable methods, and emergency contraception in the 1990s; and the hormonal patch and vaginal ring in the 2000s (Thompson 2013). In the half century or so since the pill went into widespread use, considerable research has taken place in developing new delivery methods and improving safety, but while usage remains common, and options for women are more prevalent than there were when Envoid was first debuted, concerns about side effects persist.

The power dynamics at play between women consumers and mostly male physicians is fascinating. On the one hand, women need the doctor's permission; on the other, they were usually the ones seeking it out, not the typical case for prescription medication. And there was an added consequence of more scrutiny of a woman's reproductive system, for good and for ill. Scholars of the pill's history tend to view claims that the pill invited the sexual revolution as overblown; there are too many other relevant factors. The development of hormonal birth control did, however, coincide with, and to some degree shape, a sea change in how women's bodies are viewed, literally and figuratively, by the medical profession. As Marks writes (2010, 8),

> Not only did it require medical prescription, but the fact that it interacted with the physiology of the body and that it needed to be taken by healthy women over long periods of time also meant that it necessitated greater medical supervision. In addition to turning contraception into a legitimate medical activity, the drug promoted a new form of preventive medicine. Requiring regular medical checkups, such as breast examinations and cervical smears, the pill allowed medical practitioners more scrutiny of their female patients than ever before.

As legal access to and medical advancements made oral contraceptives more widely available, concerns about its safety reemerged. Sanger and McCormick struggled mightily for a form of contraception that a woman could control, so it's striking that along with their success came claims from feminists that the pill was being used to control women, without their informed consent (Watkins 2001). In particular, activists complained that women were not being fully informed about the side effects of hormonal birth control. Their activism culminated in what became as the Nelson Pill Hearings, convened by U.S. senator Gaylord Nelson of Wisconsin in 1970 to investigate the risks of the birth control pill.

The parallels between those hearings and the more recent hearing we explore later in the book are dramatic. Previewing protests to come, feminists expressed outrage at the lack of women participating in the hearing. Activist Alice Wolfson interrupted the hearing, and the exchange is striking. Wolfson stood up from the gallery and shouted, "Why had you assured the drug companies that they could testify? Why have you told them that they could get top priority? They're not taking the pills, we are!" Senator Nelson responded, "We are not going to permit the proceedings to be interrupted in this way. . . . If you ladies would sit down . . ." Wolfson came back with, "I don't think the hearings are any more important than our lives."[8]

The protest garnered immediate media attention. Later in an interview with a reporter, Wolfson explained, "We are objecting to the fact that there are no women testifying and that there are no women on the panel. We are tired of men controlling our lives and our bodies."[9] Ultimately the women succeeded in securing an insert detailing potential side effects included with each prescription. They also organized the National Women's Health Network, a nonprofit advocacy group that seeks to amplify women's voices in health-care debates. Their protest was successful on a number of fronts, raising public awareness, galvanizing opposition, and securing policy change. The Nelson hearings illustrate once again the tensions between male expertise and women's experience, and the intersection of media, policy, gender, and who has the microphone. The next time this political issue would become high profile would be in the form of expanded coverage under the Affordable Care Act—the topic under consideration for the bulk of this volume.

Consideration of the history of the development of birth control sheds light on three key points that inform our analysis of its current politics. First, the six frames that form the backbone of our analysis of the varied ways birth control is covered, debated, and understood (religious freedom, health, reproductive rights, economics, morality, partisan/strategic game) are not new phenomena. Rather they have been ever present, to varying degrees, throughout generations of struggles over development, access, and regulation of contraception. Second, the nature of the "varying degrees" is significant; while demands for birth control, and women's usage of it in some form, has been present throughout human history, the contested nature of that practice has varied considerably. We focused largely on the key controversies here, but as we will return to in our analysis of public opinion (chapter 8), there have been periods of relative quietude in debates over birth control as well. Understanding which frames are dominant both in driving expansion and in promoting restriction, who utilizes those frames, and the high-profile politicized conflict that ensues, is therefore critical. This is the key project of this text, developed throughout the chapters that follow on policy and media framing. Finally, the reoccurring refrain of "Where are the women?" or in Wolfson's words, "We are tired of men controlling our lives and our bodies," echoes loudly in the history covered here and in the chapters that follow. We explore how and when women's voices, experience, and expertise were valued in birth control debates, and how and when they were devalued. We consider the ways in which persistent underrepresentation of women in positions of power affected rhetoric and policy, but also how, even in the minority, women played formative roles, voicing substantive concerns, pulling policy levers where and when they could. As Karpowitz and Mendelberg write, "Low numbers do not doom women to powerlessness" (2014, 331). In short, the women asking, "Where are the women?" are, in effect, answering their own question: they are there, if not always recognized or given equal time, and, as we see in the pages that follow, their voices play a significant role in the politics of birth control.

3

Contraception Coverage Policy in the States

At the time of the U.S. Department of Health and Human Services' (HHS) August 2011 announcement, twenty-eight states had already adopted policies mandating insurance coverage of prescription contraceptives for women (VanSickle-Ward and Hollis-Brusky 2013). Understanding how the birth control debate unfolded in the states is critical for a number of reasons. First, because the states were the most active source of policymaking on contraception coverage for a number of years, consideration of laws crafted at the state level is essential to a complete picture of the landscape of birth control policy in the United States. Second, the dynamics that we explore here set the stage for the debates that we consider at the federal level—indeed, regulations under the Affordable Care Act (ACA) are modeled after statutory language from state mandates. Finally, looking at the states offers a unique opportunity to consider the impact of gender on policy adoption with a considerable degree of variation in gender composition of legislative branches. Later chapters show that women were critical in shaping both policy and discussion under the ACA, but those discussions involve deep dives into how multiple actors shaped and talked about one policy. Here we have a chance to consider how women's representation affected attempts to pass comparable policies across all states—a bird's-eye view before we unpack the details on the ground at the federal level.

Toward that end, in this chapter we consider the political, religious, and ideological factors that shaped the successful passage and content of this diverse group of policies, with a particular focus on the impact of women officeholders. Specifically, we demonstrate that the gender and partisan composition of state legislatures exerted a strong influence on whether state governments enacted contraceptive mandates between 1998 and 2009. Our analysis shows that legislatures with high levels of gender parity and operating under unified Democratic control were vastly more likely to pass laws mandating birth control coverage than states with few women legislators or operating under unified

The Politics of the Pill: Gender, Framing, and Policymaking in the Battle over Birth Control. Rachel VanSickle-Ward, Kevin Wallsten, Oxford University Press (2019). © Oxford University Press.
DOI: 10.1093/oso/9780190675349.001.0001

Republican control. We also show, however, that women's power to shape state-level contraceptive mandates was not consistent across institutions or across different aspects of the policymaking process. Larger percentages of women in state legislatures were not correlated, for example, with broader protections for birth control access in successfully implemented contraceptive mandates, and having a woman governor exerted no influence whatsoever over the passage or content of laws requiring insurance coverage of contraception.

These results not only help shed light on the link between substantive and descriptive representation (see, e.g., Carroll 2001; Childs, Sarah, and Lovenduski 2013; Osborn 2012; Pitkin 1967; Reingold 2008; Swers 2002, 2013) but they also serve as a useful reminder about the importance of electing women to serve in state legislatures. Indeed, while much attention is paid to electing more women to Congress, in this chapter we demonstrate the concrete policy changes that can result from more gender equity at the state level. As importantly for our purposes here, the findings presented below provide the necessary context for understanding the factors that would come to define the 2012 debate over birth control and the ACA.

Evolution of Contraceptive Coverage Law

In 1994, nearly two decades before Congress's passage of the ACA, Sandra Fluke's testimony, and the Supreme Court's ruling in *Hobby Lobby*, California introduced the first legislation mandating coverage of contraception by insurance plans that covered other kinds of prescription drugs ("Guaranteeing Coverage of Contraceptives" 2012). Sponsored by the California Elected Women's Education and Research Institute, the legislation (AB 3749) required coverage of contraceptive management, counseling, and advice, as well as all FDA-approved prescription drugs and devices (Assembly Bill Analysis AB 3749 1994).[1] It further exempted "insurance companies that are subsidiaries of religious organizations or employers that are religious organizations from the requirement to offer forms of treatment for contraception inconsistent with the organization's religious and ethical principles."[2]

Bill analyses noted the billions of dollars in contraception costs incurred by women in their child-bearing years. Analysts cited national surveys finding that half of all "typical" plans failed to cover reversible contraceptive devices. In fact, surgical intervention, including abortion and sterilization, were covered at a higher rate than preventative contraceptive care. "Although these services are not pregnancy services," the Senate floor bill analysis stated, "they are directly related to good birth outcomes as well as the general health of women." According to the Senate analysis, the Association of California Life Insurance Companies "generally opposes" mandates that include benefits in all insurance policies because they "unfairly impose the cost for these benefits on the segment of society that can least afford it, namely, small businesses and individuals" (Senate Bill Analysis AB 3749 1994).

Debate over the bill prompted numerous advocacy organizations within the state to make public stands. The California Academy of Family Physicians came out in favor of the legislation, arguing,

> [We] have seen the cost of contraceptive care skyrocket, making it difficult for many women to practice responsible birth control. . . . Currently, only 53 percent of women with family incomes at 200 percent of the poverty level have insurance coverage for contraceptives. With data indicating that more than 50 percent of all pregnancies are unintended, and that 50 percent of those end in abortion, we believe that a clear crisis in contraceptive management exists in California, resulting in undue hardship to women and unnecessary costs to our health care system.[3]

Other women's groups and medical practitioners also voiced their support for the legislation, including the California Nurses' Association, Planned Parenthood Affiliates of California, the Commission on the Status of Women, and the American College of Obstetricians and Gynecologists. Insurance companies opposed the bill, joined by the California Catholic Conference. In the end, opponents of the mandate got their way and the bill died in the state Assembly.

The victory of the mandate's California opponents, however, would be short-lived. In 1998, many insurance plans began covering the male impotency medication Viagra ("Guaranteeing Coverage of Contraceptives" 2012). The discrepancy between insurance coverage of Viagra and the lack of coverage for birth control became a rallying cry for women's health advocates around the country (Kilborn 1998). In California, state senator Jackie Speier and state assemblyman Robert Hertzberg framed their "Contraceptive Equity Act" (which required health insurance companies that cover prescription drugs to also cover birth control) as an explicit response to insurance companies' decision to cover Viagra. As Assemblyman Hertzberg's spokesman Paul Hefner explained,

> The fact that so many insurance companies were quick to accept Viagra certainly laid bare the notion that whenever new technology becomes available for men, the insurance companies are willing to put it on their formularies but we are not doing the same for women. . . . We really see this as strictly a fairness and equity issue. Until we provide this

coverage, an unequal and discriminatory form of health care continues to exist, and we think that's dead wrong. (Chesky 1999)

During the legislative debate over the Contraceptive Equity Act, the bill's cosponsors and supporters, including the American College of Obstetricians and Gynecologists, the California Medical Association, and California Planned Parenthood, placed front and center questions of gender equity tied to insurance coverage of Viagra. American Civil Liberties Union (ACLU) attorney Michelle Welsh, for example, said, "This bill really goes a long way in closing the gender gap in health care" (Chesky 1999). Similarly, Assemblywoman Hannah Beth Jackson claimed that the coverage decisions violated a principle of "basic fairness to women" and that she was "deeply offended by the notion that men in this room [the state Assembly] are standing up here and telling us how to exercise our right of conscience" (California Healthline Daily Edition 1999).

There was, of course, opposition in the state to mandating insurance coverage of contraception. Most notably, Republicans in the legislature argued that it "would be wrong . . . to ignore the religious beliefs" of Catholic groups and Catholic-owned hospitals (California Healthline Daily Edition 1999). Although Republican opposition had successfully thwarted four previous attempts to require birth control coverage,[4] the national political environment related to contraception had changed significantly by time the California legislature was debating the Contraceptive Equity Act in the summer of 1999. Only a year earlier, in 1998 Maryland passed the first state law mandating insurance coverage of prescription contraceptives (if plans also covered prescription drugs). Perhaps more importantly, Congress mandated inclusion of FDA-approved contraceptives for plans providing coverage to federal employees under the Federal Health Benefits Plan ("Guaranteeing Coverage of Contraceptives" 2012). Republican women, most notably House member Nancy L. Johnson and Senator Olympia J. Snowe, were key sponsors of this legislation. Johnson argued that the bill "demonstrates that across the ideological spectrum, we recognize that women—and men—have to have the right to plan their families" (Kilborn 1998). These changes, coupled with the election of a Democratic governor in 1998, led California to enact the Contraceptive Equity Act in 1999.

Comparing State Laws

By mandating insurance coverage of contraception in 1999 California became part of a growing national movement to expand access to birth control. In 1999 alone, ten states passed contraceptive coverage laws. In the decade that followed, nineteen others followed suit. Other states changed their policy in the direction of coverage through nonlegislative means. Michigan's contraceptive mandate resulted from an administrative ruling, for example, and Montana's mandate followed from an attorney general opinion. While there is significant variation across these policies, the thread that ties them together is the requirement that all plans providing prescription coverage must also provide contraceptive coverage (Stabile 2004, 747; Lowell 2004, 450; VanSickle-Ward and Hollis-Brusky 2013).These state mandates typically target small-group employer benefit plans that operate through state law (Stabile 2004, 747).[5]

Despite the fact that all of these state-level statutes purport to mandate contraceptive equity, the way in which the statutory provisions are worded can significantly limit their scope and reach. For example, the definition of "contraceptives" varies from state to state. The California statute (Cal Health & Saf Code §1367.24 [2012]), for instance, mandates that plans "shall include coverage for *a variety of*" FDA approved contraceptives. The Georgia statute (O.C.G.A. § 33-24-59.6 [2011]) mandates coverage "for *any* prescribed drug or device approved by the [FDA]." The Hawaii code (HRS § 431:10A-116.7 [2011]) defines contraceptive supplies as including "*all* United States Food and Drug Administration–approved contraceptive drugs or devices used to prevent unwanted pregnancy" (emphases added). The interpretation of these slight but important differences in wording by insurance companies and third parties has determined which brands of the birth control pill women have access to (Lowell 2004–2005, 450).

The definition of "contraception" in these laws is important for women's access to particular forms of birth control. Yet the single most important factor determining the scope and reach of these contraceptive equity statutes is the inclusion of language exempting individuals or groups that have religious or moral objections to contraceptives—so-called conscience clauses. Currently, 20 states include such language in their contraceptive mandates (Guttmacher 2012a). While the exact language varies from state to state, these conscience clauses generally do three things: identify the types of entities entitled to claim an exemption based on conscience, define the grounds that form the basis of that exemption, and identify what measures those claiming an exemption can take to mitigate the deleterious effects on those needing contraceptive services (Lowell 2004–2005, 455–56). In doing so, these conscience clauses attempt to strike a balance between the states' concern for contraceptive equity and the rights of conscience secured under the Free Exercise clause of the First Amendment to the U.S. Constitution.[6] Some states err on the side of religious liberty, defining very broadly *who* qualifies for an exemption.[7] For example, the Maryland statute (Md. Insurance Code Ann. § 15-829 [2011]) uses the following language to define who qualifies for an exemption: "A religious organization may request ... an exclusion from coverage ... if the required coverage conflicts with the religious organization's bona fide religious beliefs and practices." Such broad wording qualifies church-associated hospitals, charities, universities, and even health insurers for an exemption, thereby placing the greatest number of women at risk of going without contraceptive coverage.

Other states, such as California and New York, have very narrowly carved exemptions for religious conscience, bringing church-associated hospitals, charities, and universities within the purview of the mandate. To qualify for an exemption under the California code (Cal Health & Saf Code § 1367.25 [2012]), for example, an entity needs to satisfy each of these four criteria:

(1) The inculcation of religious values is the purpose of the entity.
(2) The entity primarily employs persons who share the religious tenets of the entity.
(3) The entity serves primarily persons who share the religious tenets of the entity.
(4) The entity is a nonprofit organization as described in Section 6033(a)(2)(A)I or iii of the Internal Revenue Code of 1986, as amended.

Two of the states (California and New York) that passed laws that afforded broader levels of coverage—that is, they had narrow conscience clauses—were challenged by faith-based Catholic organizations in *Catholic Charities of Sacramento v. California* (2004)[8] and *Catholic Charities of the Diocese of Albany v. Serio* (2006).[9] The plaintiffs in these cases unsuccessfully argued that the mandate violated their right to free exercise of religion (VanSickle-Ward and Hollis Brusky 2013). Of note, these state statutes would serve as a model for the contraception coverage under the ACA (VanSickle-Ward and Hollis Brusky 2013; Lipton-Lubet 2014).

Literature Review

In chapter 1 we explained the importance of exploring links between descriptive and substantive representation, and noted some of the work done in that regard on state legislatures (Poggione 2004; Reingold and Smith 2012; Osborn 2012; Carroll 2001). As we explained, with important caveats, women legislators have been found to take distinct policy stances, introduce more bills, and invest more energy in shepherding legislation through the process (Reingold 2008). In this section, we further develop our discussion of state policymaking in general, and of state policymaking around birth control in particular.

The importance of state governments and state-level politics in shaping social policy, including health care, has been well established. A number of studies have explored the impact of political and institutional variations on legislative priorities, budgeting, and policy precision (see, for example, VanSickle-Ward 2014; Huber and Shipan 2002; Volden 2002; Tolbert and Steuernagel 2001; Weissert 2004, 2000; Weissert and Silberman 2002; Kousser 2002; Winston 2002). In addition to the multiple advantages of comparing states to one another, analysis of state policies allows us to better understand how state policymaking differs from, is informed by, and influences policy making at the federal level (VanSickle-Ward 2014).

From a comparative perspective, state-to-state variation in institutional design and political environment is ideal: significant enough to serve as fertile ground for testing meaningful research questions, but not so great that it precludes appropriate controls and generalizability (VanSickle-Ward 2014). This is particularly important in providing context for the birth control debate, since most of the focus is on federal reform. As we see in later chapters, the impact of women policymakers on federal law is significant, but only at the state level do we have the opportunity to compare how different levels of women's representation within legislative bodies lead to different outcomes on comparable bills.

While health and welfare policy have long been central concerns for policy scholars, and especially for scholars of state policymaking, the current political climate on birth control gives this topic particular urgency. The law enacting the most dramatic change in birth control coverage, the ACA[10] is in a precarious position. If congressional Republicans are successful in repealing the ACA, state-level policies will again become the primary way in which birth control accessibility is promoted and regulated. Indeed, legislatures in a number of states have already taken action to expand contraception access in anticipation of possible changes to the ACA (Villegas 2017).

So what do we know about state policymaking dynamics and birth control policy? Deb McFarlane and Kenneth Meier (2001) describe birth control issues in terms of morality policy more broadly characterized by "heterogeneous preferences with some highly inelastic demand, and differences between public pronouncements and private behavior" (5). This latter point becomes particularly salient when we consider here and elsewhere the disconnect between pronouncements of the Catholic Church, and practices of rank-and-file Catholics. McFarlane and Meier further note that "American fertility control policy permits nearly unlimited access to contraception and abortion for adults who can pay for these services from their own funds or through private insurance" (14). The wealthy, then, are relatively immune to the public policy around birth control except vis-à-vis FDA approval of certain types of contraception. The role of public policy is much more pronounced for low-income individuals. Thus, the focus here on insurance coverage as key for access is critical, rather than just policies around the development of birth control methods. Finally, contraception is usually a less controversial policy than abortion. Increased salience occurs when advocates of restricted contraception provision or use are able to tie the issue to abortion or to access to minors (McFarlane and Meier, 2001, 15). One way to tie contraception to abortion is through focus on conscience clauses, which, as we cover in more depth in the next chapter, emerged most prominently in abortion policy. This dimension is worth keeping in mind here as we examine how conscience clauses played a key role in state-level policy, and also set the stage for the center of controversy in debates over federal policy regarding birth control.

Variation in the wording of conscience clauses has received some attention in the law review literature. Scholars have debated the constitutionality of these clauses, highlighting how the variation in the wording thereof can affect the delicate constitutional balance between religious freedom and the establishment of religion (see, e.g., Stabile 2004; Bailey 2004; Gilbert 2006; Miller 2006; Kubasek, Tagliarina, and Staggs 2007). Groups concerned with women's reproductive health have also examined the proper wording, constitutionality, and possible impact of these conscience clause exemptions for women's reproductive health (ACLU 2002; Guttmacher Institute 2012a; Center for Reproductive Rights 2012).

There is limited political science work explicitly on the key drivers of state birth control policy. In their study of state-level variation in women's healthcare policy, Tolbert and Steuernagel (2001) offer a compelling analysis of the political factors promoting the adoption of contraception insurance mandates, noting that they "vary in their comprehensiveness" (7) and treat them as part of an index of women's health-care policy. More recent work has examined the level of precision in state birth control laws as a function of political and institutional fragmentation and considered the consequences of statutory specificity in court decisions (VanSickle-Ward and Hollis-Brusky 2013), and framing of the contraceptive debate in Maryland (Rasmussen 2011).

Looking specifically at the impact of women legislators on reproductive policy in the states, the results are compelling but mixed. Scholars have found an impact of women in state legislatures on abortion policy (Berkman and O'Connor 1993; Hansen 1993; Kreitzer 2015; Norrander and Wilcox 2001; Tatalovitch and Schier 1993; Wetstein 1996) and on "women-friendly policies" that includes reproductive rights (Caiazza 2004).[11] Work looking at contraceptive coverage as a part of an index of women's health found that states that had recently elected women to the legislature were more likely to adopt contraceptive coverage laws, but there was no impact on the overall health index (Tolbert and Steuernagel 2001). And, as with so many policy areas, the influence of women is heavily contextualized by party (Osborn 2012). It is also worth noting here that in addition to studies on abortion being far more prevalent than studies of contraceptive coverage, when it is considered, contraceptive policy is sometimes folded into a discussion of women's health policy (Tolbert and Steuernagel 2001; Osborn 2012), leaving work to be done on the particular politics of birth control.

Data and Methods

Extending previous work on the level of detail in contraceptive laws (VanSickle-Ward and Hollis-Brusky 2013), in this chapter we ask two distinct questions about state-level policies regarding birth control: What factors shape whether a state adopted any law mandating insurance coverage of contraception? What factors shape the "scope" of birth control mandates among those states that enacted them?

In order to measure whether a state adopted a birth control mandate, we relied on the data assembled by the Guttmacher Institute 2018; and National Conference of State Legislatures 2012.[12] As mentioned above, we were also interested in how many women were covered by the mandates enacted in each state. In order to measure this concept of legislative scope, we examined the expansiveness of conscience clauses in the bills actually passed by state legislatures. The more limited the conscience clause, the broader and more generous the mandated coverage (as fewer organizations are allowed to opt out).[13] In other words, states with limited (or no) conscience clauses have more all-encompassing coverage mandates, while states with more expansive conscience clauses have a narrower mandate (because many organizations can claim an exemption). Utilizing the measure developed by the Guttmacher Institute, we assigned each state's law a scope score, with the lowest score referring to states that passed mandates with expansive conscience clauses and the highest score referring to states that passed laws with no conscience clause exemptions at all).[14]

Our primary independent variables of interest concerned the gender composition of state governments. Based on the literature discussed above, we hypothesized that higher percentages of women in the state legislature would increase the probability that states would pass birth control mandates and that these laws, once enacted, would provide broader access to contraceptive coverage.

> H1: States with higher percentages of women serving in the legislature will have higher probabilities of enacting contraceptive mandates.
> H2: Among those states that have enacted contraceptive mandates, states with higher percentages of women serving in the legislature will have narrower conscience clause exemptions.

Due to the fact that enacting state-level laws generally requires gubernatorial approval, we hypothesized that women governors would have an analogous impact on the likelihood of passing a contraceptive mandate and on the content of an approved mandate.

> H3: States with a female governor will have a higher probability of enacting contraceptive mandates than states with a male governor.
>
> H4: Among those states that have enacted contraceptive mandates, states with a female governor will have narrower conscience clause exemptions than states with a male governor.

Debates around contraception are powerfully shaped by the long-term political and religious predispositions held by average citizens. Thus, our analysis controls for several other state-level variables, including the public's partisan identification, the public's ideological leanings, and the public's religious affiliation. To be more precise, because contraceptive mandates generally receive more support from Democrats, we hypothesized that states with larger percentages of people self-identifying with the Democratic Party and as liberals will lead to an increased probability of passing a mandate and more expansive coverage for those states that enact mandates. Given the vocal and mobilized opposition of the Catholic Church to contraception, we also hypothesized that states with larger Catholic populations would be less likely to adopt a mandate and less likely to provide broad coverage if a bill was passed.

> H5: States with larger percentages of self-identified Democrats will have higher probabilities of enacting contraceptive mandates.
>
> H6: Among those states that have enacted contraceptive mandates, states with larger percentages of self-identified Democrats will have narrower conscience clause exemptions.
>
> H7: States with more liberal populations will have higher probabilities of enacting contraceptive mandates.
>
> H8: Among those states that have enacted contraceptive mandates, states with more liberal populations will have narrower conscience clause exemptions.
>
> H9: States with larger percentages of Catholics will have lower probabilities of enacting contraceptive mandates.
>
> H10: Among those states that have enacted contraceptive mandates, states with larger percentages of Catholics will have more expansive conscience clause exemptions.

While partisanship and ideology tend to function as political identities (Mason 2018) that do not change in the short term (Johnston 2006), public support for immediate government activity is far more volatile. The most notable body of research into the public's volatility in this regard draws on Stimson's (1991) concept of a policy "mood." Measures of policy mood aggregate responses to dozens of survey questions in order to identify the public's broad preferences about the size and scope of government.[15] A large literature indicates that this mood may exert an important influence on the actions of the federal (Stimson, MacKuen, and Erikson 1995; Casillas, Enns, and Wohlfarth 2011; McGuire and Stimson 2004) and state governments (Erikson, Wright, and McIver 1993; Lax and Phillips 2012; Pacheco 2013).[16] Based on this research, we hypothesize the following:

> H11: States in a more liberal policy "mood" will have higher probabilities of enacting contraceptive mandates.
>
> H12: Among those states that have enacted contraceptive mandates, states in a more liberal policy "mood" will have narrower conscience clause exemptions.

In chapter 2 we emphasized some of the ways that race and ethnicity have been closely intertwined with debates about contraception throughout American history. As a result, it is possible that the racial and ethnic composition of a state's population will exert an important influence over its contraception policies. Unfortunately, there is relatively little empirical work on the relationship between state-level racial and ethnic diversity and contraception policy. We include it in the analyses that follow in order to control for any potential impact on birth control mandates but we cannot spell out any well-grounded hypotheses.

Our analysis was not limited to assessing attributes of the public, however. We also examined how partisan control of the government and overall state government ideology shaped legislative voting on contraceptive mandates—with the expectation that Democratic control and more liberal state governments would enhance the probability of enacting bills with limited conscience clause exemptions.

> H13: States under unified Democratic control will have higher probabilities of enacting contraceptive mandates than states that are not.
>
> H14: Among those states that have enacted contraceptive mandates, states under unified Democratic control will have narrower conscience clause exemptions.

Table 3.1 presents a list of our independent variables, along with the sources of the data and explanation of coding. Data was collected for each state for each of the variables in Table 3.1 for every year between 1998 (the year that Maryland became the first state to pass a mandate) and 2009 (the year the last mandate was enacted in Wisconsin).

Results

Before discussing the factors that shaped the passage and content of contraception mandates, it is worth saying a few words about how states scored on our dependent variables. Figure 3.1 displays the cumulative number of states passing a contraceptive mandate policy from 1998 to 2009. As Figure 3.1 shows, adoption of mandates rose consistently over time. In 1998 Maryland was the first to pass a contraceptive mandate law. Ten states followed quickly in Maryland's footsteps and adopted birth control mandates in 1999. By 2009, 28 states had enacted some version of a contraceptive mandate. As Figure 3.1 also suggests, a large number of states (22) did not pass any legislative contraception coverage statutes between 1998 and 2009.[17]

Of the 28 states that adopted mandatory birth control coverage policies, 12 passed statutes with expansive conscience clauses (Arizona, Connecticut, Delaware, Hawaii, Illinois, Maryland, Missouri, Nevada, New Mexico, Texas, Virginia, and West Virginia); six (Arkansas, Maine, Massachusetts, New Jersey, North Carolina, and Rhode Island) passed statutes with broad conscience clauses; and three passed statutes with limited conscience clauses (California, New York, and Oregon). Only seven states—Colorado, Georgia, Iowa, New Hampshire, Vermont, Washington, and Wisconsin—enacted statutes with no conscience clauses (see Figure 3.2).

Adoption of Contraceptive Mandates

In order to answer our two distinct research questions, we employed two distinct modeling strategies. First, following previous studies of gender and comparative policy adoption (e.g., Kittilson 2008; Kreitzer 2015), we employed event-history analysis (EHA). EHA (Yamaguchi 1991; Box-Steffensmeier and Jones 1997) is a commonly used methodological tool for researchers interested in "predicting the conditions under which a dichotomous dependent variable of interest switches in value from 0 (the lack of a condition) to 1 (the presence of a condition)" (Crowley 2006, 528). Although there are many different approaches to EHA, we relied on a Cox proportional hazards model. Cox models allow us

Table 3.1 **Independent Variables Explaining Contraceptive Mandate Laws**

Variable	Source	Coding
Percentage of Women in the Legislature	Center for American Women and Politics	The percentage of women in the state legislature
Female Governor	Center for American Women and Politics	0 = Male governor 1 = Female governor
Public Party Identification	Erikson, Robert S., Gerald C. Wright, and John P. McIver. (1993). *Statehouse Democracy: Public Opinion, and Policy in the American States*. Cambridge University Press.	The percentage of Democratic identifiers minus the percentage of Republican identifiers in each state.
Public Ideology	Enns, P. K., and Koch, J. (2013). "Public Opinion in the U.S. States: 1956 to 2010." *State Politics and Policy Quarterly*, 13: 349–72.	The percentage of liberal identifiers minus the percentage of conservative identifiers in each state.
Public Policy Mood	Enns, P. K., and Koch, J. (2013). "Public Opinion in the U.S. States: 1956 to 2010." *State Politics and Policy Quarterly*, 13: 349–72.	A measure of the public's preferences for the size and scope of government (with higher scores indicating more liberal preferences)
Percentage Catholic	The Longitudinal Religious Congregations and Membership File, 1980–2010	The percentage of Catholic residents in the state
Percentage Non-White	Kelly, Nathan J., and Christopher Witko. (2014). "Government Ideology and Unemployment in the U.S. States." *State Politics & Policy Quarterly*, 14(4): 389–413.	The percentage of nonwhites living in the state
Republican Unified Government	Klarner, Carl. (2013). "State Partisan Balance Data, 1937–2011."	0 = Republicans do not have unified control of the state government 1 = Republicans have unified control of the state government
Democratic Unified Government	Klarner, Carl. (2013). "State Partisan Balance Data, 1937–2011."	0 = Democrats do not have unified control of the state government 1 = Democrats have unified control of the state government

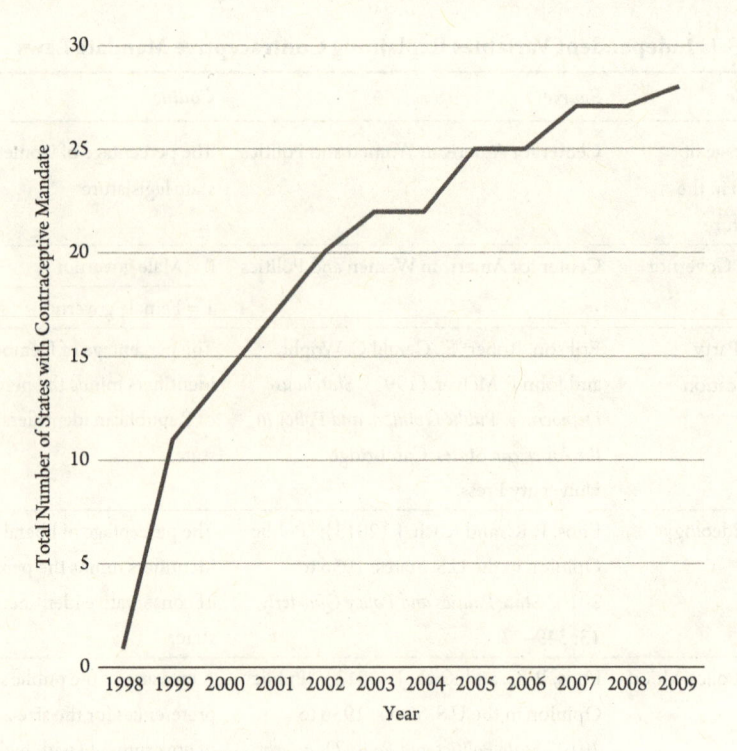

Figure 3.1 State Adoption of Contraceptive Mandates over Time

to assess which factors significantly increase or decrease a state's probability of adopting a contraceptive mandate. This probability is based on the likelihood that passage of a contraceptive mandate will occur at a certain time, given that it has not yet occurred (Yamaguchi 1991).[18]

Table 3.2 shows the results of the Cox model as hazard ratios. When the hazard ratio for a variable presented in Table 3.2 is greater than 1, it indicates that increases in that variable are associated with an increased probability of a state legislature enacting a contraceptive mandate. Alternatively, when the hazard ratio for a variable is less than 1, it indicates that increases in that variable are associated with a decreased probability of a state legislature enacting a contraceptive mandate.

We found strong support for our hypothesis (H1) that higher levels of gender diversity in state legislatures would be associated with mandating birth control coverage. As Table 3.2 shows, the percentage of women in the state legislature exerted a significant, positive, and substantively large impact on the probability that a state would enact a contraceptive mandate. Indeed, based on our analysis, a state with no women serving in the legislature was predicted to be 33 times less likely to enact a contraceptive mandate than a hypothetical state with an even number of male and female representatives.[19] This general pattern is

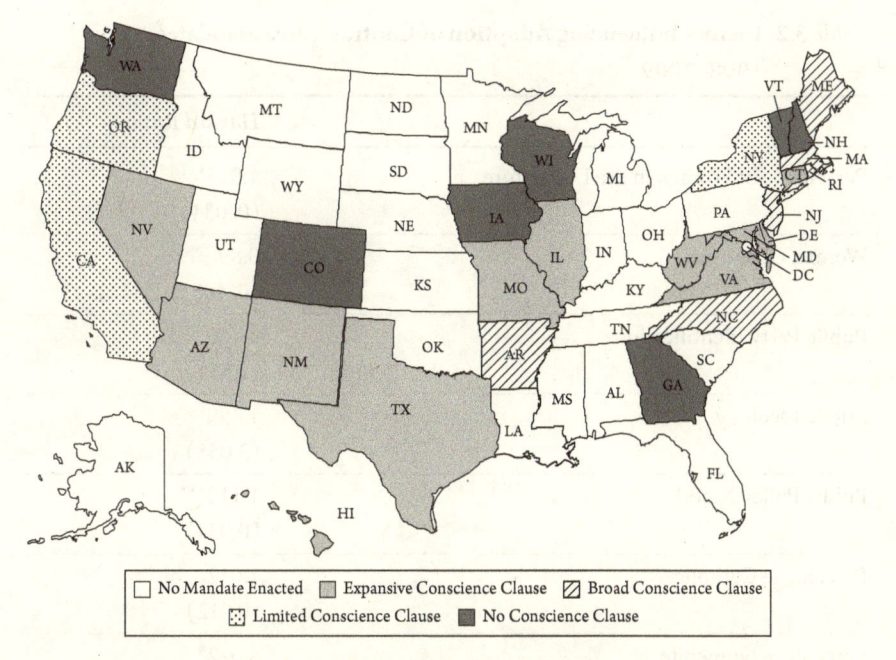

Figure 3.2 State Contraceptive Mandate Policies, 1998–2009

apparent when simply comparing the average percentage of women serving in state legislatures that passed a contraceptive mandate (25.3%) to the average percentage of women serving in state legislatures that did not enact a mandate (20.3%).

By contrast, having a woman governor did not lead states to become more likely to mandate birth control coverage. Male governors were in office when state legislatures passed 24 of the 28 contraceptive mandates enacted between 1998 and 2009, and women governors served 43 years in office across various states without successfully pushing through a mandate. As Table 3.2 also shows, this apparent lack of impact is not an illusion produced by confounding factors. Having a woman governor exerted no statistically significant influence over a state's likelihood of mandating birth control coverage even after controlling for other influences. The results of our analysis suggest, in other words, that having more gender diversity in the legislature was far more important for the adoption of contraceptive mandates than having a woman serve as governor.

We expected that more Democratic (H5), more liberal (H7), and fewer Catholic (H11) states would be more likely to enact contraceptive mandates. Although each of these variables appear highly correlated with the probability of passage at first glance (e.g. bivariate Cox analyses show that states with more Democratic Party identifiers, states with more self-identified liberal residents, and states with fewer Catholics were significantly more likely to enact a mandate),

Table 3.2 **Factors Influencing Adoption of Contraceptive Mandates, 1998–2009**

	Hazard Ratio
Percentage of Women in the Legislature	1.075*
	(0.034)
Woman Governor	0.89
	(0.408)
Public Party Identification	1.400
	(2.851)
Public Ideology	1.499
	(3.055)
Public Policy Mood	1.110***
	(0.034)
Percentage Catholic	1.012
	(0.012)
Percentage Nonwhite	5.022*
	(3.679)
Republican Unified Government	0.395
	(0.337)
Democratic Unified Government	4.885***
	(1.823)
N	373

Note: Table entries represent coefficient(estimates from Cox Regression Model. Robust standard errors in parentheses.
*$p < 0.05$, **$p < 0.01$, ***$p < 0.001$

these relationships are merely an artifact resulting from more Democratic, more liberal, and more Catholic states' tendency to elect more Democratic and more gender-diverse state legislatures (which, in turn, influence the probability of passing contraceptive mandates). As Table 3.2 shows, the relationships between the public's long-term political and religious predispositions and enacting contraceptive mandates disappear once the appropriate statistical controls are added to the model. Put differently, the values of a state's residents matter for the passage of contraceptive mandates only to the extent that they shape the composition of a state's government.

While long-term political and religious predispositions exerted only an indirect effect on birth control policy, the public's mood had a direct impact on the probability of enacting a contraceptive mandate. As Table 3.2 shows, states with populations that were in the mood for expansive government action were significantly more likely to pass a mandate even after controlling for the partisan and gender composition of the legislative and executive branches—with a state in a relatively liberal policy mood being nearly 17 times more likely to pass a contraceptive mandate than states in a relatively conservative policy mood.[20] Put differently, the long-term values of a state's residents matter for the passage of contraceptive mandates only to the extent that they shape the composition of a state's government while the shorter-term moods of residents exert a more direct influence over birth control policies.

Race and ethnicity seem to shape nearly all areas of American political life, including state-level contraception policy. As the hazard ratios in Table 3.2 show, states with fewer white residents were significantly more likely to pass contraceptive coverage mandates than states with more white residents. Our model predicts, for example, that even after controlling for all other factors, a hypothetical all-white state would be 1.6 times less likely to mandate birth control coverage than a hypothetical state with an even split between white and nonwhite residents. The racial composition of a state, in other words, was an important factor in determining whether that state expanded birth control access.

Since prior work on reproductive rights policy adoption in the states does not typically include race of state population as a variable, we are reluctant to offer a definitive interpretation of the mechanism driving this relationship here. That said, the fact that states with more nonwhite residents were likelier to adopt coverage mandates, even controlling for other factors, is worth reflecting on, particularly in the context of the complicated history around race and birth control discussed in the previous chapter. Prior scholarship suggests that spending on social welfare programs is generally lower in states with higher nonwhite populations (Grogan 1994; Kronebusch 1997). We also know that racial attitudes are a strong predictor in determining support for welfare programs among white individuals (Gilens 1996). Thus it seems possible, echoing concerns raised by some black activists around birth control more generally, that contraception coverage mandates are being adopted in states with higher proportions of nonwhite residents in lieu of more comprehensive health-care or social safety nets. Of course, our historical account also noted the role that nonwhite activists and policy elites played in expanding birth control access for their communities. This suggests a competing explanation: those advocates saw a greater need and gained more traction for expanding birth control access in more diverse states. We revisit the particular dynamics around race and support for contraception access in our discussion of public opinion in chapter 9.

H11 and H13 focused on how partisan control over a state's government might condition the probability of enacting a contraceptive mandate. At first glance, the relationship between the partisan composition of the government and the passage of contraceptive mandates is obvious: 12 contraceptive mandate laws were enacted under unified Democratic control of the government while only two mandates were approved by unified Republican governments. As Table 3.2 shows, this relationship holds up even once other factors are accounted for. When Democrats have simultaneous control of the state legislature and the state governorship, the probability of passing a contraceptive mandate significantly increases—with states under unified Democratic government being nearly five times more likely to implement a contraceptive mandate than states that were not.

Scope of Enacted Contraceptive Mandates

In addition to exploring whether states adopted a contraceptive mandate, we were interested in understanding the factors that shaped the content of the enacted mandates. Given that the text of laws did not change after passage by the legislature in any state during our period of study, we decided to pool our data and model the scope of contraceptive mandates as a function of variables for the year of enactment only.[21] The OLS regression results predicting the narrowness of birth control mandates are presented in Table 3.3.

Although greater gender parity in state legislatures exerted an important influence over a state's willingness to adopt a contraceptive mandate, it mattered very little for the scope of the mandate. Indeed, a number of states with very few women in the state legislature, such as Georgia in 1999 (18.6% women) and Iowa in 2000 (20.7% women), enacted statutes with no conscience clause exemptions, and a number of states with relatively high levels of female legislative representation, such as Arizona in 2002 (35.6% women) and Nevada in 1999 (36.5% women), passed laws with expansive conscience clauses. More importantly, as Table 3.3 shows, our measure of gender representation in the legislature (i.e., the percentage of women serving in the legislature) did not achieve statistical significance in our fully specified model. While women legislators, in other words, seem to be an essential part of ensuring the passage of contraceptive mandates, ideological and partisan predispositions in the public appear to be more important in determining their expansiveness.

Relatively few states have ever had women serve as governors. It is perhaps unsurprising, therefore, that only four of the 28 contraceptive mandates enacted by state governments between 1998 and 2009 were passed during the tenure of female governors. Two of these bills—the 1999 New Hampshire law passed under Governor Jeanne Shaheen and the 2007 Washington law passed under Governor Christine Gregoire—contained no conscience clause exemptions. The other two bills, however—the 2002 Arizona law passed under Governor

Table 3.3 **Factors Influencing Scope of Contraceptive Mandates, 1998–2009**

	Scope of Mandate
Percentage of Women in the Legislature	−0.019
	(0.014)
Woman Governor	0.281
	(0.165)
Public Party Identification	−1.854*
	(0.836)
Public Ideology	1.862*
	(0.897)
Public Policy Mood	−0.019
	(0.0106)
Percentage Catholic	0.003
	(0.004)
Percentage Nonwhite	−0.745
	(0.418)
Republican Unified Government	0.287
	(0.337)
Democratic Unified Government	0.307
	(0.185)
Constant	1.844*
	(0.724)
N	28
R-squared	0.546

Note: Table entries represent OLS regression coefficients. Robust standard errors in parentheses.
* $p < 0.05$, ** $p < 0.01$, *** $p < 0.001$

Jane Dee Hull and the 2002 Massachusetts law passed under Governor Jane Swift—both contained fairly expansive conscience clauses. Unsurprisingly, therefore, our multivariate analysis found no evidence that having a woman governor led to mandates ensuring broader access to birth control.

As discussed above, the public's political predispositions were less important than the composition of government in explaining why some states adopted contraceptive mandates and others did not. By contrast, the public's political predispositions were more important than the composition of government in explaining why some states adopted bills with narrow conscience clauses and some states adopted bills with expansive conscience clauses. Consistent with our expectations (H8), states with a relatively larger number of self-identified liberal residents were more likely to adopt bills with no or limited conscience clause exemptions. Contrary to our expectations (H6), however, states with a larger percentage of self-identified Democrats were actually more likely to pass bills with expansive conscience clauses.

As discussed throughout this book, the Catholic Church has stridently opposed the passage of birth control mandates at the state and federal levels. Based on this opposition, we hypothesized that states with large Catholic populations might pass contraceptive mandates with expansive conscience clause exemptions. We found no evidence to support this hypothesis. Three of the seven states that passed mandates with no conscience clause exemptions, for example, have populations in which more than 25% of residents are Catholic (Vermont, New Hampshire, and Wisconsin). As Table 3.3 shows, the percentage of Catholics in a state had no identifiable effect on the content of contraceptive mandates. Similar to our findings about passage of birth control laws, therefore, it appears that the Catholic Church had minimal success in limiting the scope of contraceptive mandates across the states.

We hypothesized that lawmakers may enact contraceptive mandates with narrow conscience clauses when their constituents were in a liberal policy mood but adopt more expansive conscience clauses when their constituents were feeling more skeptical about government action. As Table 3.1 shows, state legislators did not demonstrate this kind of responsiveness to constituents. The public's mood, in other words, shaped whether a contraceptive mandate was passed at all but not the specific provisions it contained.

Surprisingly, having a unified Democratic government did not lead to less expansive conscience clauses and having a unified Republican government did not lead to more expansive conscience clauses in legislatively enacted mandates. Four of the 12 mandates enacted by unified Democratic governments contained broad conscience clauses, and although Republican unified governments were responsible for passing only two of the 28 mandates enacted between 1998 and 2009, one of those mandates—Colorado's 1999 law—included no conscience clause whatsoever. As Table 3.3 shows, unified control of government did not systematically lead to the inclusion (or exclusion) of conscience clauses in contraceptive mandates.

Discussion

The debates over contraceptive mandates that played out across the United States between 1998 and 2009 foreshadowed some (but certainly not all) of the fault lines that would emerge around the issue following implementation of the ACA. In the same way, our analysis of the factors that influenced the passage and content of these state-level birth control mandates foreshadows many of the conclusions we make throughout the rest of this book. First, women played a crucially important—yet subtle and easy to mischaracterize—role in the pre-ACA, state-level attempts to mandate insurance coverage of birth control. Having women in the state legislature was indispensable for passing a mandate. For example, there were 15 states (across a combined 85 years) in which women made up less than 15% of the legislature. There was not a single contraceptive mandate approved in any of these states until gender representation in the legislature increased above 15%. High levels of gender parity had very little impact, however, on the specific content of contraceptive mandates, as having a larger percentage of women in state legislatures did not produce mandates containing fewer ways for employers to opt out based on their moral or religious objections to contraceptive use. Similarly, the gender of a state's governor mattered very little for how the politics of contraceptive mandates played out in that state. Having a woman governor did not boost a state's probability of passing a mandate nor did it lead to more or less expansive conscience clauses in mandates that were successfully proposed. In short, women's influence over the trajectory of contraceptive debates was profound but circumscribed.

Second, the Catholic Church became far more influential in debates surrounding contraception after the passage of the ACA than before it. The leadership of the Catholic Church and its affiliated organizations have staged the most organized, highest-profile, and longest-lasting fight against government efforts to guarantee comprehensive birth control coverage (most readily apparent in the Beck Fund's support for hundreds of legal challenges to such efforts) over the last two decades. We anticipated that states with a large percentage of Catholics might cater to the church's advocacy out of fear of electoral retribution and either avoid passing laws mandating birth control coverage or pass mandates that provided expansive conscience clause exemptions. The percentage of Catholics living in a state, however, had no impact on the probability of enacting a contraceptive mandate or on the inclusion of expansive conscience clauses. While it is possible that the Catholic Church was influential and that our statistical analysis missed its influence due to our failure to include any measures of church-backed lobbying, it is far more likely that religious considerations simply became more important after the passage of the ACA. The Catholic Church's influence, in other words, was a variable and not a constant.

Finally, debates around contraceptive mandates have been well described by both the "morality politics" and the "representational" models of public policy at different times (Kreitzer 2015). The morality politics model emphasizes the central role that public opinion and religious forces play in shaping policy choices on "easy" issues such as abortion, school prayer, and same-sex marriage. Because these issues are technically simple and speak to cherished values, the thinking goes, they provoke unusually high levels of citizen engagement and interest group activity (Meier and McFarlane 1993; Mooney and Lee 1995). The political pressure stemming from this heightened mobilization often compels policymakers to give special weight to public opinion and religious forces when making decisions on morality issues (Camobreco and Barnello 2008; Cohen and Barrilleaux 1993; Cook, Jelen, and Wilcox 1992; Norrander and Wilcox 2001; Wetstein and Albritton 1995; Wilcox 1989; Wlezien and Goggin 1993). The representation model, by contrast, focuses less attention on the public's advocacy and more attention on how the composition of governments (particularly in terms of gender and partisanship) shape policy outcomes (Berkman and O'Connor 1993; Hansen 1993; Norrander and Wilcox 2001; Tatalovich and Schier 1993; Wetstein 1996). From this perspective, governmental decisions on morality issues are more tied to the identities and values of policymakers than to the preferences of constituents.

During the period covered in this chapter, the politics of contraceptive mandates existed somewhere between the ideal typical images painted by the morality politics and representational models. Indeed, although birth control has always had some of the hallmark features of an easy morality issue, the question of state-level regulation connected to insurance coverage of contraception did not initially provoke the kind of intense division and rapidly expanding conflict that has come to characterize abortion, school prayer, or gay rights issues. As we show in our discussion of public opinion on contraceptive mandates (chapter 8), polling in the late 1990s and early 2000s showed widespread support for contraceptive mandates across nearly every segment of American society. The relatively uncontroversial and low-salience nature of many state-level debates over contraceptive mandates between 1998 and 2009 had the effect of freeing up representatives to make their own choices about the wisdom of regulating insurance coverage. As discussed above, whether a state passed a contraceptive mandate was largely a function of the partisan and gender composition of the government, and Catholic influence over the policymaking process appeared limited. The representational model, in short, seems to capture most of the essential features of pre-ACA debates about contraceptive mandates.

This is not to suggest, of course, that the morality politics model was an entirely poor fit for understanding these early state-level debates about contraception. As discussed above, the Catholic Church's opposition to contraceptive mandates can be traced back at least to California's 1994 attempt to require birth control coverage. In addition, this chapter's analysis of state-level mandates suggests that the public's mood was on policymakers' minds when debating contraception coverage requirements. In other words, the rough outline of the morality politics conflicts that would emerge after the ACA were evident around this issue for some time.

The dynamics explored here—policy salience, party, public opinion, how and when representation and morality politics inform the birth control debate, the influence of religion, and particularly the impact of women—continue to animate our investigation in the chapters that follow. We continue that exploration with a focus on how birth control coverage became a key component of one of the most landmark laws passed in recent decades: the ACA.

4

Contraception Coverage Policy in Congress

In the previous chapter, we explored the impact of women legislators on the adoption of state-level contraceptive coverage laws. Here we switch gears to consider federal policymaking. In this chapter we have two primary objectives: explain how birth control policy evolved at the federal level, and explain how and when women's voices mattered in the context of the birth control debate. More specifically, we provide an overview of the legislative and administrative stages of birth control policy at the federal level, with a particular focus on the Affordable Care Act (ACA), and analyze patterns in how policymaking elites framed the issue of contraceptive coverage. Our analysis relies on press accounts, transcripts from Senate floor deliberations, committee hearings, and in-depth interviews.[1] The first section briefly reviews the relevant literature on gender, policy, representation, and contraception. We then consider early federal attempts to expand contraceptive coverage, the development of the Women's Health Amendment within the ACA that laid the foundation for protecting women's preventative health care, and debates on the Senate floor over the inclusion of the Women's Health Amendment. We next turn our attention to the rules that emerged defining preventative care as including contraception, and congressional hearings debating those rules. Throughout these policymaking stages we examine how key actors employed different frames to make their case for or against mandated coverage of contraception. In the concluding section we analyze rhetorical patterns in legislative deliberations, discuss trends in how framing evolved over the course of these deliberations, and consider how the frame employed correlates with the gender of speakers. In later chapters we further probe the significance of these frames for how birth control policy was perceived and interpreted.

Overall, this chapter illustrates that women's impact on the birth control mandate was significant in a number of key ways. It was a female senator, Barbara Mikulski, who authored the Women's Health Amendment and fought for its

The Politics of the Pill: Gender, Framing, and Policymaking in the Battle over Birth Control. Rachel VanSickle-Ward, Kevin Wallsten, Oxford University Press (2019). © Oxford University Press.
DOI: 10.1093/oso/9780190675349.001.0001

inclusion in the final bill. Women's rights organizations worked closely with Mikulski and her staff, articulating the need for women's health to be proactively protected in the legislation and relaying the experiences of women who under existing law lacked coverage for birth control. When women were left out of testimony in high-profile hearings, female legislators and advocates sounded the alarm. At various points in the process, women emphasized reproductive rights and "gendered" frames more, and the religion frame less, on balance, than their male counterparts. Importantly, women made their voices heard despite being in the clear minority, and at certain points excluded altogether.

Literature

A great deal of our knowledge of how women shape policy outcomes in the United States comes from studies of legislating in general and Congress in particular (Carroll 2002; Dodson 2006; Dolan 1997; Frederick 2010; Swers 2002, 2013; Reingold 2008; Mansbridge 1999). We noted some of the primary findings drawn from this work in chapter 1; here we focus on the work most relevant for understanding deliberation of birth control—specifically work on the Senate, and work on the impact on rhetoric and deliberation of having women speakers.

The legislative activity we consider takes place mostly in the U.S. Senate. As Michele Swers explains in *Women in the Club* (2013), the Senate is hardly a place with a history of promoting equality: "in both its demographic make-up and its institutional rules, the Senate defied ideals of equal representation. For most of its history the Senate has been a white male bastion" (2). This was, as Swers notes, largely by design; the Senate was purposefully constructed by the founders to be less responsive than the House. In the words of James Madison, the Senate was constructed as "a defense to the people against their own temporary errors and delusions" as well as a "temperate and respectable body of citizens" to protect the masses from the "tyranny of their own passions" (Hamilton 1788). The Senate's removal from the masses was electorally built in for much of the Senate's history as well. Until the Seventeenth Amendment mandating direct election of senators was ratified in 1913, senators were selected by state legislative bodies, not the voters themselves.

For most of the nation's history, these "temperate and respectable" senators were white men. During the period of time most relevant for our study—that of the development of and deliberation over the ACA in 2009 and 2010, there were 17 women in the U.S. Senate (13 Democrats and four Republicans).[2] Moreover, because the health-care debate took place after Carol Moseley Braun left the body in 1999, and before 2012 when Mazie Hirono was elected, there were no women of color in the U.S. Senate.

According to Swers, "gender is a fundamental identity that affects the way that senators look at policy questions, the issues they prioritize, and the perspectives they bring to develop solutions" (2013, 3). This link between identity and policy outlook is shaped by how the senators understand public perceptions of them: "As they develop their legislative portfolio, female senators take into account long-standing public assumptions about voter stereotypes about women's policy expertise. The strong link between gender and women's issues enhances the credibility of women in these areas" (Swers 2013, 3). Several other studies have noted that women candidates are more likely to be trusted on issues that deal with caretaking and compassion, such as health care, education, and welfare (Alexander and Andersen 1993; Huddy and Terkildsen 1993; Leeper 1991; Kahn 1996). In contrast, men are more likely to be trusted on economics, public safety, and national security. Moreover the links between descriptive and substantive representation are forged through socialization and experiences and interests unique to women (Reingold 2000; Mezey 1994; Pearson and Dancy 2011).[3] As we explained in the introduction, frames are critical in political debates in four ways: policy formation, privileging of expertise, support mobilization, and opinion formation. To fully understand the impact of gender on birth control policy, then, it is essential to understand how the issue is framed.

Putting potential substantive-descriptive links in the context of framing birth control, we would expect women to emphasize more gendered or women's issue frames both because of direct experience with those aspects of the issue (as we highlighted in the introduction, birth control is an extremely common part of women's lives), and because it strategically benefits them to do so. The strategic calculation differs between the parties, however. Given the contemporary commitment of the Democratic Party to women's rights (Swers 2013; Wolbrecht 2000), for Democratic senators, policy and electoral goals are well aligned. For Republican women senators, the calculus is trickier because the core policy goals espoused by their party—namely, military strength and a probusiness agenda—do not mesh well with policies that will garner them credibility or perceived expertise based on their gender. Thus, throughout this chapter, we consider partisan perspectives in addition to gendered ones.

It is further beneficial to situate our investigation in work that considers the impact of women legislators on rhetoric and deliberation. In later chapters we consider persistent disparities in women's participation in political communication writ large. Particularly relevant here, Kathryn Pearson and Logan Dancy (2011) analyze speech patterns of members of Congress and identify a clear relationship between the gender of the speaker and gender-specific rhetoric. In other words, congresswomen of both parties reference women and girls and use associated terms more across a range of issues than their male counterparts. This also lends credence to our expectation that women policymakers will be more likely to emphasize gendered elements of the birth control debate. Before we unpack these patterns further, we provide an overview of contraception coverage as it unfolded in the ACA.

Contraceptive Coverage before the ACA

The ACA was not the first attempt to ensure coverage of contraception, but it is the most sweeping and highest profile. As we discussed in the previous chapter, most of the legislative activity prior to the ACA took place in the states. Since the mid-1990s, twenty-eight states have expanded insurance coverage of contraception through legislation or (in rare cases) administrative rule or attorney general ruling (Chapter 3). These state mandates generally target small-group employer benefit plans that operate through state law, requiring that where such a plan provides prescription coverage it must also provide contraceptive coverage, and often include some form of exemption or "conscience clause" for religious entities (Stabile 2004–2005, 747; Lowell 2004–2005, 450; VanSickle-Ward and Hollis-Brusky 2013). Previewing what would become a national conversation, 20 states included conscience clause language in their contraceptive mandates (Guttmacher 2012).

Federal attempts to require coverage for contraception prior to the ACA were relatively modest (for a timeline of significant developments, see Table 4.1). Early federal attempts such as Equity in Prescription Insurance and Contraceptive Coverage (EPICC) failed to gain the necessary support for

Table 4.1 **Timeline of Events in Contraception Policy**

Coverage of Contraceptives in Federal Health Benefits Plan	July 1998
Equal Employment Opportunity Commission (EEOC) ruling	December 2000
Women's Health Amendment adopted (Senate floor debate)	December 3, 2009
ACA signed into law	March 23, 2010
ACA rule first announced	August 1, 2011
House Oversight Hearing	February 12, 2012
ACA modified rule announced (modifications ongoing)	February 15, 2012
***Hobby Lobby* decided**	June 30, 2014

passage. Shortly thereafter, Congress mandated inclusion of FDA-approved contraceptives for plans providing coverage to federal employees under the Federal Health Benefits Plan ("Guaranteeing Coverage of Contraceptives" 2012). In 2000 the Equal Employment Opportunity Commission (EEOC) ruled that denying coverage for preventative contraceptives but covering other "drugs, devices and preventative care" violated the Pregnancy Discrimination Act. This ruling was less legally binding than statutory or administrative law to begin with, and it was further diluted by subsequent appellate rulings (Brooker 2012, 15). It is, nevertheless, still in effect and frequently used in regulating employer practice.[4] The Putting Prevention First Act of 2004, later reintroduced as the Equity in Prescription Insurance and Contraception Act in 2007, failed to reach a floor vote. Notably, the 2007 bill contained no religious exemptions (Brooker 2012).

"With Respect to Women"—Contraceptive Coverage through the ACA

The ACA added language to the existing Public Health Service Act (also incorporated under the Employee Retirement Income Security Act and the Internal Revenue Code) that required health plans to cover preventative care services with no cost-sharing imposition on the insured individual (Brougher 2012). Later designated the "Women's Health Amendment," the provision was the first significant Senate amendment to the ACA, and was approved by a 61-39 vote margin on December 3, 2009 (*Congressional Record* 155, no. 78). Senator Barbara Mikulski (D-MD), widely regarded as the dean of women in the Senate, drafted the amendment in consultation with a coalition of stakeholders (including Planned Parenthood, the National Partnership for Women, the American College of Obstetricians and Gynecologists, and the National Women's Law Center) in response to concerns about gaps in women's health coverage in existing ACA language on preventive care.

The importance of filling these gaps came up frequently in interviews with the stakeholders involved in the early drafting stages of the ACA, as did the point that birth control was one of these gaps, although certainly not the only one. This latter point becomes important when we consider how and why birth control became the most politicized. Gretchen Borchelt, vice president of health and reproductive rights at the National Women's Law Center, described how concerns about birth control coverage arose from women reporting their experiences:

We also have long had a hotline that women can call if they aren't getting birth control coverage. So we work with women individually to get the coverage that they need. We would help them file a complaint, or talk to their insurance company, or talk to their employer. That meant we were hearing from women directly, too, about why this coverage mattered . . . not just on birth control, but on other women's health needs that weren't covered.[5]

Building on related sections that covered preventive care more generally, the Women's Health Amendment focused on preventive care specifically relevant to women, stating, "with respect to women, such additional preventative care and screenings . . . as provided for in comprehensive guidelines supported by the Health Resources and Services Administration" (42 USC 300gg-13(a)(4)) (Brougher 2012). A gendered framing was thus explicit from the start. Emily Stewart, national director of public policy for Planned Parenthood Federation of America, recalled the excitement of advocates as they watched the amendment pass the Senate Committee on Health, Education, Labor, and Pensions (HELP), particularly because it was so explicitly focused on women: "I remember that being a really exciting day, for us as advocates, because it was the first time in a long time that we were getting a pro–women's health amendment that's being voted on as a women's health thing."[6]

Interestingly, while the amendment had initially already been adopted in the HELP Committee markup of the bill, it was dropped when the health committee version was merged with the finance committee version. The gender dynamics at work in response were clear. According to her staff, Senator Mikulski "went to the Democratic caucus. Prior to that she had contacted all the other female senators and told them what had happened, and said that this was unacceptable and raised a ruckus in caucus, to say this should not have happened, and got everyone on board."[7] Senator Harry Reid (D-NV), the Democratic Senate Leader, then allowed the amendment to be brought to the floor, and as a result it garnered greater attention and set the tone for the version of the bill that would become law. When asked why the amendment was initially dropped, one inside observer noted that there were "no women at the table."[8]

"Health Care Is a Woman's Issue"—Floor Debate on the Women's Health Amendment

What became known as the Women's Health Amendment was the first substantive amendment to the ACA to be debated on the Senate floor. Animating the debate was a discussion of the extent to which women's unique preventative health-care needs warranted explicit protection above and beyond the preventative care language already in the bill (linked to recommendations by the U.S. Preventative Services Task Force). The amendment's backers highlighted the number of ways in which women's health was sidelined. Senator Mikulski, the amendment's author, opened her remarks by stating that "health care is a woman's issue."[9] She continued with a focus on the economic burdens faced by women seeking health care.

> Many women don't get these services because, first of all, they don't have health insurance; and, number two, when they do have it, it means these services are either not available unless they are mandated by states or the copayments are so high that they avoid getting them in the first place. The second important point about my amendment is it eliminates deductibles and copayments. So we eliminate two big hurdles: having insurance in the first place, which is the underlying bill, as well as copayments and deductibles.

Democratic women in the Senate credited Mikulski for her leadership and reiterated the women's health frame—emphasizing the unique health-care challenges women faced, and the importance of the amendment in ensuring adequate screening and treatment. Senator Murray (D-WA) captured this dynamic in her Senate floor remarks:

> We have to make sure we cover preventive services, and this takes into account the unique needs of women. Senator Mikulski's amendment will make sure this bill provides coverage for important preventive services for women at no cost. Women will have improved access to well-women visits—important for all women; family planning services; mammograms, which we have all talked about so many times, to make sure they maintain their health.

Democratic senators, men and women, linked preventative health to other disparities in women's health care, as the following excerpts illustrate:

> Women of childbearing age pay on average 68 percent more for their health care than men do. We have so many instances in which insurance companies are standing between women and their doctors right now in making decisions—decisions not to cover preventive services, such as a mammogram screening or a cervical cancer screening, decisions to call pregnancy a preexisting condition so women cannot get health insurance, decisions not to cover maternity care so that women and their babies can get the care they need so that babies can be successful in life, both prenatal care and postnatal care. [Senator Debbie Stabenow (D-MI)]

> Under her amendment, the Health Resources and Services Administration will be able to include other important services at no cost, such as the well woman visit, prenatal care, and family planning.... Prevention is just one of the ways this bill will improve women's health. It also ends insurance companies' practice of charging women more because they happen to be women, or denying coverage based on a history of pregnancy, C-section, or domestic violence. We need to pass this bill this year to ensure comprehensive, affordable care for women throughout the country. [Senator Al Franken (D-MN)]

Several male Democrats spoke in favor of the amendment. Notably, they sometimes couched their support in terms of lessons learned from, and responsibilities to, their female colleagues and family members.

> Senator Mikulski said: If you look at the research being done at NIH, it is almost all done on men and not on women. I remember that some years ago, and all of a sudden a lightbulb went off in my head. I said: You are right. So we had to start changing the focus of a lot of the research done to focus on the unique situations faced by women. [Senator Tom Harkin (D-IA)]

> And we need to include this amendment because I want to be able to look my wife in the eye, I want to be able to look my daughter in the eye—my son, too—and my future grandchildren in the eye and say we did everything we could in this bill to improve women's health. [Senator Al Franken (D-MN)]

What became the flashpoint in debates over preventative care—birth control—only came up a handful of times in the floor debate, and was universally referred to as "family planning." There did not appear to be any mystery that birth control was a likely contender for the yet unwritten preventative care recommendations. The supporters certainly had it in mind. In addition, one senator, Ben Nelson (D-NE), ultimately opposed the amendment because it did not specify that it would not cover abortion, but emphasized that he did support the "underlying goal of furthering preventative care including ... family planning." Senator Bob Casey Jr. (D-PA) also raised concerns about abortion coverage but voted for the bill after emphatic assurances from Senator Mikulski that "neither legislative intent nor legislative language would cover abortion." Opposition to the amendment focused predominantly on cost, and on who should decide what constitutes preventative measures. Opponents largely argued in favor of a competing amendment by Senator Lisa Murkowski (R-AK), which called for guidelines from private insurance companies. The central frames that emerged in the floor debate were health (specifically, women's health) and economic considerations. Religion, which would become the unmistakably dominant frame after the bill's passage, was never brought up at all.

Notably, given the bitterly partisan dynamics at play during debate over the ACA as a whole, the amendment received a degree of bipartisan support. Two Republican women voted for it—Susan Collins and Olympia Snowe (Snowe was also a cosponsor)—as did David Vittner (R-LA), whose support was linked to a related discussion of mammogram coverage (Mikulski 2009). Democratic senators Ben Nelson and Russ Feingold (WI) voted against the amendment. Controversy quickly emerged, however, over how the broadly written amendment would be interpreted and, in particular, how conscience clauses would be applied.

Implementation Controversy

After the ACA passed, the U.S. Department of Health and Human Services (HHS) directed the Institute of Medicine (IOM) to put forward suggested preventative services for potential inclusion under the law in July 2011. IOM head Dr. Linda Rosenstock testified before congressional hearings to explain the process and the final recommendations:[10]

> The committee defined preventive health services as measures—including medications, procedures, devices, tests, education and counseling—shown to improve well-being, and/or decrease the likelihood or delay the onset of a targeted disease or condition. (Rosenstock, Judiciary Committee hearings, February 28, 2012)

> The recommendations are based on a review of existing guidelines and an assessment of the evidence on the effectiveness of different preventive services. The committee identified diseases and conditions that are *more common or more serious in women than in men or for which women experience different outcomes or benefit from different interventions*. (Rosenstock, Committee on Oversight and Government Reform, February 16, 2012, emphasis added)

Here again, gender is explicitly invoked in the policy narrative. In addition to comprehensive lactation support, screening for gestational diabetes, and prenatal care visits, the IOM's recommendations included "the full range of Food and Drug Administration–approved contraception methods, sterilization procedures, and patient education and counseling for women with reproductive capacity" ("Clinical Preventive Services for Women" 2015). The Departments of HHS, Treasury, and Labor announced their guidelines modeled on the IOM report and endorsed by the Health Resources and Services Administration (Brougher 2012). Mikulski had argued throughout the debate and since for the importance of leaving definitions of preventative care to nonpartisan scientists ("Mikulski Calls for Continued Action" 2014).

While birth control was presumed to be a potential recommendation, the laserlike focus on birth control after the passage was a surprise even to the bill's key architects. As one key player explained,

> [The goal] really was comprehensive women's health, knowing that one of the gaps was birth control, hoping that one of things that would be addressed would be birth control, but the goal was never just birth control, it was never all about that, it become known as the birth control amendment, and that of course becomes the most well-known and talked-about provision ... but that was never the intent. [Interview by author in person]

As the previous chapter illustrated, similar laws were already on the books in twenty-eight states. But as we discuss more fully in the next section, the religious exemption initially put forward by the administration was more targeted than the broadly worded conscience clause in many states. Moreover, the ACA and subsequent rules applied to smaller groups and organizations that self-insure, thereby closing a loophole that had allowed some religiously affiliated institutions in the independent market to deny contraceptive coverage (Sonfield and Pollack 2013).

Birth control was a somewhat minor issue during the debate over preventative care while the ACA was being deliberated, but it was an explosive one during implementation. According to the *New York Times*, "the tortured history of the [birth control coverage] rule has played out in several chapters" (Pear 2013). On August 1, 2011, the departments of Health and Human Services, Labor, and the Treasury jointly announced rules implementing the preventative services portions of the ACA (Interim final regulations, August 3, 2011, 76 FR 46621). Echoing language from the IOM, the agencies' rollout of these rules specifically referenced the potential benefits to women's well-being and gender equality, noting that increased access to contraception "improves the social and economic status of women by reducing disparities between men and women in terms of out-of-pocket costs" (IRS, EBSA, and HHS 2013, 39,873, cited in English 2015, 12).

Pushback was swift and focused predominantly on the exemption in the HHS mandate for employers who object to contraception on moral or religious grounds—the so-called conscience clause exemption (Rassbach 2013). Because the initial conscience clause exemption in the HHS rule was narrowly tailored, it did not exempt religiously affiliated universities, hospitals, and charities from providing coverage for contraception in their group insurance plans.[11] Opponents (most prominently the Catholic Church) criticized the HHS mandate in the media as an egregious affront to religious liberty. Proponents and advocates of reproductive rights and women's health, on the other hand, applauded the mandate as a necessary step to safeguard the reproductive health of women (VanSickle-Ward and Hollis-Brusky 2013). In response to the controversy, the administration offered modifications to the rules.[12] The initial modification stated that these non-exempt employers with religious objections would be granted a yearlong "safe haven" from enforcement, during which time the federal government would "work with stakeholders to develop alternative ways of providing contraceptive coverage."

President Barack Obama previewed these modifications in February 2012, and subsequently, in July 2013, the agencies promulgated rules that simplified and clarified the definition of "religious employer." They eliminated the first three prongs, leaving the definition from the Internal Revenue Code, and articulated an additional accommodation whereby other nonprofit religiously affiliated organizations (e.g., universities, hospitals, or charities) would be exempted from directly providing contraceptive coverage for their employees. The rule facilitates insurance companies covering contraceptive care directly without any cost to employees or to the objecting religious organizations that had self-certified as exempt.[13] Finally, in response to the *Hobby Lobby* and *Wheaton College* court decisions (discussed in more detail in the next chapter), the Obama administration proposed two additional accommodations. First, an eligible nonprofit could notify HHS directly of its exempt status, rather than contacting the insurance company. Second, the rules extended the workaround previously offered to nonprofits to the closely held for-profits at issue in *Hobby Lobby* (CMS Fact Sheet).

Rulemaking is not typically a high-profile component of public policymaking, but here it was both substantively important and high salience. Attention to the rules that emerged from the Women's Health Amendment, specifically as they related to birth control coverage, was remarkably high. According to a Gallup poll taken in 2012, a significant percentage (60%) of Americans reported "following the news story very closely or somewhat closely" (Saad 2012, also cited in English 2015). Nearly half a million public comments were submitted (472,082) during the public comment period by organizations and individuals, and through form letters (solicited by groups including NARAL, Planned

Parenthood, and the U.S. Conference of Catholic Bishops (English 2015). Appeals to women's rights and women's health were very common in these comments. In her excellent discussion of the nature of how women's interests were presented in these rules, Ashley English explains the downsides of the description of women in "broad, universal terms":

> This focus on women and their families often obscured references to more controversial subsets of women such as unmarried women, women of color, low-income women, and LGBTQ women making it difficult to understand their unique experiences with contraception and the complicated ways these women may have approached the contraception issue. (2015, 51)

Thus as we unpack the patterns in how men and women approach and are affected by contraceptive coverage, it is worth keeping in mind that women's experiences are far from universal.

Conscience Clauses

Central to the HHS mandate controversy was a debate over so-called conscience clauses. These provisions typically allow physicians and other healthcare providers to opt out of performing a procedure, or some other function of their occupation, due to a religious or moral objection. Conscience clauses (or "refusal clauses") in health-care provision have existed formally since the mid-1970s, most clearly in response to *Roe v. Wade* in 1973 (Lynch 2010). While initially focused predominantly on physicians objecting to abortion, the scope has expanded both in terms of objectionable services and those doing the objecting (Lynch 2010). Before objections to traditional forms of contraception attracted nationwide attention, controversy emerged over contested 2008 Federal Drug Administration (FDA) regulations allowing (at least under some interpretations) pharmacists to refuse provision of emergency contraception based on religious objections. Key to the controversy was ambiguity in how these clauses were worded, particularly with regard to the procedures to which the clause applied. As one women's health advocate argued, in a statement typical of opponents' concerns, "The officially proposed rule is broad and ill-defined enough to leave considerable room for debate about what it would mean in practice if approved" (Walden 2008).

A variety of other cases have emerged as well, highlighting the concerns among religious organizations that their religious liberty is being threatened as well as the restrictions that women face when health professionals are given exemptions from performing medical procedures as a result of conscience clauses. The following excerpt from an American College of Obstetricians and Gynecologists (ACOG) report illustrates the belief among women's health professionals that the consequences for women's reproductive health are dramatic and in some cases life-threatening:

> In Texas . . . a pharmacist rejected a rape victim's prescription for emergency contraception, arguing that dispensing the medication was a "violation of morals." In Virginia, a 42-year-old mother of two was refused emergency contraception, became pregnant, and ultimately underwent an abortion she tried to prevent . . . In California a physician refused to perform intrauterine insemination for a lesbian couple, prompted by religious beliefs and disapproval of lesbians having children. In Nebraska a 19-year-old woman with a life-threatening pulmonary embolism at 10 weeks of gestation was refused a first-trimester pregnancy termination when admitted to a religiously affiliated hospital. . . . At the heart of each of these examples is a claim of conscience—a claim that to provide certain service would compromise the moral integrity of a provider or institution. (ACOG Committee on Ethics 2007)

The idea seems to have gained traction even beyond the medical profession: a bus driver in Texas sued his former employer for firing him after he refused to take a passenger to Planned Parenthood, claiming that he could not make the trip "in good conscience" and that the dismissal therefore violated his religious freedom (Ford 2010).

"Where Are the Women?"—Congressional Oversight Hearings

In the midst of the evolution of the regulations regarding contraception coverage and conscience clauses, Congressman Darrell Issa (R-CA), chairman of the House Committee on Oversight and Government Reform, held a hearing on the topic in February 2012. Provocatively titled "Lines Crossed: Separation of Church and State—Has the Obama Administration Trampled on Freedom of Religion and Freedom of Conscience?" the hearing invited testimony from religious leaders and sought to, in Issa's words, "hear from people who have spent their entire life pondering these very questions of faith and conscience."[14] ("Lines Crossed", 2).

As noted in chapter 1, the opening panel famously included no women. In fact, no women were even invited to testify before the committee. Planned Parenthood tweeted a picture of an all-male panel testifying in opposition to the birth control mandate before a congressional committee with the message "What's wrong with this picture?" and the hashtag #WhereAreTheWomen? As the picture went viral, female members of the committee expressed anger over the exclusion, posing the same question. Before leaving the hearing with two of her colleagues in protest (Abad-Santos 2012), Representative Carolyn Maloney (D-NY) asked,

> What I want to know is: Where are the women? When I look at this panel, I don't see one single woman representing the tens of millions of women across the country who want and need insurance coverage for basic, preventative health care services, including family planning, Where are the women? ("Lines Crossed" 2015)

Maloney's sentiments and attempts to reframe the issue by highlighting women's perspectives were echoed by some of her colleagues, male and female, including the ranking House Minority Leader, Representative Elijah Cummings (D-MD):

> But there is another core interest we must consider, and that is the interest of women. The pill has a profound impact on their well-being, far more than any man in this room can possibly know. It has allowed women to control their lives and make very personal decisions about how many children to have and when to have them. . . . In my opinion, this committee commits a massive injustice by trying to pretend that the views of millions of women across this country are meaningless or worthless or irrelevant to the debate.

This focus on women's health and agency was roundly rejected by the witnesses and other members of Congress, some of whom explicitly pushed back on the narrative suggested by Maloney and Cummings. Representative Joe Walsh argued "*This is not about women. This is not about contraceptives. . . .* This is about religious freedom" ("Lines Crossed", 110, emphasis added). According to Representative Maloney, this position was proffered by Committee Chairman Issa himself: "Your staff told us you personally rejected [Georgetown law school student] Ms. Fluke's testimony, saying, 'The hearing is not about reproductive rights and contraception.' Of course this hearing is about rights, contraception, and birth control" (Lines Crossed 2015, 4). Other responses focused on religious convictions held by both men and women, and the good work being done by religious organizations on behalf of women. Often, however, the framing embraced by witnesses elided women altogether in favor of an emphasis on religious liberty. Indeed, even when including the queries of members of Congress (who were more likely to reference the absence of women and highlight women's health), mentions of "religion" and "religious" in the hearing outpaced mentions of "women" and "woman" by a factor of more than three to one (354–96).

After the hearing, Issa's staff countered the "where are the women" complaint. Noting that two women appeared on a second panel, Issa's spokeswoman Becca Watkins countered that criticism was "either ill-informed or arrogantly dismissive of women who don't share her views" (Flock 2012). She was not the only woman to take issue with the "where are the women" refrain. Speaking directly to arguments about policy framing, Ann Marie Buerkle (R-NY), the only Republican woman on the committee, insisted that contraception was not the main issue at hand: "I really find it so objectionable that my colleagues on the other side of the aisle would characterize this as something so narrow as being about contraception. This is a fundamental assault on one's conscience" (Koppelman 2012). There are clear examples, then, of conservative women rejecting the idea that women were rendered voiceless in this debate. Nonetheless, the image of the first all-male panel had received thousands of comments and shares, been spoofed on the *Daily Show*, and galvanized supporters of expanded contraception access (*Jon Stewart's Eye on the Ladies* 2015).

Frustrated by the tone and witness roster of the Issa hearing, the House Democratic Steering and Policy Committee held its own hearing shortly after ("Women's Health and Contraception" 2015).[15] Titled "Hearing on Women's Health and Contraception," the hearing included only four congressional members, all Democrats (Nancy Pelosi [D-CA], Cummings [D-MD], Maloney [D-NY], and Eleanor Holmes Norton [D-DC]), and one witness, Sandra Fluke, a Georgetown Law student and former president of the Georgetown Law Students for Reproductive Justice. Democratic members had requested Fluke's inclusion at the first hearing, but their request had been denied.

According to Congressman Issa and his staff, Fluke was not qualified to testify because she was not a member of the clergy and because contraception was not at issue in the hearing: "As the hearing is not about reproductive rights but instead about the administration's actions as they relate to freedom of religion and conscience, he believes that Ms. Fluke is not an appropriate witness" (Flock 2012; "Women's Health and Contraception" 2015). Dan Lungren (R-CA), the Republican chair of the House Administration Committee, declined to broadcast the "protest hearing," a decision Pelosi deemed an "effort to silence women on the topic of women's health" (Marinucci and Garofoli 2012).

While the hearing clearly carried no real policy weight, it does give us the opportunity to examine a very different framing of contraceptive coverage. Representative Pelosi opened the hearing by highlighting gender and calling attention to the public nature of the debate:

> I think it's important ... to inform you, Sandra, that following your rejection by the Republicans from the panel, which the Democrats had suggested you as their witness, that we've heard from over 300,000 people saying we want women's voices to be heard on the subject of women's health.

Fluke's testimony focused on threats to women's health when contraception access was limited. Relying on stories from fellow students who had been denied coverage for contraceptive devices and services, or put through onerous hurdles to obtain them, she characterized restrictions placed on access by Catholic universities as "untenable burdens" on health, economic well-being, and academic success. "This is the message that not requiring coverage of contraception sends," Fluke argued. "A woman's reproductive health care isn't a necessity, isn't a priority." Pushing back against the religious framing, she maintained, "Ours is not a war against the church. It is a struggle for access to the health care we need" ("Women's Health and Contraception" 2012).

Shortly after the hearings, Senator Roy Blunt (R-MO) sponsored legislation that would have amended the ACA to allow employers to refuse contraception coverage based on religious or moral objections. In other words, the amendment sought to add a conscience clause. Commentary from party leadership echoed the now well-established frames of women's health and religious liberty (Parkinson 2012). The Senate tabled the amendment by a vote of 51-48.[16] At this point, a series of legal challenges to the HHS mandate with similar goals were already under way in federal courts ("HHS Mandate Information Central" 2015).

Evolution of Frames

The qualitative discussion presented thus far illustrates sharp divisions in both the policy details of contraceptive coverage and in the frames used to understand the issue of birth control regulation. In this section we further examine the question of how the contraceptive mandate was framed by examining testimony delivered during the two most prominent public legislative discussions about the contraceptive mandate—the Senate floor deliberation and the House oversight hearings—for the relative importance of each of the six frames introduced in chapter 1: religion, health, reproductive rights/women's rights, economics, morality, and partisanship/strategic. We identified these six frames as the most common and relevant to understanding various perspectives on birth control coverage after extensive investigation into policy debates around birth control and media coverage of the debate. The health, religion, and women's/reproductive rights frames were self-evident given the topic. We included the economics frame due to fundamental link between insurance coverage, central to the mandate, and economic considerations. We included the morality frame because, as we discussed in the previous chapter, birth control has traditionally been viewed as morality policy (McFarlane and Meier 2000). Finally, we added the partisanship/strategic frame based on the frequency with which is emerged in media coverage, and the relevance of this frame in literature on media coverage of policy more broadly (see Chapter 7).

How the Frames Are Measured

We gathered the population of framing statements made during these two deliberations by searching the hearing transcripts for keywords indicative of our six frames (listed in Appendix A). We populated our list of keywords with the terms we considered to be the best indicators of each frame based on our qualitative analysis. For example, "hospital," "health," and "physician" were used to identify health framing statements; "faith," "religion," and "god" were used to identify religion framing statements. We also noted the gender and either the party or the position (for or against the mandate) for each speaker.[17]

Once the population of framing statements was identified, we translated the raw scores for each separate framing category into relative percentages of total framing statements. We did this for each speaker, and aggregated for the hearing or debate as a whole. In other words, the frames are discussed in terms of proportions—how often statements in one frame were used relative to all relevant statements across frames. Importantly, this means if that the length of time a speaker speaks is controlled for, one speaker talking longer than another does not skew the analysis of which frames were more or less emphasized. This measure, which we employ in the next chapter as well, allowed us to assess which frames were most prominent in discussing the mandate during interactive deliberations with multiple speakers, such as congressional hearings.[18]

Based on the literature reviewed at the outset of this chapter, we expected women speakers to be more likely than their male counterparts to employ two frames in particular—health and reproductive rights, because their direct experience with these aspects of birth control provisions makes these elements more salient, and because they are more likely to be perceived as credible on these topics. Moreover, we expected women on balance to be more likely to use gendered frames, frames that explicitly highlight gender (i.e., women's health, reproductive rights, and morality) versus nongendered themes (i.e., religious freedom, economics, and horserace). Again the logic here is twofold; women are invested in the gendered elements of the policy given their identity, and women are perceived as more expert, and can more easily claim credit on issues, when they frame them as explicitly "women's issues."

Results

There are four striking takeaways from our analysis of the frames employed in legislative deliberation. The first is how dramatically congressional debate shifted from being predominantly about health care to predominantly about religion between December 2009 and February 2012. As Figure 4.1 shows, the religious frame was essentially nonexistent in Senate floor deliberations over the women's health amendment—accounting for less than 1% of all statements employing a frame. By contrast, discussions of health (53% of framing statements), women's rights (25% of framing statements), and economic considerations (18% of

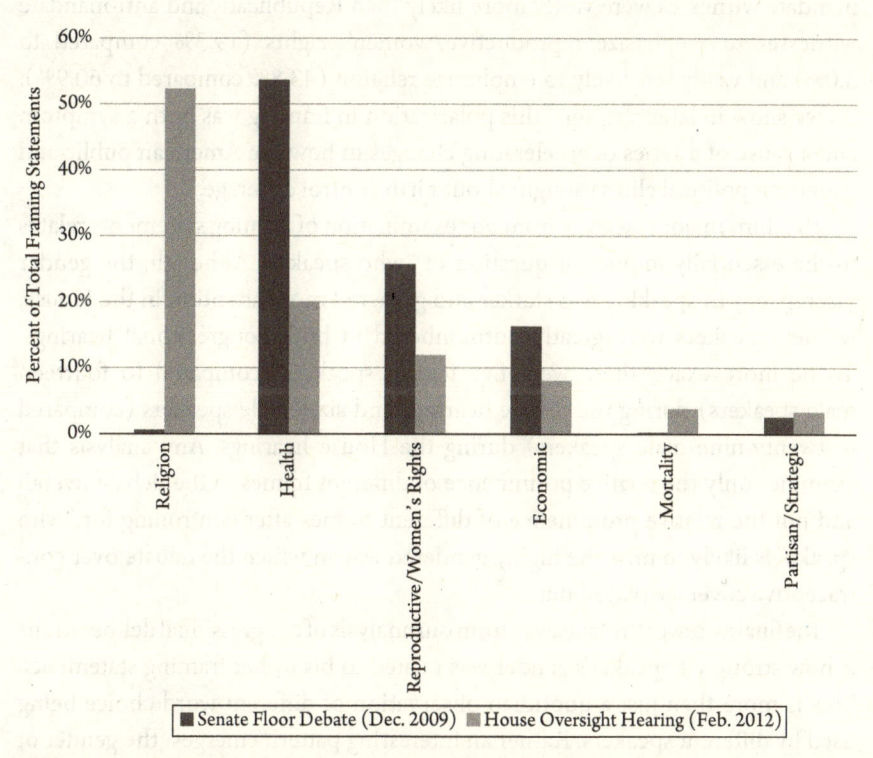

Figure 4.1 Relative Prominence of Congressional Deliberation Frames

framing statements) dominated the Senate's debate. The difference between these statements and those made during the 2012 oversight hearing was stark. As Figure 4.1 shows, in that venue, religion was the clearly dominant frame (51% of framing statements), more than doubling discussions of health (20% of framing statements) and outpacing references to women's rights and reproductive rights (13%) by a factor of roughly four to one. Put simply, what started as a conversation almost exclusively about health and women's rights in 2009 became a conversation primarily about religious liberty in 2012. As we see in the next chapter, the increasing prominence of religion vis-à-vis health and women's rights is a trend that would only accelerate as the contraceptive mandate was challenged on First Amendment grounds in the Supreme Court.

The second major takeaway from this analysis is that the debate around the ACA's contraceptive mandate became much more dramatically shaped by partisanship between 2009 and 2012. Partisan differences in framing statements were small to nonexistent during the Senate hearings. In fact, the percentage of framing statements made by Republicans and Democrats was within 3% on four of our six framing categories (religion, health, morality, and partisan/strategic). By 2009, there were vast differences in how the contraceptive mandate was being framed by opposing sides of the debate. Most notably, Democrats and pro-mandate witnesses were vastly more likely than Republicans and anti-mandate witnesses to emphasize reproductive/women's rights (19.3% compared to 5.0%) and vastly less likely to emphasize religion (43.8% compared to 60.9%). As we show in later chapters, this polarization in framing was both a symptom and a cause of a series of accelerating changes in how the American public and American political elites thought about birth control coverage.[19]

The third major takeaway from our examination of framing statements relates to the essentially important question of "who speaks?" Although, the gender discrepancy in speaking was starker and garnered more attention in the House, women speakers were greatly outnumbered in both congressional hearings. To be more exact, there were five female speakers (compared to fourteen male speakers) during the Senate hearings and six female speakers (compared to twenty-nine male speakers) during the House hearings. Any analysis that examines only the relative prominence of different frames in the debate overall and not the relative prominence of different frames after controlling for "who speaks" is likely to miss the highly gendered way in which the debate over contraceptive coverage played out.

The final noteworthy takeaway from our analysis of congressional deliberations is how strongly a speaker's gender was related to his or her framing statements. This is more than just a quotidian observation of different word choice being used by different speakers. Rather an interesting pattern emerges: the gender of the speaker matters for which frame is emphasized. In the Senate floor debate

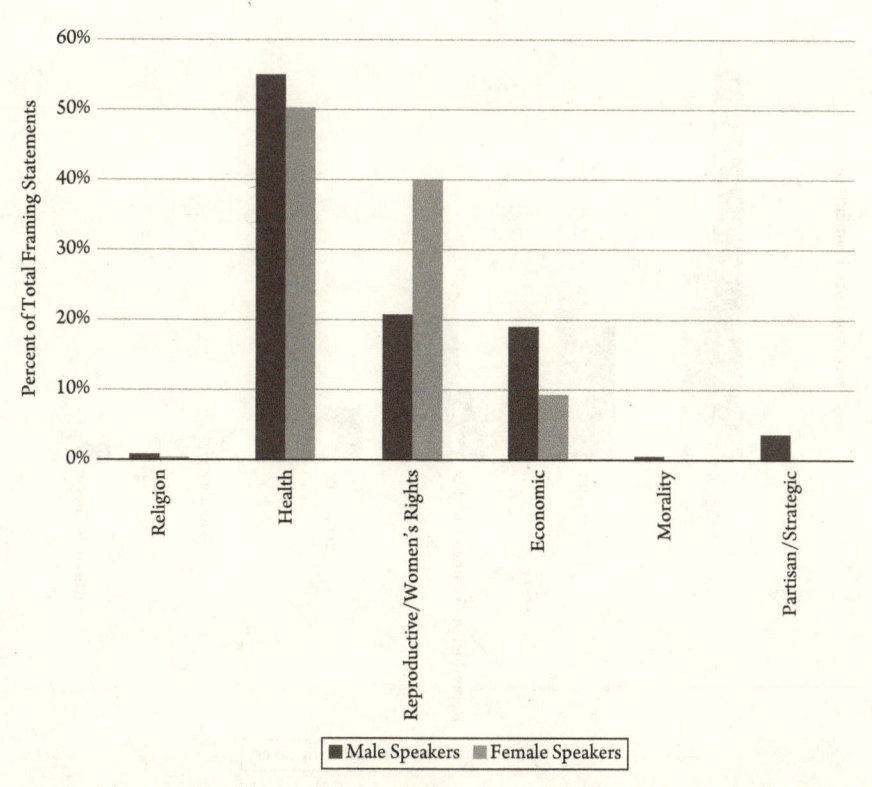

Figure 4.2 Relative Prominence of Congressional Deliberation Frames in the Senate by Gender

(Figure 4.2), the most notable difference in the framing statements made by men and women was in relative prominence of reproductive/women's rights: women employed this frame nearly twice as often as men did in their comments (39.8% of all framing statements versus 20.8%). Interestingly, men were slightly more likely during the Senate hearings than women (54.9% of all framing statements compared with 50.2%) to bring up health-related considerations and dramatically more likely to emphasize economic concerns (19.0% of all framing statements compared with 9.4%). Perhaps more remarkably given the debate that was to come, neither men nor women invoked religion in 2009.

As Figure 4.3 shows, these speaking patterns would shift dramatically during the course of the 2012 oversight hearings. Most notably, religion was transformed from a nonconsideration to the primary consideration for male and female speakers alike—with more than half of all framing statements referencing religious considerations. Contrary to the Senate hearings, women in the House hearings were more likely to focus on health, though the difference between genders here was not as large (24.4% versus 19.4%). Similar to the Senate

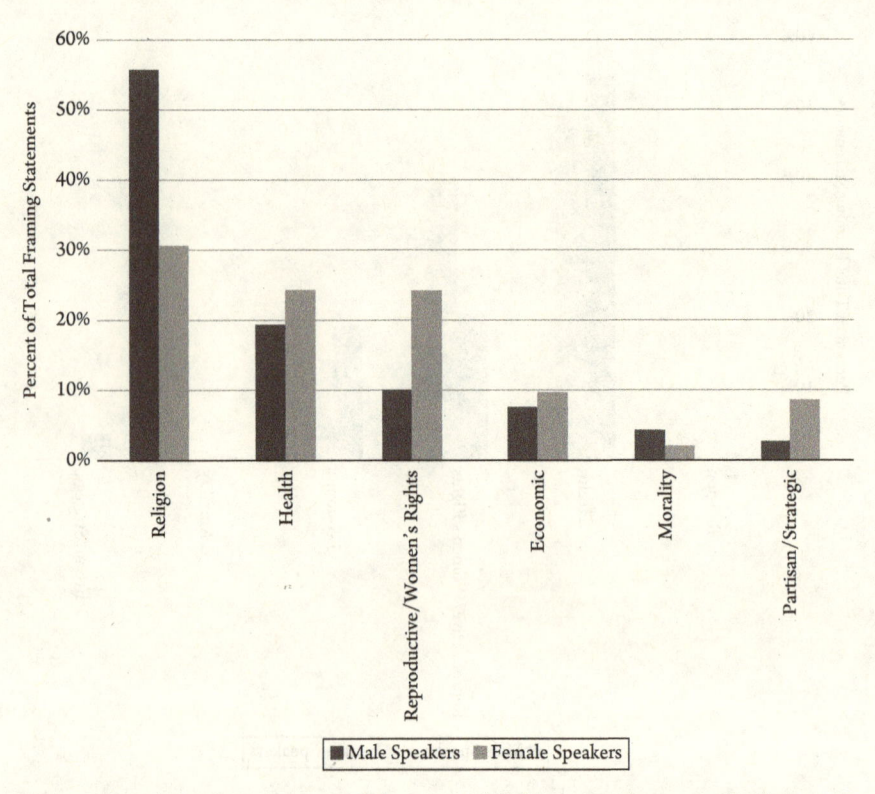

Figure 4.3 Relative Prominence of Congressional Deliberation Frames in the House by Gender

hearings, however, the share of women's framing statements that emphasized reproductive/women's rights was two and a half times greater than that of male speakers (24.4% versus 10.0%). Regardless of the hearing in question, therefore, women were much more likely than men to invoke issues related to reproductive and women's rights.

We considered that this apparent gender effect was simply masking the effect of partisanship on framing choices, given that most of the women participating in these two congressional deliberations were Democrats (three of the five women speaking in the Senate and three of the four women representatives speaking in the House were Democrats). In order to address this possibility, we examined within-party differences in framing based on gender during both the Senate and the House hearings. The three Democratic women senators discussed reproductive/women's rights far more in their framing statements than their male counterparts (45.3% versus 22.8%) and economics far less (8.8% versus 13.4%). The same disparity existed across the aisle—with Republican women talking more about reproductive/women's rights (31.7% versus 18.9%) and less about economics (10.1% versus 24.6%) than men in their party.

Our analysis of debate in the House revealed nearly the same pattern. Among House Democrats and pro-mandate witnesses, 39.6% of framing statements made by women were about reproductive/women's rights (compared to 15.2% for men), 27.7% were about health (compared to 16.5% for men), and 19.2% were about religion (compared to 48.8% for men). These framing choices were mirrored among House Republicans and anti-mandate witnesses—with 9.2% of framing statements made by women focused on reproductive/women's rights (compared to 4.4% for men), 32.1% of framing statements made by women focused on health (compared to 16.5% for men), and 42.2% of framing statements made by women focused on religion (compared to 63.6% for men). To put all of this more simply, because there are large differences *within each party* for how men and women chose to discuss the contraceptive mandate we are confident that it was gender (and not just partisanship) that drove framing choices.

The fact that gender exerted an influence on framing choices independent of partisanship makes an important contribution to the literature on women and politics. It is common in the existing literature to see gendered effects on policy eclipsed by partisan ones. The fact that gender was significantly correlated with framing decisions both when the debate was on a less salient and more bipartisan issue as well as when it became a polarized lightning rod points to the importance of closely examining gender's influence on other policy issues.

The overarching takeaway here, however, is that, despite their minority status, women's participation in policy debates on birth control mattered both for how the policy was developed, and for how it was understood and discussed—and, as we note throughout this book, the development and framing of policy are themselves fundamentally linked. In some cases, this connection was evidenced by individual women using their formal or informal power in key ways: Senator Barbara Mikulski's efforts to make sure that the Women's Health Amendment was included in the first place, then House Democratic Leader Nancy Pelosi using her position to provide a forum for Sandra Fluke's testimony. In other cases, we begin to see the contours, albeit from a small sample, of more general patterns in how women framed the issue in the legislative branch. In the next chapter, we consider similar dynamics in a judicial context, and see the ways in which these patterns persist.

5

Contraception Coverage in the Courts

> I never thought when I started this whole process that this would become something that was argued before the Supreme Court. It just goes to show how political birth control really is.
> —Mona Shah, senior health policy adviser to Senator Barbara Mikulski[1]

The previous chapter detailed the legislative process at work in crafting the Women's Health Amendment of the Affordable Care Act (ACA), which would become the foundation for the contraception coverage mandate. We illustrated how critical female actors were in ensuring the survival of the amendment, and unearthed patterns in how women and men framed discussions of the issue.

In this chapter we conduct a similar analysis of the framing of the mandate from the perspective of the courts. More precisely, we review the major developments in how the courts responded to contraceptive coverage under the ACA, focusing specifically on the two most prominent cases to reach the Supreme Court: *Hobby Lobby* and *Zubik v. Burwell* (hereafter *Zubik*).[2] We discuss the primary frames used at each stage—amici curiae briefs, oral arguments, decisions, and dissents. Where possible, we analyze the dynamics of how gender—more specifically, the gender or gender composition of the speaker or author(s) at each stage—shaped the framing of the legal debate around birth control coverage.

Literature on Gender and Framing in the Courts

As we noted in the introduction, scholarship on how women's presence in the courts has shaped outcomes is more limited than comparable work in the legislative branch. The work that has been done is fascinating but somewhat conflicting. Recent scholarship has found that women impact outcomes on appellate courts even when they are in the minority (Farhang and Wawro 2004) and that women serving as district court judges reach settlement in their cases with greater frequency and alacrity than male judges (Boyd, Epstein, and Martin 2010). Studies such as these often emphasize that the effects are restricted to particular areas of law, such as sexual discrimination and sexual harassment (Boyd, Epstein, and Martin 2010; Peresie 2005). But a number of other studies reveal no impact on judicial decisions and case outcomes (Ashenfelter, Eisenberg, and Schwab 1995; Kulik, Perry, and Pepper 2003; Segal 2000). Even some of the accounts that find some impact are careful to note that it's a narrow one (for example, Epstein Boyd and Martin 2010) find effects in only one, on sex discrimination, out of 143 cases they study; Walker and Barrow [1985] note gender difference in sympathy to certain types of claims and claimants). Other work emphasizes the impact of female judges on judicial processes and outcomes not based on sex as an individual variable but gender as dynamic social process "always contested ... continually renegotiated, fluid and variable within social groups, across cultures, and across time" (Kenney 2012, 16).

These analyses described above are illuminating, but we are left with a puzzle of how gender impacts judicial outcomes, with some important pieces missing. First, as noted earlier the findings on whether gender matters are somewhat conflictual. On balance, it's fair to say that answer is "sometimes," but it's a fairly cautious "sometimes," and several studies are skeptical of any impact at all. Second, the existing literature on the impact of gender on the courts, with rare exception (Kenney 2012), focuses almost exclusively on the actions of judges, with impact measured by rulings. In this chapter we seek to expand the lens, considering the impact of gender not just on rulings but on arguments and frames, and analyzing not just the justices but legal advocates—specifically the attorneys and interested parties who file briefs in an attempt to influence the outcome of the case at hand. This is critical because the way in which cases are framed can have long-term, path-dependent consequences, shaping future cases and arguments (Silverstein 2009; Hollis-Brusky 2015). Relatedly, there is a "first move" advantage when it comes to framing and court decisions; the way in which a case is initially framed dictates the area of law considered relevant in deciding that case, making particular outcomes more likely than if the case were framed another way.

Framing is further essential in a judicial context because legal reasoning is used to uphold judicial legitimacy, and especially for the federal courts, legitimacy is the coin of the realm. Since so many critical judicial actors do not face electoral constraints on or consequences for their decisions—federal judges and justices are lifetime appointments—promoting the legitimacy of their decisions is paramount. Legitimacy is why the nature of the arguments used is so significant in judicial decision making, and hence why amicus briefs and written options are worth serious consideration in judicial analysis.

Finally, there is limited analysis of how gender shapes court rulings in concert with other policy developments on one particular issue. As we have discussed throughout this book, since the vast majority of studies of the impact of gender are constrained to one venue, it's hard to know how trends travel across institutional constraints.

As we noted in the introduction, our discussion here covers amici curiae briefs, oral arguments, opinions, and dissents. While the import of Supreme Court rulings is fairly self-evident, the relevance of oral arguments and amici curiae briefs may be less so.[3] It is worth taking a moment then, to describe what they are and why they matter. Our analysis includes extensive discussion of amici curiae (friends of the court) briefs. They are filed by organizations or individuals who have expertise, strong opinions, or both about the case at hand, but no formal standing. They typically advocate strenuously for either the petitioner or the respondent in a given case. Existing research illustrates that amicus briefs are frequently cited in, and are consequential to the outcome of, Supreme Court decisions. More specifically, scholars have shown that briefs have an impact because they provide relevant information to the court (Collins 2004) as well as a pathway for formative ideas to travel to clerks and justices (Hollis-Brusky 2015, 26). Prior scholarship on the impact of amicus briefs on the highest court has illustrated that the submission of amicus briefs make it more likely the case will be granted certiorari (in other words, that the court will agree to hear the case) (Collins 2004; Caldeira and Wright 1988; Perry 1991). There is also evidence that amicus briefs increase the overall likelihood of litigant success (Kearney and Merrill 2000; McGuire 1990, 1995; Puro 1971; Collins 2004).[4] We know that amicus briefs in support of respondents are more effective than those supporting petitioners, and that numbers matter: small disparities have an impact; larger disparities produce diminishing returns and even counterproductive outcomes (Kearney and Merrill 2000). We know very little, however, about how the gender of the author correlates with positions taken in an amicus brief, and how it shapes the rhetoric employed. In keeping with the thread of the book, we consider how gender composition of amicus brief authors affects frame selection. The analysis of amicus briefs is also helpful because, as discussed above, it allows us to flesh out the impact of gender beyond the few key players on the court. Put another way, studies that focus exclusively on rulings are missing a subtler but potentially very important way in which gender dynamics shape policy development.

Oral arguments offer the legal representation to the parties in a given case the opportunity to orally present their arguments to the justices, and allow the justices the chance to ask questions in response to those claims.[5] They are typically an hour long and open to the public. Just how impactful they are on judicial outcomes is a matter of some scholarly debate. There is evidence that the quality of arguments can influence final votes (Johnson, Wahlbeck, and Spriggs 2006) and that the information gathering that happens in oral arguments shapes the policy choices made by justices (Johnson 2001). Prominent scholars of judicial behavior Segal and Spaeth (2002), however, contend that while oral arguments provide a "valuable source of information," it does not naturally follow that "oral arguments regularly, or even infrequently determine who wins and who loses" (Segal and Spaeth 2002). Importantly for our purposes, oral arguments clearly have signaling significance, both to court watchers gauging where the justices stand (Shullman 2004; Roberts 2005; Johnson et al. 2009; Black, Wedeking, and Johnson, 2012), and as a form of communication from justices to one another (Black et al. 2012). In other words, whether oral arguments change the outcome of a case or not, they provide important cues for how justices and attorneys are framing a case, which, as we have argued throughout, is significant for the ruling at hand as well as future rulings and policy development beyond the judicial branch.

Methodology

As noted earlier, in this chapter we consider oral arguments, opinions (and in the case of *Hobby Lobby*, the dissent) and amicus curiae briefs. The bulk of the analysis here focuses on the briefs because they offer us the most variation to consider in terms of gender and frame. Justice Ruth Bader Ginsburg's dissent is searing, and moments of oral argument are dramatic, but neither one dissent nor a terse exchange in oral arguments allows us to conclusively judge the role that gender played in shaping perspective.

Parallel to the approach used in our preceding chapter on congressional deliberations, we code the briefs, oral arguments, opinions, and dissents from *Hobby Lobby* and *Zubik* for framing statements and for author or speaker gender.[6] A bit more detail on exactly how the briefs and oral arguments were coded and analyzed is helpful here. For each brief, we coded a number of elements. First, who wrote the brief? Second, what position did they take—for the petitioner or the respondent? Third, what was the gender breakdown of the authorship? For this component, we recorded the gender of each author, then calculated an overall percentage for each brief—in other words, if the brief was authored by one man and one woman it was coded "50% women authored." Finally, we coded the relative importance of each of the six frames discussed in chapter 1 by recording the frequency of framing statements associated with each frame, and dividing those by the overall number of framing statements.[7] Thus, for every document—and for those documents where the speaker is identified, for every speaker—we have a proportional measure of the relative importance of the religious, reproductive/women's rights, health, economics, morality, and partisanship/strategic game frames. Using this measure, we can identify a dominant frame in each brief and gauge how dominant it was relative to all others.[8] More importantly, we can also conduct a series of bivariate and multivariate analyses to track the relationship between the gender of authors and the frames employed.

For oral arguments, we conducted a similar content analysis for each framing statement made by each speaker. Since we are dealing with a smaller set of actors, however, our discussion of oral arguments does not include a multivariate analysis of the impact of gender of speaker on frame selection. Rather we highlight particularly noteworthy exchanges, and offer a quantitative analysis of the major themes and a qualitative discussion of their relevance to how the policy unfolded. It is worth reiterating here that the analysis of frames is based on a proposition of words selected relative to all words included across frames. Thus, as we noted in the last chapter, the fact that some speakers talk more often or longer than others in oral arguments is controlled for in the discussion of overarching framing trends.

Hobby Lobby: Venturing into a Minefield

The controversy over contraception care prompted the second trip to the Supreme Court for the ACA.[9] But while the first yielded a surprising opinion from Chief Justice Roberts to uphold the law, the *Hobby Lobby* 5-4 decision fell along predictably ideological lines. At issue in the case was whether the birth control mandate violated the federal Religious Freedom Restoration Act (RFRA). According to the RFRA, "Government shall not substantially burden a person's exercise of religion even if the burden results from a rule of general applicability," except when furthering a "compelling government interest" in the "least restrictive means" available (42 U.S. Code § 2000bb–1). Families owning Hobby Lobby and Conestega Wood Specialties claimed a religious objection to covering four types of birth control out of the 24 approved by the FDA (specifically, IUDs and morning-after pills). In other words, *Hobby Lobby* constituted a continuation of the conscience clause exemptions raised in the previous chapters: who should be able to opt out of providing birth control coverage based on a religious objection? Thus far, the crux of that conversation had been which organizations could be classified as religious (churches? charities and hospitals run by churches?). *Hobby Lobby* pushed the conversation even further: what about nonreligious private businesses, like Hobby Lobby and Conestoga Wood, whose owners claimed personal religious exemptions? The court's ruling concluded that they were also eligible for a religious exemption.

Hobby Lobby—Oral Arguments

Oral arguments in the case began with Solicitor Paul D. Clement emphasizing the "religiously sensitive" nature of the case. According to Clement, "When a Federal Government agency compelled employers to provide something as religiously sensitive as contraception, it knew that free exercise in RFRA claims would soon follow." Almost immediately, as is common in oral arguments, Clements was interrupted by a Justice, in this case Justice Sonia Sotomayor, pressing him on what constituted "sensitive materials":

> Is your claim limited to sensitive materials like contraceptives or does it include items like blood transfusion, vaccines? Some religions, products made of pork? Is any claim under your theory that has a religious basis, could an employer preclude the use of those items as well?

As Clement continued, Justice Elena Kagan returned to this line of questioning, pressing Clement on vaccinations and later raising the possibility of religious objection to "really, every medical treatment." These slippery-slope concerns were well established before the case went to the Supreme Court and continued well after the ruling. According to the account of one stakeholder, vaccination was a valid slippery-slope concern:

> We did a report at the one-year anniversary of *Hobby Lobby* where we looked at all the instances that *Hobby Lobby* has been cited to try and get out of other kinds of requirements. So one was a vaccination requirement where a student said, a paramedic student said, "I don't want to comply with my school's vaccination requirement, it's my religious beliefs, *Hobby Lobby*."

But beyond slippery-slope concerns, it is notable that from the earliest moments of oral arguments we see an initial and emphatic religious liberty framing followed immediately by an equally emphatic health framing offered by two of the Court's female justices.

Figure 5.1 breaks downs the frames used in oral arguments. By far the most dominant frames in oral arguments for *Hobby Lobby* were religion and economics; each constituted 37% of total framing statements. References to health care constituted only 15% of framing statements, and women's rights and morality references made up only 5% each. In other words, both economics and religion separately received more attention than all of the other frames put together. The focus on religion is hardly surprising. Since the question at hand was

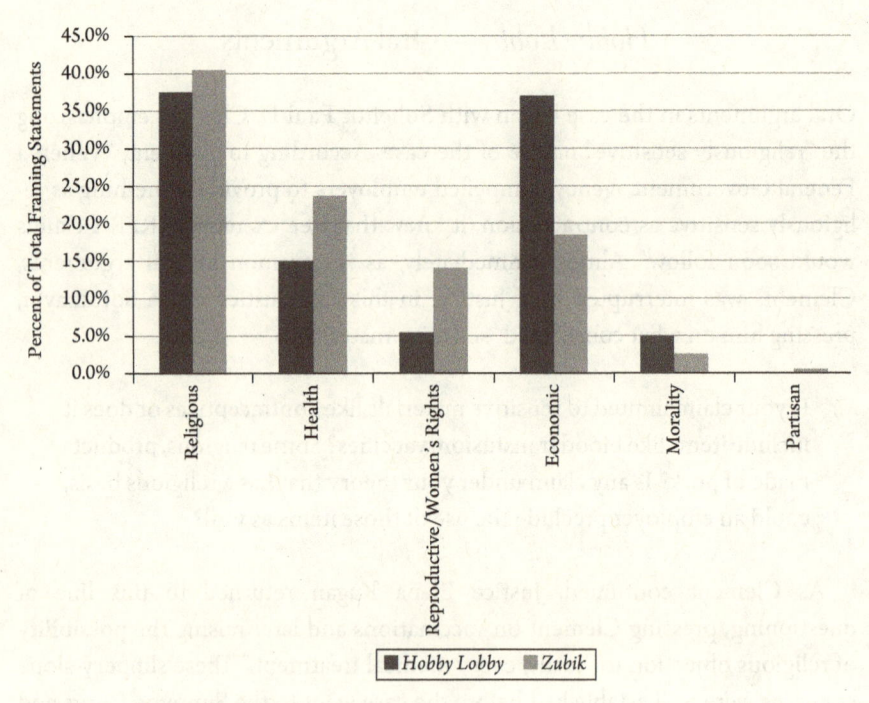

Figure 5.1 Frames Employed in Oral Arguments

whether the mandate violated the federal RFRA, religious liberty was obviously going to play a key role. While perhaps less obvious, the economic focus makes sense as well, given the centrality of topics like insurance and costs to a discussion of whether privately held companies would be compelled to cover birth as part of an employee health-care package. It is important to note, though, that the focus on costs to the employee, or women in general, were relatively rare. Much more common were references to costs to the employer, and discussions of whether corporations were entitled to religious protection. Indeed, nearly half (64 out of 143) of the framing statements linked to economic considerations were references to a corporation or corporations. While many reproductive rights' advocates had sought to emphasize the economic burden placed on women denied easy access to contraception, this was not a primary focus of the economic discussion in *Hobby Lobby*.

Indeed, women in general were not a primary focus of oral arguments in *Hobby Lobby*. As noted above, only 5% of framing statements were focused on women's rights or reproductive rights. The word "women" shows up only four times; the word "woman" only three. "Female," "reproductive," "reproduction," and "autonomy" were not used at all. Half of the references to "she" (four out of eight) were when a justice referred to another female justice. For comparison, references to "religious," "religion," or "religions" occurred 111 times in oral arguments. The dearth of references to women (except, as we explain later, in the dissent) is striking. One asking "Where are the women?" when considering the court's commentary would not readily find them, at least rhetorically, in oral argument.

The health-care frame fared a bit better—receiving 15% of the total share of framing statements. Mostly these were direct usage of the word "health," but also occasional references to "health care," "medical," and "doctors." "Preventive," which is fundamentally linked to the reason why the coverage was mandated in the first place, came up six times. While larger than the remaining frames (reproductive/women's rights and morality), the relatively limited use of the health-care frame is noteworthy considering how dominant it was—constituting over 50% of framing statements—when the statutory language that would ultimately authorize the mandate was discussed on the Senate floor.

Hobby Lobby—Opinion and Dissent

The limited attention to women and health would continue in the written opinion. The court's majority, citing the Dictionary Act, concluded that these for-profit companies could be viewed as "persons" and were thus eligible for protection under RFRA. The majority further found that the requirement to cover all forms of FDA-approved birth control constituted a substantial burden on the ability of the corporations to freely exercise their religion, particularly in terms of the financial costs.

Authored by Justice Samuel Alito, the decision gave relatively short shrift to the question of whether requiring the coverage of contraception constituted an "important government interest." As one expert court watcher put it, the majority "assumed—without actually deciding—that the government has good reasons for requiring employers to provide their female employees with no-cost access to the four kinds of birth control to which Hobby Lobby and Conestoga object" (Howe 2014). But the decision did emphasize that less restrictive means of accomplishing that goal existed, specifically by providing the coverage directly and/or offering the exemptions already provided for nonprofit religious entities.

As was the case in oral arguments, the majority opinion was decisively framed in terms of economics and religious liberty (Figure 5.2). Mentions of "religion" (46 times) and "religious" (147) far outweighed mentions of "women" (13) and "woman" (1). The phrase "women's health" only came up once. In total, framing statements related to religious considerations constituted 39% of all framing statements, and economic mentions constituted 44%. By contrast, health-related framing statements constituted 10% and reproductive/women's rights–related statements constituted only 3%.

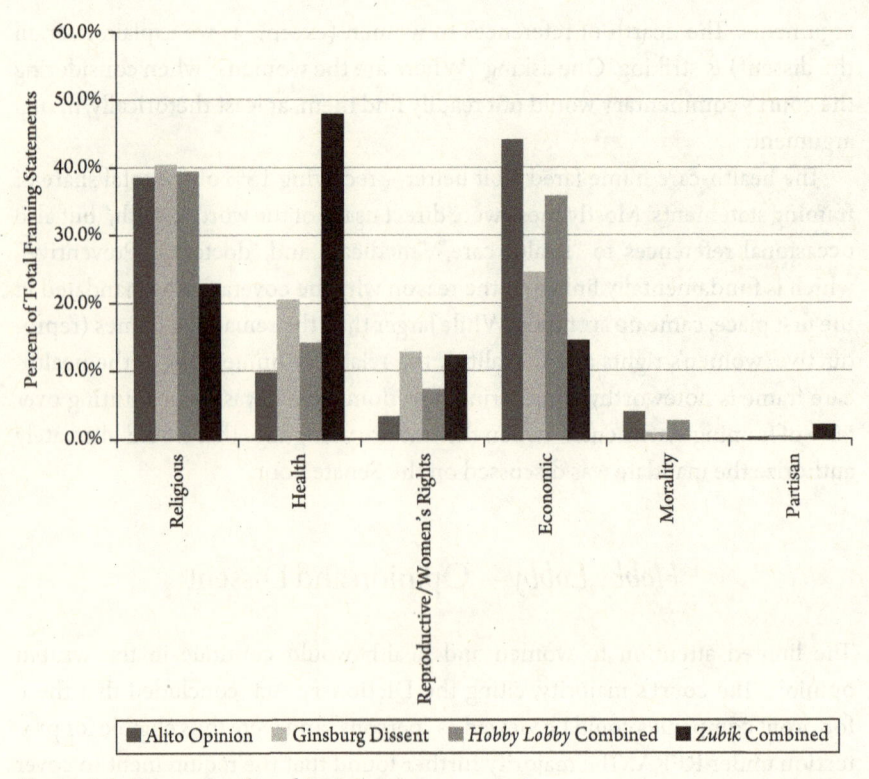

Figure 5.2 Frames Employed in Opinions

Before and after the ruling, defenders of the mandate, both those involved with the case and outside observers, made a series of slippery-slope claims. These challenges informed and then built on the line of argument pursued by Justice Sotomayor in oral arguments. If religious employers could opt out of providing birth control coverage based on RFRA, they argued, what would stop denials of other health-care benefits on religious grounds? What about blood transfusions, vaccinations, and psychiatric benefits? Beyond health care, could corporate heads simply refuse to abide by laws prohibiting discrimination based on race or sexual orientation if the laws counter their religious convictions (VanSickle-Ward 2014)? Justice Samuel Alito, writing for the majority, addressed the issue of scope explicitly, stating, "Our decision in these cases is concerned solely with the contraceptive mandate." He continued that not only should the ruling not apply to vaccinations, but that it also did not threaten compliance with taxation and racial discrimination law.

Justice Ginsburg forcefully disagreed, arguing in an oft-quoted dissent that the decision's "startling breadth" evidenced a court that had "ventured into a minefield."[10] Ginsburg focused directly on the issues of women's health as a compelling government interest, arguing that even if there were a burden on the for-profit corporation (which she does not concede), the government's interest is nonetheless persuasive:

> ACA provides further compelling interests in public health and women's well-being. Those interests are concrete, specific, and demonstrated by a wealth of empirical evidence. To recapitulate, the mandated contraception coverage enables women to avoid the health problems unintended pregnancies may visit on them and their children (Ginsburg 2014, 24).

Ginsburg also dedicates a considerable portion of her dissent to detailing the process by which the Women's Health Amendment was adopted, and the subsequent rules developed. Quoting extensively from the floor debate over the amendment, Ginsburg embraces the frames employed by amendment's authors and supporters that women needed special attention for preventative health care because they were so often left out:

> Women paid significantly more than men for preventive care, the amendment's proponents noted; in fact, cost barriers operated to block many women from obtaining needed care at all. See, e.g., id., at 29070 (statement of Sen. Feinstein) ("Women of childbearing age spend 68 percent more in out-of-pocket health care costs than men."); id., at 29302 (statement of Sen. Mikulski) ("co-payments are [often] so high that [women] avoid getting [preventive and screening services] in the first place").
> And increased access to contraceptive services, the sponsors comprehended, would yield important public health gains. See, e.g., id., at 29768 (statement of Sen. Durbin) ("This bill will expand health insurance coverage to the vast majority of [the 17 million women of reproductive age in the United States who are uninsured].... This expanded access will reduce unintended pregnancies.") (Ginsburg 2014, 3–4).

Ginsburg's share of framing statements dedicated to religion was comparable to Alito's. Again, in a case focusing on the application of the Religious Freedom Restoration Act religion will inevitably be a dominant theme. The more striking aspect of the dissent is the dramatically increased attention to health and women's rights. Proportionally speaking, Ginsburg emphasizes health care more than twice as often as Alito (21% compared to 10%), and women's rights and reproductive rights nearly four times as often (13% compared to 4%). Ginsburg is notably less likely to focus on economic considerations overall in her dissent than is Alito in the majority opinion (25% compared to 44%). But when she does so, she is much more likely to focus on costs to and burdens on women, rather than costs to and burdens on companies, as is evidenced by the excerpt above. The differences are key for two important reasons. First, as noted earlier in the chapter, frames, even those in dissents, can matter a great deal for future cases. Second, the extent to which Ginsburg explicitly invokes Senate deliberation is a clear example of frames traveling across venues, even when the dominant frame changes dramatically.

How significant was the gender of the justice here? More pointedly, did the fact that Ginsburg is a woman make a difference in how she ruled, or how she articulated her dissert? It is hardly shocking, of course, that a dissent would emphasize different frames than a majority opinion, or that Ginsburg, who built her legal career as an advocate for gender equity, would emphasize women's health as a compelling government interest. It is noteworthy, however, that Ginsburg so forthrightly views her own gender as providing insights. In the introduction we noted that Katie Couric interviewed Ginsburg about the case shortly after the ruling. In that interview, Ginsburg asserted that "Contraceptive protection is something that every woman must have access to, to control her own destiny." Couric asked Ginsburg if she believed "that the five male justices truly understood the ramifications of their decision." Ginsberg replied, "I would have to say no" ("Exclusive" 2015). Ginsburg has expressed skepticism in the past about the impact of a judge's sex on the nature of opinions (Kenney 2012; Bazelon 2009).[11] In this case, she readily agrees that most of the male justices had a "blind spot" ("Exclusive" 2015).

Zubik v. Burwell

Hobby Lobby was not quite the last word on contraception from the Supreme Court. The issue returned in *Zubik v. Burwell* in 2016—meaning that two of the four challenges to the ACA to reach the Supreme Court during this period focused on the birth control coverage mandate. As this section explains, the decision in *Zubik* was far less dramatic than *Hobby Lobby*, and the opinion issued was relatively brief. We therefore do not spend as much time here delving into the details of oral arguments and the opinion issued. We do, however, provide a brief overview of key elements and include *Zubik* in our discussion of frames at each stage.

At issue in *Zubik* was the so-called accommodation. After *Hobby Lobby*, the Obama administration allowed closely held for-profit companies the same arrangement that had already been granted to religious organizations: insurance companies would cover contraceptive care directly without any cost to employees or to the objecting religious organizations that had self-certified as exempt.[12] This compromise was unacceptable to religious organizations that believed that the process still made them culpable in the provision of contraception and thus still constituted an abrogation of their religious convictions, as well as a violation of the RFRA. A group of religious organizations challenged the accommodation cases that became consolidated under the name *Zubik*, one of the challenging institutions in Pennsylvania.[13] The debate over the appropriateness of the compromise was especially striking and controversial because during *Hobby Lobby*, Alito (to some extent) and Kennedy (even more explicitly) expressed support for the accommodation as a way for the government to provide coverage but steer clear of trampling on religious liberty. That the conservative justices later abandoned that position drew stinging criticism from the three female justices in response to a court order in a challenge (Wheaton College) that came between *Hobby Lobby* and *Zubik*. As Sotomayor, who authored the dissent, argued, "Those who are bound by our decisions usually believe they can take us at our word. Not so today" (Liptak 2014).

Notably *Zubik* came after the death of Justice Scalia and before a replacement had been confirmed. Advocates on either side hoping for a decisive opinion were disappointed. The *Zubik* decision was issued per curium (by the consensus of the court). The ruling was essentially a compromise that directed six federal courts to reevaluate the thirteen cases under their jurisdiction in light of the arguments brought to bear under *Zubik*.[14]

In some ways *Zubik* illustrated a continuation of the key themes raised in *Hobby Lobby*, and as the compromise decision illustrates, in the end none of the justices fundamentally changed their position on the centrality of religious liberty or women's health. That said, there was a discernable shift in frames, most notably the reemergence of the health frame and, to a less dramatic extent, the reproductive rights and women's rights frame. In oral arguments as well as the opinion, there was greater emphasis in *Zubik*, relative to *Hobby Lobby*, on health and women's rights (see Figures 5.1 and 5.2). In the *Zubik* opinions, health-related references constituted 48% of the total coded mentions; in *Hobby Lobby* health constituted only 14%. Indeed, health was the most prominent frame in the *Zubik* combined opinions, and the emphasis is particularly strong in the concurring opinion authored by Sotomayor and joined by Ginsburg (both female justices), where it made up 59% of framing statements. The reproductive/women's rights frame, which was used in 7% of the *Hobby Lobby* opinions, nearly doubles to 12% of the share of total framing statements in *Zubik*. A similar pattern emerges in oral arguments. Health was emphasized 24% of the time in *Zubik* (relative to 15% in *Hobby Lobby*), and women's rights and reproductive rights 14% of the time (relative to 5% in *Hobby Lobby*).

In other words, while the outcome of the case was a compromise ruling, the frames employed seemed to indicate a resurgence of the frames preferred by supporters of the mandate: health and reproductive/women's rights. Ginsburg made a point to emphasize those frames in her *Hobby Lobby* dissent, despite the dominance of the religious frame, and she and other female justices made a point of raising these frames throughout the process. This point links to a reoccurring theme in this volume as a whole; efforts made by women to assert certain frames—even when they, and the frames they promote, are in the minority—nevertheless affect the direction of conversation on policy and the policy itself. In this case, frames raised in the dissent in *Hobby Lobby*, but neglected in the majority opinion, became more central in *Zubik*.

It is important to remember, of course, that this is not entirely a function of gender. In the case of oral arguments, for example, the lion's share of these references came neither from a female justice nor any justice, but from male attorney Donald B. Verrilli, the U.S. solicitor general charged with representing the administration. Clearly, position on the mandate matters a great deal for which frame is preferred. As we explore through amicus briefs in the next section, however, there is evidence that gender mattered even when controlling for position.

Amicus Curiae Briefs

We now turn to a discussion of the amicus briefs. As discussed extensively at the introduction of the chapter, the briefs not only afford us a larger dataset, they also provide important insights into how advocates frame the legal arguments. The sheer number of briefs filed in these cases was striking—87 for *Hobby Lobby* and 70 for *Zubik*. The average numbers of briefs filed across all cases in the years these cases were decided were 12 and 13, respectively.[15] For further context, the cases garnering the highest number of amicus briefs during this time period were same-sex marriage in 2015 (148) and the ruling upholding key components of the ACA in 2013 (136).[16] In other words, while not at the level of the highest-profile cases of the day, the number of briefs clearly indicates a much higher than average level of attention paid by advocacy groups to these cases.

It is important to note from the outset of this discussion the stark gender disparities in brief authorship. As Table 5.1 illustrates, men were more likely overall to author briefs; women constituted 31% of brief authors in *Hobby Lobby* and 35% of brief authors in *Zubik*. In both *Hobby Lobby* and *Zubik*, women were much more likely to be arguing on the side in favor of the mandate. In *Hobby Lobby* women constituted 55% of authors writing briefs in support of the mandate (the petitioner, in the case of *Hobby Lobby*), compared to 23% of authors who opposed the mandate. In other words, three-quarters of the brief authors

Table 5.1 **Percentage of Women Authors in Briefs on** *Hobby Lobby* **and** *Zubik*

Position on Mandate	Hobby Lobby	N	Zubik	N
Anti-mandate	23.0%	58	22.9%	41
Neutral	6.3%	4	n/a	
Pro-mandate	55.2%	25	53.1%	29
Total	31.5%	87	35.4%	70

in opposition to the mandate were men and slightly less than half of those who supported the mandate were men.

A similar pattern emerges for *Zubik*. Fifty-three percent of the authors of briefs in support of the mandate (the respondent, in the case of *Zubik*) were women. Only 23% of those who wrote in opposition to the mandate were women. In total, women constituted about a third (35%) of brief writers. Before we move on to a discussion of frames, it is worth taking note of how striking these disparities are. Women were more than half of the voices in support of the mandate but less than a quarter of voices in opposition to it. Viewed simply as percentages, there is a clear gender division in these cases.

Amici curiae briefs were filed predominantly by religious organizations, but also by state governments, members of Congress, women's rights groups (such as the National Women's Law Center), women's health organizations, general health-care groups (such as the American Academy of Pediatrics), and civil liberties organization (such as the American Civil Liberties Union). Opponents of the mandate celebrated the significant degree to which the number of briefs favored their side (more two to one in *Hobby Lobby*) and kept the focus on religious liberty. Lori Windham, senior counsel at the Becket Fund, asserted, "Religious freedom is at stake here.... The broad support shows that Americans of many faiths and backgrounds want to see religious freedom protected."[17]

Bivariate and Multivariate Analysis: Gender and Frames

For this section, we first computed a series of bivariate correlations to assess the relationship between the percentage of authors who were women and the percentage of framing statements that were devoted to each of our six frames. Mirroring the hypotheses articulated in the previous chapter, we expected that briefs authored by a larger percentage of women would be more likely to emphasize gendered frames—namely, health and women's/reproductive rights.

Gender of authorship in amici briefs (measured by percentage of authors who were women) was significantly correlated with frames in both *Hobby Lobby* and *Zubik*. On balance, briefs with a higher percentage of women authors were more likely to make framing statements emphasizing health and reproductive rights and women's rights considerations. As Table 5.2 shows, briefs with a higher percentage of women were also less likely to highlight religious concerns.

Of particular note, these relationships generally persist when controlling for which side of the issue the briefs are on. This is important, because as we discussed earlier in the chapter, women were much more likely to be authoring briefs in favor of the mandate than they were in opposition to it. An obvious assumption is that the gender effect is simply explained away by the position of the brief. In other words, perhaps the difference in frames is most fundamentally linked not to the gender of the author(s) of the briefs themselves but to the missions of the organizations on whose behalf the briefs are written.

In tackling this question, we should first be clear that there are indeed consistent patterns in the position of briefs and the frames employed. We would hardly expect otherwise, as we have noted throughout the discussion of the evolution of this policy, supporters and opponents of the mandate, and birth control access in general, emphasize, overall, decidedly different frames on this issue. And supporters are, on balance, more likely to be women. This is clear for example in the competing hearings described in the previous chapter.

What is also clear, however, is that gender of brief authorship has a persistent effect even when holding constant the position of the briefs. This relationship is evidenced by a series of multivariate analyses where we included both gender percentage of brief authorship and the position taken in the brief as independent variables.

Table 5.2 **Gender of Authorship in Amici Briefs and Frames**

Frame	Hobby Lobby	Zubik
Religious	−.405**	−.443**
Health	.474**	.305**
Women's/Reproductive Rights	.434**	.411**
Economics	.199*	0.152
Morality	−0.025	−0.156
Partisan	−0.111	0.009
Combined "Gendered"	.505**	.420**
N	88	70

* $p < 0.05$, ** $p <\_ 0.01$, *** $p < 0.001$

The OLS regression models presented in Tables 5.3 and 5.4 illustrate that gender shaped frame selection in significant ways, even controlling for the position taken in a brief.[18] In the case of *Zubik*, the positive correlation between the percentage of women authors and the percentage of framing statements emphasizing reproductive/women's rights remained statistically significant and substantively important—with a 12.4% greater emphasis on reproductive/women's rights predicted between an all-male-authored brief and an all-woman-authored brief.

Table 5.3 **Impact of Author Gender and Brief Position on Frame Prominence:** *Zubik*

	Religion	Health	Reproductive Rights	Combined Gender
Percentage Women	−.227*	.108	.124*	.213*
	(.088)	(.068)	(.048)	(0.085)
Pro-mandate Position	−.183*	.092	.068*	.144*
	(0.061)	(.048)	(.034)	(.059)
Constant	.575***	.155***	.068*	.299***
	(0.041)	(.032)	(.022)	(.039)
N	70	70	70	70

Standard errors in parentheses
* $p < 0.05$, ** $p < 0.01$, *** $p < 0.001$

Table 5.4 **Impact of Author Gender and Brief Position on Frame Prominence:** *Hobby Lobby*

	Religion	Health	Reproductive Rights	Combined Gender
Percentage Women	−.202*	.182***	0.117**	0.104***
	(.067)	(.048)	(0.035)	(0.024)
Pro-mandate Position	−.101*	.078*	.047	.031
	(0.213)	(.037)	(.027)	(.018)
Constant	.493***	.068***	.038*	.051***
	(0.030)	(.021)	(.015)	(.011)
N	86	86	86	86

Standard errors in parentheses
* $p < 0.05$, ** $p < 0.01$, *** $p < 0.001$

Similarly, the relationship between female authorship and religious framing statements also remains important. For this set of framing statements, the predicted impact of moving from all male authors to all female authors is a more than a 20% decline. The relationship between gender of authorship and the relative prominence of health frames is still positive, albeit just below conventional levels of statistical significance.

The effect of female authorship is even more consistent in the case of *Hobby Lobby*. Higher percentages of women in brief authorship had a significant and positive relationship with the relative importance of health and reproductive/women's rights even after controlling for the position taken in the brief. As Table 5.4 shows, higher levels of women as authors also make the briefs significantly less likely to employ a religious frame. In other words, taking into account the position of the briefs is very important for understanding the frame selected, as we would expect. But it is not the full story. On the contrary, the impact of author's gender on frame is also significant. Regardless of stance, gender composition of authorship matters for how the issue is framed. Indeed, in several cases, such as the driving forces behind use of the health, reproductive rights, and combined gender frames in *Hobby Lobby*, gender appears to matter more than position taken for frame selection.

Gender of authorship in amicus briefs (measured by percentage of authors who are women) was significantly correlated with framing statements in both *Hobby Lobby* and *Zubik*. Importantly, these relationships persisted in almost every case, even after controlling for which side the brief was filed. In other words, gender has a strong, independent influence on frame selection decisions. As noted in the previous chapter, findings such as this are noteworthy because evidence of the impact of gender is often "explained away" by partisanship and ideology. Moreover, in this case, women were much more likely to be heard from on the side arguing for more expansive coverage of birth control. This point is important in its own right; there are clear asymmetries to the participation of women in this debate. But it is also true that women were more likely to emphasize certain contours of the debate and less likely to emphasize others, regardless of which side of the issue they supported.

Conclusion

The evolution of the contraception coverage under the ACA, from the introduction of the Women's Health Amendment covered in the last chapter to the Supreme Court rulings covered here, tells a dramatic story with two key takeaways. First, what began as a health-care debate transitioned into a religious one in *Hobby Lobby*. Health care reemerged in *Zubik*, but religion remained prominent. Some additional context is important here. Religious objections did not come out of nowhere; advocates for religious organizations had been fighting contraceptive coverage in the states for years before the ACA. Moreover, we know from existing scholarship that broadly worded statutes frequently encounter controversy after passage; indeed, dodging that controversy is often why they were broadly worded in the first place (VanSickle-Ward 2014). It is nonetheless striking that the religious frame is so absent in the initial debates and so dominant after the passage.

Second, gender clearly shaped framing in persistent ways that transcended both issue position and venue. Women were more likely to emphasize gendered frames than men in both legislative and judicial settings and even when controlling, where possible, for their party, views on the mandate, or both. Here we see the advantage of a cross-venue approach. The impact isn't identical across venues; for example, the impact of gender in promoting the health frame is more striking in the judicial context particularly when health is being downplayed otherwise, than it was in the legislative context. But considering how much else changed—the venue, the key players, the rules and norms for speaking, the dominant frames—the consistency with which women, on balance, emphasized different frames that related tangibly to their rights and experiences tells a powerful story about representation. Having established the role that gender plays in legislative as well as executive contexts, in subsequent chapters we turn to a discussion of how gender affected reporting on the birth control debate, how public opinion evolved on this issue, and how that opinion may be a function of which frame is highlighted.

PART II

MEDIA AND PUBLIC OPINION

6

Media Sourcing

As discussed in chapters 1 and 4, Republican representative Darrell Issa turned down a request to include Georgetown Law student Sandra Fluke on his February 2012 panel about "Freedom of Religion and Freedom of Conscience." Answering calls to "Let Sandra Speak" (Lipton-Lubet 2014, 366), House Democrats invited Fluke to testify in front of their Steering and Policy Committee. During this testimony, Fluke argued that, despite their moral opposition to birth control, Catholic universities such as Georgetown should be compelled to offer contraception to their students without a copay. In making her case, Fluke claimed that 40% of Georgetown Law School's female population experienced financial hardship from the student health insurance program's decision to not cover birth control, which could cost more than $3,000 over the course of obtaining a degree.

On his February 29, 2012, show, conservative radio pundit Rush Limbaugh devoted a full segment to Fluke's testimony and, in particular, her assertion that "contraceptives can cost a woman over $3,000 during law school" (Bey 2012). Specifically, Limbaugh wondered,

> What does it say about the college co-ed Susan [sic] Fluke, who goes before a congressional committee and essentially says that she must be paid to have sex, what does that make her? It makes her a slut, right? It makes her a prostitute. She wants to be paid to have sex. She's having so much sex she can't afford the contraception. She wants you and me and the taxpayers to pay her to have sex. What does that make us? We're the pimps.

Elected officials from both sides of the aisle swiftly rebuked Limbaugh's remarks. Republican senator John McCain, for example, said Limbaugh's comments were unacceptable "in every way" and "should be condemned" by all Americans, regardless of political affiliation. Similarly, Republican Speaker of the House John Boehner called the segment "inappropriate" (Thorp, Russert,

The Politics of the Pill: Gender, Framing, and Policymaking in the Battle over Birth Control. Rachel VanSickle-Ward, Kevin Wallsten, Oxford University Press (2019). © Oxford University Press.
DOI: 10.1093/oso/9780190675349.001.0001

and O'Brien 2012). David Frum, former special assistant to President George W. Bush, wrote that "Limbaugh's verbal abuse of Sandra Fluke set a new kind of low. I can't recall anything as brutal, ugly and deliberate ever being said by such a prominent person" (Frum 2012). Democrats were even stronger in their admonitions. Democratic House Minority Leader Nancy Pelosi denounced Limbaugh's "vicious and inappropriate attacks" (Geiger and Memoli 2012). Seventy-five congressional Democrats signed an open letter calling Limbaugh's rhetoric "sexually charged, patently offensive, obscene," and "an abuse of public airwaves" (Bassett 2012). President Obama referred to the statements as "disappointing" and "reprehensible" (Geiger and Memoli 2012).

The seemingly unending torrent of controversy unleashed by Issa's all-male panel produced a dramatic spike in media coverage. As Figure 6.1 shows, the number of newspaper articles mentioning "birth control" or "contraceptives" between August 1, 2011—the announcement date of a Health and Human Services (HHS) rule requiring that providers of group health insurance cover the costs of contraception as part of the Affordable Care Act (ACA)—and August 1, 2012—the date a modified mandate requiring that new health plans provide contraceptives without a copayment was enacted—changed suddenly in early 2012. Indeed, the debate over the ACA's contraceptive mandate received only sparse and inconsistent coverage prior to the House's "religious freedom" hearing. During February 2012, however, newspapers published 80 separate

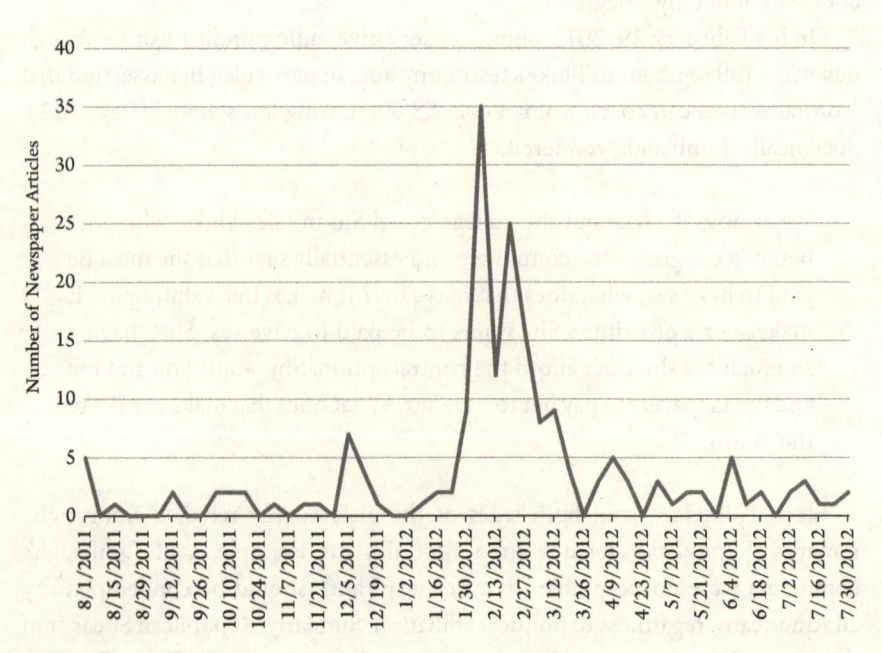

Figure 6.1 Newspaper Coverage of Contraceptive Mandate

articles on birth control and the ACA. By mid-March 2012, the controversy began to wane, and the nation's attention began shifting back to the looming presidential election. Between May 1 and August 1, 2012, there were only 25 total stories on the mandate.

What was the content of this news reporting? Which sources shaped it? How was it framed? What impact did it have on public opinion? Until this point we have focused exclusively on the evolution of birth control policy and explored the ways in which gender shaped framing and decision making across policy-making contexts. Over the course of the next four chapters, we turn our attention to media coverage and public opinion about the birth control debate. In this chapter we examine how the presence (or absence) of female reporters and gender-balanced newsrooms shaped sourcing patterns in news coverage of the ACA's contraceptive mandate. Examining newspaper coverage from August 1, 2011, through August 1, 2012, we find strong evidence that gender matters for the substance of the media's reporting. Specifically, we find that men and official sources were quoted more frequently than women and unofficial sources. Perhaps more importantly, we find that the tendency to rely on men was significantly dampened in reports written by female authors and in reports appearing in newspapers with more gender-balanced staffs. These findings provide support for the increasingly vocal concerns of media watchdog organizations that lobby for increased newsroom diversity and offer a clear answer to the oft-repeated question of whether having more women in the media leads to a qualitatively different kind of reporting on issues affecting women.

Literature Review

Source Diversity in News Coverage

Shoemaker and Reese (1996) define *news sources* as "external suppliers of raw material, such as speeches, interviews, corporate reports and government hearings" (178). According to Franklin, Lewis, and Williams (2010), "An understanding of the relationship between journalists and their sources sits at the heart of journalism studies" (202). Unsurprisingly, therefore, researchers have conducted numerous studies of who gets cited in news coverage and who does not (Althaus, Edy, Entman, and Phalen 1996; Benson and Hallin 2007; Galtung 2006; Zaller and Chiu 1996). Many of these studies implicitly assess the amount of "source diversity" in news coverage (Hansen 1991; Kurpius 2002). According to Voakes, Kapfer, Kurpius, and Chern (1996), "Source diversity is a dispersion of the representation of affiliations and status position of sources to create a news product. The more even the dispersion of the representation among source affiliations, status, and proximity in a given story or medium, the greater the diversity" (583). In other words, news reports that provide perspectives from a large variety of people have more source diversity than those that quote relatively few kinds of people.

A consistent theme of the research into the media's source diversity is that journalists have a clear preference for accessible sources who occupy official positions of power within formal institutions or that represent influential segments of society (Berkowitz and Beach 1993; Ericson, Baranek, and Chan 1989; Gans 1979; Lemert 1989; Sigal 1973). These studies have shown that while journalists occasionally reference a diverse array of occupational affiliations in their reporting, including interest groups (Kurpius 2002; Danielian and Page 1994), anonymous individuals (Martin-Kratzer and Thorson 2007), and policy experts (Lasorsa and Reese 1990), a small group of government sources tends to dominate most of the media's political coverage (Entman and Rojecki 1993; Sigal 1973; Smith 1993).

Diversity, of course, is not defined wholly in occupational terms. Another type of source diversity relates to the gender of individuals cited in news articles. While the disparities between men and women appear to be largest in sports and business reporting, existing research shows that media outlets consistently quote, reference and photograph men more frequently than women in all kinds of news stories (Armstrong 2004; Brown et al.1987; Craft, Wanta, and Lee 2003; Len-Rios, Rodgers, Thorson, and Yoon 2005; Potter 1985; Rodgers and Thorson 2000; Rodgers, Thorson, and Antecol 2000; Zoch and Turk 1998). While part of the overrepresentation of men is a function of the media's reliance on government officials (who are disproportionately male), a gender bias in citations also exists independent of status affiliation (Carpenter 2008; Graber 2006). Indeed, the growing number of women holding leadership positions in business and government has not significantly increased the percentage of women cited as news sources (Armstrong 2004). Overall, these studies suggest that the news media have a significant diversity problem in terms of its sourcing practices.

Source diversity in news coverage is important for three reasons. First, high levels of source diversity are necessary for legitimizing marginalized actors within the realm of political discourse. Media organizations bolster the legitimacy and notoriety of the individuals whom they quote in their reporting (Armstrong 2004; Manning 2001; Sigal 1973; Soloski 1989). When high-profile media organizations frequently cite certain types of individuals in news reports, they send a message to audience members that these actors are legitimate players in the political game who deserve to have their perspectives heard (Gans 1979; Kim and Weaver 2003). When high-profile media organizations systematically exclude certain types of individuals from political coverage, the opposite message is sent. To take just one example, Tuchman, Daniels, and Benet (1978) argue that the dominance of men in media coverage has led to the "symbolic annihilation" of women in a variety of spheres, including politics. As a result of the fact that women are rarely asked to comment on political developments and frequently appear only in stories about parenting, education, or gardening (Armstrong and Gao 2011; Ross 2007), news audiences are signaled that women are not important contributors to public discourse and are unfit to hold leadership positions within government.

Second, sources play a vital role in media "agenda building" (Dominick 2009; Scheufele 2000)—the process by which news outlets decide which issues to cover—and "frame building" (de Vreese 2005)—the process by which news outlets choose which elements of a particular issue to highlight. As we discuss at length in the next chapter, when reporters are consulting a diverse array of sources, there is a strong chance that the media will cover a diverse array of issues in a diverse array of ways. Indeed, because norms of objectivity and neutrality actively discourage journalists from strategically selecting and framing news stories, the sources to whom reporters turn inevitably exert a strong influence on the content of news coverage (Gans 1979; Cook 1998; Entman 2004; Scheufele 1999). Numerous studies of election coverage (Berkowitz and Adams 1990; Weaver and Elliott 1985), for example, have found that the media's reliance on official government and campaign sources results in reporting that focuses disproportionately on "game strategic" themes (Aalberg et al. 2012) and ignores alternative perspectives and counterframes. Understanding the sourcing decisions that news outlets make, therefore, becomes essential to understanding why the media focuses attention on certain areas.

Finally, the reputation of news outlets may depend on the kinds of sourcing decisions they make. Data from numerous survey organizations reveal that, over the course of the last 50 years, the media has become one of the most reviled and mistrusted institutions in the United States (Cook and Gronke 2001; Gronke and Cook 2007; Ladd 2009). Gallup's long-running series on the public's views toward news organizations, for example, shows that the percentage of people expressing a "great deal" or a "fair amount" of "trust and confidence" in the media dropped from 72% in 1976 to 40% in 2014. Similarly, the General Social Survey's battery of items on social and political institutions reveals a substantial decrease in the percentage of people expressing "a great deal" or "some" confidence in the press—from 84% in 1973 to 51% in 2012. Data for 2016—released by the Media Insight Project, a partnership between the Associated Press–NORC Center for Public Affairs Research and the American Press Institute—revealed that only 6% of Americans reported having a high level of trust in the press. As Ladd (2009, 29) succinctly put it, "Today, most Americans dislike the news media as an institution."

Unsurprisingly, academic research has attempted to uncover the origins of these negative evaluations. While explanations range from the media's reliance on "horserace journalism" (Cappella and Jamieson 1997; Patterson 1993) to politicians' relentless criticism (Ladd 2011), recent work points to sourcing decisions as a potential cause of declining media trust. A March 2017 study by the Pew Research Center, for example, found that sourcing decisions are the single most important factor in the perceived credibility of news reports—with half of the American public stating that "the sources a story cites" has a "large impact" on whether they think a news story is trustworthy. According to Vos and Wolfgang (2018), a significant amount of the growing disconnect between Americans and the media can be explained by a lack of diversity among journalists' sources. Indeed, as former *San Jose Mercury News* editor David Yarnold (2002) has written, "If readers don't see themselves and hear their voices in your pages, they won't view you as a credible source of information" (55). Diversifying the sources appearing in news coverage, in other words, may hold the key to restoring the media's damaged and diminishing reputation.

Influences on Source Diversity

Given the importance of sourcing decisions, what factors influence a reporter's choices about which sources to cite? A large body of work exists on the factors that shape how journalists report the news. The earliest studies argued that journalists' opinions, experiences, and social characteristics exerted a definitive influence over the kinds of news stories they report and how they report them (see, e.g., White 1950). In response, subsequent work emphasized the role that newsroom policies, organizational routines, and occupational norms play in shaping media coverage (Breed 1955; Geiber 1956). Shoemaker and Reese's (1996) hierarchical model synthesized these various perspectives. Their approach argued that five factors, operating at different levels of analysis, shape news content: the personal attributes of journalists, professional routines, organizational influences, external pressures, and ideology. Reese and Shoemaker's model guides our approach in this chapter and the next to analyzing the print media's coverage of the ACA's contraceptive mandate.

Personal Attributes

A great deal of the research on sourcing has focused on the personal attributes level in Shoemaker and Reese's hierarchy. The idea driving this work is that the social characteristics of journalists shape who gets quoted by news organizations and who does not. So, which personal attributes matter most? Although a vast literature has explored how age (Beam 2008), race and ethnicity (Poindexter, Smith, and Heider 2003; Zeldes and Fico 2005; Zeldes, Fico, and Diddi 2007), sexual orientation (Rosenkrantz 1992), and role conceptions (Weaver and Wilhoit 1996) influence a journalist's reporting, gender has received the most attention. Underlying nearly all studies of gender in journalism is the assumption that male and female reporters will make different decisions about news coverage as a result of their distinct values, interests, and identities (Rodgers and Thorson 2006). Research from a wide array of academic disciplines has shown, for example, that socialization processes lead men and women to have different ideas about "moral thinking" (Grant 1988), different "gender-linked" languages (Mulac, Bradac, and Gibbons 2001), different work priorities (Betz and O'Connell 1989), different conceptions of interpersonal relationships (Andersen and Urban 1997), different views on cooperation (Haugen and Brandth 1994), and different approaches to carrying out their career responsibilities (Aven, Parker, and McEvoy 1993). When coupled with feminist beliefs that encourage advocacy on behalf of women's interests (North 2009), the thinking goes, these different gender orientations should produce differences in nearly every aspect of the news coverage that male and female reporters produce.

Testing this assumption, a voluminous body of research explores whether women's reporting is more representative in its sourcing than men's reporting. The findings of this work are inconsistent. Numerous studies of news coverage, for example, show that female reporters quote female sources more frequently than male reporters (Armstrong 2004; Zoch and Turk 1998; Rodgers and Thorson 2003; Freedman and Fico 2005; Zeldes and Fico 2005; Zeldes, Fico, and Diddi 2007). Analyses of sourcing decisions on explicit women's issues, such as Title IX (Hardin, Whiteside, and Garris 2007) and the HPV vaccine (Correa and Harp 2011), suggest that these gender disparities may be particularly pronounced in coverage that directly affects the lives of women. A number of other studies, however, have contradicted the conclusions of this work and found that male reporters are actually more likely than female reporters to include quotes from women in their stories (Freedman, Fico, and Durisin 2010; Len-Rios et al.2008). Still other research (Freedman, Fico, and Love 2007; Liebler and Smith 1997; Ross 2007) has failed to find any important differences between male and female correspondents in their choice and treatment of sources. What's more, survey research has shown that reporters do not strategically or consciously choose which sources to cite based on the source's gender (Powers and Fico 1994). In short, despite good theoretical reasons for expecting differences in the news coverage authored by men and women, the empirical literature contains no hard and fast conclusions about the relationship between reporter gender and source diversity.

Professional Routines

According to Shoemaker and Reese's model, professional routines—the "repeated practices and forms that media workers use to do their jobs" (1996, 100)—are also an important influence on news content. Many of the media's professional routines are designed to help journalists cope with the time constraints of the news business by establishing consistent channels of reliable information. Most importantly, journalists are supposed to "interview credible sources, attribute their remarks and avoid expressing overt opinions" (Shoemaker and Reese 1996, 15).

While these routines were not intended to limit source diversity, most have the effect of enhancing the role that official sources play in news coverage at the expense of nonofficial sources. Journalists value official sources not only because they have little time to search out new sources (Brown et al. 1987; Powers and Fico 1994; Schudson 2003; Sigal 1973) but also because official sources are likely to respond to media queries in the kind of clear, quick, and quotable fashion that helps journalists do their jobs efficiently (Dimitrova, Kaid, Williams, and Trammell 2005; Gans 1979 Steele 1995). In many cases, official sources even proactively provide "information subsidies" (Gandy 1982; Berkowitz and Adams 1990), such as political advertisements, direct mail, speeches, press releases, and webpage content, that grease the skids of the writing process for reporters. Moreover, journalistic values about what constitutes "good" reporting suggest that reporters seek out the opinions of those who occupy positions of power within society because those opinions can be taken as "fact" without the need to research the veracity of that "fact" (Berkowitz 2009; Ericson 1999). From this perspective, quotations from women (who are less likely to hold leadership positions) and nonofficial actors are predictably rare.

Professional routines matter for sourcing decisions not only because they set the bounds of who constitutes a "good" source but also because they act as a "conformity mechanism" (Berkowitz 2009, 110) that tempers the influence of a reporter's personal attributes on the stories produced. While professional routines drive the reporting of all journalists to converge around a common set of sources, some research shows that routines exert a particularly strong influence over the stories written by women who work in male-dominated newsrooms (Rodgers and Thorson 2003; Weaver et al. 2007; Berkowitz 2009). According to Pease (1990), the socialization of journalists into professional routines inevitably leads well-intentioned attempts at diversifying newsrooms to fail in their goal of diversifying media coverage.

Organizational Influences

Shoemaker and Reese's model also identifies a number of organizational influences, most notably the composition of newsroom staff, on media content. One of the most consistent findings from the extensive literature about gender's role in media coverage is that women are significantly underrepresented in U.S. newsrooms. While there is no shortage of academic work on the topic, the most current data on the status of women in journalism comes from the numerous media watchdog organizations committed to diversifying newsrooms. The American Society of Newspaper Editors (ASNE), for example, has been tracking newsroom diversity since 1997. Much like its previous 16 reports, ASNE's "2014 Census" found that women are greatly outnumbered in media companies, making up less than 38% of newspaper employees. Striking a similar chord, the Women's Media Center's (WMC) 2014 "Status of Women in the U.S. Media" report found that female staffers constituted only 36% of newsrooms at major broadcast and print media outlets, and that male opinion-page writers outnumbered female opinion-page writers four to one at the nation's most prestigious newspaper syndicates. More surprisingly, the WMC found that female reporters were responsible for only one-third of all bylines on political stories in 2015. Echoing the ASNE and WMC findings, a 2014 Radio Television Digital News Association survey found that women made up just 31% of TV news directors and 20% of general managers. Collectively, these results led the Neiman Foundation for Journalism to echo Issa's critics and author a report asking, "Where Are the Women?" (Griffin 2014).

Unfortunately, empirical investigations of the relationship between the gender diversity of newsrooms and the gender diversity of sources are infrequent and inconclusive. In a study of male and female editors, for instance, Craft and Wanta (2004) suggested that the gender parity of newspaper editorial teams could indirectly influence sourcing practices by shaping which reporters were assigned to cover certain stories. Specifically, editorial teams with relatively few women were less likely to assign female journalists to report on political events than editorial teams with a relatively large number of women. Given that female reporters may cite more women in their articles, these reporter assignments could, in turn, lead to more gender diversity in sourcing. In a more direct test of the impact of editorial diversity, Freedman, Fico, and Durisin (2010) found that newspapers with female editors did not use more female sources than newspapers with male editors. Analyzing the gender composition of the entire newsroom, Freedman, Fico, and Love (2007) found that more diverse newspapers were actually less likely to cite female sources. The limited research thus far, in other words, has presented a very mixed picture of how gender diversity in newsrooms shapes media coverage.

External Pressures

Personal attributes, professional routines, and organizational influences are not the only factors that matter for sourcing decisions. Reporters' perceptions of their audience—the so-called external pressures of Shoemaker and Reese's model—also shape choices about whom to quote. Marketing researchers have long argued that the most effective approach to creating a profitable media enterprise is to produce content that appeals to the largest possible audience (Armstrong 2004; Graber 2006). As Altschull (1984, 254) argues, "The content of the press is directly correlated with the interests of those who finance the press. The press is the piper, and the tune the piper plays is composed by those who pay the piper." Because audiences, and the advertisers they attract, pay the piper in the media business, news content is inevitably affected by the preferences that those in the news business perceive audiences and advertisers to have (White 1950).

In practice, the need to attract readers or viewers has often meant that news organizations focus on covering state- or national-level events in a way that is as neutral as possible. Indeed, according to some observers, the media's desire to reach a mass audience produces low-quality coverage because it encourages reporters to ignore local issues and rely too heavily on a small number of official sources (Tuchman 1978). This is not to suggest, however, that news companies are immune from local pressures. Research has shown that perceptions of audience demands can mitigate the tendency to ignore local concerns and limit source diversity (Armstrong 2002; Brown et al. 1987; Jeffres, Cutietta, and Lee 1999). Most recently, Rodgers and Thorson (2003) found that female reporters at small local newspapers used a greater diversity of sources than female reporters at larger national papers. In short, how those involved in the news business view their audiences matters greatly for the issues covered and the sources used.

Although Shoemaker and Reese's approach guides most research into sourcing patterns, very few studies empirically assess the variables that operate at each of the model's five levels (journalists' personal attributes, professional routines, organizational influences, external pressures, and ideology). In fact, the vast majority of published work collects data on only one level, such as reporter attributes, and assesses the impact of this level after controlling for a small number of story-specific attributes, such as placement of the article. Here, we attempt to improve on these studies by measuring variables associated with multiple levels of Shoemaker and Reese's model.

Hypotheses

In this chapter we test six hypotheses about sourcing in the media's contraceptive mandate coverage. First, in line with decades of research into sourcing patterns, we hypothesize that articles about the contraceptive mandate will display limited levels of occupational diversity. We expect that "official" sources—meaning people holding formal positions within government, interest groups, universities, media companies, or religious organizations—will be quoted far more frequently than individuals who hold no positions of power within a formal organization.

H1: Official sources will be cited more frequently than nonofficial sources.

The second set of hypotheses guiding our analysis has to do with the number of male and female sources found in the media's reporting. On the one hand, nearly every study of sourcing patterns ever conducted has shown a strong bias in favor of male sources. Freedman and Fico (2005), for example, found that women made up less than 10% of nonpartisan sources cited in newspaper coverage of gubernatorial campaigns, and Bridge (1995) found that quotes from female experts were almost entirely absent in major newspaper stories. On the other hand, research has also demonstrated that journalists cater coverage to their perceived audiences. As a result of the fact that health-care news in general is a "female consumer-oriented news topic" (Len-Rios et al. 2012, 77) that is likely to appeal to more women than men, we might expect that news coverage on birth control will feature more female than male sources. In light of these diverging studies, we test the accuracy of the following hypothesis:

H2: Male sources will be cited more frequently than female sources.

Our primary interest in this chapter is to assess how byline and newsroom diversity influence source diversity. As suggested above, evidence is mixed on the role that a reporter's gender plays in shaping sourcing decisions. While some studies have found that women are cited more frequently when female reporters write stories (Armstrong 2004; Zoch and Turk 1998; Rodgers and Thorson 2003; Freedman and Fico 2005; Zeldes and Fico 2005; Zeldes, Fico, and Diddi 2007) and, in particular, when female reporters write stories about women's issues (Correa and Harp 2011; Hardin, Whiteside, and Garris 2007), other research suggests that news values, organizational hierarchies, routines, and professional socialization may standardize journalists' work (Rodgers and Thorson 2003). This contradictory set of empirical findings compels us to test the following hypothesis:

H3: Women authors will cite more women as sources than male authors.

Relatively few studies have explicitly linked newsroom diversity to sourcing decisions. As a result, it is possible to state three competing hypotheses regarding the gender composition of newsroom staffs. Gender diversity may exert little influence over sourcing decisions because female journalists have been strongly socialized into the same, "masculine" set of professional norms (Liebler and Smith 1997; Rodgers and Thorson 2000; Van Zoonen 1998) and "macho newsroom culture" (Ross and Carter 2011) as men. By contrast, large numbers of women working in a newsroom might create a "critical mass" (Correa and Harp 2011) that overpowers the norms, routines, and cultures that limit source diversity. It is also possible that, consistent with Freedman, Fico, and Love (2007), more gender diversity in newspaper staffs will lead to less gender diversity in sourcing. In other words, we need to further examine the validity of the following proposition:

> H4: Newspapers with more gender-balanced staffs will cite more women as sources than newspapers with more male-dominated staffs.

Finally, previous work has shown that circulation size and national orientation influence the reporting found in newspapers. Their larger and more diverse audiences may cause national newspapers to attempt to diversify the sources they cite in their coverage (Carpenter 2008; Hansen 1991). This attempt to diversify could lead to more occupational and gender-based parity in citation counts.

> H5: Newspapers with larger circulation sizes will cite more women as sources than newspapers with smaller circulation sizes.
> H6: Newspapers with larger circulation sizes will cite more unofficial actors as sources than newspapers with smaller circulation sizes.

Methods
Dependent Variables

Articles for this study were collected via LexisNexis's Newspapers and Wires database, which contains extensive archives of articles published in approximately 300 American newspapers. Although LexisNexis includes content from the vast majority of national, regional, and local newspapers in the United States, a number of notable publications are not included in their database. Most notably, articles from the *Wall Street Journal*, the *Chicago Tribune*, and the *Los Angeles Times* were not available when data for this study were collected. Even with these exclusions, however, the LexisNexis database is the single most comprehensive archive of news stories in the United States. Unsurprisingly, therefore, it is the most widely used source for gathering data in the social sciences about media coverage (Deacon 2007).

In order to collect a sample of news stories on controversies surrounding the ACA and reproductive rights, we searched the "headline/lead paragraph" section of articles contained in the LexisNexis Newspapers and Wires database for the term "birth control" or "contraceptives" in the headline or lead paragraph of their archived articles between August 1, 2011—the announcement date of an HHS rule requiring that providers of group health insurance cover the costs of contraception as part of the ACA—and August 1, 2012—the date a modified mandate was enacted that required new health plans to provide contraceptives without a copayment. This search yielded 191 unique news reports.

Once this population of articles was collected, we employed a variation of the coding schemes used in previous studies of sourcing patterns (Armstrong 2004; Carpenter 2008). Specifically, we classified three features of each article. First, the number of sources in each article was recorded. Following Carpenter's (2008) operationalization, a news source was defined as "a provider of attributed textual information" (15). Coders, therefore, were instructed to record the total number of individuals, organizations, and documents in each article to whom information was attributed. To be considered a news source, the individual, organization, or document cited in the article had to be identified with a "verb of attribution," which is a statement of direct or indirect communication (Carpenter 2008, 15). Direct communication included verbs such as "reported," "stated," "said," "claimed," and "argued," while indirect communication included verbs such as "hopes," "believes," "thinks," and "feels."[1]

Second, each cited news source was categorized based on gender. Coders were instructed to determine the gender of each source mentioned in each article by looking at the first name, courtesy title, and pronoun reference provided in the news report. Following Freedman et al. (2010), if the gender was not made clear by any of these indicators, the source was coded as "other/unknown." The most common kind of "other/unknown" source was an organizational or institutional actor, such as the U.S. Conference of Catholic Bishops, Teva Pharmaceuticals, or the Obama administration.[2]

Third, the source's title was recorded and placed into one of eight mutually exclusive categories:

(1) politicians (including elected officials, candidates, spokespeople, and political parties);
(2) government employees, bureaucrats, and judges;[3]
(3) representatives of churches and religiously affiliated organizations;[4]
(4) interest group representatives;[5]
(5) academics and researchers;[6]
(6) media professionals (including journalists, bloggers, and commentators);

(7) unofficial/noninstitutional actors (such as private citizens, church members, and protestors); and

(8) other/unknown individuals or organizations.[7] Consistent with previous research, "official sources" included any individual or organization included in categories 1 through 6, while "unofficial sources" were individuals or organizations falling into categories 7 and 8.

We aggregated these data into two separate dependent variables capturing different dimensions of the source diversity concept: the percentage of cited sources in an article who were women and the percentage of sources cited in an article who were "unofficial."

Independent Variables

Our primary independent variables of interest were the gender of the news article's reporter and the gender diversity of the publishing newspaper's staff. Using the same approach employed for categorizing sources, each article was placed into one of three categories: male-only authorship, female-only authorship, and unknown/mixed authorship. Our measure of gender diversity in newsroom staffs came from the ASNE 2012 Newsroom Employment Census.[8] ASNE has tracked racial and gender diversity on American newspaper staffs since 1997 by reporting the percentage of women and African Americans working in newsrooms each year. While the Newsroom Employment Census sends surveys to every newspaper in the country, the yearly response rate is only 65%. In 2012 the census received data on gender diversity from 985 newspapers. Unfortunately, a number of the newspapers that reported on the contraceptive mandate during the time frames of our study did not respond to ASNE's survey request. Specifically, 19 of the 62 newspapers appearing in our search results (accounting for 34 of our 191 stories) failed to provide data on the diversity of their staffs.

To isolate the influence of reporter gender and newsroom diversity on sourcing patterns, we also collected data on a number of other factors identified by previous research as influencing citation decisions. The first variable we measured was newspaper circulation. For each of the newspapers in our study, we gathered the average weekday circulation in 2013.[9] According to previous research, these circulation numbers serve as a useful proxy for a newspaper's prominence, prestige, and popularity (Lacy, Fico, and Simon 1989). Circulation numbers also allow us to take into account whether a newspaper is catering to a national, regional, or local audience.

Previous studies suggest that a reporter's perceptions of her audience shape sourcing decisions (Carpenter 2008; Hansen 1991). To account for these perceptions, we also measured two attributes of the states in which newspapers reside: attitudes toward reproductive rights and citizen political ideology. The

National Abortion and Reproductive Rights Action League (NARAL) maintains a report card listing the grades each state earns on the basis of state policies related to reproductive rights. This score, which ranges from A+ to F, serves as a measure for how progressive a newspaper's home state is on reproductive rights. In addition, we also included citizen ideology scores for each state in our analyses (Berry, Ringquist, Fording, and Hanson 1998). Similar to the more specific NARAL scores, this state-level ideology measure allows us to assess whether sourcing decisions are shaped by the ideology of the reporter's presumed consumer.

Results

Journalism is a "male-dominated" profession. Despite the fact that women have made up more than half of all journalism graduates every year since 1977 (Bennet and Ellison 2010; Len-Rios et al. 2012), the ASNE, the WMC, the Global Media Monitoring Project, and many other watchdog organizations have repeatedly found that the vast majority of journalists, editors, and producers working in the news industry are men. Moreover, male print reporters are more than twice as likely as female reporters to cover high-profile stories, win assignments to write on political developments, and receive a published byline (Layton and Shepard 2013). Existing research suggests that these disparities result from the fact that newsrooms can often be subtly or overtly hostile to women, leading them to occupy few managerial positions, receive less pay than their male counterparts, and leave journalism as a career at a relatively young age (Elmore 2007; Everbach and Flournoy 2007).

Perhaps unsurprisingly, therefore, male-authored reports on the ACA's contraceptive mandate outnumbered female-authored reports in American newspapers during the period of our study. The gender disparity in bylines was, however, far less pronounced than previous studies of women in journalism would lead us to expect. Indeed, between August 2011 and August 2012, 54.5% of newspaper articles published by an author with a clearly identifiable gender were written by male reporters and 45.5% of such articles were written by female reporters. Given that the 43 papers included in our study actually had somewhat less gender diversity in their newsroom staffs than the ASNE national average (34.9% female employees vs. 37.1% female employees), this is a considerable degree of byline parity.

In total, 586 different sources were quoted in the 191 newspaper articles on contraception published between August 2011 and August 2012. While the number of sources ranged widely—from zero to 14—the majority of articles cited between two and six sources. Consistent with the predictions spelled out in H1, we found that "official" sources were far more likely to be cited than "unofficial" sources. Indeed, as Figure 6.2 shows, politicians (31.4% of sources), government

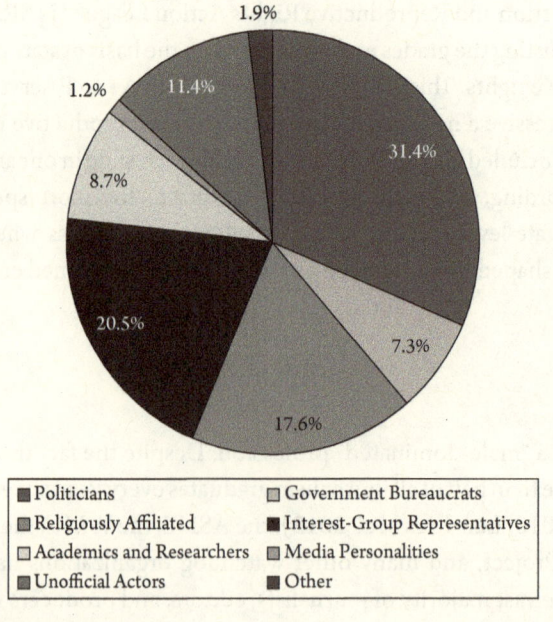

Figure 6.2 Sources in Newspaper Stories by Type

bureaucrats (7.3%), interest-group representatives (20.5%), and religious leaders (17.6%) received far more attention than "average" members of the public who were not speaking on behalf of an organization (11.4% of sources). The dominance of politicians, interest-group representatives, and religious leaders is not surprising given that the contraceptive mandate was a controversial government policy that mobilized churches and reproductive rights organizations. What is surprising, however, is how infrequently the media sought out the perspectives of average citizens whom changes to birth control policy were likely to affect.

The fact that contraception is primarily a woman's issue led us to speculate that women may be quoted more than men in news coverage despite a long tradition of work showing the underrepresentation of female sources in political reporting. This speculation turned out to be unwarranted. In line with the consensus of previous research on sourcing, men were quoted far more frequently than women in the media's coverage. Overall, after excluding the 30 sources that were documents, collective attributions, organizational statements, or individuals whose gender could not be determined, 56.7% of quoted sources (315 of 556) were men and 43.3% were women (241 of 556). Given the significance of birth control in women's lives, this gender gap in citations is a striking finding.

Digging further into our sourcing data, it becomes clear that the gender gap in citations resulted primarily from the media's desire to present the views of politicians and clergy members on the ACA's contraception mandate. As Figure 6.3 illustrates, women representing interest groups and government

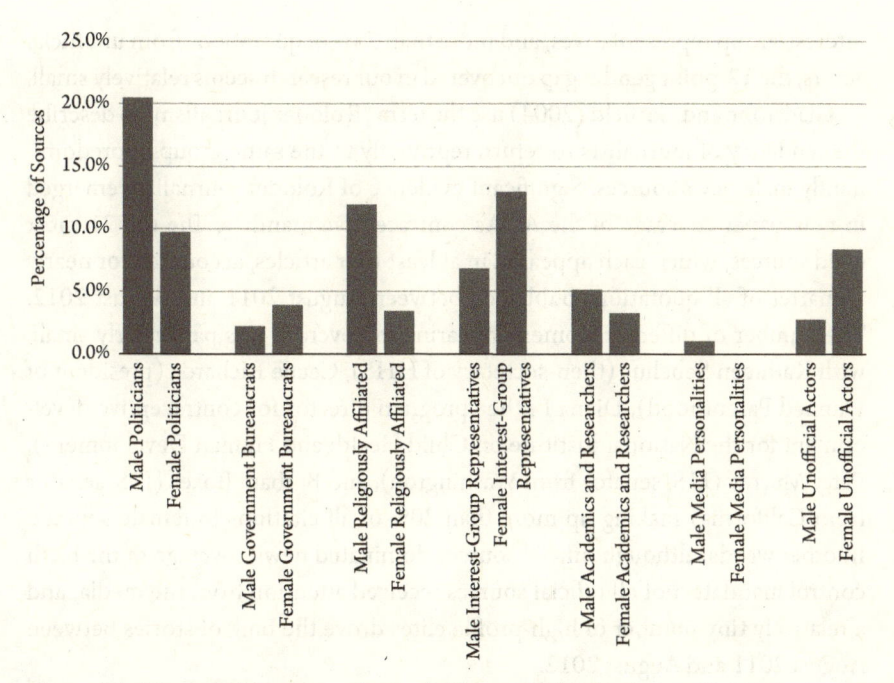

Figure 6.3 Sources in Newspaper Stories by Type and Gender

agencies were actually cited far more frequently than their male counterparts. Additionally, news reports quoted unofficial women over four times more than unofficial men. The overall quotation disparity between men and women, therefore, was mostly driven by decisions to seek information from areas where women have been historically underrepresented: paid political work and church leadership positions.

An important note here, however, is that female politicians and religious leaders may have actually been overrepresented in birth control coverage during the period of our study. Women, of course, are notoriously underrepresented in the upper echelons of politics and religion in the United States. During the year of our study (2011–2012), women made up only 30% of federal cabinet-level appointees (Bialik 2016), 24% of state legislators, 22% of statewide elected executive office positions, and 17% of the U.S. Congress (Gillibrand 2012). Similarly, a 2016 report by the Pew Research Center found that while many large religious organizations in the United States formally allow women to hold leadership positions, very few women have actually served at the top, and significant barriers prevent women from advancement (Sandstrom 2016). Despite these large disparities, women constituted 30.4% of citations to politicians and 22.2% of citations to religious leaders in coverage of the ACA's contraception mandate. When considered alongside the fact that women made up more than 60% of quotations from government bureaucrats, more than 65% of quotations from interest-group representatives, and more than 75% of quotations from unofficial actors, the 12-point gender gap uncovered in our research seems relatively small.

Gladstone and Garfield (2004) use the term "Rolodex journalism" to describe the tendency of journalists to return repeatedly to the same group of predominantly male news sources. Significant evidence of Rolodex journalism emerged in newspaper coverage of the ACA's contraceptive mandate. The top 21 most cited sources, which each appeared in at least four articles, accounted for nearly a quarter of all quotations published between August 2011 and August 2012. The number of different women appearing in coverage was particularly small, with Kathleen Sebelius (then-secretary of HHS), Cecile Richards (president of Planned Parenthood), Diana Blithe (program director for contraceptive development for the National Institute on Child Health and Human Development), Patty Murray (U.S. senator from Washington), and Barbara Boxer (U.S. senator from California) making up more than 20% of all citations to female sources. In other words, although official sources dominated news coverage of the birth control mandate, not all official sources received attention from the media, and a relatively tiny number of high-profile elites drove the bulk of stories between August 2011 and August 2012.

Media observers and a large body of previous research suggest that a lack of byline and newsroom diversity might lead to a lack of source diversity. Did a reporter's gender or a newsroom's composition matter for the sources discussed in coverage of the contraceptive mandate? Table 6.1 presents the findings from a series of OLS regression models predicting the percentage of attributions made to female and nonofficial sources.[10] In addition to reporter gender and newsroom diversity, each of the models includes the theoretically important control variables described above: daily newspaper circulation, NARAL scores, and citizen ideology.

Consistent with the predictions of H3, female sources were more visible in stories written by women than by men. Overall, a majority of the sources (52.1%) cited in female-authored stories on the contraceptive mandate were women, while less than 40% of sources in male-authored stories were women ($p = 0.02$). As Table 6.1 shows, even after controlling for other influences on sourcing decisions, female reporters quoted a much larger percentage of women than male reporters during the period of our study. Articles written by women contained nearly 15% more citations to female sources than articles written by men; put differently, women-authored articles included an average of approximately 0.5 more quotes from female sources. At least on this particular women's issue during this particular period, therefore, female reporters made sourcing decisions that significantly amplified the voices of other women.

Newspaper reports on contraception published under female bylines were also far more likely to quote women than those published under unknown or

Table 6.1 **OLS Regression Results for Source Diversity**

	Female Sources Percent	Unofficial Sources Percent
Male Authorship	–14.88***	–2.509
	(4.117)	(4.260)
Unclassified/Organizational Authorship	–31.47**	–9.352*
	(10.28)	(3.634)
Circulation	–0.339	0.187
	(0.647)	(0.524)
Citizen Ideology	–0.450	0.295
	(0.265)	(0.256)
NARAL Score	0.130	–0.714
	(0.757)	(0.580)
Percent Female in Newsroom	1.044*	–0.0398
	(0.407)	(0.258)
Constant	41.41	–3.379
	(22.41)	(11.97)
N	138	138
adj. R^2	0.090	0.002

Robust standard errors in parentheses
* $p < 0.05$, ** $p < 0.01$, *** $p < 0.001$

mixed-gender bylines. As Table 6.1 shows, articles in our unknown or mixed-gender authorship category included 31% fewer female sources than articles written by women. Given that 22 of the 24 articles in our unknown/mixed-authorship category were published by wire services (e.g., Bloomberg News, Washington Bureau, Associated Press) rather than by mixed-gender reporting teams, it seems safe to conclude that these disparities represent differences in the reporting styles recommended for articles receiving anonymous and individualized bylines. More specifically, these differences suggest that female sources were marginalized in the contraception debate when newspapers relied on wire services rather than their own reporters to provide coverage or the ACA's mandate.

While female reporters provided more gender diversity in their sourcing than male reporters, they did not produce reports with significantly more occupational diversity. As Table 6.1 shows, there were no meaningful differences in the percentage of unofficial sources included in birth control mandate reports authored by women and authored by men. As Table 6.1 also shows, however, important differences existed in the percentage of unofficial sources included in the birth control mandate reports published under female and organizational bylines. Specifically, articles attributed to women included, on average, 9.3% more unofficial sources than articles attributed to wire services and other anonymous entities. When considered alongside the findings about gender diversity in sourcing, these data suggest that the differences between source diversity found in female and organizational reports are just as large and substantively important as the differences in source diversity found in female and male reports.

The effect of gender diversity in newsrooms on sourcing decisions has received little scholarly attention. As a result, we were unsure whether gender parity in news staffs would influence which kinds of people were quoted. According to our data, having more women employed at a newspaper encourages more gender diversity in sourcing but not more occupational diversity. As Table 6.1 illustrates, increases in the percentage of women employed at a newspaper significantly raised the percentage of women quoted in articles about the contraception mandate but did not exert any influence over the percentage of unofficial sources quoted. Moreover, newsroom diversity failed to exert an indirect effect on sourcing decisions by enhancing the probability of female authorship. Indeed, the percentage of women employed at a newspaper was uncorrelated with the probability of an article being authored by a man, a woman, or an organizational entity.[11] Overall, therefore, newsroom diversity encouraged a small and direct increase in source diversity by increasing the prominence of women in contraception stories between August 2011 and August 2012.

Contrary to H5 and H6, we found little evidence that a newspaper's size and national prominence influenced its sourcing practices. Indeed, although our data contained evidence that larger newspapers cited more sources than small local papers,[12] there was no evidence that these sources were more diverse. As the results in Table 6.1 show, a newspaper's circulation was not significantly correlated with its propensity to quote either female sources or unofficial sources. These results contradict previous research suggesting that large national papers try to appeal to their more diverse audiences by diversifying who is quoted in their stories. Although we cannot determine whether this finding applies to all women's issues, we can conclude that readers of large papers did not hear from dramatically different sources than readers of small papers on the issue of contraception.

Discussion

One of the press's primary democratic responsibilities is to inform the public about a range of political perspectives by presenting a diversity of viewpoints about current events (Porto 2007).[13] Whether the media is actually fulfilling this responsibility depends on one's definition of "diversity." According to Ferree et al. (2002), two different normative standards related to sourcing decisions exist for evaluating the media's performance on the diversity criterion.[14] In a representative liberal model, source diversity simply refers to whether political elites are quoted in a way that is proportionate to their relevance in government institutions. Omission of viewpoints beyond those articulated by elected representatives is unproblematic from this perspective because those who matter most for policymaking are allowed to speak and be heard. Alternatively, in a participatory liberal model, the notion of source diversity is expanded to include communication by nonelite actors. Under this model, if the media is to communicate diverse perspectives, it must provide a wide range of individuals within and outside the halls of power with the opportunity to speak.

Regardless of whether it is defined in representative liberal or participatory liberal terms, the media appears to have failed in providing a meaningful level of source diversity to its readers during the early months of the debate over the contraceptive mandate. As discussed above, the media did not regularly call on the nonelite women most affected by birth control policy decisions to speak about contraception coverage under the ACA, instead relying heavily on politicians and government bureaucrats to source their reports. Displaying a strong tendency toward Rolodex journalism, the number of unique politicians and government bureaucrats quoted in news reports was also quite small and drawn overwhelmingly from the ranks of high-profile, national leaders. Furthermore, the data provide little evidence that any of the variables from Shoemaker and Reese's (1996) hierarchical model—ranging from the reporter's gender to the political views of the news audience—exerted any influence at all over the media's propensity to privilege elite voices over the input of the masses. It is quite clear, in other words, that source diversity was greatly limited in the media's coverage of the contraception mandate.

Source diversity is not just about occupations, however. According to Hartley (1982, 146) the "news is not simply mostly about and by men, it is overwhelmingly seen through the eyes of men." We found mixed evidence for this argument in our examination of contraception coverage. On the one hand, although they make up more than 50% of the overall U.S. population, women wrote only 45% of contraception articles and accounted for only 41% of quoted sources. Given that contraception is a "female consumer-oriented news topic" (Len-Rios et al. 2012, 77) that primarily affects women, the size of this disparity in bylines and citations raises important questions about how well the media is actually serving its audience and fulfilling its democratic responsibilities to represent diverse viewpoints. Our work in this area is not alone. A 2013 report by 4thEstate.net found that women were dramatically underrepresented in election coverage during 2012—making up only 26% of quoted sources in election stories about

Planned Parenthood, 19% of quoted sources in election stories about birth control, and 12% of quoted sources in election stories about abortion. Taken together, these results suggest the possibility of serious systemic and structural problems in the way the American media cover women's reproductive rights.

On the other hand, however, women appear to be slightly overrepresented in news coverage relative to their numbers among the population of politicians, government bureaucrats, clergy members, and citizens. Indeed, if journalists attempted to populate their reports on the contraceptive mandate with quotes by representatively sampling each of these groups, the views of significantly fewer women would have appeared in newspaper stories than actually did. When coupled with the fact that women authored a higher percentage of articles on contraception (45.5%) than their numbers in newsroom staffs would lead us to expect (34.9%), this level of female visibility suggests that American newspapers were taking conscious steps to portray the ACA's contraceptive mandate through the eyes of women.

Overall, our evidence suggests that news organizations strategically assigned female reporters to cover the birth control issue and that these female reporters diversified sourcing patterns by quoting more women. Our evidence also shows, however, that these efforts failed to produce an equal distribution of bylines and quotations. There are two main reasons for this failure. First, there are simply not enough women in journalism to produce byline parity on the reporting of political issues. Female reporters' propensity to cite other women more than men means that this shortage contributes, in turn, to a lack of source diversity. Second, journalistic norms dictating that journalists turn first and most frequently to politicians and government officials act as a "conformity mechanism" (Berkowitz 2009, 110) by compelling all reporters, regardless of gender, to seek information from male-dominated domains. To put all of this more simply, the gender gap in news sourcing is likely to persist as long as women remain underrepresented in journalism *and* politics.

Regardless of its causes, the underrepresentation of women in the media is not a minor issue, and most major American media watchdog organizations explicitly advocate for diversifying the news industry. As Rodgers and Thorson (2003, 685) note, however, "Although anecdotal evidence supports the hiring of more female journalists, empirical evidence supporting this notion is less common." The findings presented here answer Rodger and Thorson's call and provide strong empirical backing for the idea that hiring more women would be beneficial to news organizations that care about diversifying the content of their political reporting. As shown here also, female reporters significantly enhanced the visibility of other women—with women constituting a majority of the sources quoted in female-authored articles (52%). Whether the preference for citing other women is the result of female reporters having more diverse professional networks (Armstrong 2004), pursuing a deliberate strategy of seeking out female experts (Craft, Wanta, and Lee 2003), or feeling a "gender-based camaraderie" with other women (Berkowitz 2009, 110), this finding implies that assigning more women to write on women's issues will organically result in more diverse sourcing practices. Furthermore, given that higher levels of gender parity in newsrooms were strongly and positively associated with higher levels of source diversity, newspapers should also be able to increase the number of women appearing in their news reports by simply hiring more women to their staffs. In short, our findings affirm the repeated calls of the ASNE, the WMC, the Neiman Foundation for Journalism, and many others to hire more women to work in the press and provide more women with the opportunity to report on politics.

Closely related to our findings about the importance of diversifying bylines and newsrooms, our analysis also reveals the pitfalls of newspapers' increasing dependence on wire service reports to populate their pages. While American newspapers have always relied heavily on organizations like the Associated Press, Reuters, and United Press International to provide some of their content (Graber 2008), the precipitous collapse of the print media's subscription- and advertising-based business model has enhanced the role that wire services play in the reporting of the news. Indeed, with revenue and newsroom staffs at their lowest levels in decades (Mitchell and Holcomb 2016), many newspapers cannot produce their own coverage of newsworthy events and must turn to wire service reports. A report by the Pew Research Center (2015), for example, found that wire services now account for a majority of the government news coverage that local newspapers provide.

Our analysis suggests that source diversity is likely to be one of the main casualties of the newspaper industry's reliance on wire service reports. Stories published under organizational bylines were dramatically less likely than stories published by female reporters to include women as sources. Additionally, stories attributed to wire services were significantly less likely than stories attributed to male and female journalists to include unofficial sources. To the extent that newspapers continue to use wire services for their reporting and to the extent that wire services continue stylistic practices that encourage minimal levels of source diversity, female and unofficial voices are likely to remain marginalized in the news.

Conclusion

Studies of sourcing patterns all revolve around the question of "who gets a voice" in news coverage (Berkowitz 2009, 110). Despite the centrality of contraception to women's lives and to recent political debates, no studies assess who gets a voice in the media's reporting on birth control issues. In this chapter we examined exactly who was given a voice on the contraceptive mandate by tracking newspaper sources between August 2011 and August 2012. In line with previous research showing that women and nonelite actors are marginalized in the American media, particularly by daily newspapers (Armstrong 2004), we found that women and unofficial sources were quoted less frequently than men. Our findings also show, however, that news organizations have the power to mitigate some of these tendencies, if they so choose, by hiring more women to work in newsrooms and report on women's issues.

While this chapter's analysis charts significant new territory by identifying exactly how gender diversity—both in the story byline and in the newsroom—matters for the media's coverage of a fundamentally important women's issue, important questions remain. As suggested earlier, studies into sourcing patterns assume that increases in source diversity will produce corresponding increases in content diversity—defined by Voakes et al. (1996, 585) as the dispersion of "ideas, perspectives, attributions, opinions or frames within a news product, and within the context of one particular issue." Unfortunately, almost no empirical work directly tests this assumption or attempts to parse out the relative importance of reporter gender, newsroom composition, and source characteristics. In the next chapter we address directly the consequences of source diversity. Specifically, we tackle the question of whether source diversity influences content diversity by exploring the frames employed in the media's coverage of the debate over the birth control mandate.

7

Media Frames

The Republican-led congressional hearings of February 2012 triggered a series of cascading conflicts on gender, morality, economics, and religion that forever altered the national debate over who should pay for access to contraception. As we illustrated in the previous chapter, the Affordable Care Act's (ACA) contraceptive mandate was thrust from the margins to the mainstream in the weeks immediately preceding and following Congressman Darrel Issa's all-male "Lines Crossed" panel—receiving detailed coverage in well over 100 newspaper articles between early February and mid-March 2012. Liberal and conservative media watchdog groups both tracked and critiqued closely this outpouring of reporting. If the statements issued by these watchdogs are any indication, major American news organizations were seemingly not making anyone happy during this period.

The conservative-friendly Media Research Center, for example, complained extensively about the broadcast and print media's emphasis on the political consequences of the contraception fight. There were, in fact, dozens of reports on how the debate was playing with the potential voters in the upcoming 2012 election. Indeed, a brief glance of some of the headlines published by American newspapers during just the six-week period between February 6 and March 19 demonstrates the impressive scope of the media's concern with the political fallout generated from debating contraception coverage:

> "Battling over Birth Control; Both Sides Seize Issue to Increase Support, Cash" —*Spokesman-Review* (Spokane, WA) (February 9, 2012)
>
> "Parties Eye Advantage in Contraceptives Fight; Poll Finds Americans Evenly Divided over Obama's Edict" —*Washington Times* (February 24, 2012)
>
> "Democrats Use Birth-Control Clash to Get Money, Votes" —*Daily Camera* (Boulder, CO) (March 1, 2012)

The Politics of the Pill: Gender, Framing, and Policymaking in the Battle over Birth Control. Rachel VanSickle-Ward, Kevin Wallsten, Oxford University Press (2019). © Oxford University Press.
DOI: 10.1093/oso/9780190675349.001.0001

"GOP on Losing Side of Birth Control; 30% in Party Back Obama's Stance" —*Washington Times* (March 2, 2012)

"Romneys Court Women Alienated by Contraception Issue" —*New York Times* (March 19, 2012).

Interestingly, the Media Research Council seemed to object more to how the reports characterized the winners and losers of this "Holy War" over birth control than on its framing primarily as a political game. In March alone, for example, the council posted articles on its website titled "NYT Poll Blows Away Slanted Assumptions of NYT Reporters: Social Conservatism Not Hurting GOP with Women," "New York Times Plays Up GOP Worries over Women's Issues on Front Page, Buries Anti-Obama Poll Data," and "Another Bogus NYT Story Baselessly Assumes Contraception Fight Hurting the GOP." The Media Research Council, in other words, was more intent on making sure the horserace was accurately called than on challenging the more fundamental assumption that it was a race at all.

Although left-leaning watchdog groups largely turned a blind eye to the coverage of most major broadcast and print outlets, they were equally troubled by the conservative media's decision to emphasize religious liberty and economic considerations at the expense of discussions about women's health and reproductive rights. On February 8 and February 9, 2012, alone, for instance, Media Matters posted articles titled "Fox's Tantaros Avoids Fact That Contraception Coverage Is a Women's Health Issue," "Fox's Gutfeld Equates Providing Affordable Birth Control to Women with 'Class Warfare,'" "Fox Goes Cherry-Picking in Attempt to Keep Its Phony 'War on Religion' Claim Alive," and "O'Reilly on Birth Control: 'There Are a Million Clinics around That Will Give It to You Free . . . So What's the Beef?'" In short, observers from across the political spectrum believed that media organizations were highlighting the wrong dimensions of the contraceptive mandate controversy and that these organizations should be publicly shamed into making better framing choices.

Which frames actually dominated the media's extensive coverage of contraception during the debate over the ACA's mandate? Why did news organizations and individual reporters make the framing choices they did? In this chapter we attempt to answer these questions by examining the frames employed in the print media's coverage of the birth control mandate between August 2011 and August 2012. Building on the data our study of sourcing patterns in chapter 3, we trace the frames used in every newspaper article between August 1, 2011, and August 1, 2012, that mentioned the term "birth control" or "contraceptives" in the title or lead paragraph. After showing that newspaper coverage framed the ACA's mandate as a strategic game and religious freedom issue far more frequently than an economic, women's health, or reproductive rights issue, we assess the impact that byline, newsroom, and source diversity had on a news article's dominant frame.

Similar to our findings in chapter 3 about sourcing, we show here that gender diversity in bylines mattered a great deal for which aspects of the contraceptive mandate were highlighted in news reports. Specifically, we show that female journalists were significantly more likely than male reporters to employ gendered frames (i.e., women's health, reproductive rights, and morality) in their reporting. Additionally, our data show that female authorship exerted an important indirect influence on news frames by increasing the proportion of women quoted in articles about the contraception mandate. Unlike our findings from the previous chapter, however, we also found that articles published by diverse newspaper staffs were largely indistinguishable from those published by homogeneous staffs. In other words, creating a backdrop of representation in news organizations has a less direct impact on content diversity than simply ensuring that women will have the opportunity to speak directly on contraception issues through authoring news reports.

Literature Review

Framing—Concept

Two distinct concepts of framing exist in the academic literature: individual frames and media frames (Scheufele 1999). *Individual frames* refer to "internal structures of the mind" while *media frames*, the focus of this chapter, refer to "devices embedded in political discourse" (Kinder and Sanders 1990, 74). The empirical research on media framing has been guided by many different yet closely related definitions (Callaghan and Schnell 2001; Entman 1993; Iyengar 1991; Matthes 2009; Semetko and Valkenburg 2000; Tankard, Hendrickson, Silberman, Bliss and Ghanem 1991; Tuchman 1977). Here, we adopt Entman's (1993) definition of *media framing* as selecting "some aspects of a perceived reality to make them more salient, thus promoting a particular problem definition, causal interpretation, moral evaluation, and/or treatment recommendation" (52).

Framing—Dependent Variable

In this chapter, we are interested in media "frame building" (de Vreese 2005)—the process by which news organizations choose which frames to employ in their coverage of political events. Unfortunately, the empirical literature on frame building in the press is not as developed as the empirical literature on other aspects of news coverage. As Snow et al. (2007, 385) write, "In the context of the print media, we know little about the factors that account for variation in frames, particularly with respect to the same event, object or issue." Once again, therefore, we turn to Shoemaker and Reese's (1996) hierarchical model for guidance, emphasizing the role that reporter attributes, professional routines, organizational influences, external pressures, and ideology play in shaping news content.

The existing empirical studies on frame building are not evenly distributed across the various levels that Shoemaker and Reese (1996) identify. Indeed, most accounts of how media outlets select frames for their news coverage focus on either the personal attributes of individual journalists or the selection of sources dictated by professional routines (Vliegenthart and Van Zoonen 2011). The effects of other variables are largely ignored or consciously excluded from the analysis (e.g., Dimmick and Coit 1982; McQuail 2000; Lowrey, Becker, and Punathambekar 2003; Van Zoonen 1998). With these limitations in mind, we focus in the next few sections on reviewing the existing literature for how variables at each level of the Reese and Shoemaker model might influence news frames on contraception.

Personal Attributes

As Rodgers and Thorson (2003, 660) write, "Female reporters, like females in other professions, are expected to bring different values, interests, and priorities to the newsroom that will affect the manner in which news stories are researched, framed, and written." Much like the conclusions from research into sourcing patterns we discussed in the previous chapter, however, the empirical findings on the role that a reporter's gender plays in shaping framing decisions do not paint a consistent picture. On the one hand, a number of empirical studies show that male and female journalists emphasize very different aspects of the same issue in their reporting. In a study of gubernatorial campaign coverage, for example, Devitt (1999) found that male reporters discussed the personality, private lives, and physical appearances of female candidates far more regularly than those of male candidates. The same was not true of reports authored by female journalists. Similarly, in their analysis of news coverage during the 2000 Republican presidential nomination race, Aday and Devitt (2001) found that male reporters were about half as likely as female reporters to include a discussion of issue positions in their stories about Elizabeth Dole. Instead, male reporters focused attention on Dole's personal characteristics. More recently, Nelson and Signorielli (2007) found significant differences in reporting about hormone therapy to relieve menopausal symptoms based on the gender of the reporter authoring the story—with women being more likely than men to employ a self-help frame. These quantitative studies are backed up by qualitative work suggesting that men and women differ in their propensity to highlight gendered subjects in their reporting (Mills 1985; Armstrong 2004; Gallagher 2001).

On the other hand, a nontrivial number of studies show only minimal differences between the news coverage produced by male and female reporters. In a study of editorials, for example, Goodrick noted striking similarities in the language and arguments that male and female opinion writers used to discuss the women's issues of child care and pay equity. More generally, a disparate group of studies imply that a reporter's gender is irrelevant for the substance of their reporting because all journalists are socialized into the same set of "masculine" professional norms (Liebler and Smith 1997; Rodgers and Thorson 2000; Turk 1987; Van Zoonen 1998) and subject to the same conformity pressures imposed by a "macho newsroom culture" (Ross and Carter 2011). The simplest conclusion to distill from all of this work, then, is that the influence of a reporter's gender is not a constant but instead is a variable that likely depends on the time, place, and issue under examination.

Professional Routines

The frame-building process is not dictated, however, entirely by the social characteristics of reporters. News frames are also affected by professional routines that make journalists highly susceptible to source influences. As mentioned in the previous chapter, Shoemaker and Reese (1996, 178) define *news sources* as "external suppliers of raw material, such as speeches, interviews, corporate reports and government hearings." Beginning with the work of Sigal (1973), numerous studies have attempted to clarify the role that these external suppliers play in structuring media coverage. Most notably, Gans (1979) described the relationship between journalists and their sources as a complicated yet mutually beneficial dance—where sources seek out journalists to reach the media's large audience and journalists nurture relationships with sources to establish reliable channels of access to newsworthy information. According to Gans, the heavy informational demands and tight time constraints of the news business inevitably mean that sources lead this dance rather than journalists.

As a result of the fact that journalists so frequently follow their lead, sources are seen to be essential components of the frame-building process (Berkowitz 1987). In a cross-national comparison of newspaper frames about the 2005 riots in France, Snow, Vliegenhart, and Corrigall-Brown (2007), for example, found that differences in media frames could largely be explained by differences in sourcing practices—with official government sources being far less involved in diagnostic framing efforts than local residents. Entman and Rojecki's (1993) content analysis of news coverage of the nuclear freeze movement found that stories using unofficial sources are more likely to raise critical questions than those that rely on official sources. More germane to our purposes here, Freedman, Fico, and Durisin (2010) demonstrated that the gender of sources used in newspaper coverage of U.S. Senate races was highly correlated with an article's dominant frame. Specifically, the researchers found that male sources were far more likely than female sources to appear in horserace and issues stories during the 2006 campaign. To put all of this in terms of the concepts we employ here, the existing research shows a clear and direct relationship between source diversity and content diversity in political news coverage.

Related to these studies on sourcing, communications and public relations scholars have consistently shown that the "information subsidies" (Gandy 1982; Berkowitz and Adams 1990) proactively provided to journalists by campaign organizations and interest groups can have a particularly strong influence on the content of the news media's reporting (Danielian and Page 1994; Roberts and McCombs 1994; Turk 1986; Turk and Franklin 1987; Tedesco 2002, 2005). Callaghan and Schnell (2001), for example, found that interest groups were often able to place their preferred frames on gun control directly in television news broadcasts by issuing persuasively written press releases. Andsager (2000) also found that press releases exerted a significant influence on how journalists chose to frame abortion coverage between 1995 and 1996. Interest-group sources, in other words, may be particularly important to the frame-building process due to their provision of information subsidies that journalists can use to craft their reporting.

Organizational Influences

Although almost no empirical studies exist of how gender diversity in staffing shapes framing decisions in particular, some evidence suggests that having more women in newsrooms leads to different kinds of reporting. Craft and Wanta (2004), for example, found that newspapers with a large number of female editors covered issues more positively and did not relegate women to as many stereotypical beats as in male-dominated newsrooms. Echoing these findings, Correa and Harp (2011) found important differences in the thematic content of HPV vaccine reports published by male-dominated and gender-diverse newsrooms. Studying the balance of newspaper coverage in U.S. Senate races during the 2004 campaign, Fico, Freedman, and Love (2006) found that newsrooms with higher levels of gender parity gave more favorable treatment to Democrats. Reaching a different conclusion from a study of the 2006 campaign, Fico and Freedman (2008) found that newspapers with a greater proportion of female reporters tended to provide more evenly balanced treatment of candidate assertions.

Importantly, however, not all research finds evidence that newsroom gender diversity exerts an influence on media content. In an early study of newsroom staffs, Bleske (1991) found that gender shaped coverage only "when last-minute extra space opens in the newspaper." In surveying newspaper editors, Splichal and Garrison (1995) found that male and female newsroom managers did not have fundamentally different views about whether and how to cover the private lives of politicians. More recently, Everbach (2005) found that the presence of female editors and executives did not change media representations of women. To repeat a common refrain in our discussion of gender's role in journalism thus far, the research presents a very mixed picture about how gender diversity in newsrooms might shape the media's political coverage.

External Pressures

In the American media system, news organizations attempt to create profits by producing content that appeals to the largest possible group of readers or viewers (Armstrong 2004; Graber 2006). This commercial imperative has often meant that news organizations frame political events in a way that prioritizes their entertainment value and highlights their gamelike and strategic components (Kalb 1998). Indeed, according to most studies of the American media, the strategic game frame now dominates nearly all mainstream political news coverage (Cappella and Jamieson 1997; Fallows 1997; Farnsworth and Lichter 2011; Jamieson 1993 Patterson 1993). The dominance of this game strategy frame makes a great deal of sense from the perspective of trying to sell news audiences on political coverage in an increasingly competitive media marketplace. In a study of the actual choices news consumers make when selecting political stories, Iyengar, Norpoth, and Hahn (2004) found that horserace and strategy reports were far more popular than substantive reports about the issues.

Media outlets appear to take more than just their audience's preferences for entertaining political coverage into account when framing news stories. Both Lee (2007) and Pease (1990), for example, have speculated that a desire to attract elite white readers has led to low levels of content diversity among large national newspapers. In particular, several scholars (Fallows 1997; Lawrence 2000; Patterson 1993) have argued that strategic game frame coverage is far more likely to occur in national or Washington-based newspapers than in more regional or local outlets. Whether casting politics as a strategic game or emphasizing specific issue elements that appeal to the perceived preferences of local consumers, news organizations appear to try to frame their reports in a way that maximize profits by attracting the largest possible audiences.

In sum, most analysis of the frame-building process implicitly assumes that an individual reporter's personal characteristics and the ideas communicated by news sources determine which elements of an issue are highlighted and which are ignored. Organizational influences, external pressures, and ideological commitments have received far less systematic attention in the literature, and there have been almost no attempts to statistically sort out the relative importance of variables at each of the different levels of Reese and Shoemaker's model. In this chapter, we provide one of the first empirical assessments of the roles that reporter gender, source characteristics, newsroom diversity, and audience preferences play in framing decisions by analyzing the media's coverage of the birth control mandate.

Methods

Measure of the Dependent Variable—Frames

While there are countless ways to classify the media's framing choices, most studies implicitly distinguish between "issue-specific" and "generic" frames (Aalberg, Strömbäck, and de Vreese, 2011). According to Semetko and de Vreese (2004, 93), *issue-specific frames* are "pertinent only to specific topics or events." Studies analyzing media frames from this perspective emphasize that every political issue has its own distinct set of issue-specific frames (De Vreese et al. 2001). In a study of news coverage about U.S. national budget deficits, for example, Jasperson, Shah, Watts, and Faber (1998) distinguish between "crisis," "impasse," "fight," and "talk" frames. Similarly, Shah, Watts, Domke, and Fan's (2002) content analysis of the Monica Lewinsky scandal classified news stories as employing a "Clinton behavior," a "conservative attacks on Clinton," or a "liberal defense of Clinton" frame.

Generic frames "transcend thematic limitations and can be identified in relation to different topics, some even over time and in different cultural contexts" (Semetko and de Vreese 2004, 93). In one of the earliest attempts to measure commonly used media frames, for example, Iyengar (1991) argued that all news coverage adopts either an "episodic" frame, which portrays political issues as specific events caused by the actions of individuals, or a "thematic" frame, which portrays political issues as systematic problems caused by the structure of society. Similarly, Semetko and Valkenburg's (2000) study of newspaper and television coverage of European politics suggested five generic media frames: conflict, human interest, economic consequences, morality, and responsibility.

As Semetko and de Vreese (2004, 93) write, an "issue-specific frame approach allows for a profound level of specificity of details relevant to the event or issue under investigation." Given our interest in fully understanding the role that gender played in shaping the public debate over the ACA's contraceptive mandate, we chose to adopt an issue-specific framing approach for the analysis that follows. We assigned[1] every American newspaper story that used the phrase "birth control" or "contraceptives" in the headline or lead paragraph between August 1, 2011, and August 1, 2012, to one of the six mutually exclusive framing categories we identified in chapter 1: religious freedom, health, reproductive rights, economics, morality, partisan/strategic game.[2]

Once the data on frames were collected, we conducted three different kinds of analyses to test the hypotheses spelled out below. First, we examined the bivariate relationships between framing choices and each of the presumed causal variables discussed above: reporter gender, newsroom diversity, source diversity, press releases, circulation size, citizen political ideology, and state-level reproductive rights policy. Second, we fit a logistic regression model that compared the likelihood of a newspaper article framing its contraceptive mandate coverage using explicitly gendered themes (e.g., women's health, reproductive rights, and morality) to the likelihood of a newspaper article framing its coverage using nongendered themes (e.g., religious freedom, economics, and strategic game). Finally, we ran a number of multinomial logistic regression models that compared the likelihood of a newspaper article using each one of the six individual frames separately relative to one of the other individual frames (for a total of 30 different comparisons). We discuss the main findings from these different analyses below.

Hypotheses

The literature on frame building led us to test seven distinct hypotheses using the data described above. First, Entman (2004) draws a distinction between "procedural" media frames, which emphasize political strategy; "horserace" updates and power struggles among elites; and "substantive" media frames, which emphasize the real-world consequences of issues and events for average news audiences. Research into media framing demonstrates that procedural or, more commonly, strategic game frames (Aalberg, Strömbäck, and de Vreese 2012 are "embedded in virtually every aspect of political news, dominating and driving it" (Patterson 1993, 69). Following this work, we hypothesize as follows:

> H1: Articles employing the procedural or strategic game frame will outnumber articles employing substantive frames (e.g., religious freedom, women's health, reproductive rights, economics, and morality).

As discussed earlier, the existing research fails to find a consistent effect for a reporter's gender on framing choices. While some work shows that their unique values, interests, and identities lead female reporters to emphasize systematically different aspects of an issue than male reporters, other work demonstrates that professional norms act as a "conformity mechanism" (Berkowitz 2009, 110) that suppresses individual differences in reporting and standardizes the content of news. As a result of this lack of clarity, we decided to test the following hypothesis:

> H2: Articles written by female reporters will employ gendered frames (e.g., women's health, reproductive rights, and morality) more frequently than those written by male reporters.

Similar to the existing research on reporter gender, the current body of work on newsroom diversity provides little guidance regarding the influence that gender parity in staffing has on framing choices. With some studies pointing to differences in the frame-building process based on the amount of gender diversity in newsrooms and other studies concluding that the percentage of women on staff makes little difference on news coverage, we decided to assess the following hypothesis:

> H3: Articles published by newspapers with higher levels of gender diversity will employ gendered frames (e.g., women's health, reproductive rights, and morality) more frequently than those published by newspapers with lower levels of gender diversity.

Because they are so frequently able to determine or "shape" the way a story is presented to the public through their efforts at strategic communication, some studies of the media refer to sources as "news shapers" (Soley 1989). Assuming that the unique interests, values, and identities of female news shapers lead them to shape news coverage in different ways than male news shapers, we hypothesize as follows:

> H4: Articles with a higher percentage of female sources will employ gendered frames (e.g., women's health, reproductive rights, and morality) more frequently than those with a lower percentage of female sources.

Similarly, assuming that news shapers who do not hold formal positions of power in business, religion, or politics offer different perspectives than those who do, we expect that articles relying on unofficial sources will emphasize different areas of the contraceptive mandate than articles relying on official sources. More precisely, given work showing that official sources are especially prominent in game strategy stories (Freedman et al., 2010), we hypothesize as follows:

> H5: Articles with a higher percentage of unofficial sources will employ a game strategy frame less frequently than those with a lower percentage of unofficial sources.

Information subsidies in general and press releases from prominent interest groups in particular have been shown repeatedly to influence the frame-building process. Following previous work on interest groups (Andsager 2000; Callaghan and Schnell 2001), we test hypotheses about the press releases of interest groups on both sides of the debate over the ACA's contraceptive mandate: Planned Parenthood and the United States Conference of Catholic Bishops (USCCB). Given that each of these organizations is likely to emphasize very different aspects of the issue, we state two different hypotheses:

> H5: Articles published immediately after a press release by Planned Parenthood will employ gendered frames (e.g., women's health, reproductive rights, and morality) more frequently than those not published immediately after a release by Planned Parenthood.
>
> H6: Articles published immediately after a press release by the United States Conference of Catholic Bishops will employ a religious freedom frame more frequently than those not published immediately after a release by the United States Conference of Catholic Bishops.

Finally, based on work by Fallows (1997), Lawrence (2000), and Patterson (1993), we predict that large national newspapers will emphasize the horserace features of the ACA's mandate far more than regional or local outlets.

> H7: Articles published by large national newspapers will employ a game strategy frame more frequently than those published by small regional or local newspapers.

Results

What were the most common frames used in the media's coverage of the birth control mandate? According to Iyengar, Norpoth, and Hahn (2004), "The evidence is consistent and unequivocal that the media invariably highlight the horserace and strategic aspects of politics at the expense of providing meaningful information about policy and governance" (157). As Figure 7.1 shows, our data back up this assertion. Specifically, slightly more than one-third of all stories (33.5%) on the ACA's contraceptive mandate between August 2011 and August 2012 focused on questions of who was winning and losing at any given moment or the strategies and tactics being employed by politicians, parties, and interest groups. Put differently, it appears that the ACA's contraceptive mandate was covered by American newspapers in the same, primarily nonsubstantive way as most other political issues in the United States.

The dominance of the strategic game frame was not unexpected given the impressively vast literature on the media's tendency toward horserace political coverage. Indeed, framing politics as a strategic game not only provides journalists with a steady stream of novel stories but it also gives them the occasion to maintain their "enduring focus on drama, conflict and negativity" (Aalberg, Strömbäck, and de Vreese 2011, 164). What was surprising, however, was how consistently newspapers emphasized these considerations. According to Lawrence (2000), the strategic game frame is "less likely to be applied to public policy issues when they are discussed in news about the implementation phase of public policy making" and "most likely to be applied to public policy issues when they are discussed in national election news" (93). Despite the fact that the media coverage component of our study exclusively covered the implementation phase of the ACA's birth control mandate, strategic game considerations still dominated news reports. Furthermore, there was no more or less coverage framed around strategic considerations in late 2011 than in the summer before the 2012 election. In other words, although news coverage of the ACA's contraceptive mandate was similar to many other issues in that it emphasized strategic considerations over policy substance, it was surprisingly immune

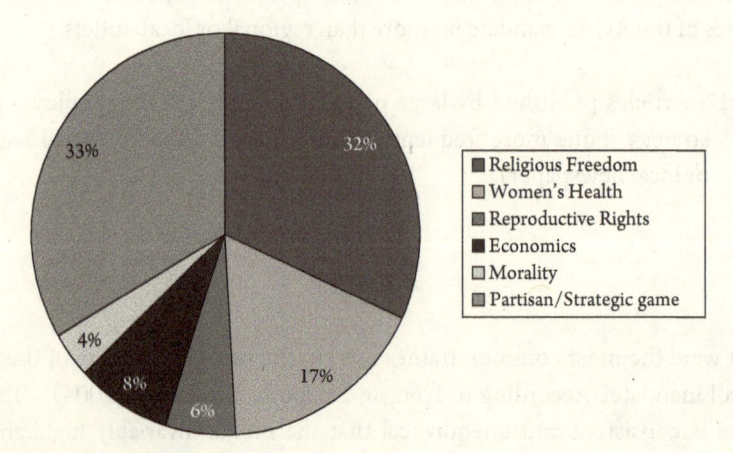

Figure 7.1 Frames in Contraception Coverage

from the standard contextual influences that normally push journalists toward less horserace coverage.

As Figure 7.1 shows, religious freedom was the second-most-popular frame among reporters between August 2011 and August 2012, with nearly one-third of all newspaper stories (31.9%) on the contraceptive mandate emphasizing the tension between the First Amendment's promise of religious liberty and government regulation of the health insurance marketplace. Overwhelmingly, articles employing a religious freedom frame focused on the objections of the Catholic Church—with 22 of the 191 articles framed around religious freedom explicitly mentioning the Catholic Church or its affiliated institutions—such as Catholic-run hospitals, universities, and nonprofits—in the headline. An additional nine articles mentioned church leadership in their headlines without specifically referencing the Catholic Church itself. Far more than discussing contraception as an issue of women's health, reproductive rights, economics, or morality, the American print media chose to define the ACA's mandate as a First Amendment, religious liberty issue.

Noteworthy, however, is that the media's tendency to emphasize religious freedom did not take root until well after the formal announcement of the mandate. Indeed, during the first five months of our study (between August 1, 2011, and January 1, 2012), only four of the 31 stories published in American newspapers (13.3%) emphasized religious freedom. During the last seven months of our study, questions of religious liberty accounted for more than 25% of stories in every month and more than 35% of stories overall. The ACA's contraceptive mandate, in other words, did not become a question of religious freedom in the eyes of media outlets until long after its announcement.

While nearly two-thirds of newspaper reports on the contraceptive mandate between August 2011 and August 2012 employed either a strategic game or religious freedom frame, the American media rarely used reproductive rights, economics, and morality frames during the period of our study—accounting for only 5.8%, 7.8%, and 3.7% of articles, respectively. Interestingly, unlike the economics and morality frames, journalists employed the reproductive rights frame during very specific times in the debate over contraception. Specifically, over 80% of articles framed around reproductive rights were published in either December 2011 (45.5%) or February 2012 (36.4%), and every reproductive rights article appeared between December 2011 and May 2012. Overall, however, the American press contained relatively little content diversity during the first year of debate over the ACA's contraception mandate.

As discussed above, a variety of factors are likely to shape the frame-building process. Along these lines, we asked whether a journalist's gender influenced the frame the writer chose to use when reporting on the birth control mandate. Our findings clearly show that a reporter's gender was a central factor in shaping the frames employed in news stories on the contraceptive mandate. As Table 7.1 demonstrates, female authors were significantly more likely to frame stories around gendered themes than their male counterparts. Specifically, the predicted probability of a female reporter using one of the three gendered frames discussed earlier was 0.38, while that for a male author was only 0.16, a decline of nearly 60%.[3] What's more, the relationship between a reporter's gender and a story's frame was consistent even when examining the six frames separately. As Figure 7.2 shows, stories written by female reporters were considerably more likely than stories written by male reporters to employ women's health and morality frames. Male reporters, by contrast, were far more likely than female reporters to employ religious rights and strategic game frames.[4] These results suggest either that female reporters choose to frame similar events in different ways than male reporters or that female reporters are assigned to cover different kinds of stories than men, thereby producing organic differences in the nature of the reporting.

We were also interested in whether reporters working in newsrooms with more gender diversity selected different frames from those working in more male-dominated newsrooms. Overall, as Table 7.1 shows, increases in the percentage of women working in a newsroom had no impact on the probability that the paper would frame its reporting on the contraception mandate around gendered themes after controlling for reporter gender. Comparing the influence of newsroom diversity across our six different frames tells a similar story. High levels of gender diversity, for example, did not make newspapers more or less likely to use religious freedom, women's health, reproductive rights, or morality frames instead of a strategic game frame. Similarly, gender parity on newspaper staffs did not encourage journalists to emphasize religious freedom, women's health, economics, or morality instead of reproductive rights in their reporting. Diversifying newsrooms, in other words, is unlikely to produce diverse framing choices unless the gender diversity of newsrooms is also reflected in who authors news reports on contraception.

Previous research suggests that sourcing decisions can shape the frames that journalists use in their reporting. Consistent with this research, our results also show that the gender of who was quoted mattered a great deal for the frame that newspapers employed. As Table 7.1 shows, even after controlling for all other influences on framing choices, the percentage of female sources exerted a large and positive impact on the probability that an article was framed around gendered themes. To put Table 7.1's coefficients in perspective, the predicted probability of an article without any female sources being framed around gendered themes was only 0.15, while the predicted probability of an article with all female sources being framed around gendered themes was nearly three times greater, at 0.44. Moreover, higher levels of source diversity were strongly associated with our gendered frames when considered separately. Our multinomial

Table 7.1 **Factors Influencing Newspaper Article Frames on the Contraceptive Mandate**

	Gendered vs. Nongendered Frame
Female Author	1.291**
	(0.405)
Unknown Author	0.508
	(1.144)
Circulation Size (in 100,000s)	0.105***
	(0.0237)
Citizen Political Ideology	−0.0241
	(0.0161)
NARAL Score	0.0673
	(0.0537)
Newsroom Gender	−0.0121
	(0.0423)
Percent of Sources (Female)	1.732**
	(0.668)
Percent of Sources (Unofficial)	−0.228
	(0.897)
U.S. Conference of Catholic Bishops—Press Release	−0.966
	(0.591)
Planned Parenthood—Press Release	0.228
	(0.429)
Constant	−1.118
	(1.771)
N	136

logistic regression analyses show that larger percentages of female sources were associated with lower probabilities of framing coverage around religious freedom ($b = -3.85$, $p < 0.04$), economics ($b = -3.37$, $p < 0.07$), and strategic game considerations ($b = -3.57$, $p < 0.05$) relative to reproductive rights. It also led, relative to morality, to lower probabilities of framing coverage around religious freedom ($b = -4.48$, $p < 0.00$), economics ($b = -4.01$, $p < 0.01$), and strategic game considerations ($b = -4.2$, $p < 0.00$). Although it is difficult to determine with any precision whether diverse sources determined the frame or the frame determined the diversity of the sources, this evidence suggests that sourcing decisions and framing choices are closely related.[5]

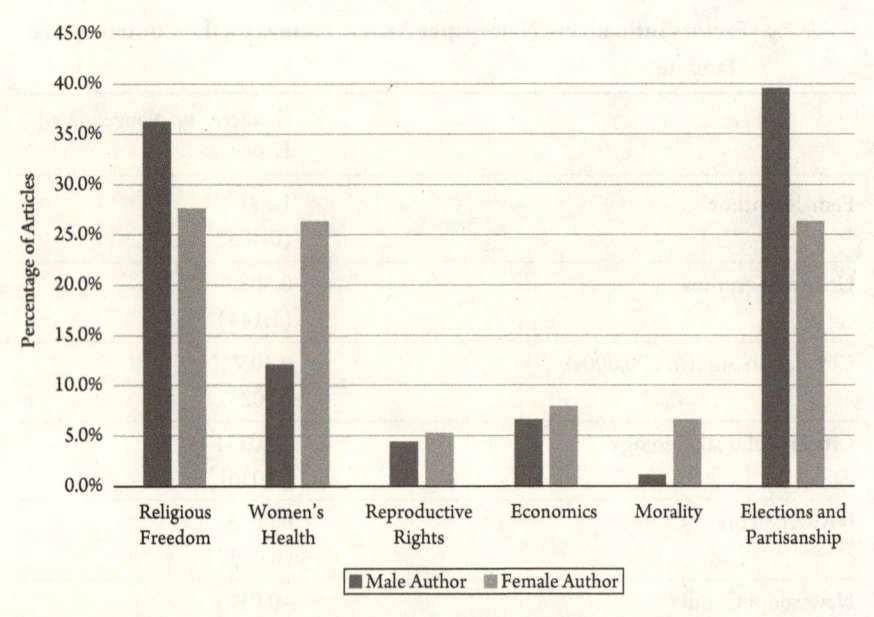

Figure 7.2 Frames in Birth Control Coverage by Reporter Gender

While gender diversity in sourcing mattered for the types of frames used in newspaper coverage, occupational diversity did not. Having a larger percentage of unofficial sources was not a significant predictor of using a gendered as opposed to a nongendered frame. Other than increasing the likelihood that an article was framed around economics ($b = 8.84, p < 0.03$) and morality ($b = 11.81, p < 0.05$) relative to women's health, more occupational diversity in sourcing mattered very little for framing decisions. Contrary to H5, therefore, unofficial sources did not produce more game strategy reporting, and gender diversity in sourcing is far more important for framing decisions than occupational diversity.

Previous work suggests that information subsidies provided to journalists by interest groups could shape media coverage in ways that are consistent with the group's goals. The USCCB and Planned Parenthood were both active in their efforts to shape news coverage through press releases between August 2011 and August 2012—with each organization sending out, on average, well over one press release per month on the mandate. Predictably, the USCCB and Planned Parenthood focused on very different themes in these press releases. Applying the same coding scheme used in our analysis of media coverage, we found that while the USCCB narrowly focused its messaging on religious freedom, Planned Parenthood chose to employ a broad array of frames. Specifically, while 88.4% of press releases by the USCCB focused on religious freedom, Planned Parenthood's statements were more evenly distributed between women's health (50%), reproductive rights (33.3%), and economics (16.7%).

The question, of course, is whether the USCCB's attempts to persuade news outlets to emphasize religious freedom and Planned Parenthood's attempts to persuade news outlets to emphasize women's health and reproductive rights were successful. Our data suggest that the press releases issued by these stakeholder organizations had a complicated relationship with media frames between August 2011 and August 2012. As Table 7.1 shows, statements released by the USCCB and Planned Parenthood had no relationship to gendered versus nongendered framing choices on the day of their release, the day after their release, or two days after their release. Examining each of these organizations and each of these frames separately, however, tells a different story. As discussed above, the vast majority of Planned Parenthood's press releases emphasized women's health and reproductive rights concerns. Although this messaging was very ineffective at shifting media frames from nongendered to gendered overall, it was very successful in directing attention toward reproductive rights concerns. Indeed, Planned Parenthood's public statements led news organizations to focus more attention on reproductive rights than on religious freedom ($b = -3.58, p < 0.04$), economics ($b = -4.21, p < 0.02$), and strategic game considerations ($b = -3.23, p < 0.08$). Unfortunately, perhaps, from Planned Parenthood's perspective, their press releases were also associated with a lower probability of newspapers emphasizing women's health ($b = -4.20, p <. 0.02$) than reproductive rights. It seems, therefore, that Planned Parenthood was most compelling to journalists when they emphasized the ways in which the ACA's contraceptive mandate hurt women's reproductive rights.

Nearly all of the USCCB's 26 press releases on the contraceptive mandate between August 2011 and August 2012 centered on religious freedom. There is some evidence that these releases did, in fact, compel the media to begin covering the mandate through the lens of religious freedom. Specifically, in the days following a USCCB press release, news organizations became dramatically more likely to frame their coverage as a potential threat to religious freedom than as a potential threat to reproductive rights ($b = 16.54, p < 0.00$). While this result was likely consistent with the bishops' goals, it is important to point out that journalists did not become more likely to emphasize religious freedom than any of our other frames. Indeed, there were no significant differences between the likelihood of a story adopting a women's health, economics, morality, or strategic game frame relative to a religious freedom frame in the three days after a press release from the USCCB. Somewhat surprisingly, the main effect of the media message by the Catholic bishops was to greatly diminish the significance of reproductive rights themes compared to all other themes. In addition to making a religious freedom framing more likely, a USCCB press release was associated with a greater probability of emphasizing women's health ($b = 15.83, p < 0.00$), economics ($b = 18.29, p = 0.00$), morality ($b = 17.69, p < 0.00$), and strategic game considerations ($b = 15.98$, $p < 0.00$) relative to reproductive rights. Although it was not likely the bishops' public communications strategic goal, their messaging about religious freedom seems to have drawn media attention away from reproductive rights considerations.

Larger, national papers chose different frames for their coverage of the birth control mandate than smaller regional or local papers. As Table 7.1 illustrates, higher daily circulation numbers were, in general, associated with an increased likelihood of selecting a gendered, instead of a nongendered, news frame—with the predicted probability of employing a women's health, reproductive rights, or morality frame increasing from 0.21 at the lowest levels of circulation to 0.54 at the highest. These overall differences were largely a function of the fact that larger circulation numbers were associated with lower probabilities of framing coverage around religious freedom ($b = -0.54$, $p < 0.00$), economics ($b = -0.98$, $p < 0.00$), and strategic game considerations ($b = -0.48$, $p < 0.00$) relative to morality. This finding runs counter to the conclusions of previous work that national newspapers employ the strategic game frame more frequently than regional or local outlets (Fallows 1997; Lawrence 2000; Patterson 1993). Given that audience characteristics were, to some extent, controlled for in our models through the inclusion of local ideology and NARAL scores, these findings also suggest that the news staff of larger, national papers had systematically different approaches to reporting on the contraceptive mandate than the news staff of smaller local papers.

Discussion

One of the primary functions of the press in a democratic society is to serve as a forum for the communication of diverse viewpoints on public affairs (Graber 2008). Most media observers assume that high levels of byline, newsroom, and source diversity are needed to provide democratic publics with the requisite amount of content diversity. Increasing female and minority representation in bylines, newsrooms, and quotations, therefore, becomes a central area of inquiry and advocacy for media observers and academics alike. As the research discussed earlier demonstrates, however, the relationship between a reporter's gender, a newsroom's composition, an article's sources, and a media segment's content diversity is an empirical question whose answer cannot be simply assumed; it must be answered through an investigation of the data on an issue-by-issue basis.

In chapter 5 we showed that newspapers with more gender parity in their staffing and articles authored by female reporters featured a broader array of sources in their coverage of the ACA's contraceptive mandate. Based on this analysis, we concluded that the only genuinely effective approach for newspapers seeking to diversify the substance of their political coverage is to hire more women and publish more articles written by female reporters. Following the recommendations of Baden and Springer (2017), in chapter 5 we operationalized content diversity as the number of different frames employed in the print media's coverage of the birth control mandate between August 2011 and August 2012. Operating with this understanding of content diversity, we have further explored the relative importance of newsroom and byline diversity. Unlike our results in chapter 5, female authorship revealed itself to be a far more important influence on the content of political reporting than gender parity in newsroom staffing. Indeed, while female reporters emphasized the gendered components of the birth control debate far more frequently than male reporters, articles published by newspapers with relatively high percentages of women on staff were largely indistinguishable from articles published by newspapers with newsrooms dominated by men. In short, content diversity in political reporting is primarily a function of byline diversity, not newsroom diversity.

One of the primary differences associated with female authorship was an emphasis on substantive concerns, particularly about women's health and sexual morality, over game strategy themes. Specifically, while only 26% of the stories authored by women emphasized the strategic game aspects of the ACA's birth control mandate, nearly 40% of the stories authored by men did. Male reporters also provided far less content diversity in their coverage than female reporters, with more than three-quarters of male-authored reports using either a game strategy or religious freedom frame. The origins of these disparate approaches to reporting the contraceptive mandate are difficult to sort out. Male reporters may have systematically different interests than female reporters when it comes to political debates, and these different interests might be inevitably reflected in the details reporters choose to highlight. Alternatively, male reporters could be more likely than female reporters to develop an expertise, receive an assignment from an editorial team, or work a beat that requires a focus on horserace themes. Unfortunately, our data do not allow us to adjudicate between these various explanations.

Regardless of the factors driving the disparity, however, the tendency of male and female reporters to highlight different elements of the same story, when coupled with the fact that men authored significantly more articles (91) than women (76) during the period of our study, may have had negative consequences for the public discourse surrounding the contraceptive mandate. Indeed, concerns about horserace journalism arise from the assumption that framing politics as a strategic game has negative consequences for the functioning of democratic government (Cappella and Jamieson 1997; Jamieson 1993 Patterson 1993). While the empirical research is somewhat mixed, a number of scholars have found that exposure to strategic game frames can inhibit the acquisition of political knowledge (Cappella and Jamieson 1997; Valentino et al. 2001b), reduce overall levels of political engagement (Blumler and Coleman 2010; Patterson 1993) and activate latent political cynicism (De Vreese 2004; Rhee 1997; Valentino et al. 2001a, 2001b). It is possible that the large percentage of game strategic stories produced by the disproportionately male group of reporters covering the contraception mandate had similar effects on news audiences between August 2011 and August 2012.

In chapter 8 we return to the specific question of whether low levels of content diversity and high levels of game strategic framing in reporting about the contraception mandate increased disengagement and cynicism among members of the public. More generally, however, our findings suggest that having more women author news stories may dampen the tendency to highlight strategic concerns and, in doing so, potentially minimize the harmful consequences of exposure to horserace journalism. Put differently, from the perspective of democratic governance, female reporters may not just provide different coverage than male reporters; they may provide better coverage.

In addition to directly influencing the selection of news frames, a reporter's gender also exerted an indirect effect on which components of the contraceptive mandate were highlighted by shaping decisions about sourcing. As we demonstrated in the previous chapter, female reporters quoted significantly more female sources than male reporters. In this chapter, consistent with a large body of previous research on frame building, we found that who was quoted in a story about the birth control mandate was strongly and independently related to how the policy was framed—with articles quoting more female sources being more likely to emphasize gendered themes even after controlling for a reporter's gender. Considered together, these findings suggest that providing more female reporters the opportunity to write on women's issues is the quickest and surest path to promoting content diversity in the news media. Women authors not only appear to provide a different perspective on issues but they also locate, interview, and quote different sources. While organizational efforts to alter sourcing practices and guidelines will likely diversify frames by itself, the change to news reporting will be far subtler than if women are simply asked to report more often on the issues that directly affect them.

Conclusion

In a widely cited review of the framing literature, Scheufele (1999, 109) states, "No evidence has yet been systematically collected about how various factors impact the structural qualities in news in terms of framing." In this chapter, we have shown that when women published reports on the contraception mandate, news audiences were exposed to a qualitatively different kind of coverage than when men published reports on that issue. Indeed, women cited more female sources in their articles than men, and these female sources helped produce more gendered coverage of the ACA's birth control mandate between August 2011 and August 2012. As noted earlier, Semetko and de Vreese (2004, 93) write that an "issue-specific frame approach allows for a profound level of specificity of details relevant to the event or issue under investigation." They also point out, however, that "the high degree of issue sensitivity makes analyses drawing on issue-specific frames difficult to generalize and compare" (Semetko and de Vreese 2004, 93). Future work should explore whether our findings are unique to the question of contraceptive coverage or reflective of a broader trend in framing decisions on women's policy issues.

8

Public Opinion

In this chapter we trace the ebb and flow of public opinion toward birth control over the last 60 years and toward the contraceptive mandate between 2011 and 2014. We argue that access to birth control is the quintessential "easy" issue (Carmines and Stimson 1980, 1989) for most Americans: it is symbolic rather than technical, focused on ends rather than means, and has been a matter of public scrutiny for a very long time rather than recently appearing on the political scene. Contrary to some other "easy" political issues, we show that large segments of the American public—including significant majorities of both parties, both genders, and all races and religious affiliations—have had relatively strong and stable opinions over the last 60 years on whether women should have access to birth control and whether contraceptives are "morally acceptable."

We also show, however, that the 2012 debate over the Affordable Care Act's (ACA) contraceptive mandate politicized the much harder issue of who should pay for birth control—quickly opening yawning partisan, gender, and "God-based" gaps in public support for requiring health insurance coverage of contraceptives that persist today. Indeed, while early attempts to mandate birth control coverage attracted widespread support from the public, major divisions between Democrats and Republicans, men and women, and the religious and secular sectors emerged in early 2012. We attribute these growing divisions to a shift in the public's framing of the issue. Whereas contraceptive mandates were framed primarily as providing access to valuable health care in the early 2000s, Republican Party leaders and Catholic clergy members shifted the debate during 2012 to include considerations about the size of government and protections for religious liberty. Evidence of this shift can be found not only in media coverage of the mandate (chapter 6) but also in the questions asked and answers given in surveys between 2011 and 2014. In short, we argue that partisanship, gender, and religiosity interacted with elite rhetoric during early 2012 to polarize mass-level opinions on the hard questions that the ACA's contraceptive mandate presented.

The Politics of the Pill: Gender, Framing, and Policymaking in the Battle over Birth Control. Rachel VanSickle-Ward, Kevin Wallsten, Oxford University Press (2019). © Oxford University Press.
DOI: 10.1093/oso/9780190675349.001.0001

Aggregate Public Opinion on Access to Birth Control

The 2012 debate over the ACA's contraceptive mandate occurred against the backdrop of widespread and longstanding support for legal access to birth control information, medication, and instrumentation. The earliest survey data on birth control was collected in the 1930s. In one of the first polls to tap opinions on access to contraceptive information, Gallup (1939) found that 71% of Americans supported the idea that government health-care clinics should provide information about birth control to married couples. Subsequent surveys by Gallup in the 1940s and 1950s found similarly large majorities of the American public endorsing married people's access to contraceptive-related information. When Gallup expanded its question wording to include the provision of birth control information for nonmarried couples in the 1950s and 1960s, the public's support did not waiver. Surveys from this period suggest that the public drew no meaningful distinctions between access to birth control information for married couples and for single people. Indeed, questions that asked respondents about the provision of contraception information to married couples, those that asked respondents about the provision of contraception information to "anyone who wants it," and those that simply asked respondents whether the provision of birth control information should be legal in general all received similar levels of public support. By the time the Supreme Court formally legalized access to birth control for married couples in 1965's *Griswold v. Connecticut* and single people in 1972's *Eisenstadt v. Baird*, 81% of Americans already believed that everyone, single or married, should have legal access to birth control information. As Figure 8.1 shows, access to birth control information was so consistently uncontroversial—with more than 90% of Americans expressing support—that survey organizations stopped asking the question in the 1980s.

Importantly, no dramatic differences existed between how various kinds of Americans thought about access to birth control between the 1950s and 1980s. The polls fielded by the General Social Survey (GSS) in 1974, 1975, 1977, 1982, and 1983 paint the clearest picture of the American public's stable, deep, and widespread support for birth control access during this period. Pooling the results of these five surveys shows, for example, that 91.2% of men and 92.6% of women supported making "birth control information" "available to anyone who wants it." Similarly, 92.4% of Democrats, 91.9% of independents, and 91.2% of Republicans endorsed the idea that access to birth control information should be legal. Even income exerted relatively little influence over opinions on birth control access, with more than nine in 10 members of every income group

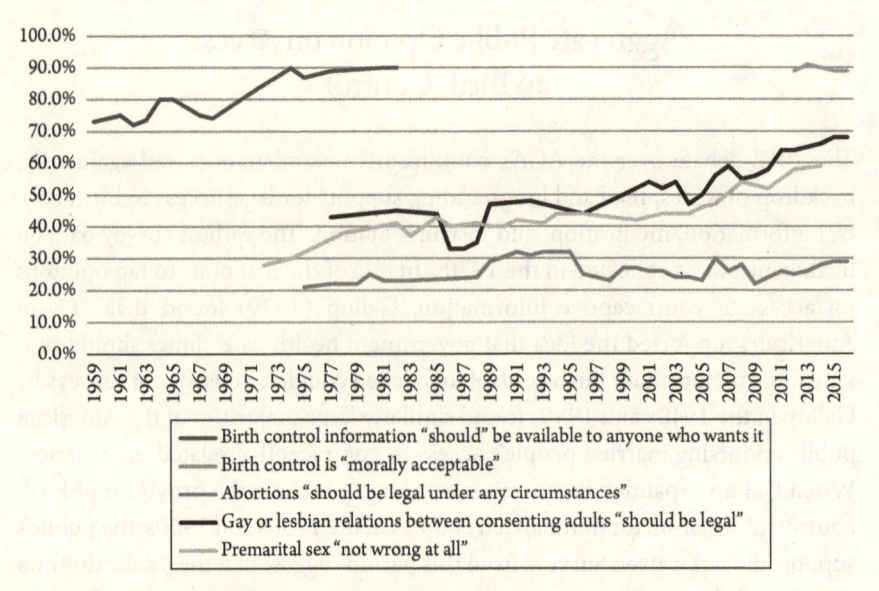

Figure 8.1 Attitudes toward Birth Control Accessibility

measured in the GSS expressing support for widespread and legal access to birth control information.

Two politically salient dimensions of individual identity deserve particular attention here: religious affiliation and race. Between the 1950s and the 1980s, more than 85% of Americans identified themselves as either Protestant or Catholic (Newport 2009). While Protestant denominations had a decidedly mixed and difficult-to-pin-down public stance on birth control during this period (Campbell 1960), the Catholic Church remained consistently steadfast in their opposition to contraception throughout the 1950s, 1960s, 1970s, and 1980s. Most notably, Pope Paul VI's 1968 encyclical *Humanae vitae* articulated the Catholic Church's official view that "artificial birth control" was an intrinsic evil that single and married people alike should avoid.

Given the Catholic Church's persistent and vocal opposition to contraceptive use, we might expect American Catholics to be considerably less supportive of birth control than members of other denominations. Surprisingly, however, there is little evidence that Catholic parishioners heeded the calls of their clergy members on birth control. In a pair of surveys from 1964, for example, only 14% (Gallup) and 15% (Harris) of Catholics expressed opposition to birth control. In a 1968 Gallup poll, a mere 14% of Catholics favored *Humanae vitae*'s call to "ban artificial methods of birth control." In the five surveys conducted by the GSS during the mid-1970s and early 1980s, Catholic support for widespread and legal access to birth control information was nearly indistinguishable from that of Protestant (91.5%) and nonreligious (94.2%) respondents.

African Americans have had a long and complicated relationship with contraceptives. Between 1920 and 1945, most African American leaders supported expanding access to birth control as a strategy for enhancing the general health and economic status of the black community (Gamble and Houck 1994; Rodrique 1991). Mistrust among African Americans toward contraceptives began growing in the 1960s and 1970s, however, as the country's disturbing history of coercive sterilization practices against black and poor women came to light. In the 1974 case *Relf v. Weinberger*, for example, a federal district court found that up to 150,000 poor women a year, including many African Americans, were sterilized under federally funded programs. As Brown and Eisenberg (1995) wrote, "This historical legacy of distrust profoundly affected black Americans' attitudes toward family planning. Many viewed the increased availability of oral contraceptives not solely as a matter of individual choice but also as a reflection of a government policy to decrease their numbers."

Concerns about "racial genocide" (Brown and Eisenberg 1995) enacted through contraception provision left a small but unmistakable mark on African American attitudes toward birth control between the 1950s and 1980s. In every survey during the period, African Americans were slightly less supportive than whites on the question of legalizing and expanding access to birth control information. In a 1961 Gallup poll, for instance, 67.7% of African Americans (compared to 76.0% of whites) supported access to birth control information. A follow-up poll conducted by Gallup three years later also found that African Americans were less supportive of legalizing birth control information than whites (74.3% to 82.1%). By the 1970s and 1980s, the racial gap in attitudes toward birth control had diminished but not disappeared. Specifically, in the five GSS surveys, there was less than a 5-point difference (92.6% to 88.1%) between whites' and blacks' support for access to birth control information. Despite their somewhat lower levels of support, however, the overwhelming majority of African Americans have endorsed access to birth control information since at least the 1960s, and support has increased over time in a way that has reduced the gap with whites.

Given that support for access to contraceptives was broadly shared by nearly all of America's diverse demographic groups throughout the second half of the 20th century, there was relatively little interest in measuring the public's views on birth control in the 1990s and early 2000s. The Republican Party's long-standing opposition to abortion—coupled with its newer objections to federal funding for Planned Parenthood, the ACA's contraceptive mandate, and laws punishing workplace discrimination—prompted House Minority Leader Nancy Pelosi to accuse the GOP of waging a "war on women" in 2011 (Epstein 2011; Lillis 2012). Following Pelosi's lead, prominent Democrats, including President Barack Obama, repeatedly echoed the "war on women" refrain throughout the

2012 campaign season. Most notably, the Obama campaign ran a number of campaign advertisements in the run-up to the 2012 election that characterized Republican presidential nominee Mitt Romney as "extreme" and "really out of touch on women's health issues." One ad even went so far as to claim, "This is not the 1950s. Contraception is so important. It's about a woman being able to make decisions" (Politifact 2012). For their part, Republicans accused Democrats of being hostile to religion and attempted to frame the contraceptive mandate as being a violation of the First Amendment's protections for religious liberty. After decades on the sidelines, in other words, the events of 2012 placed birth control back in the center of the political agenda.

In response to the increasing salience of contraception, survey organizations began asking the American public whether they "personally believe that in general it is morally acceptable or morally wrong" to use birth control. As Figure 8.1 shows, the American public's views on birth control did not seem to change much between 1983 (the last year the GSS polled on the issue of legal access to birth control information) and 2012 (the first year Gallup asked its morality question). Indeed, the vast majority of Americans surveyed between 2012 and 2016 were unbothered by the use of birth control—with an average of more than 90% reporting that birth control is morally acceptable. As with the question of access to birth control, support for the notion that contraceptives are morally acceptable was nearly uniform across the American public. Specifically, recent surveys by Gallup (2016) and Pew Research Center (2016) show no substantively meaningful partisan, gender, or religious differences in attitudes toward the appropriateness of birth control—with less than 10% of nearly every conceivable segment of the American public believing contraception is morally wrong.

In light of this evidence, access to birth control is clearly an "easy" issue (Carmines and Stimson 1980) for the American public. According to Carmines and Stimson (1980), "easy" issues are distinguished from "hard" issues in three ways: (1) easy issues are symbolic, while hard issues are technical; (2) easy issues focus on ends, while hard issues focus on the means to achieve ends; and (3) easy issues have been on the political agenda for a long time, while hard issues are more recent entrants into public debate. Similar to other questions about social and sexual behavior, the issue of access to contraceptives is symbolic, focused on ends rather than means, and has been the focus of public attention for a very long time. However, the American public's overwhelming endorsement of access to birth control has not been accompanied by similarly permissive views toward other easy matters related to personal sexuality. As Figure 8.1 shows, Americans' opposition to premarital sex has remained high and stable over the last four decades, and despite some softening in recent years, a significant segment of the American public still believes that gay and lesbian "relations" between consenting adults "should be illegal." Most importantly, support for the use of birth control has been far less controversial than access to abortion. As Figure 8.1 shows, the public has been divided since the 1970s on whether abortions should be legal. Access to birth control, in other words, is the rare easy issue related to private sexual behavior that Americans do not seem to view through a strongly moral lens.

Aggregate Public Opinion on Paying for Birth Control

While there is a widespread and relatively stable consensus among the American public that women should have access to birth control, there has been less consistent agreement about who should pay for it. In 1998 Congress debated a bill that would have required all health insurance plans with prescription drug coverage to pay for one of six different forms of FDA-approved birth control (pills, intrauterine devices, Norplant implants, diaphragms, cervical caps, and Depo-Provera). Although the bill failed to win much support in Congress at the time, a number of states enacted similar laws during the late 1990s and early 2000s that mandated insurance coverage of various methods of birth control. Early polling motivated by the passage of these state-level laws suggested that the American public was highly supportive of contraceptive mandates. A 1998 Kaiser Family Foundation survey, for example, found that three-quarters of Americans endorsed a legal requirement that health insurance plans cover birth control—with 45% expressing "strong" support and only 16% expressing any opposition at all. Similarly, in a 2001 poll by the American Civil Liberties Union, 79% of respondents agreed with the statement that "insurance plans that cover prescription drugs in general should be required to cover birth control pills, regardless of the insurance company's religious objections to contraception."

The large, clear, and widespread polling majorities in favor of contraceptive mandates as an answer to the question of who should pay would not last. State and federal attempts to compel insurance companies to cover the cost of birth control triggered an increasingly contentious debate about whether insurance companies, health-care providers, privately held companies, and religious organizations could secure moral exemptions to mandate laws. In particular, concerns about religious freedom, which had lingered in the background for much of the early debate over contraceptive mandates, took center stage in the months following the Obama administration's August 2011 announcement that employers would be required to cover certain forms of birth control for their female employees under the ACA.

The foregrounding of First Amendment religious liberty questions in late 2011 and Democratic denunciations of the GOP's so-called "war on women" generated a political firestorm that sparked more than a year of repeated public opinion polling on the question of contraception coverage. Between August 10, 2011, and October 3, 2012, 12 different polling organizations asked 31 survey questions about various interpretations of the mandate. After the presidential election of 2012, polling slowed considerably. In fact, only four polls asked contraceptive mandate–related questions between November 2012 and March 2014. By mid-2014, most polling organizations had moved on entirely from their brief obsession with surveying the American public about contraception policy. Indeed, despite *Burwell v. Hobby Lobby*'s obvious significance for federal policymaking, only one pollster—the Kaiser Family Foundation—even bothered asking a question about the contraceptive mandate after the Supreme Court issued its ruling in July 2014.

As the survey toplines in Table 8.1 show, the public's views on who should pay for birth control in the period bookended by the Department of Health and Human Services' (HHS) August 2011 announcement of the contraceptive mandate and the Supreme Court's decision in *Burwell v. Hobby Lobby* varied widely across time, exemption type, and question wording. A February 2012 CBS News / *New York Times* poll, for example, found that 66% of Americans expressed support for the "recent federal requirement that private health insurance plans cover the full cost of birth control for their female patients." A Quinnipiac University (2012) poll sampling respondents during the week immediately following the close of the CBS News / *New York Times* survey, however, found that only 47% of Americans believed that "the federal government should require private employers to offer free birth control coverage as part of their health insurance benefit plans." Backing up Quinnipiac's findings in a sample collected two months later, the Marist College Institute for Public Opinion concluded that a majority of Americans were opposed to the birth control mandate. Specifically, Marist Poll (2012) found that only 46% of the American public backed the belief that "medical professionals, hospitals, or insurance companies" should not be allowed to "opt out" of providing birth control pills for "religious reasons." Four months later, a survey by the Institute of Politics at Harvard University (2012) suggested an entirely different distribution of opinion on the mandate than the Quinnipiac and Marist polls—with 72% of its sample claiming to be "closer" to the statement that "doctors, hospitals, and insurance companies should provide birth control to all women who want it" than to the statement that "doctors, hospitals, and insurance companies should not have to provide birth control if they object to it on moral or religious grounds." In other words, American polling organizations did not have a clear sense of how to frame the contraceptive mandate for their respondents, and in turn, the American public did not seem to express a consistent preference for government regulation on the question of birth control provision.

Table 8.1 **Public Opinion Surveys on the ACA's Contraceptive Mandate**

Question	Start Date	Organization	Support
In general, do you support or oppose the new federal requirement that private health insurance plans cover the full cost of birth control and other preventive services for their female patients?	8/10/2011	Kaiser Family Foundation Poll: August Kaiser Health	66
(Now as I read some statements, please tell me if you completely agree, mostly agree, mostly disagree, or completely disagree with each one.) ... All employers should be required to provide their employees with health-care plans that cover contraception or birth control at no cost.	2/1/2012	Public Religion Research Institute PRRI/ RNS Poll	56
(There is currently a debate over what kinds of health-care plans some religious organizations should be required to provide.) Do you think ... churches and other places of worship should be required to provide their employees with health-care plans that cover contraception or birth control at no cost, or not?	2/1/2012	Public Religion Research Institute PRRI/ RNS Poll	36
There is currently a debate over what kinds of health-care plans some religious organizations should be required to provide. Do you think ... religiously affiliated colleges and hospitals should be required to provide their employees with health-care plans that cover contraception or birth control at no cost, or not?	2/1/2012	Public Religion Research Institute PRRI/ RNS Poll	49

(*continued*)

Table 8.1 **Continued**

Question	Start Date	Organization	Support
And what about for religiously affiliated employers, such as a hospital or university—do you support or oppose a recent federal requirement that their health insurance plans cover the full cost of birth control for their female employees?	2/8/2012	CBS News / *New York Times* Poll	61
Do you support or oppose a recent federal requirement that private health insurance plans cover the full cost of birth control for their female patients?	2/8/2012	CBS News / *New York Times* Poll	66
In general, do you support or oppose the new federal requirement that private health insurance plans cover the cost of birth control?	2/13/2012	Kaiser Health Tracking Poll	63
Do you think the federal government should require private employers to offer free birth control coverage as part of their health insurance benefit plans or not?	2/14/2012	Quinnipiac University Poll	47
Do you think that health insurance plans should cover birth control as preventive care for women or not?	2/14/2012	Quinnipiac University Poll	71
As you may know, President [Barack] Obama recently announced a new policy on health insurance and birth control. Under the rule, if a religiously based institution, such as a Catholic hospital or university, objects to providing coverage for its workers for birth control, its insurance company must pay for the coverage instead. What about you . . . do you support or oppose this requirement?	2/23/2012	United Technologies / National Journal Congressional Connection Poll	49

Table 8.1   **Continued**

Question	Start Date	Organization	Support
(Now I have a few questions about the health-care law that Congress passed in 2010.) ... The health reform law also requires employers providing health insurance for their workers to cover other medical services, such as birth control, free of cost. Some members of Congress have proposed legislation that would allow employers to deny coverage for any medical service that violates the employer's moral convictions or religious beliefs. What about you ... do you support or oppose this legislation?	2/23/2012	United Technologies / National Journal Congressional Connection Poll	40
(As you may know, the Obama administration announced a new policy concerning health insurance plans provided by employers and how they handle birth control and contraceptive services. The new policy requires that these services are available as part of the preventative care women would receive. Now, please tell me whether you favor or oppose each of the following, or if you do not have an opinion one way or the other.) ... The federal government requiring health insurance plans for the employees at Catholic and other religiously affiliated hospitals and colleges to offer free birth control coverage and mandate that the health insurance company pays for that cost	2/29/2012	NBC News / *Wall Street Journal* Poll	38

(*continued*)

Table 8.1 **Continued**

Question	Start Date	Organization	Support
(As you may know, the Obama administration announced a new policy concerning health insurance plans provided by employers and how they handle birth control and contraceptive services. The new policy requires that these services are available as part of the preventative care women would receive. Now, please tell me whether you favor or oppose each of the following, or if you do not have an opinion one way or the other.) . . .The federal government requiring employers to offer free birth control coverage as part of their health insurance benefit plans	2/29/2012	NBC News / Wall Street Journal Poll	55
(As you may know, the Obama administration announced a new policy concerning health insurance plans provided by employers and how they handle birth control and contraceptive services. The new policy requires that these services are available as part of the preventative care women would receive. Now, please tell me whether you favor or oppose each of the following, or if you do not have an opinion one way or the other.) . . . The federal government requiring employers to offer free contraceptive services, including the morning-after pill, as part of their health insurance benefit plans	2/29/2012	NBC News / Wall Street Journal Poll	43
Do you think health insurance companies should or should not be required to cover the full cost of birth control for women?	3/7/2012	ABC News / Washington Post Poll	62

Table 8.1 **Continued**

Question	Start Date	Organization	Support
What if the insurance is provided through an employer who is affiliated with a religious institution that opposes birth control? This could be a religious-affiliated university or hospital, for example. In this case, do you think health insurance companies should or should not be required to cover the full cost of birth control for women?	3/7/2012	ABC News / Washington Post Poll	79
Do you think health insurance plans for all employers should have to cover the full cost of birth control for their female employees, or should employers be allowed to opt out of covering that, based on religious or moral objections?	3/7/2012	CBS News / New York Times Poll	40
What about for religiously affiliated employers, such as a hospital or university? Do you think their health insurance plans should have to cover the full costs of birth control for their female employees, or should they be allowed to opt out of covering that based on religious or moral objections?	3/7/2012	CBS News / New York Times Poll	36
(There is currently a debate over what kinds of health-care plans employers, including religiously affiliated employers, should be required to provide.) Do you think . . . churches and other places of worship should be required to provide their employees with health-care plans that cover contraception or birth control at no cost, or not?	3/7/2012	PRRI/RNS Religion News Survey	42

(*continued*)

Table 8.1 **Continued**

Question	Start Date	Organization	Support
(There is currently a debate over what kinds of health-care plans employers, including religiously affiliated employers, should be required to provide.) Do you think... privately owned small businesses should be required to provide their employees with health-care plans that cover contraception or birth control at no cost, or not?	3/7/2012	PRRI/RNS Religion News Survey	53
(There is currently a debate over what kinds of health-care plans employers, including religiously affiliated employers, should be required to provide.) Do you think... publicly held corporations should be required to provide their employees with health-care plans that cover contraception or birth control at no cost, or not?	3/7/2012	PRRI/RNS Religion News Survey	62
(There is currently a debate over what kinds of health-care plans employers, including religiously affiliated employers, should be required to provide.) Do you think... religiously affiliated hospitals should be required to provide their employees with health-care plans that cover contraception or birth control at no cost, or not?	3/7/2012	PRRI/RNS Religion News Survey	57
(There is currently a debate over what kinds of health-care plans employers, including religiously affiliated employers, should be required to provide.) Do you think... religiously affiliated social service agencies should be required to provide their employees with health-care plans that cover contraception or birth control at no cost, or not?	3/7/2012	PRRI/RNS Religion News Survey	52

Table 8.1 **Continued**

Question	Start Date	Organization	Support
There is currently a debate over what kinds of health-care plans employers, including religiously affiliated employers, should be required to provide. Do you think . . . religiously affiliated colleges and universities should be required to provide their employees with health-care plans that cover contraception or birth control at no cost, or not?	3/7/2012	PRRI/RNS Religion News Survey	52
(I'm going to read several types of services medical professionals, hospitals, or insurance companies may not want to provide because it goes against their religious beliefs. For each one, please let me know if you think medical professionals, hospitals, or insurance companies should or should not be allowed to opt out of providing the service for religious reasons.) . . . Birth control pills	5/10/2012	Knights of Columbus / Marist Poll	51
(Please tell me in your view if each of the following situations ought to be allowed or not.) . . . A religiously affiliated university denies its employees and students insurance coverage for birth control on the grounds that birth control is a sin. (If Allow/Not allow, ask.) Do you feel that way strongly or somewhat?	9/12/2012	ACLU / Catholics for Choice Religious Exemptions Survey	69
(There is currently a debate over what kinds of health-care plans some religious organizations should be required to provide.) Do you think . . . churches and other places of worship should be required to provide their employees with health-care plans that cover contraception or birth control at no cost, or not?	9/13/2012	Public Religion Research Institute American Values Survey	45

(continued)

Table 8.1 **Continued**

Question	Start Date	Organization	Support
(There is currently a debate over what kinds of health-care plans some religious organizations should be required to provide.) Do you think... churches and other places of worship, even if they have religious objections should be required to provide their employees with health-care plans that cover contraception or birth control at no cost, or not?	9/13/2012	Public Religion Research Institute American Values Survey	48
(There is currently a debate over what kinds of health-care plans some religious organizations should be required to provide.) Do you think... religiously affiliated colleges and hospitals, even if they have religious objections, should be required to provide their employees with health-care plans that cover contraception or birth control at no cost, or not?	9/13/2012	Public Religion Research Institute American Values Survey	56
There is currently a debate over what kinds of health-care plans some religious organizations should be required to provide. Do you think... religiously affiliated colleges and hospitals should be required to provide their employees with health-care plans that cover contraception or birth control at no cost, or not?	9/13/2012	Public Religion Research Institute American Values Survey	56
Which statement comes closest to your own view regarding birth control?... Doctors, hospitals, and insurance companies should provide birth control to all women who want it. Doctors, hospitals, and insurance companies should not have to provide birth control if they object to it on moral or religious grounds.	9/19/2012	Attitudes Toward Politics and Public Service Survey	72

Table 8.1 **Continued**

Question	Start Date	Organization	Support
As you may know, in 2012 President [Barack] Obama announced a new policy on health insurance and birth control. Under the rule, if a religious-based institution, such as a Catholic hospital or university, objects to providing birth control coverage to its workers, its insurance company must pay for the coverage instead. Do you support or oppose this requirement?	2/27/2013	Quinnipiac University Poll	51
Do you think health insurance plans for all employers should have to cover the full cost of birth control for their female employees, or should employers be allowed to opt out of covering that, based on religious or moral objections?	12/4/2013	CBS News / New York Times Poll	37
Some say employers must be required to cover birth control because it is an important part of women's health care. Others say employers should not be required to cover all forms of birth control if the company opposes it. Which comes closer to your view?	12/9/2013	Fairleigh Dickinson University's PublicMind Poll	48
In general, do you support or oppose the (2010) health-care law's requirement that private health insurance plans cover the full cost of birth control?	3/14/2014	Kaiser Health Tracking Poll	58
Do you think religious-affiliated organizations should have to cover the cost of prescription birth control for their female employees as part of their health insurance plans, or should religious-affiliated organizations be able to opt out of covering that, based on religious objections?	3/20/2014	CBS News Poll	35

(continued)

Table 8.1 **Continued**

Question	Start Date	Organization	Support
What about companies and non-religious organizations? Do you think these employers should have to cover the cost of prescription birth control for their female employees as part of their health insurance plans, or should these employers be able to opt out of covering that, based on religious objections?	3/20/2014	CBS News Poll	51
In general, do you support or oppose the (2010) health-care law's requirement that private health insurance plans cover the full cost of birth control?	4/15/2014	Kaiser Health Tracking Poll	61
(There is currently a debate over what kinds of health-care plans employers, including religiously affiliated employers, should be required to provide.) Do you think... churches and other places of worship should be required to provide their employees with health-care plans that cover contraception or birth control at no cost, or not?	5/14/2014	Public Religion Research Institute Religion & Politics Tracking Survey	42
(There is currently a debate over what kinds of health-care plans employers, including religiously affiliated employers, should be required to provide.) Do you think... privately owned corporations should be required to provide their employees with health-care plans that cover contraception or birth control at no cost, or not?	5/14/2014	Public Religion Research Institute Religion & Politics Tracking Survey	57
(There is currently a debate over what kinds of health-care plans employers, including religiously affiliated employers, should be required to provide.) Do you think... privately owned small businesses should be required to provide their employees with health-care plans that cover contraception or birth control at no cost, or not?	5/14/2014	Public Religion Research Institute Religion & Politics Tracking Survey	51

Table 8.1 **Continued**

Question	Start Date	Organization	Support
(There is currently a debate over what kinds of health-care plans employers, including religiously affiliated employers, should be required to provide.) Do you think... publicly held corporations should be required to provide their employees with health-care plans that cover contraception or birth control at no cost, or not?	5/14/2014	Public Religion Research Institute Religion & Politics Tracking Survey	61
(There is currently a debate over what kinds of health-care plans employers, including religiously affiliated employers, should be required to provide.) Do you think... religiously affiliated hospitals should be required to provide their employees with health-care plans that cover contraception or birth control at no cost, or not?	5/14/2014	Public Religion Research Institute Religion & Politics Tracking Survey	56
There is currently a debate over what kinds of health-care plans employers, including religiously affiliated employers, should be required to provide. Do you think... religiously affiliated colleges and universities should be required to provide their employees with health-care plans that cover contraception or birth control at no cost, or not?	5/14/2014	Public Religion Research Institute Religion & Politics Tracking Survey	52
In general, do you support or oppose the (2010) health-care law's requirement that private health insurance plans cover the full cost of birth control?	7/15/2014	Kaiser Health Tracking Poll	60
Do you favor, oppose, or neither favor nor oppose a requirement that health insurance plans cover the full cost of birth control pills and other contraceptives for women?	10/16/2014	Associated Press / GfK Knowledge Networks Poll	55

If there is any pattern across this diverse population of polling results, it is that explicitly mentioning religious organizations—such as churches, places of worship, or religiously affiliated colleges and hospitals—as the targets of the policy seems to depress support for the mandate. The best illustration of this pattern can be found in the Public Religion Research Institute's (PRRI) various surveys about birth control policy. In its first survey on the mandate (February 2012), PRRI found that support for requiring employers "to provide their employees with health-care plans that cover contraception or birth control at no cost" declined from 56% when no specific organizations were mentioned to 49% when "religiously affiliated colleges and hospitals" were mentioned to 36% when "churches and other places of worship" were mentioned. Similarly, in its May 2014 polling, PRRI found that the mandate's popularity declined from 61% for "publicly held corporations" to 57% for "privately owned corporations" to 56% for "religiously affiliated hospitals" to 52% for "religiously affiliated colleges and universities" to 42% for "churches and other places of worship." Overall, questions that explicitly mention religiously affiliated universities, hospitals, or churches had an average level of support of 48.4%, compared to an average level of support of 56.7% for questions that did not mention these organizations.

When policy opinions fluctuate erratically over time and are subject to a variety of question wording and question ordering effects, the public is said to lack "true attitudes" (Converse 1970; Zaller and Feldman 1992; Zaller 1992) on the issue. According to Zaller's (1992) account of "nonattitudes," the policy opinions captured by surveys are best understood not as genuine reflections of committed belief but instead as short-term articulations guided by a random selection of whatever considerations happen to be at the "top of the head" when a polling question is posed. Research into nonattitudes has shown that some Americans lack true attitudes even on easy issues related to the culture war. Zaller (1992, 32, 92–93) and Bartels (2003, 64), for example, use variation in responses to questions about abortion to show that most people do not hold crystallized attitudes on the topic. On "hard issues," which require "contextual knowledge, appreciation of often subtle differences in policy options, a coherent structure of beliefs about politics, systematic reasoning to connect means to ends, and interest in and attentiveness to political life" (Carmines and Stimson 1989, 12), nonattitudes are more prevalent and the opinions measured by surveys even more unstable.

Based on the results presented in Table 8.1, Americans clearly lacked true attitudes on the contraceptive mandate between August 2011 and July 2014. The presence of these nonattitudes is the result of the fact that the question of who should pay for birth control is a much harder issue than the question of who should have access to birth control—involving a relatively new set of debates that go beyond simple symbolic disagreements about the ends of government action. More specifically, the variation in survey questions and the variation in results produced by these survey question variations suggest a deep fissure in the public's thinking about contraceptive mandates. When mandate questions are framed in a general and nontargeted way, Americans seem to view the issue primarily as a question of access to valuable health care for women (that is, very similarly to questions about birth control access and whether contraceptives are "morally appropriate"). When mandate questions are framed in a way that targets religious entities and suggests an expansion in the size of government, doctrinal and ideological considerations are activated in a way that complicates the issue for most Americans.

To assess the evolution of opinion on the ACA's contraceptive mandate over time while controlling for some of the problems presented by these nonattitudes, we limited our assessment to the data provided by survey organizations that asked the same survey item on the contraceptive mandate three or more times—namely, the Kaiser Family Foundation and the PRRI. As Table 8.1 shows, the timing of the surveys and the questions posed to respondents by these two pollsters were very different. The Kaiser Family Foundation question was one of the most general asked by any of the polling organizations conducting surveys on the issue. Specifically, the Kaiser Family Foundation's polls repeatedly asked, "Do you support or oppose the new federal requirement that private health insurance plans cover the full cost of birth control and other preventive services for their female patients?" The Kaiser Family Foundation was also the only pollster to capture opinions throughout the entirety of the debate over the contraceptive mandate—asking its respondents its broad policy question at five different points between August 2011 and July 2014. Standing in stark contrast to the Kaiser Family Foundation's general approach, PRRI tapped feelings about whether "churches and other places of worship should be required to provide their employees with health-care plans that cover contraception or birth control at no cost, or not" four separate times between March 2012 and May 2014.

Consistent with the idea that mentioning churches and religiously affiliated organizations dampens aggregate approval of the mandate across polls, the gap between public support as measured by the Kaiser survey's nonspecific question and public support as measured by PRRI's church-specific question was never less than 13% and was as high as 27%. While aggregate public opinion on the mandate as measured by both organizations shifted early in the debate, it remained relatively stable between April 2012 and July 2014. In the first poll conducted following HHS's announcement, for example, the Kaiser Family Foundation found that 66% of Americans supported "the new federal requirement that private health insurance plans cover the full cost of birth control and other preventive services for their female patients." Support for the mandate was lower (63%) in Kaiser's March 2012 polling and consistently hovered around

60% in each of their subsequent surveys—coming in at 58% in March 2014, 61% in April 2014, and 60% in July 2014. Similarly, after revealing an initial uptick in support, the PRRI data showed almost no change at all between 2012 and 2014 in the public's willingness to apply the mandate to "churches and other places of worship." As Table 8.1 shows, acceptance for applying the mandate to "churches and other places of worship" jumped from 36% in February 2012 to 42% in March 2012 but remained at 45% in September 2012 and 42% in May 2014.

The early shifts in public opinion identified by the Kaiser Family Foundation and PRRI are somewhat confusing. While Kaiser's data show a decline in general support for the mandate in the months following the HHS announcement, PRRI's surveys suggest that the public became more willing to impose a birth control requirement on religious organizations during this period. What might explain this inconsistency? Part of the story almost certainly has to do with the public's high level of attentiveness to the media's coverage of the mandate during the first few months of 2012. Kaiser's February 2012 survey, for example, found that 60% of the American public had heard "a lot" or "some" about "the debate over whether certain categories of religiously affiliated employers, such as Catholic hospitals or universities, should be required to include birth control in their health insurance coverage" and a March 2012 *USA Today* poll found that 59% of Americans were following the debate over the contraceptive mandate "very closely" or "somewhat closely."

A large literature in political science and mass communication has shown that media frames can influence political opinions by changing the considerations that news consumers use to formulate their issue evaluations (e.g., Berelson et al. 1954, 253–73; Nelson et al. 1997 Scheufele 1999, 117; Zaller 1992). As discussed in chapter 6, the media did not adopt a dominant or consistent approach to its framing of the contraceptive mandate, and news reports emphasized different aspects at different moments in time. Specifically, the prominence of the religious freedom and reproductive rights frames ebbed and flowed significantly during the course of our one-year study—with reproductive rights receiving more attention in the final months of 2011 and religious freedom receiving more attention in January, February, and March 2012. Reflecting these competing narratives, a CBS News / *New York Times* poll from March 2012 found that 37% of Americans defined the issue of the contraceptive mandate as one of "religious freedom," while 51% thought about it as a matter of "women's health and their rights." Unsurprisingly, 81.4% of those saying "religious freedom" opposed the mandate, while only 31.5% of those saying "women's health and their rights" opposed the policy. This difference in opinion suggests that the lack of a dominant or consistent news frame in the media's coverage, coupled with high levels of public attentiveness, may help explain the early and somewhat contradictory shifts in public opinion toward the mandate. In the next chapter we examine this possibility in more detail by empirically assessing the relationship between media frames and public opinion on the mandate.

The Structure of Opinion on the ACA's Contraceptive Mandate

Two previous studies have examined the individual-level determinants of opinions toward the mandate. Using data from a November 2013 survey of the American public, Moniz, Davis, and Chang (2014) examined the factors shaping whether respondents believe that "all health plans in the United States should be required to include coverage for birth control medications." Consistent with other similarly worded survey items about the mandate (questions not explicitly referencing religious institutions), Moniz, Davis, and Chang (2014) found that 69% of respondents supported a policy of required birth control coverage in health plans. More importantly, in a multivariate regression analysis that did not control for religious affiliation, religiosity, political ideology, or partisanship, the researchers show that support for a contraceptive mandate was significantly higher among women, African Americans, and Hispanics.

In a more thorough test of the factors shaping individual attitudes toward the contraceptive mandate, Deckman and McTague (2015) conducted a multivariate regression analysis on one of PRRI's September 2012 two mandate questions—the item asking whether "religiously affiliated colleges and hospitals should be required to provide their employees with health-care plans that cover contraception or birth control." They found that nonwhite, lower-income, younger, and less religious Americans were more likely to express support for the mandate. Most importantly, they found that women and Democrats were significantly more supportive of the mandate than men and Republicans—with the predicted probability of backing the law increasing by 13 percentage points for women over men and 39 percentage points for Democrats over Republicans. These results suggest that the insurance coverage of birth control was both highly gendered and highly partisan in the fall of 2012.

While providing some initial insight into the individual-level determinants of opinions on the contraceptive mandate, these studies are limited in three important ways. First, both studies rely on polling data collected during a single moment in time. As a result, they cannot shed light on how the relative importance of variables such as gender, race, or education may have changed over time. Second, both analyses leave important variables out of their regression models. Most importantly, both studies fail to control for political ideology and religious affiliation. Finally, both studies focus exclusively on a single survey question to draw general conclusions about the determinants of support for the mandate.

Given the varied responses to the differently worded questions described earlier, this necessarily limits our understanding of the dynamics of American thinking on the contraceptive mandate.

In the following sections, we address these weaknesses by reviewing the survey data collected by both the Kaiser Family Foundation and PRRI. Given that some of the polls conducted by these organizations did not ask questions about a number of our key independent variables, we limit our analyses here to the three Kaiser Family Foundation surveys (February 2012, May 2014, July 2014) and the three PRRI surveys (March 2012, September 2012, May 2014) that contained measures of gender, race, age, income, education, partisanship, political ideology, and religious affiliation. Tables 8.2 (Kaiser Family Foundation surveys) and 8.3 (PRRI surveys) present the results of a series of logistic analysis regression models in which the dependent variable is scored 1 for support for the contraceptive mandate and 0 for opposition to the contraceptive mandate.

Partisanship

A long-standing consensus in political science research claims that information, ideas, and issue frames follow a one-way path from political elites and the mainstream media to the mass public. Beginning with the early work of Berelson, Lazasfeld, and McPhee (1954) and Downs (1957), numerous scholars have hypothesized that the "rational ignorance" of ordinary citizens leads them to pay little attention to political affairs and to rely instead on cues from political elites when forming their political judgments. As a result, individual attitudes and aggregate public opinion respond in highly predictable ways to the messages communicated by political elites through the mass media. This so-called elite opinion theory (Lee 2002) has come to dominate the study of American public opinion. According to Lee and Schlesinger (2001, 5), "The idea that public opinion is fundamentally top-down and elite-driven is virtual orthodoxy among political scientists."

A key aspect of elite opinion theory concerns the characteristics of elite messages. According to Zaller (1992), when elite messages are unified (i.e., all elites agree concerning an issue at hand), all politically aware members of the public will receive the message, and this message will shape their individual opinion. On the other hand, when the elites present conflicting messages on the same issue, then the opinion of politically aware members of the public reflects the elite message that is most in line with partisan or ideological identifications of the individual in question. Zaller (1992) says of the characteristics of elite messages, "When elites uphold a clear picture of what should be done, the public

Table 8.2 **Determinants of Mandate Support in Kaiser Data**

	February 2012	May 2014	July 2014
Female	0.407*	1.266***	0.712***
	(0.176)	(0.192)	(0.199)
Party ID	1.423***	2.066***	1.873***
	(0.236)	(0.294)	(0.285)
Ideology	1.027***	0.501	1.445***
	(0.257)	(0.277)	(0.314)
African American	0.136	−0.313	0.371
	(0.345)	(0.362)	(0.376)
Latino	1.138**	0.418	0.563
	(0.367)	(0.311)	(0.359)
Education	0.541	−0.236	−0.0256
	(0.281)	(0.268)	(0.265)
Age	−0.0178**	−0.0253***	−0.0266***
	(0.00558)	(0.00584)	(0.00602)
Catholic	−0.488*	−0.0292	0.0753
	(0.193)	(0.214)	(0.233)
Church Attendance	−1.313***	−1.648***	−1.309***
	(0.317)	(0.344)	(0.326)
Constant	0.716	0.895*	0.640
	(0.415)	(0.390)	(0.408)
N	1211	852	871

Standard errors in parentheses
*$p < 0.05$, **$p < 0.01$, ***$p < 0.001$

tends to see events from that point of view.... When elites divide, members of the public tend to follow the elites sharing their general ideological or partisan predisposition" (8). Thus, an environment characterized by polarized elite messages on the birth control mandate may elicit polarized opinions on this issue among politically aware Democrats and Republicans.

The Democratic and Republican Parties have diverged considerably in their positions on issues affecting women over the last decade (Deckman and McTague 2015). These diverging views culminated in the intense debate over the ACA's contraceptive mandate and the broader "war on women" during the 2012 campaign. Given the large body of research supporting elite opinion theory and the widely acknowledged differences between the Democratic and Republican Parties on the issue, it is perhaps unsurprising that partisanship was a major determinant of opinions about the mandate. As Tables 8.2 and 8.3 show, regardless of the framing of the survey question, party identification was a statistically significant predictor of support for birth control requirements even after controlling for all other influences on policy views, with Republicans expressing considerably less support for the mandate than Democrats. Additionally, as Figure 8.3 shows, the partisan gap between Democrats and Republicans increased as the differences between the parties at the elite level became clearer to members of the mass public. According to the Kaiser Family Foundation surveys, for example, Democrats were only 17.9% more supportive of the mandate in August 2011 than Republicans. In the wake of the widely covered congressional debate over the mandate, the partisan gap increased to 40.9% in February 2012 and to 46.1% in July 2014. Similarly, the gap between Democrats and Republicans increased from 11.4% to 33.9% to 36.7% to 37.4% in the four surveys conducted

Table 8.3 **Determinants of Mandate Support in PRRI Data**

	February 2012	September 2012	May 2014
Female	0.445**	0.289*	0.368*
	(0.167)	(0.126)	(0.152)
Party ID	0.956***	1.609***	1.147***
	(0.213)	(0.178)	(0.220)
Ideology	0.0787	1.551***	1.503***
	(0.0526)	(0.290)	(0.266)
African American	−0.0613	0.0582	−0.000550
	(0.253)	(0.218)	(0.209)
Latino	0.914**	0.159	0.112
	(0.282)	(0.226)	(0.253)
Age	−0.0205***	−0.0106**	−0.0115**
	(0.00456)	(0.00360)	(0.00386)
Catholic	−0.335	−0.218	0.00788
	(0.209)	(0.155)	(0.182)
Education	0.284	−0.169	−0.260
	(0.286)	(0.196)	(0.262)
Constant	−0.647*	−1.193***	−1.174***
	(0.329)	(0.260)	(0.288)
N	753	1298	860

Standard errors in parentheses
*$p < 0.05$, **$p < 0.01$, ***$p < 0.001$

by PRRI. Consistent with the predictions of elite opinion theory, therefore, mass-level opinions on the contraceptive mandate quickly polarized along partisan lines in 2012 after Republican and Democratic elites expressed their diverging views on the issue.

Gender

Gender has been repeatedly shown to exert an important influence on political opinions and behaviors. Academic research has found that, in general, women hold more liberal policy preferences (Cook and Wilcox 1991; Norrander and Wilcox 2008), are more likely to identify with the Democratic Party (Kaufmann and Petrocik 1999; Norrander 1997; Norrander 1999), and are more likely to vote for Democratic candidates than men. Importantly, these differences, commonly referred to as the "gender gap" (Conover 1988; Kaufmann 2006), do not hold across all political issues. In fact, research shows that the gender gap is largest on redistributional questions that involve the government's role in providing social welfare benefits. On culture-war issues such as abortion, feminism, and school prayer, where concerns about the size of the federal government are secondary, researchers find relatively few differences in opinion between men and women (Cook, Jelen, and Wilcox 1992; Cook and Wilcox 1991; Kaufmann 2002; Kaufmann and Petrocik 1999; Shapiro and Mahajan 1986).

We had good reasons to suspect that men and women would hold different views about the ACA's contraceptive mandate between August 2011 and June 2014. First, previous research suggests that the American public viewed the birth control mandate early in the debate as less of a culture-war issue and more of a role-of-government issue (Deckman and McTague 2015). All other things being equal, this should increase the differences in opinion between men and women. Second, as pointed out above, the Democratic Party and its allies explicitly attempted to activate gender identity and considerations of gender-based interests among female voters by emphasizing the Republican Party's so-called "war on women" throughout the 2012 campaign. According to political reporter Michelle Goldberg (2012), for example, "Obama was unique in foregrounding women's health, turning Planned Parenthood's Cecile Richards and Georgetown Law graduate Sandra Fluke into major campaign surrogates." To the extent that appeals from these sources were successful, men and women should have reached different conclusions on the contraceptive mandate.

So was there a gender gap on the issue of the contraceptive mandate? As Tables 8.2 and 8.3 show, women were consistently more supportive of the mandate than men across time and across surveys even after controlling for standard demographic characteristics (such as race), religious affiliation, and political orientation. As Figure 8.2 shows, men and women both had very positive feelings toward the contraceptive mandate immediately following the HHS announcement. In fact, more than 70% of male and female respondents in Kaiser's initial survey supported the mandate, and the gender gap was relatively small—a mere 5.1%. Consistent with the hypothesis that gender became a more important influence on opinions as religious organizations began challenging the framing of the mandate in terms of women's health and reproductive rights, the gender gap increased significantly in size between February 2012 and April 2014 (from 5.7% to 9.1%). When the mandate was reintroduced to the political agenda in the wake of oral arguments in *Burwell v. Hobby Lobby Stores*, opinions quickly polarized along gender lines. Indeed, the gender gap in support for the mandate jumped more than 10 percentage points—from 9.1% to 19.6%—in the space of only three weeks. Interestingly, the vast gap that opened up between men and women in the final weeks of April 2014 was driven both by women becoming much more supportive of the mandate and men becoming much less supportive. Specifically, support among women increased 3.5% and support among men dropped by 7.0% in the final weeks of April 2014. The Supreme Court's final ruling in *Burwell* appeared to push men and women, once again, in opposite directions. Male support for the mandate increased over five percentage points between May 2014 and July 2014 while female support declined by nearly four percentage points.

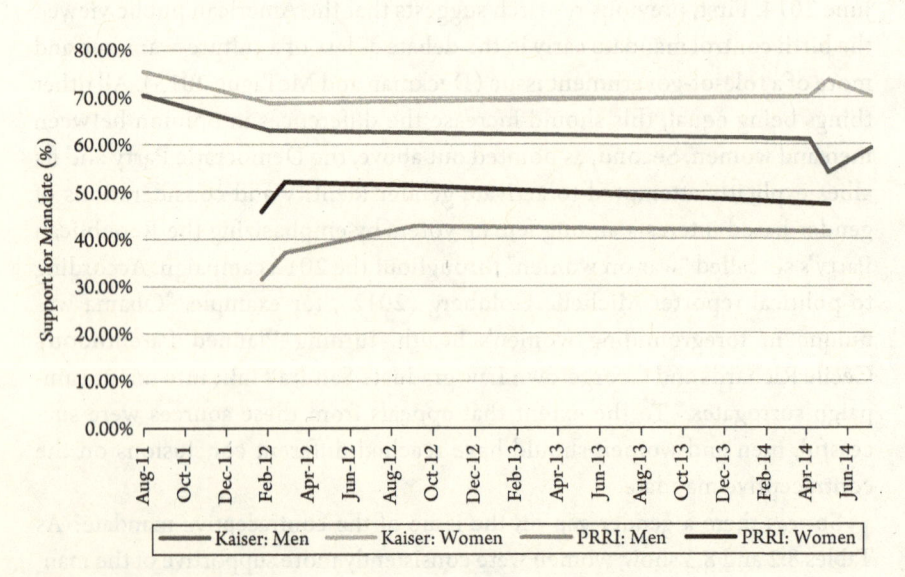

Figure 8.2 Support for the Contraceptive Mandate by Gender

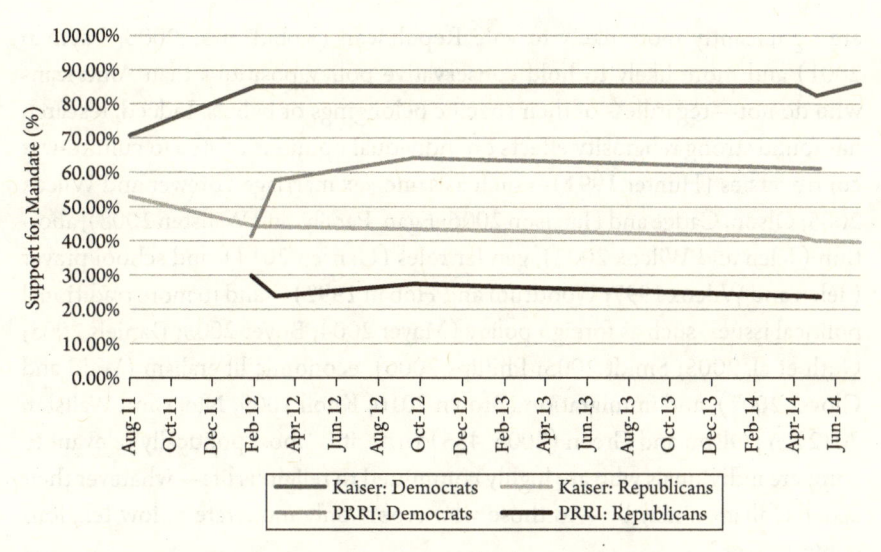

Figure 8.3 Support for the Contraceptive Mandate by Partisanship

While the gender gap on the general question of the mandate increased over the course of the debate, the gender gap on the more tailored question of whether "churches and other places of worship" should be required to cover birth control narrowed significantly. As Figure 8.2 shows, women (45.8%) were initially far more supportive of applying the contraceptive mandate to "churches and other places of worship" than men (31.5%). After the spring of 2012, however, male support increased and female support decreased, resulting in a significant decline in the size of the gender gap—falling from 14.9% in March 2012 to 8.5% in September 2012 to 5.8% in May 2014. It appears, therefore, that different gender dynamics drove the public's thinking on the mandate in general and the mandate as applied to churches.

Religious Affiliation and Religiosity

A considerable body of social science evidence suggests that individuals calibrate their positions on cultural issues to conform with their deeply socialized religious predispositions (Leege et al. 2002; Djupe and Gilbert 2009; Wald and Glover 2007). Specifically, previous research (Guth et al. 1997; Layman 2001) has suggested that religion's political influence must be understood in three distinct yet interrelated ways: belonging (i.e., which affiliation an individual claims), believing (i.e., which specific theological and eschatological beliefs an individual endorses), and behaving (i.e., the religious practices in which an individual takes part). The growing consensus of this work is that Americans who frequently attend church, pray, and report high levels of religious commitment are significantly more likely to vote Republican (Kohut et al. 2000; Layman 2001) and more likely to hold conservative policy positions than Americans who do not—regardless of their specific belongings or beliefs. Indeed, research has found strong religiosity effects on individual opinions related to culture-war controversies (Hunter 1991)—such as same-sex marriage (Brewer and Wilcox 2005; Olson, Cadge and Harrison 2006; Egan, Persily, and Wallsten 2008), abortion (Jelen and Wilcox 2003), gender roles (Hansen 2014), and school prayer (Jelen and Wilcox 1997; Woodrum and Hoban 1992)—and to more traditional political issues, such as foreign policy (Mayer 2004; Boyer 2005; Daniels 2005; Guth et al. 2005; Smidt 2005; Phillips 2006), economic liberalism (Wald and Glover 2007), and immigration (Brown 2010; Knoll 2009; Nteta and Wallsten 2012). As Olson and Green (2006, 455) write, it is "most politically relevant to compare individuals who are highly committed to religious life—whatever their actual affiliation may be—to those who report only moderate to low religious commitment."

In addition to this body of work, a voluminous literature attempts to assess the extent to which the religious context that individuals inhabit shape their political attitudes (Gilbert 1993; Huckfeldt, Plutzer, and Sprague 1993; Huckfeldt and Sprague 1995; Wald, Owen, and Hill 1988). Generally speaking, early scholarship on this topic found that the messages communicated in churches exercised an important influence over the political views of congregation members (for a review, see Djupe and Calfano 2013). In a detailed study of Protestant parishioners, for example, Wald, Owen, and Hill (1988) found that an individual's level of political conservatism was partly determined by the theological conservatism of his congregation. Similarly, Huckfeldt, Plutzer, and Sprague (1993) demonstrated that the partisanship of Protestant congregations has a considerable impact on an individual's partisan loyalties. As Chris Gilbert (1993) summarized in *The Impact of Churches on Political Behavior*, the early data "clearly support the hypothesis that churches are significant sources of political cues, and that churches do affect the political actions and beliefs of their members" (171).

More recent scholarship has reached conflicting conclusions about the influence of clergy speech on public opinion. On the one hand, some of this research has uncovered evidence for strong clergy effects. In his study of Anabaptist denominations, for example, Fetzer (2001) showed that pastors reinforced and converted their congregation's political views on issues of war and peace. Bjarnason and Welch (2004) used a survey of Catholic parishioners and priests to demonstrate that religious leaders can exert a significant influence on the way their congregations think about the death penalty. In their study of the Episcopal Church and the Evangelical Lutheran Church in America, Djupe and Hunt

(2009) found that clergy messages on the environment played an important role in shaping the views of church members.

Other research, by contrast, has discovered that the influence of religious leaders is more limited and contingent upon characteristics of the message, the context of the communication, and the clergy member who is communicating. In a specific test of Zaller's (1992) model of elite influence, Campbell and Monson (2003) found that Mormons are likely to "follow their leaders" only when endorsement by and agreement among Latter-Day Saints church leaders exist on political issues. Employing Bjarnason and Welch's (2004) methodological framework, Smith (2008) showed that only liberal Catholic pastors exert a significant impact on the attitudes of lay Catholics. Pairing data about the quantity and quality of political messages from clergy members with surveys of congregation members, Djupe and Gilbert (2009) found little support for the idea that religious leaders persuade their parishioners. Most recently, Wallsten and Nteta (2016) found that, unlike Methodist, Southern Baptist, and Evangelical Lutheran Church in America leaders, members of the Catholic clergy were unable to persuade their denominations to think differently about immigrants as a group and about immigration policy. The recent surge in scholarly attention on the impact of clergy pronouncements has not, in other words, produced a consistent set of findings regarding the scope and reach of the clergy's influence over their congregation's political attitudes.

The United States Conference of Catholic Bishops (USCCB) and other leaders within the church fiercely opposed the mandate and actively sought to shape the public debate over it. In a multifaceted strategy that involved issuing press releases, granting interviews to news organizations, and testifying before congressional committees, clergy members repeatedly emphasized the church's objection to the ACA's mandate on religious freedom grounds, particularly during late 2011 and early 2012. As shown in chapter 6, there was some evidence in favor of the efficacy of this strategy. Specifically, news organizations became dramatically more likely to frame their coverage as a potential threat to religious freedom than as a potential threat to reproductive rights in the days following a press release from the USCCB.

Did the combination of clergy messages and media stories emphasizing religious liberty concerns push Catholics to oppose the mandate? Neither the Kaiser nor the PRRI data provide much support for the idea that any of the church's campaigning was persuasive to parishioners. As Tables 8.2 and 8.3 show,[1] identifying as a Catholic (relative to not identifying as a Catholic) was only a significant predictor of opposition to the contraceptive mandate in the February 2012 Kaiser Family Foundation data. In each of Kaiser's subsequent surveys and in all of the PRRI surveys, Catholics were no more or less supportive of the mandate than those claiming any other religious affiliation. In short, consistent with previous work on clergy attempts at opinion leadership (e.g., Wallsten and Nteta 2016), we find little evidence that the Catholic Church persuaded its members to oppose the mandate.

Even after controlling for religious affiliation, an individual's level of religiosity (as measured by the frequency of their attendance at church services) had a significant, substantial, and negative effect on an individual's support for the contraceptive mandate. As Table 8.2 shows, attending church more frequently significantly depressed support for the mandate in all three of the Kaiser Family Foundation surveys asking questions about religion. Unfortunately, the February 2012 and May 2014 PRRI surveys did not include similar measures of religiosity. In the lone PRRI survey to ask a question about religiosity (September 2012), however, church attendance was also a significant and negative predictor of support for the mandate, with opposition increasing by more than 13% for frequent attendees relative to nonattendees. Similar to many other political issues, it appears that the so-called God gap (Olson and Cadge 2006) that separates Americans with high levels of religiosity from those with low levels of religiosity was an important factor in understanding opposition to the contraceptive mandate.

Conclusion

The conventional wisdom in political science research suggests that Americans ground their opinions on abortion, gay rights, and school prayer in longstanding, deep-seated partisan loyalties and religious commitments (Johnston 2006; Jelen 2009). In this chapter, we have shown that while this characterization does not generally extend to questions of access to birth control, it describes quite well the state of opinion toward the ACA's contraceptive mandate after 2012. Prior to 2012, contraceptive mandates were for most Americans relatively easy issues that did not activate any concerns other than whether it was moral for women to have access to birth control. Consequently, few partisan, religious, or gender differences existed in support for requiring health insurance providers to cover contraception. Beginning in late 2011, however, American political discourse was saturated with diverging signals about where political parties and religious leaders stood on the ACA's contraceptive mandate. As a result, the debate over contraceptive mandates shifted from the question of whether people should have access to birth control to the question of who (if anyone) should be forced against their will to pay for other people's birth control. Public opinion on this much harder question split along partisan, gender, and religious lines—with Republicans, men, and the religious expressing more opposition than Democrats, women, and the secular.

The above analysis makes some strong but largely unsubstantiated claims about the impact of shifting elite-level frames on mass opinion. In the next chapter we empirically demonstrate how changes in the media's framing can produce large changes in the distribution of public opinion on issues related to insurance coverage of birth control. Specifically, in a series of survey experiments that systematically manipulate the content of fabricated news reports, we show that a gendered framing of the ACA's contraceptive mandate (emphasizing women's health, reproductive rights, and sexual morality) produces much higher levels of support for mandatory coverage of birth control than a religious freedom framing. The results of these survey experiments further underscore the importance of byline diversity by linking authorship to public opinion through the influence of frame choices.

9
Experiment
Frames and Public Opinion

We have shown in previous chapters that the media's coverage of contraceptive policy was shaped in important ways by the presence or absence of female voices. We demonstrated, for instance, that female journalists included significantly more women as news sources (chapter 6) and chose to frame contraception issues around gendered themes far more frequently than male journalists (chapter 7). Additionally, we presented evidence that quoting more female sources exerted an independent influence on which aspects of the Affordable Care Act's (ACA) contraceptive mandate were highlighted in a given news report—with higher levels of gender parity in sourcing predicting the use of more gendered news frames (chapter 7). Collectively, these results make a compelling case that byline, source, and content diversity were all deeply connected in the media's discussion of the contraception issue.

Do byline, source, and content diversity exert an influence over the American public? Specifically, does having more female reporters, more female news sources, or more gendered coverage matter in any way for how news consumers think about politicians, the press, or the question of who should pay for contraception? In the analysis presented in this chapter, we attempt to provide an empirical answer to this question. Using a set of survey experiments, we assess the impact that female underrepresentation in the bylines and texts of contraceptive mandate reports had on news consumers by measuring how exposure to the kinds of articles produced by male and female reporters influenced media trust, political cynicism, and opinions about birth control policy.

The results of our experimental manipulations show that the consequences of marginalizing women in media discussions of birth control policy extend far beyond the content reported by the press. How the public thinks about health insurance coverage of contraception, how the public perceives the news media, and how the public relates to government are all directly and indirectly shaped by the presence of female voices. More specifically, our data show that women

The Politics of the Pill: Gender, Framing, and Policymaking in the Battle over Birth Control. Rachel VanSickle-Ward, Kevin Wallsten, Oxford University Press (2019). © Oxford University Press.
DOI: 10.1093/oso/9780190675349.001.0001

presented with female-authored articles on the contraceptive mandate rated the news media's credibility significantly higher than women presented with male-authored articles. Even more importantly, we found that exposure to strategic game coverage, which was the most common type of male-authored story on the contraceptive mandate, decreased perceptions of media credibility, enhanced feelings of political cynicism, reduced issue-specific information retention, and encouraged more frequent expressions of negativity among all experimental participants. Consistent with a large body of previous studies, our experiments also revealed the power of news frames to shape policy opinions—with male, but not female, respondents decreasing their support for the contraceptive mandate in response to reading an article emphasizing religious freedom and all respondents increasing their support in response to reading an article emphasizing women's health, reproductive rights, and sexual morality.

Literature Review

Three separate bodies of work serve to inform the analysis presented in this chapter: research on perceptions of media credibility, research on the impact of substantive news frames on policy opinions, and research on the consequences of exposure to strategic game reporting. We address each of these literatures in turn.

Media Credibility

Credibility refers to the "amount of believability" (Bracken 2006, 724) an audience assigns to a message communicator (Sternadori and Thorson 2009). Since the 1950s, scholars of mass communication and journalism have devoted thousands of pages in academic books and peer-reviewed journals to understanding the amount of believability the American public assigns to news sources, news products, news organizations, and the news media as an institution (e.g., Appelman and Sundar 2015; Gaziano and McGrath 1986; Sundar and Nass 2001; Kiousis 2001; Armstrong and Nelson 2005; White and Andsager 1991). Beyond a general agreement that the concept should be measured in a number of different ways, this voluminous literature has produced little scholarly consensus about how to best operationalize media credibility (Bucy 2003). The earliest studies on media credibility, for example, suggested there were only four dimensions to the concept: knowledge, trustworthiness, attractiveness, and dynamism (Berlo et al. 1969; Markham 1968; Singletary 1976). Subsequent research rejected this narrow focus and began expanding the inventory of questions designed to tap the news media's amount of believability. The list of items commonly found in contemporary studies of media credibility now includes measures of fairness, balance, completeness, bias, accuracy, goodwill, and concern for community (Fico, Richardson, and Edwards 2004; Flanagin and Metzger 2000; Gaziano and McGrath 1986; Greer 2003; Johnson and Kaye 1998; Meyer 1988; Brann and Leezer Himes 2010; Kamins, Brand, Hoeke, and Moe 1989; Kenton 1989; McCroskey and Teven 1999; Ohanian 1990; Kertz and Ohanian 1992). As a result of this ever growing body of work, there are nearly as many different approaches to measuring media credibility today as there are studies examining it.

Regardless of how it is measured, however, most empirical studies on the subject are interested in identifying the factors that bolster media credibility at the individual, organizational, and institutional levels. Research into how a message communicator's (i.e., a reporter's or a news source's) gender shapes an audience's perceptions of credibility is a particularly popular area of inquiry. This body of work reveals a complicated relationship between media credibility assessments and the gender of a reporter or the gender of a quoted news source. A number of studies show, for example, that news consumers deem the information communicated by men as significantly more credible than information communicated by women. Most notably, analyses of "hard news" broadcasts have repeatedly shown that television viewers evaluate male newscasters as more credible than female newscasters (Balon, Philport, and Beadle 1978; Brann and Himes 2010; Weibel, Wissmath, and Groner 2008). Social media content attributed to male authors is also viewed as more credible than social media content attributed to female authors (Armstrong and McAdams 2009). Overall, these studies suggest that widely held gender stereotypes may make it difficult for women in the news media to be viewed as credibly as their male counterparts (Armstrong and Nelson 2005).

Other work, however, suggests that gender stereotypes may, in certain circumstances, actually bolster an audience's perceptions of the credibility of information communicated by female reporters and news sources. Research dating back to the 1970s demonstrates that people hold powerful stereotypes about men and women (Dolan and Lynch 2014). Women, for example, are believed to be more honest, compassionate, expressive, and consensus-oriented than men (Burrell 1994). Large majorities of the public also perceive women to be more ideologically liberal than men (Alexander and Andersen 1993; Huddy and Terkildsen 1993) and more capable of dealing with education, health care, the environment, and issues concerning seniors, children, and families (Alexander and Andersen 1993; Kahn 1996; Lawless 2004; Koch 1999; Leeper 1991). While these stereotyped-based assessments can hurt the perceived credibility of women attempting to communicate on traditionally male-dominated topics, such as foreign policy, defense, and crime (Fox and Oxley 2003; Kahn

1994), they may provide a boost to the perceived credibility of female reporters and news sources speaking on women's issues (Shaw, Cole, Moore, and Cole 1981). In other words, gender stereotypes can sometimes pose obstacles and sometimes prove advantageous for women in the media.

Still other research suggests that female reporters and interviewees may, in fact, be seen as more credible sources of information than male reporters and interviewees but only among other women. According to social identity theory (Postmes, Spears, and Lea 1998; Spears and Lea 1992; Tajfel 1979; Tajfel and Turner 1986), people have an innate tendency to rate members of their ingroups more positively than members of their out-groups. Extending this line of thinking to media attitudes, credibility assessments should be significantly enhanced when high levels of similarity exist between those sending and those receiving messages (Bochner 1994; Brock 1965). Unsurprisingly, gender, as one of the most readily identifiable individual traits, has been shown to shape how people respond to media content. White and Andsager (1991), for example, found that while news audiences did not view columns written by authors of their gender more credibly, women did strongly prefer reading content produced by other women. To put all of this differently, credibility assessments may be a function of how message sender and message receiver traits interact rather than a function of sender traits alone.

Substantive Framing Effects

Studies of the media frame-building process often distinguish between strategic game reporting and substantive or policy-oriented coverage (Aalberg, Strömbäck, and de Vreese 2011; Entman 2004). As discussed in Chapter 6, news coverage employing the strategic game frame relies heavily on polling results, war metaphors and analyses of political optics (Jamieson 1993; Cappella and Jamieson 1997). At the core of strategic game reporting is the assumption that politicians are primarily self-interested actors who take positions on issues not because they are interested in solving policy problems but, instead, because they are interested in winning elections (Valentino, Beckmann, and Buhr 2001a). The centerpiece of substantive news coverage, by contrast, is a detailed discussion of how various courses of government action will affect average citizens. News reports adopting this substantive frame often portray politicians as "sincere" public servants motivated to represent their constituents' interests and make responsible social policy (Valentino et al. 2001).

Over the last several decades, hundreds of academic research articles have used dozens of different research methods to demonstrate the existence of substantive framing effects on countless political issues (e.g., Chong and Druckman 2007; Edelman 1993; Entman 1991; Gamson 1992; Iyengar and Simon 1993;

McLeod, Kosicki, and McLeod 1994; McLeod and Detenber 1999; Nelson and Oxley 1999; Price et al. 1995; Semetko and Valkenburg 2000; Tewksbury et al. 2000; Zaller 1992). The main idea guiding this body of work is that media frames exert an influence on news audiences by increasing the salience of some attributes of an issue at the expense of others. In an early study of framing effects, for example, Iyengar (1991) demonstrated that how news audiences attribute responsibility for societal-level problems, such as crime, poverty, terrorism, unemployment, and racial inequality, was heavily dependent upon whether journalists reported about these problems using an "episodic" or "thematic" frame. Similarly, Nelson, Clawson, and Oxley (1997) found that experimental participants who viewed a news story emphasizing free speech considerations expressed far more tolerance for a planned Ku Klux Klan rally than participants who viewed a story highlighting safety and public order. As Semetko and Valkenburg (2000, 94) suggest, "How people think about an issue, especially a political issue that is inherently ambiguous, is dependent on how the issue is framed by the media."

Despite the fact that framing effects have been documented in nearly every conceivable context, there are important constraints on the news media's ability to shape their audience's political opinions. According to Chong and Druckman (2007, 109), "Strong predispositions reduce framing effects by increasing one's resistance to disconfirming information." While Chong and Druckman's discussion was focused primarily on the conditioning influence of political knowledge (e.g., Kinder and Sanders 1990; Haider-Markel and Joslyn 2001; Nelson et al. 1997; Slothuus 2005; Miller and Krosnick 2000) and values (e.g., Druckman 2001; Haider-Markel and Joslyn 2001; Barker 2005; Lau and Schlesinger 2005; Shen and Edwards 2005), ascriptive characteristics such as race and gender are also commonly considered "predispositions" in many studies of public opinion (Lee 2003). In general, therefore, existing research suggests that media framing effects may be strongly attenuated by the political predispositions of audience members.

Strategic Game Framing Effects

The strategic game frame's presence has been documented in studies of news coverage for more than three decades (Aalberg, Strömbäck, and de Vreese 2011), including our analysis of newspaper stories on the ACA's contraceptive mandate (chapter 6). Scholars and media observers have long worried that this approach to political reporting, with its relentless depiction of politicians as cynical opportunists who have little interest in solving policy problems, will seriously undermine the public's faith in the news media and in the political process (Fallows 1997; Farnsworth and Lichter 2003; Lichter and Noyes 1996; Patterson 1993). Empirical tests of this so-called spiral of cynicism hypothesis (Valentino et al. 2001a; de Vreese 2005) have largely validated these concerns. In a seminal set of experiments, for example, Cappella and Jamieson (1997) linked consumption of strategic game news coverage to higher levels of political cynicism and lower levels of political trust. They also found that the framing of election reporting affected the kinds of information that news audiences took away from a story, with subjects exposed to strategic game coverage retaining only strategy-based information about the campaign. Similarly, Rhee (1997) found that strategy-based news encouraged potential voters to give a strategic interpretation of the 1992 presidential election campaign while issue-based news encouraged potential voters to provide an issue-oriented interpretation. Building on this work, Valentino, Beckmann, and Buhr (2001a, 2001b) found that reading strategic campaign coverage enhanced political cynicism, depressed retention of policy-based information, and encouraged negative commentary about the electoral process. More recently, de Vreese (2004) used a two-wave experimental design to show that exposure to "strategic" reporting about EU enlargement contributed to the development of political cynicism, though the effects of this coverage did not persist unless participants were exposed to additional news framed in a similar way.

Hypotheses

Credibility

The existing literature leaves us with competing expectations about the role that reporter and news source gender will play in shaping perceptions of media credibility. On the one hand, there is some evidence that women may be seen as less credible than men when writing about and speaking on hard political news stories such as the contraceptive mandate (Balon, Philport, and Beadle 1978; Brann and Himes 2010; Weibel, Wissmath, and Groner 2008). Exposure to an article written by a woman or an article quoting a large number of women may, therefore, undermine perceptions of credibility. On the other hand, however, the contraceptive mandate is the quintessential women's issue, and it falls squarely under the broader rubric of health-care policy, an area where women are widely believed to have more expertise than men. If respondents are presented with a female-authored article or an article quoting a large number of female sources, the alignment between stereotyped beliefs and gender cues could actually produce a boost to perceptions of credibility. We are compelled, therefore, to examine the validity of the following two hypotheses:

H1: Individuals exposed to articles written by a female reporter will rate the news story, the newspapers, and the news media in general as more credible than individuals exposed to articles written by male reporters.

H2: Individuals exposed to articles quoting a large number of female sources will rate the news story, the newspaper, and the news media in general as more credible and trustworthy than individuals exposed to articles quoting a small number of female sources.

Social identity theory (Tajfel 1979; Tajfel and Turner 1986) posits that people view members of their in-groups far more positively than they view members of their out-groups. Applying this principle to our analysis of media attitudes suggests that gender similarities between the receiver of a message and the source of a message may positively influence credibility assessments (O'Keefe 1990). However, while we have some evidence to support the idea that opposite-sex credibility evaluations tend to be less favorable than same-sex evaluations (White and Andsager 1991; Bochner 1994), some data also suggests that the reverse is true (Flanagin and Metzger 2003). As a result, we tentatively propose the following hypotheses:

H3: Women exposed to an article written by a female reporter will rate the publishing newspaper and the news media in general as more credible and trustworthy than women exposed to articles written by male reporters.

H4: Women exposed to articles featuring female sources will rate the publishing newspaper and the news media in general as more credible and trustworthy than women exposed to articles featuring male sources.

Framing

The research on framing effects leads us to formulate two distinct sets of hypotheses: one focusing on the impact of substantive news frames and another focusing on the impact of strategic game coverage. First, according to Nelson, Clawson, and Oxley (1997, 568), "substantive" frames "shape individual opinion concerning an issue by stressing specific elements or features of the broader controversy, reducing a usually complex issue down to one or two central aspects." The typical approach to studying substantive framing effects is to conduct a one-sided experiment in which participants are randomly exposed to a fabricated news story emphasizing a single set of issue-based concerns. For example, in experimental studies of American's tolerance for public demonstrations by hate groups such as the Ku Klux Klan, subjects are often presented with articles defining the issue either as a matter of free speech or as a matter of public safety. The opinions of these two groups are then compared to determine whether the media's framing matters for how the public thinks about protests and First Amendment issues (Chong and Druckman 2007; Sniderman and Theriault 2004). Using this basic approach, scholars have demonstrated framing effects across a dizzying range of political issues, including welfare (Haider-Markel and Joslyn 2001), campaign finance (Grant and Rudolph 2003), government spending (Jacoby 2000), evaluations of foreign nations (Brewer et al. 2003), and support for the Supreme Court (Nicholson and Howard 2003).

With this research as our guide, we hypothesize that exposure to different news frames will activate a different set of concerns for news readers and, in doing so, produce a different distribution of opinion on the contraceptive mandate. More specifically, we hypothesize that reading a story highlighting gendered themes such as women's health, reproductive rights, and sexual morality while ignoring religious freedom considerations will lead news audiences to be more supportive of a birth control mandate. Similarly, we hypothesize that reading a story emphasizing religious freedom to the exclusion of gendered concerns will lead news audiences to be less supportive of a birth control mandate.

> H5: Individuals exposed to a gendered news frame will express more support for a contraceptive mandate policy than individuals not exposed to a gendered news frame.
> H6: Individuals exposed to a religious freedom news frame will express less support for a contraceptive mandate policy than individuals not exposed to a religious freedom news frame.

We also suspect that the framing effects spelled out in H5 and H6 might be conditioned by individual-level predispositions. Previous research has demonstrated that the framing of a policy can mitigate the impact of framing by activating concerns about group-based interests (e.g., Kinder and Sanders 1996; Nelson and Kinder 1996) and that religious values can serve as a counterweight to media influence on issues with a strong moral dimension (Jelen and Wilcox 2003). This research leads us to the following pair of addendums to H5 and H6:

> H5a: Highly religious individuals exposed to a gendered news frame will express less support for a contraceptive mandate policy than nonreligious individuals exposed to a gendered news frame.
> H6a: Women exposed to a religious freedom news frame will express less support for a contraceptive mandate policy than men exposed to a religious freedom news frame.

Second, to examine the consequences of exposure to strategic game coverage, we test specific propositions derived from the spiral of cynicism hypothesis. As discussed above, this hypothesis suggests that the public's vanishing trust in the media and in political leaders is the result of news organizations' obsession with strategic game reporting (Cappella and Jamieson 1997; Crigler et al. 2002; Rhee 1997). Some research has even found that exposure to strategically framed coverage alienates news audiences so profoundly that it minimizes their ability to recall the factual information presented in campaign coverage (Valentino et al. 2001). Based on this work, we test the following four hypotheses about trust in the media, cynicism toward politics, retention of issue-based information, and expressions of negativity:

> H7: Individuals exposed to a strategic game news frame will view the news story, the newspaper, and the news media as less credible than individuals not exposed to a strategic game frame.
>
> H8: Individuals exposed to a strategic game news frame will express more political cynicism than individuals not exposed to a strategic game frame.
>
> H9: Individuals exposed to a strategic game news frame will retain less substantive information about the contraception issue than individuals not exposed to a strategic game frame.
>
> H10: Individuals exposed to a strategic game news frame will express more negative commentary about the contraceptive mandate policy than individuals not exposed to a strategic game frame.

Methods

Amazon's Mechanical Turk (MTurk) is an online marketplace for crowd-sourced task completion. Researchers can solicit respondents for participation in experiments by offering compensation for completing surveys. Social scientists are increasingly turning to MTurk as it provides an opportunity to easily gather samples that are only slightly less representative than national telephone surveys and significantly more representative than traditional convenience samples (Berinsky, Huber, and Lenz 2012; Weinberg, Freese, and McElhattan 2014). Perhaps more importantly, there is evidence that the results of well-established survey experiments can be replicated using the MTurk subject pool (Crump, McDonnell, and Gureckis 2013; Rand 2012). Additionally, MTurk workers are as attentive to Internet-based survey experiments as participants in lab-based studies, and their ability to follow instructions is on par with respondents in other modes of survey experimentation (Buhrmester, Kwang, and Gosling

2011; Goodman, Cryder, and Cheema 2012; Paolacci, Chandler, and Ipeirotis 2010; Grose, Malhotra, and Van Houweling 2015).

Using MTurk's recruitment platform, we conducted two separate survey experiments: one focused on the impact that a reporter's gender and the gender of quoted news sources has on an audience's perceptions of news media credibility and another focused on the attitudinal consequences of exposure to different news frames on the contraceptive mandate. The advertisements for recruitment into both of these experiments mentioned only a "brief survey" on "current events," and made no mention of politics, birth control, gender, the ACA, the media, or any other phrases that could cause selection bias in our sample. Participants were paid $0.75 for completion of our experiments, and each survey took less than 10 minutes from start to finish.

Before discussing the results of our two studies, a note of caution about MTurk survey experiments is in order. Although experimental research designs are the best way to assess whether a set of independent variables—in our case, the gender of a reporter, the gender of news sources, and the type of news frame—cause changes in the dependent variables of interest (Kinder and Palfrey 1993), they are typically limited in their ability to generalize to the real world. Two particularly important limitations on external validity exist in our experiments. First, our sample of respondents was highly unrepresentative of the American public. Gathering representative samples to read or view experimentally manipulated news coverage is a notoriously difficult task in the academic study of media effects, and most previous studies rely entirely on students enrolled in mass communications courses at one or two universities (e.g., Armstrong and McAdams 2009; Fico et al. 2004). As Sears (1986) argues, using these "narrow databases" may seriously bias the conclusions of experimental research because college students have "less-crystallized attitudes, less-formulated sense of self, stronger cognitive skills, stronger tendencies to comply with authority and more unstable peer group relationships" (515). Our use of MTurk as a recruitment mechanism was designed, in part, to avoid this "college sophomore problem" (Sears 1986). Despite greater demographic variation than found in previous experimental work, however, our samples were still younger, more educated, and more politically liberal than the population as a whole. Additionally, our sample contained more Asians and fewer blacks than we might expect from a strictly random sample of the American citizenry (see Appendix E).[1] While not necessarily surprising, these deviations from representativeness limit our ability to draw broad generalizations about the impact of gender and news frames on media perceptions, political cynicism, and policy opinions.

Second, both of our MTurk experiments involved presenting a single fabricated news article to respondents in a highly artificial context that is a very poor analog for how Americans actually gather their news. Unlike the real world, where news consumers selectively expose themselves to reporting on a very narrow range of topics from a very narrow range of sources, our respondents were explicitly asked to read one article on an issue of our choosing during a 10-minute survey experiment. If, as previous research suggests, framing effects depend on a mix of factors, including the strength and repetition of the frame, the competitive environment, and the individual news consumer's interest in the topic under examination, our results about news frames may not generalize to the broader public very well. The same caveats would apply to our conclusions about authorship and sourcing. Future work, therefore, should build on the results presented here by collecting more representative samples and tracking the effects of news consumption in less artificial environments.

With these caveats in mind, we discuss the design and results for each of our two experiments below.

Experiment #1—Reporter and Source Gender

Our first MTurk experiment, fielded between July 18 and July 21, 2017, attracted 378 respondents. In this experiment, participants were directed to a mock screen shot of a hypothetical newspaper article concerning the impact of the ACA's contraceptive mandate on the rate of abortions in the United States. The article, which was titled "Abortion Rates Decline to Historic Low, with Obamacare a Likely Contributor, Study Says," was based substantively and stylistically on an actual story published by the *Los Angeles Times* (see Appendix C). In addition to clearly displaying a reporter byline and photograph immediately under the title, each treatment article included 12 quotations attributed to a mix of politicians, researchers, and interest-group representatives (e.g., "State Assembly Representative," "obstetrician," "spokesperson for Americans United for Life"). Consistent with the formatting of the original *Los Angeles Times* story, each treatment article also featured a photograph of a pregnant woman and of birth control pills. The formatting of this article was designed to enhance the external validity of our experiment by mimicking the appearance of a typical online news story.

Using this setup, we manipulated the gender of the article's reporter by switching the name and photograph provided in the byline from a stereotypical male name and image (i.e., "Kevin Ward" presented alongside a white male headshot) to a stereotypical female name and image (i.e., "Rachel Ward" presented alongside a white female headshot).[2] Similarly, we manipulated the gender of the article's news sources by assigning either stereotypically male names (e.g., "Jason Bradley," "David Williams," "Jonathan Overton") or stereotypically female names (e.g., "Jennifer Bradley," "Diane Williams," "Linda Overton") to the individuals quoted in the story.[3] Each of the articles used in our experiment contained quotes attributed to entirely male names, entirely female names, or an even mix of male and female names. The result of these various manipulations created six distinct and mutually exclusive treatment conditions:

(1) a news article written by a female author featuring all female sources;
(2) a news article written by a female author featuring all male sources;
(3) a news article written by a female author featuring a mix of female and male sources;
(4) a news article written by a male author featuring all male sources;
(5) a news article written by a male author featuring all female sources; and
(6) a news article written by a male author featuring a mix of female and male sources.

Just prior to being randomly assigned to read one of these six hypothetical news stories, we instructed our respondents to "read the following article very carefully from start to finish." To avoid priming respondents about the purposes of the experiment and to prevent them from paying more attention to the reporter's gender and the gender of the quoted sources, we did not include any special instructions to focus on these aspects of the story. In addition, we attempted to mask our study's intentions by not presenting respondents with any political or demographic questions prior to the administration of our experiment. In fact, respondents were only asked four generic questions about their news consumption habits before receiving the treatment article.

Immediately after reading our hypothetical news story, respondents were asked to identify the gender of the report's author and approximately how many of the quoted individuals in the story were women. These manipulation check items were then followed by a series of questions designed to tap respondents' perceptions of news story, newspaper, and news media credibility. Approaches for measuring these different kinds of credibility have varied widely over the years (see, e.g., Bucy 2003; Shaw 1973; Gaziano and McGrath 1986; Meyer 1988; Flanagin and Metzger 2000; Johnson and Kaye 1998), and each new empirical study on media attitudes seems to rely on its own idiosyncratic mix of survey questions (Appelman and Sundar 2015). To measure the respondents' perceptions of the treatment article, we adopted a subset of the 13 items used in Sternadori and Thorson's (2009) work on news credibility. Specifically, we asked our subjects for their level of agreement with the following four statements: (1) "The story was complete"; (2) "The story was fair"; (3) "The story was interesting"; (4) "The story was informative." Responses were given on a 5-point Likert scale ranging from 1 (strongly agree) to 5 (strongly disagree) and then added to create a "News Story Credibility" Index. Following Meyer (1988) and Fico, Richardson, and Edwards (2004), our measure of newspaper credibility was created from five items asking participants to rate on a 1–5 Likert scale how much they agreed with the statement that the newspaper that published the article they just read was "fair," "biased," "accurate," and "trustworthy," and "told the whole story."[4] Responses to each of these items were summed to form an additive "Newspaper Credibility Index."[5] Finally, we measured attitudes toward the news media in general by asking respondents, "How much trust and confidence do you have in the mass media—such as newspapers, TV, and radio—when it comes to reporting the news fully, accurately, and fairly?"

A major concern with online experiments is that subjects will not pay close enough attention to "receive" the intended treatments. To control for a lack of attentiveness among our subjects, our experiments included two separate attention check items. Near the end of the survey, respondents were presented with the following "question": "to help us calibrate our survey, please leave the following blank and do not select an answer." Respondents who were not carefully reading each question might fail to leave this blank. Additionally, the surveys concluded with a self-reported measure of distraction.[6] Together, these attention checks allow us to refine the sample and limit our analysis only to those respondents who were paying close attention to the task at hand.

Experiment #2—Substantive and Strategic Game Frames

Our second MTurk experiment, fielded between August 1 and August 8, 2017, attracted 267 respondents. Similar to our study on authorship and sourcing, the focal point of our framing experiment was a fabricated newspaper article written in the tone and displayed in the style of the *Los Angeles Times*. Instead of identifying an individual reporter under the headline, each article's byline attributed the report to anonymous journalists in the "Capitol Staff" (see Appendix D). Each of our 700-word treatment articles begins by describing a campaign speech in which one of the candidates for a state senate seat announces their position on a fake bill to instate a contraceptive mandate (SB 122). After this introductory paragraph, the article quotes a contrasting message on the contraceptive mandate from a press release issued by the candidate's opponent. A fictitious expert on political campaigns ("Professor David Stuart" of the "University of California") then responds to the comments and interprets the motivations behind the candidates raising the issue. The treatment articles each end with approximately 300 words of common text detailing facts about contraception use, health insurance costs, and the history of the legislative contraceptive mandates at the state and federal levels.[7] The experimental manipulations described below consisted only of changing each article's title, introductory paragraphs, and expert comments.

Given our interest in assessing the effect of media framing choices on news readers' political attitudes, we created three different treatment articles—each emphasizing different aspects of the debate over the contraceptive mandate while also including the common content described above. Using the approach spelled out in Valentino et al.'s (2001) experimental work, we produced a strategic game frame treatment article that included a discussion of politicians' tactical motivations, an analysis of public opinion polling, and the use of war and sports metaphors. Specifically, our strategic game article, which we chose to title "Miller and Peterson Go to War Over Birth Control Mandate," began with a sentence using the language of battle: "State Senator John Miller today blasted his opponent, local businessman Steven Peterson, as 'cowardly' and pledged his support for SB 122—a proposed law requiring that all employers that provide health insurance to their employees cover the entire cost of contraceptives in their health insurance plans." Miller is then described as "going on the attack" and taking a "no holds barred, bare knuckled approach in the increasingly contentious fight to force health insurers to provide contraceptive coverage for women." Miller is then quoted as telling the crowd that "We will not be defeated. We are going to win." Similar war and sports metaphors were employed to discuss Miller's opponent, local businessman Steven Peterson, and his press release on SB 122.[8]

A major component of the strategic game frame is an emphasis on polling and on the calculating nature of politicians. To capture these dimensions of coverage, we included an entire paragraph discussing a new survey from the fictitious "Public Opinion Institute." The article's discussion of these polling results were followed by an analysis of how both candidates "have reputations as shrewd politicians who know how to use the health care and birth control issues to gain votes." A quote from our imaginary expert, "University of California political scientist David Stuart," then stated, "This is a war. Both sides see the contraceptive mandate issue as a good way to win votes for themselves and bury their opponent." The article concluded with the 300 words of shared content on contraception use, health insurance costs, and the history of contraceptive mandates.

In addition to this strategic game frame treatment, we created two separate "sincere" (Valentino et al. 2001) and substantive (Entman, 2004) news articles: one emphasizing religious freedom and the other emphasizing women's health, reproductive rights, and sexual morality. Unlike the strategic game frame articles, these substantively framed articles contained no discussions of politicians' strategic motivations, no mention of public opinion polling, and no war or sports metaphors. Instead, the titles of these two articles reflected substantive concerns about the contraceptive mandate—"Women's Health Drives Disagreement over Proposed Birth Control Mandate" and "Religious Freedom Drives Disagreement over Proposed Birth Control Mandate"—and the candidates were described as sincere, not calculating, in their approach to the issue (e.g., "Both have repeatedly stated that they see access to contraception as an important public health issue" and "It is uncommon to have a race where both candidates care so deeply about an issue"). In the religious freedom treatment article, the narrative and quotations were centered entirely on "the Constitution," "the First Amendment's freedom of religion," and "religious objections" to the contraceptive mandate. No references were made to women's health, reproductive rights, or sexual morality. By contrast, in the gendered treatment article, the narrative and quotations were focused entirely on "preventative care," "access to contraception," and "the reproductive autonomy of all women." No references were made in this article to religious freedom. Once again, with the exception of the titles, the introductory paragraphs, and expert comments, the stories in each of the three treatment conditions were identical.

These manipulations created three possible treatments: (1) the strategic game frame news article, (2) the substantive and sincere religious freedom frame news article, and (3) the substantive and sincere gendered news article. We also chose to include a control group that received an article containing only the 300 words of factual content common to both the strategic game and gendered news articles (titled "Birth Control Mandate an Ongoing Issue"). The inclusion of this group allows us to establish an overall treatment effect for each of the three different frames in our experiment (Chong and Druckman 2007; Druckman 2001).

After reading the article, respondents in our treatment groups were presented with the same battery of questions about news story, newspaper and news media credibility posed to participants in our authorship and sourcing experiment. In addition, we also asked our respondents a series of questions designed to tap feelings of political cynicism. Although scholarly consensus is lacking on how to best measure political cynicism (Acock, Clark, and Stewart 1985; Craig, Niemi, and Silver 1990), a number of experimental studies on the consequences of exposure to strategic game coverage have used a four-item index composed of questions about the character and motivations of elected officials (Cappella and Jamieson 1997; de Vreese 2004). Adapting the specific content of these four-item indices for the particulars of the contraceptive mandate debate, we asked respondents how strongly they agreed or disagreed with the following statements: (1) "Politicians are too superficial when dealing with contraception issues"; (2) "Politicians are too concerned with public opinion about contraception"; (3) "The debate about contraception is more about strategy than content"; and (4) "Politicians are clear and honest in their arguments about contraception." The responses were recoded and averaged to form a scale of political cynicism ranging from 1 to 5.

We measured policy-specific information retention by tracking how well respondents could correctly answer factual questions derived from material found in the treatment articles. Each of the treatment articles mentioned that "99% of women aged 15–44 who have ever had sexual intercourse have used at least one contraceptive method," that "there are 10 million women on the birth control pill in the United States," and that "[p]rior to the passage of the Affordable Care Act (ACA) in 2010, twenty-eight states had mandates requiring health insurance providers to cover the cost of prescription contraceptives." We included three questions in the survey questionnaire that required respondents to accurately identify these statistics from among four response alternatives. Based on these responses, each respondent was given an information retention score ranging from 0 to 3.

Finally, to test the effect of substantive (Entman 2004) and strategic game frames on opinions toward birth control policy, we presented respondents with two traditional, close-ended survey questions about the contraceptive mandate and one open-ended, thought listing item. Our close-ended questions were modeled closely after the polling discussed in chapter 8. Specifically, we asked, (1) "Do you think religious-affiliated organizations, such as churches and hospitals, should have to cover the cost of prescription birth control for their female employees as part of their health insurance plans or should religious-affiliated organizations be able to opt out of covering that, based on religious objections?"; and (2) "What about companies and nonreligious organizations? Do you think these employers should have to cover the cost of prescription birth control for their female employees as part of their health insurance plans or should these employers be able to opt out of covering that, based on religious objections?"

In an attempt to more qualitatively measure reactions to different framings of the contraceptive mandate, we followed these close-ended questions with an open-ended thought-listing question. Following the lead of other experimental studies on media framing effects (e.g., De Vreese 2004; Price et al. 1997; Tewksbury et al. 2000; Valentino, Beckmann, and Buhr 2001a; Valkenburg, Semetko, and de Vreese 1999), we asked, "We are interested to hear how you think about laws requiring religious organizations and employers to cover the cost of prescription birth control for their female employees (i.e., the 'contraceptive mandate'). Please briefly list your thoughts and feelings about the contraceptive mandate." The responses to this item were then coded for whether they mentioned religious freedom, gendered concerns (e.g., women's health, reproductive rights, sexual morality), or strategic political considerations.[9] Each response was also coded for the presence of negativity.[10] Examples of each response category are displayed in Table 9.1.

Table 9.1 **Open-Ended Responses**

	Example of Open-Ended Responses
Gendered commentary	"I am glad to see that women's health is being taken seriously finally. Women need birth control a lot more than men need Viagra but somehow men can get their Viagra but women can't get birth control? That is just unfair and should be stopped immediately."
	"This is ridiculous. Try putting 'Viagra' on that list and now suddenly the politicians will have a different story. This is about controlling women, plain and simple."
Religious freedom commentary	"There is a war on religion and it is unfair with the 1st Amendment. Stop trying to force people to pay for things that violate their bible's commandments."
	"The contraceptive mandates basically makes religious individuals accessories to the crime of murder, in my opinion. It is an utterly terrible blow to religious freedom."
Strategic political commentary	"We need less polarization in this country. This issue makes things worse."
	"I don't understand why it can't be required that people pay a copay. I used to pay $30 out of pocket for my pills and I managed to stay on them and not get pregnant. I think people need to be more responsible for themselves and I also think this is a nonissue that involves a lot of virtue signaling and showboating."
Negative commentary	"Religion is made up bullcrap. The GOP believing in some leper-healing carpenter shouldn't matter. All healthcare, including birth control, should be universal."
	"They are not exempt from the law. I am a firm believer that churches should pay tax in this day and age, but apparently conservative dipshits disagree."

Results

Experiment #1—Reporter and Source Gender

We designed our first MTurk study to shed light on how a reporter's gender and the gender of sources quoted in an article about the contraceptive mandate might influence reader perceptions of news story, newspaper, and news media credibility. Three main findings emerged from our experimental manipulations. First, female perceptions of news story, newspaper, and news media credibility were significantly higher after reading an article written by a woman than they were after reading an article written by a man. Consistent with the predictions spelled out in H3, women exposed to a female-authored article scored higher on the News Story Credibility Index, the Newspaper Credibility Index, and the single-item measure of general news media trust than women exposed to a male-authored article. As Figure 9.1 shows, the differences in media credibility assessments between women in our three "female author" treatment conditions and our three "male author" treatment conditions were relatively small but consistently positive and statistically significant. There appears to be, in other words, clear evidence of a "similarity effect" (Flanagin and Metzger 2003) or "gender

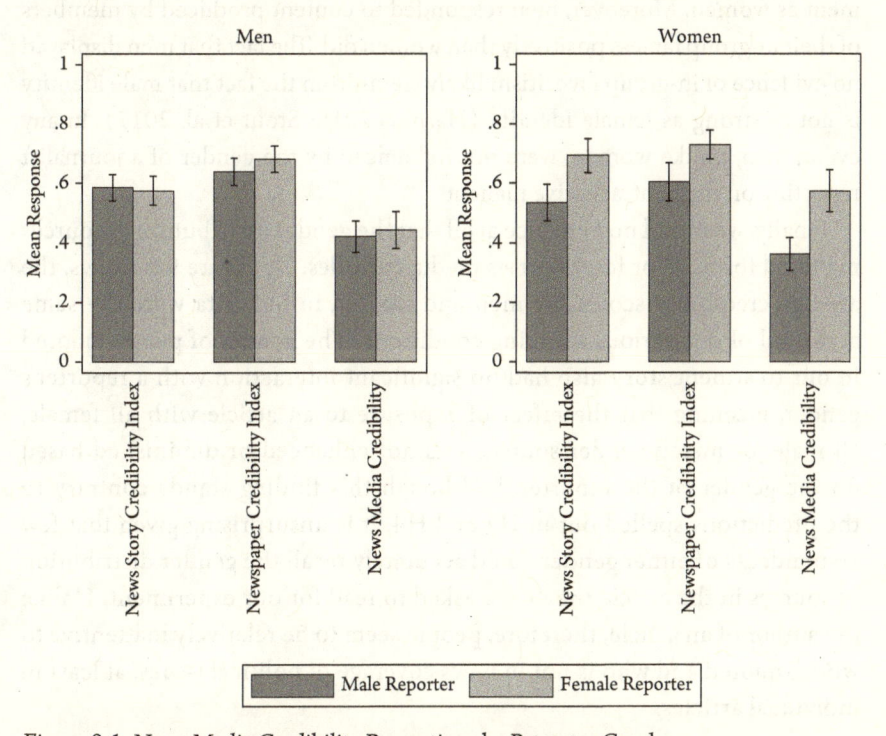

Figure 9.1 News Media Credibility Perceptions by Reporter Gender

affinity effect" (Dolan 2008) operating for women in the news media's reporting on contraception issues.

Second, men's media attitudes were entirely unaffected by the gender of an article's reporter. As Figure 9.1 shows, men reading an article attributed to a female reporter were statistically indistinguishable in their perceptions of media credibility from men reading an article attributed to a male reporter. There are, of course, two possible explanations for the attitudinal similarities among men in our various treatment groups. On the one hand, authorship may not shape male news media attitudes in the same way that it shaped female news media attitudes because men may have not noticed the reporter's gender as frequently as women did. As Flanagin and Metzger (2003) point out, "similarity effects" or "gender affinity effects" (Dolan 2008) can only emerge when receivers of a message actually recognize that a message sender is substantially similar to them. On the other hand, it is possible that men could have noticed the reporter's gender but did not let this color their perception of credibility. Our data strongly suggest the latter explanation. Contrary to previous research showing that female audiences are more aware than male audiences of how often women appear in news stories (Grabe, Samson, Zelenkauskaite, and Yegiyan 2011; Len-Rios, Rodgers, Thorson, and Yoon 2005), we found that just as many men correctly identified their reporter's gender in our MTurk experiment as women. Moreover, men responded to content produced by members of their in-group far less positively than women did. The fact that men displayed no evidence of in-group favoritism likely stems from the fact that male identity is not as strong as female identity (Harnois 2015; Stout et al. 2017). In any event, men, unlike women, were not influenced by the gender of a journalist reporting on the contraceptive mandate.

Finally, we found no evidence at all that the gender distribution of sources mattered for male or female news media attitudes. As Figure 9.2 shows, the average credibility scores for men and women in our data were the same across all of our various sourcing conditions. The gender of people quoted in our treatment story also had no significant interaction with a reporter's gender, meaning that the effect of exposure to an article with all female, all male, or mixed-gender sources was not enhanced or diminished based on the gender of the reporter.[11] Although this finding stands contrary to the predictions spelled out in H2 and H4, it is unsurprising given that few respondents of either gender could accurately recall the gender distribution of sources in the article they were asked to read for our experiment. Unlike the author of an article, therefore, people seem to be relatively inattentive to who is quoted and who is not in news coverage of political issues, at least in individual articles.

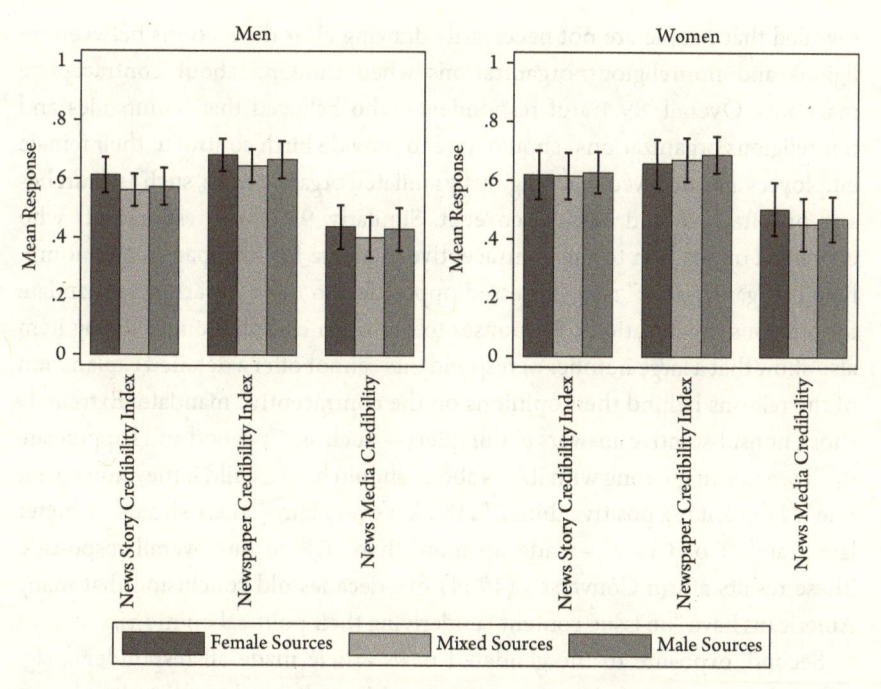

Figure 9.2 News Media Credibility Perceptions by Source Gender

Experiment #2—Substantive and Strategic Game Frames

Substantive Frames and Policy Opinions

In their review of decades of empirical research on media effects, Chong and Druckman (2007, 109) wrote, "Frames in communication matter—that is, they affect attitudes and behaviors." We designed our second experiment to test this proposition in the context of news coverage about the contraceptive mandate. To be more precise, our second MTurk experiment aimed to assess whether substantive news frames shape policy opinions on birth control issues and how strategic game news frames color perceptions of politicians and the news media. Our selection of specific substantive and strategic game frames for this experiment were designed to help us better understand the dynamics of public opinion on birth control issues (see chapter 8) by matching the treatments to the content of actual news reports on the ACA's contraceptive mandate (described in detail in chapter 7).

Our experimental data revealed three things in particular about the consequences of the news media's substantive framing for policy views on the contraceptive mandate. First, many Americans do not have particularly nuanced or well-developed views on the contraceptive mandate. Our close-ended items revealed that people are not necessarily drawing clear distinctions between religious and nonreligious organizations when thinking about contraceptive mandates. Overall, 89.4% of respondents who believed that "companies and nonreligious organizations" should have to provide birth control to their female employees also believed that religiously affiliated organizations, such as churches and hospitals, should have to cover it. Similarly, 95.7% of respondents who expressed opposition to the contraceptive mandate for "companies and nonreligious organizations" also expressed opposition to the contraceptive mandate for religious organizations. Responses to our open-ended, thought-listing item also show that a large number of respondents cannot offer a detailed explanation of the reasons behind their opinions on the contraceptive mandate. Extremely short, nonsubstantive answers to our query—such as, "It's good and I appreciate it," "I see nothing wrong with it," "Nobody should have a child if they don't want one," "I think it is a positive thing," "I think it's very fair," "There should be better laws," and "Don't care"—made up more than 10% of our overall responses. These results affirm Converse's (1964) five-decades-old conclusion that many Americans have "no issue content" underlying their political opinions.

Second, exposure to the gendered news article made all respondents significantly more supportive of a policy requiring religiously affiliated and nonreligious organizations to cover the cost of prescription birth control for their female employees as part of their health insurance plans. Respondents asked to read a news story where women's health, reproductive rights, and morality were emphasized to the exclusion of other considerations endorsed the contraceptive mandate for all organizations at a much higher rate (mean of index = 0.80) than those asked to read a news story with no mention of these considerations (mean of index = 0.55). As Figure 9.3 shows, these overall differences were not the result of women or the nonreligious responding more to the article's framing than men or the highly religious. Indeed, relative to the control group, the average support among both male and female respondents in the gendered coverage condition increased by more than 0.2 on our 0 to 1 index of opinions on the contraceptive mandate. Similarly, the average support among both the secular and the devout respondents in the gendered condition also increased by more than 0.2 relative to the no-frame condition. In other words, when gendered concerns became the "central organizing idea or story line" (Gamson and Modigliani 1987, 143) about the contraception mandate, all people—men and women, the religious and the secular—became more supportive of the policy.

Additionally, respondents in our gendered frame condition were much more likely than respondents in our other experimental conditions to mention gendered considerations as a factor influencing their opinions on the contraceptive mandate. Indeed, while mentions of "women's health care," "women's autonomy," and "sexual health" were very common across all experimental conditions

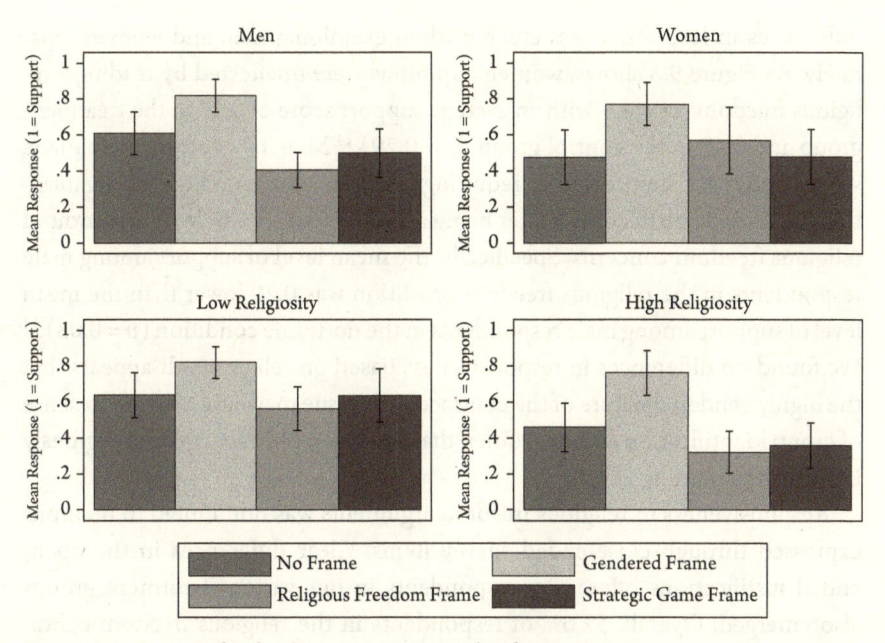

Figure 9.3 Support for the Contraceptive Mandate by News Frame

(being mentioned in 36.1% of our open-ended questions), they were an especially important component of the explanations offered by respondents reading an article focused exclusively on gendered themes. Mimicking the results of our close-ended responses, evidence of a framing effect in our open-ended items was not limited to a single subset of respondents. Women, men, the most religious, and the least religious members of our sample all showed high levels of responsiveness to the gendered framing presented by our news article—with treatment group subjects citing "women's health" and "reproductive rights" considerations an average of 20% more than control group subjects. Perhaps most importantly, mentioning gendered considerations as a factor in one's thinking about the contraceptive mandate was strongly, significantly, and positively correlated with support for the policy ($p = 0.00$).[12] Together, the results of our close-ended and open-ended survey items suggest that news reports emphasizing the gendered components of the contraceptive mandate exert a powerful influence on the public's thinking about the issue.

Third, consistent with the idea that gender acts as conditioning predisposition, exposure to an article about how religious freedom factors into the debate over insurance coverage of birth control mattered for the policy opinions of men but not women. While the religious freedom treatment and the no-frame control groups in our overall sample were statistically indistinguishable from each other in terms of their opinions about the contraceptive mandate (0.44 and 0.55 average levels of support for the policies, respectively), pronounced gender differences in responsiveness emerge when examining men and women separately. As Figure 9.3 shows, women's opinions were unaffected by reading a religious freedom article—with an average support score of 0.57 in the treatment group and 0.48 in the control group ($p = 0.29$).[13] Men, by contrast, were made significantly less supportive of requiring religious and nonreligious organizations to provide birth control after being asked to read an article framed around religious freedom concerns. Specifically, the mean level of support among male respondents in the religious freedom condition was 0.20 lower than the mean level of support among male respondents in the no-frame condition ($p = 0.03$).[14] We found no differences in responsiveness based on religiosity. It appears that the highly gendered nature of the contraception issue may have activated a sense of group identification among women that acted as a bulwark against religiously based media framing effects.

Responsiveness to religious freedom arguments was not limited to opinions expressed through close-ended survey items. Clear differences in the open-ended justifications offered by respondents in our various treatment groups also emerged. Overall, 52.6% of respondents in the religious freedom condition mentioned considerations such as the "First Amendment," "church and state," and "freedom of religion," compared to only 22.7% of respondents in the control condition, 20.0% of respondents in the strategic game condition, and 21.5% of respondents in the gendered condition. Much like the effect of reading a gendered article on discussions of women's health and reproductive rights concerns, exposure to a religious freedom news story produced a uniform tendency among men, women, the religious, and the secular to mention religious liberty as an important part of their thinking about the contraceptive mandate. Women in our experiment were particularly affected by religious freedom arguments; discussions of religious liberty more than doubled among our female respondents in our religious freedom condition relative to the control group (46.5% to 22.5%).

Mentions of religion among women, however, were mostly dismissive in tone and made primarily to undermine the legitimacy of religious concerns in the policy debate. Indeed, contrary to discussions of religious freedom among male, religious, and nonreligious respondents, mentions of religious freedom made by female respondents were entirely uncorrelated with opposition to the contraceptive mandate ($p = 0.21$).[15] A few examples of the open-ended responses illustrate the way many women in our sample invoked religious liberty arguments in order to reject them. According to one female respondent in our religious freedom condition, "It [birth control] is health care and should not be treated differently than any other medication. Religious freedom is less important than my health." As another female respondent put it, "I feel that contraception is clearly part of health care, and as such should be covered for all women.

Religious organizations refusing to cover those costs for their employees are in fact imposing their religious stance on others, who might even be of another religion. I find that imposition to be at least as much of a problem, or worse, than organizations having to protect their employees' well-being." Overall, therefore, religious freedom was a much less convincing argument about the contraceptive mandate among women than among men.

Strategic Game Frame, Credibility Assessments, and Political Cynicism

The spiral of cynicism hypothesis states that public distrust in journalists and elected officials is fueled by the media's consistent framing of political news as a strategic game. In our framing experiment, we tested this hypothesis by exposing respondents to a contrived news story that used polling data and war metaphors to depict competing politicians either as strategic actors, motivated exclusively by electoral success, or as sincere public servants, motivated by a desire to represent the interests of their constituents. Because assignment to the treatment and control groups was determined by random assignment, an intuitive way to discuss the results of our experimental manipulation is in the form of a multiple regression. Within the regression models, each of the treatment conditions can be represented by a simple dummy variable, which is coded 1 if the respondent received the treatment in question and 0 if the respondent did not receive the treatment. As a result of the fact that the strategic game condition is excluded from the model, the coefficient for each of the dummy variables represents the differences in means between the particular treatment and strategic game groups (Ladd 2010). The results of these analyses are presented in Table 9.2.[16]

Our experimental manipulation of news frames revealed clear evidence in favor of the predictions spelled out in H7 and H8. Respondents in the strategic game framing condition scored significantly lower (indicated by the positive coefficients in Table 9.2) than respondents in all three of our other experimental conditions on the News Story Credibility Index, the Newspaper Credibility Index, and the measure of general news media trust. Strategic game respondents also scored much higher on our measure of political cynicism than respondents in our pure control group and substantive treatment conditions. Notably, no meaningful differences in perceptions of news media credibility or feelings of political cynicism occurred between respondents in the religious freedom and gendered treatment groups. There were, however, significant differences between respondents in both of these substantive coverage conditions and in the pure control group. As Table 9.2 also shows, exposure to the religious freedom and gendered articles had a much larger impact on perceptions of news media credibility and feelings of political cynicism than exposure to the frameless control article. Although we cannot definitively attribute this difference to any one

Table 9.2 **Media Attitudes and Political Cynicism by News Frame**

	News Story Credibility Index	Newspaper Credibility Index	News Media Trust	Political Cynicism
No frame	0.139***	0.070+	0.118*	−0.124**
	(0.039)	(0.039)	(0.055)	(0.038)
Religious freedom frame	0.203***	0.112**	0.240***	−0.192***
	(0.039)	(0.038)	(0.055)	(0.038)
Gendered frame	0.169***	0.145***	0.224***	−0.186***
	(0.040)	(0.039)	(0.055)	(0.039)
Constant	0.360***	0.389***	0.352***	0.692***
	(0.050)	(0.049)	(0.071)	(0.049)
N	246	246	246	246
adj. R^2	0.126	0.058	0.296	0.101

Note: Standard errors in parentheses. All models also included a control for gender in order to correct for unbalanced assignment to treatment conditions.

+$p < 0.10$, * $p < 0.05$, ** $p < 0.01$, *** $p < 0.001$

factor, it seems likely that the artificial nature of the no-frame control article led to the slightly lower levels of attitude change. Overall, however, we can conclude that strategic game coverage of the birth control mandate seriously undermines the public's trust in politicians as well as the press.

Implied by the spiral of cynicism hypothesis is that strategic game coverage might coarsen political discourse by exacerbating the public's feelings of frustration with politics. Our open-ended, thought-listing question allowed us to explore this possibility by comparing the reactions of respondents exposed to a strategic game story to the reactions of respondents exposed to other kinds of news articles. Although name-calling, swearing, and hyperbolic accusations were relatively rare in our data (appearing in only 13.6% of responses overall), they were most commonly found in the answers provided by respondents asked to read strategic game coverage of the contraception mandate (appearing in 19.3% of their responses). One respondent in our strategic game condition, for example, wrote, "Conservatives feel these mandates encroach upon their religious freedoms. By that they mean I'm christian and therefore dumber than fuck. If you believe litteraly [sic] in a god than in my opinion you arent capable of critical thought on these issues. . . . Does anyone else have a problem with the mandates?" Another wrote, "I also think this is a non issue that involves a lot of virtue signaling and showboating. The people who really need to use birth control, the extremely poor with four or five kids who live off the government, won't go near a pack of birth control pills. But no one wants to talk about that."

Strategic game news frames, in short, appear to produce far more negativity than substantive frames.

Closely related to this kind of negativity are assessments that issues matter only for their political consequences. Much like negative commentary, discussions of such political considerations were very rare in our open-ended responses (only 4.2% of all responses), but when they appeared, they were found almost entirely in the strategic game condition (7.4% of responses). One respondent in the strategic game condition, for example, used the open-ended response to claim, "Democrats are trying to divide men and women. They first used abortion and now they are trying to use this issue also. Government should keep out of this and people should pay for their own birth control." Another respondent asserted, "This whole issue is a ploy by Democrats to further divide the country. It is a wedge issue that they are using to win votes with women." As Valentino et al. (2001a, 349) argued, "Strategic news tends to propagate strategic thinking about politics."

Related to concerns about news media credibility, political cynicism, and negativity, some observers worry that news organizations fail to fulfill one of their primary democratic functions—informing the public—when they deemphasize the substantive dimensions of policy debates. Our experimental results provide only the most tentative of validation for these concerns. We found that while reading strategic game coverage instead of substantive reporting on the contraceptive mandate did, in fact, depress information retention among our respondents, the differences were slightly smaller than what would be required to reach conventional levels of statistical significance. Specifically, respondents in our strategic game condition correctly answered an average of 0.30 fewer factual questions than respondents in our women's health and reproductive rights condition ($p = 0.07$) and an average of 0.28 fewer factual questions than respondents in our religious freedom condition ($p = 0.08$).[17] Respondents in the no-frame control group averaged 0.55 more correct answers than respondents in the strategic game condition ($p = 0.00$).[18] Overall, therefore, our results are very similar to experimental findings presented elsewhere (Valentino et al. 2001), and the strategic game frame does appear to slightly reduce the likelihood that citizens remember the policy-relevant information presented in news stories.

Discussion

The results presented above shed important light on the dynamics of public opinion about the contraceptive mandate. As detailed in the previous chapter, public support for requiring religious and nonreligious organizations to provide birth control for their employees has varied fairly dramatically over time and across surveys. The findings presented here strongly suggest that changes in the dominant media narrative on the contraceptive mandate may be behind these variations. Consistent with the idea that news frames change political opinions by altering the underlying considerations used in one's evaluation of an issue (e.g., Berelson et al. 1954, 253–73; Nelson et al. 1997; Scheufele 1999, 117; Zaller 1992), we found that exposure to gendered and religious freedom arguments shifted the opinions and considerations of our experimental subjects. When asked to read an article that highlighted only gendered themes, our respondents expressed more support for the contraceptive mandate and became much more likely to identify women's health and reproductive rights as reasons for their support. When asked to read an article that highlighted only religious freedom concerns, nonfemale respondents expressed more opposition to the contraceptive mandate and all respondents became much more likely to discuss the role of religious liberty in their thinking about the policy. For most Americans, it appears that both religious freedom and gendered concerns are legitimate and persuasive considerations that can be easily brought to the "top of the head" (Zaller 1992) by news organizations covering the debate over who should pay for contraception.

In light of these findings, fluctuations in public backing for the contraceptive mandate are probably best understood as a response to the media's frequently changing framing of the issue. Our content analysis of newspaper coverage between August 2011 and August 2012 (chapter 7) showed that news reports emphasized different aspects of the contraceptive mandate at different moments in time. Specifically, the prominence of the religious freedom and reproductive rights frames ebbed and flowed significantly during the course of our one-year study—with reproductive rights receiving more attention early in the debate and religious freedom receiving more attention later. Assuming that these particular news frames also advanced and receded at other points in the long debate over contraception, we may be able to understand most of the instability in public opinion through an analysis of media coverage. Unfortunately, surveys on the contraceptive mandate were not conducted at narrow enough time intervals over the last decade to definitively identify a correlation between news frames and public opinion. When considered alongside our experimental results, however, the fact that both public opinion and news frames about the contraceptive mandate fluctuate considerably over time raises the strong possibility that public support shifts based on which aspects of the issue receive the most media attention and which aspects are highlighted in survey questions.

The fact that media frames can exert a powerful influence over the policy opinions of news consumers by promoting "particular definitions and interpretations of political issues" (Shah et al. 2002, 343) affirm the wisdom of the aggressive media-oriented strategies of Planned Parenthood and the United

States Conference of Catholic Bishops. As detailed in chapter 7, both of these well-financed interest groups attempted to reframe news coverage of the ACA's birth control mandate through a series of press releases, "backgrounders" and formal interviews. More specifically, between August 2011 and August 2012 each organization sent out, on average, well over one press release per month on the mandate—with 88.4% of press releases from the USCCB focusing on religious freedom and 83.3% of press releases from Planned Parenthood focusing on either women's health (50%) or reproductive rights (33.3%). If exposure to a single fabricated news article in the artificial context of an online survey experiment can significantly affect both the considerations people bring to bear in their thinking on birth control issues and on their overall opinions on these issues, interest groups have powerful incentives to lobby journalists about their reporting.

The findings discussed above also speak to important debates about the American public's growing distrust of the news media. Data from respected polling organizations, such Gallup and the General Social Survey, show that trust in the press as an institution has dropped more than 30 percentage points over the past 40 years, implying that the American public is far more skeptical about what they see and read in the news today than they were in the 1970s, 1980s, and 1990s (Cook and Gronke 2001; Fallows 1997 Gronke and Cook 2007; Ladd 2010). Moreover, survey evidence shows that the public's distrust is not limited to the news media as an institution. According to the Pew Research Center's polling, credibility scores for major newspapers have also suffered broad-based declines in recent years. Indeed, the "believability rating" for every national newspaper tracked by Pew has suffered a double-digit drop over the last decade. Positive believability ratings for the *Wall Street Journal* fell from 77% in 2002 to 58% in 2012. *USA Today*'s believability ratings dropped by a comparable rate—from 67% to 49% between 2002 and 2012.

Unsurprisingly, a great deal of research in political science, journalism, and mass communication has attempted to uncover the origins of these increasingly negative evaluations. Yet "there is no scholarly consensus on which factors shape attitudes toward the news media and thus might help to explain why these attitudes have become so negative over time" (Ladd 2009, 30). The findings presented above directly contribute to this line of academic inquiry by identifying the important role that byline diversity may be playing in driving the American public's growing antipathy for the news media. Our experimental results show clear evidence that the relatively tiny number of female-authored reports on "women's issues" such as the contraceptive mandate hurts overall perceptions of media credibility by preventing news organizations from taking advantage of the similarity (Flanagin and Metzger 2003) or gender affinity (Dolan 2008) effects that boost trust among female news consumers.

Additionally, given that female journalists were significantly less likely than male journalists to author the kinds of strategically framed news reports (chapter 8) that dampened credibility assessments among our experimental subjects, a lack of byline diversity is also indirectly reducing the media's amount of believability. When coupled with evidence that women's issues, such as abortion, health care reform, and the wage gap, have occupied an increasingly prominent position on the nation's political agenda, our findings suggest that scholars turn their attention toward the minimal amounts of byline diversity when attempting to explain the news media's well-documented credibility problems.

With that said, promoting gender parity in newspaper bylines alone is unlikely to be an effective panacea for the ailing American press. Journalistic norms compel women to frame many of their stories around the political horserace, widespread gender stereotypes may mean that female reporters actually hurt (rather than help) credibility assessments by reporting on nonwomen's issues, and most of the factors shown to enhance public skepticism toward the press—ranging from anonymous comments on newspaper websites (Wallsten and Tarsi 2016) to disparaging comments from politicians (Ladd 2010)—have nothing to do with gender diversity. In other words, while growing disaffection with the media may be partly a result of the fact that women are underrepresented in political reporting on women's issues, larger issues are clearly at work, and diversifying newsrooms is no silver bullet.

While our findings bolster the case for studying byline diversity as a factor driving declining media perceptions, they undermine the case for sourcing diversity. As mentioned in chapter 6, Vos and Wolfgang (2016) suggest that the growing disconnect between the media and the American public could be a function of the fact that journalists often fail to quote a large number of diverse sources when reporting the news. Our data contained very little to support this line of thinking. Despite the fact that half of the American public claims that "the sources a story cites" has a "large impact" on whether they think a news story is trustworthy (Barthel and Mitchell 2017), very few respondents in our survey experiment could correctly identify the gender breakdown of the people quoted in our contraceptive mandate articles. If news audiences are so inattentive to the gender of quoted news sources that they fail to recognize when an article on a woman's issue references only men or only women, we have to question whether diversifying sourcing practices would truly bolster the media's credibility. More, regardless of whether they correctly recalled the gender distribution of news sources, we found no direct evidence that our respondents' perceptions of news story, newspaper, or news media credibility were influenced by who was quoted.

A one-time exposure to a fabricated news article is, of course, a very poor proxy for the way people consume news in the hurly-burly of the real world. Repeatedly reading stories with consistent citation disparities might, over time, be recognized by news consumers and exert significant downward pressures on their credibility assessments. Additionally, even if they fail to have a direct influence on media perceptions, sourcing practices still do matter indirectly for public opinion through their influence on news frames (chapter 7). Quoting more female sources may also have "symbolic value" (Braden 1993) completely apart from its influence on credibility assessments insofar as it communicates to news consumers that women's opinions are worth taking seriously. Our finding that an article's amount of source diversity had no influence on media perceptions, however, does raise serious doubts about the practical importance of diversifying sourcing practices from the perspective of news organizations.

Finally, our findings suggest that an obsessive focus on the strategic game elements of policy debates may, in fact, be contributing to the American public's high level of political ignorance and low levels of political trust. Consistent with many other assessments of the media's performance (e.g., Fallows 1997; Lichter and Noyes 1996; Farnsworth and Lichter 2003), our experiments show that strategic game reporting negatively colors the public's views about the press and about politicians—with perceptions of news story, newspaper, and news media credibility being lower and feelings of political cynicism being higher among respondents reading an article emphasizing warlike metaphors, polling results, and the strategic motivations of politicians. Exposure to strategic game coverage also depressed retention of factual information about birth control and increased the negativity of respondents' open-ended explanations. These findings make a strong case for changing the norms governing political journalism and assigning more women (who are less likely to employ strategic game frames) to cover politics.[19]

Conclusion

As we discussed in chapter 6, female journalists cited other women as news sources far more frequently than male journalists in their reporting about the ACA's contraceptive mandate. Chapter 6's analysis showed that female journalists were also less likely than male journalists to author strategic game news coverage and much more likely to frame their reports around the substantive and highly gendered themes of women's health, reproductive rights, and sexual morality. But what were the consequences of exposure to this kind of coverage for average American news consumers? How did it matter for the way men and women thought about the contraceptive mandate, the news media, and the political system more generally?

The experiments presented in this chapter were designed to simultaneously assess whether the kind of byline, source, and content diversity identified in previous chapters mattered for how news audiences thought about the media, politicians, and the question of who pays for birth control. The experimental results presented above show that byline diversity plays an important role in shaping perceptions of news media credibility, political cynicism, information retention, and support for the contraceptive mandate. Specifically, female journalists boosted credibility assessments among female news consumers and were more likely than male journalists to produce the highly gendered coverage that informed and persuaded consumers exposed to it. Gender diversity in quoted sources, however, was much less important than the gender of news reporters. Although source diversity indirectly shaped public opinion by encouraging the publication of more gendered coverage, it had no direct effect on the attitudes of news consumers.

Over the last three decades, researchers have done an excellent job documenting a concurrence of disturbing trends in American political life: the persistent unrepresentativeness of news organizations, the increasing vacuousness of political reporting, and the public's declining satisfaction with the major institutions of representative democracy. Unfortunately, few studies to date have empirically linked these parallel developments in the context of a single political issue. As a result, definitive conclusions about what causes what are in shorter supply in the academic literature than informed speculation. This chapter has addressed this weakness.

10

The Politics of the Pill: Looking Forward

Donald Trump's election reignited the still simmering controversy around the Affordable Care Act (ACA). In March 2017 Trump and Vice President Mike Pence met with members of the House Freedom Caucus to discuss the Republican Party's proposal to repeal and replace the ACA. The meeting included discussions about the fate of essential health benefits under the ACA, which cover, among other items, maternity care. Vice President Pence enthusiastically tweeted a picture of the meeting (Terkel 2017). Twenty-five participants were visible. None appeared to be women. A few weeks later, Senate Majority Leader Mitch McConnell convened a Senate Republican working group to lead discussions of the health care legislation (Pear 2017). The group included thirteen members. Once again, none were women.

The decision to exclude women from these meetings did not go unnoticed. Cecile Richards, president of Planned Parenthood, tweeted in response to the working group announcement: "When women aren't at the table, we're on the menu." Newly elected senator Kamala Harris (D-CA) tweeted as well: "the G.O.P is crafting policy on an issue that directly impacts women without including a single woman in the process. It's wrong."[1] Senator Patty Murray (D-WA), ranking member of the Health, Education, Labor, and Pensions Committee, penned an op-ed expressing similar sentiments:

> As a female Senator, someone who's been in the Senate since the days my male colleagues tried to keep policy negotiations to just the men's locker rooms, I've seen how much it matters to have a diversity of perspectives at the table. And I know firsthand, that when women don't have a seat at the table, their voices just aren't heard. It's true on all issues—education, budget negotiations, foreign policy, and so much more. But it's especially true when it comes to discussions about the future of our health care system and women's access to care. (Murray 2017)

The Politics of the Pill: Gender, Framing, and Policymaking in the Battle over Birth Control. Rachel VanSickle-Ward, Kevin Wallsten, Oxford University Press (2019). © Oxford University Press.
DOI: 10.1093/oso/9780190675349.001.0001

When efforts to repeal the ACA failed shortly after these all-male meetings, several observers noted that it was due primarily to the opposition of moderate Republican women in the Senate. In the words of Associate Press Reporter Alan Fram, the crucial "no" votes from Senators Susan Collins (R-ME), Shelley Moore Capito (R-WV), and Lisa Murkowski (R-AK) constituted the "revenge of the GOP women" (Golshan 2017).

Around the same time that attempts to repeal the ACA were losing steam, the Trump administration issued an executive order indicating that organizations would be provided "regulatory relief" from the law's contraception requirements if birth control ran counter to their "religious beliefs" or "moral convictions" (Nedelman, Luhby, Jarrett, and Lee 2017). Five months later, in October 2017, the Department of Health and Human Services (HHS) issued a number of formal rules that would allow a wide swath of employers, including private firms, publicly traded companies, and nonprofit organizations, to drop coverage of birth control under their insurance plans if they have "sincerely held religious beliefs" or if they have objections "on the basis of moral conviction which is not based in any particular religious belief" (Nedelman, Luhby, and Lee 2017). In December 2017 federal district court Judge Wendy Beetlestone granted the state of Pennsylvania's request for a preliminary injunction against HHS's new rules about the ACA. Beetlestone's decision rested on the argument that Pennsylvania would suffer "serious and irreparable harm" because the proposed rules would inevitably produce "an increase in unintended pregnancies" (Colliver 2017). The Trump administration, responding in part to this ruling, announced the creation of a Conscience and Religious Freedom Division in January 2018 to provide "HHS with the focus it needs to more vigorously and effectively enforce existing laws protecting the rights of conscience and religious freedom" (White House Fact Sheet 2018). At the time of this writing, groups such as the American Civil Liberties Union, the National Women's Law Center, and the Center for Reproductive Rights are pursuing a number of legal challenges to the new rules.

While the particular actors and events driving this latest round of controversies are new, the frames employed to understand them are not. Much like during the period examined throughout the bulk of this book, supporters of the ACA's contraceptive mandate are framing their arguments around gendered considerations, such as women's health, reproductive rights, and morality. For example, Dr. Haywood L. Brown, president of the American Congress of Obstetricians and Gynecologists, criticized the Trump administration rules by saying, "HHS leaders under the current administration are focused on turning back the clock on women's health. Reducing access to contraceptive coverage threatens to reverse the tremendous progress our nation has made in recent years in lowering the unintended pregnancy rate" (Nedelman et al. 2017). Similarly, Planned

Parenthood president Cecile Richards, said, "Nine out of ten women of reproductive age will use birth control in their lifetime. This administration is carrying out a full-scale attack on birth control. We cannot allow President Trump to roll back the progress women have made over the past century" (Nedelman et al. 2017).

The frames proffered by opponents of the mandate should also have a familiar ring to this book's readers. President Trump, for instance, explained his May 2017 executive order by saying, "We will never, ever stand for religious discrimination. Never, ever" (Nedelman et al., 2017). Similarly, Attorney General Jeff Sessions defended the Trump administration's moves on the contraceptive mandate by saying, "President Trump promised that this administration would 'lead by example on religious liberty,' and he is delivering on that promise" (Nedelman et al. 2017). In announcing their October 2017 rules, HHS officials also explicitly dismissed concerns about women's health, arguing that "99.9% of women" in the United States would be unaffected by the policy change (Nedelman et al. 2017).

The future of birth control coverage under the ACA, and of birth control access in general, is uncertain at the moment of this writing. The lessons provided in this book, however, suggest that what happens moving forward will depend significantly on who is at the table. Indeed, the debates that have unfolded during the first year of the Trump administration only further confirm the importance of representation and its policy implications. In this conclusion, we summarize some of the key findings from the book's preceding chapters and place them in a broader policy and political context.

Summary of Key Findings

Who Speaks?

At the outset of the book we posed three questions relating to contemporary contraception politics: Who speaks? What do they say? Does it matter? In the chapters that followed we answered these questions in separate but interconnected empirical studies of state legislatures, Congress, the Supreme Court, the media, and the public. In terms of who speaks, we found that men largely dominated public debates about birth control—in legislative hearings, media commentary, oral arguments, and beyond. Given the importance of birth control in women's lives, the frequency with which their voices were excluded from the debate is striking, troubling, and unfortunately, unsurprising. Women have been politically marginalized for most of American history. Formal barriers—including laws barring women from voting, running for office, testifying in court, and serving on juries—were frequently combined with less institutionalized forms of disparagement, intimidation, and violence to prevent women from participating in the political process. A 1916 *New York Times* editorial, for example, effectively encapsulated the prevailing sentiment toward women's participation in public affairs throughout most of 18th, 19th, and early 20th centuries: "The grant of suffrage to women is repugnant to instincts that strike their roots deep in the order of nature. It runs counter to human reason, it flouts the teachings of experience and the admonitions of common sense.... [Women] have never possessed or developed the political faculty."[2]

While the formal and informal obstacles to women's engagement in the political sphere have largely been removed in the United States over the course of the last 100 years, less overt barriers persist. In their excellent work on political voice, *The Silent Sex: Gender, Deliberation, and Institutions* (2014), political scientists Christopher Karpowitz and Tali Mendelberg explore the ways in which women's voices are often diminished in public political discourse. The roots of these disparities are multifaceted. Women's "silence" is due, in part, to lack of effective role modeling; women do not see themselves in political power structures and, as a result, do not believe they belong there (Burns, Schlozman, and Verba 2001). Motivation plays a role as well: women and girls consistently report lower levels of political interest, political efficacy, and political ambition, even after controlling for capacity and access to resources (Burns, Schlozman, and Verba 2001; Niemi and Junn 1993; Karpowitz and Mendelberg 2014; Lawless and Fox 2010).

According to Karpowitz and Mendelberg (2014), gender differences in motivation stem partly from the dismissal, devaluation, and stereotyping of women's voices that takes place in educational settings and via the media landscape (see also Hansen 1997; Kahn 1994, 1996; Falk 2008). What's more, women who voice their opinions too assertively or too confidently (i.e., in too "masculine" a way) often end up paying a social or professional price. An extensive psychology literature, for example, demonstrates that women are perceived more negatively than men for expressing anger or appearing forceful or assertive (Brescoll and Uhlmann 2008). These effects are particularly pronounced when men are evaluating women in leadership roles (Eagly and Carli 2003). In professional as well as political settings, then, women face a likability/competence trade-off; appearing too likeable makes a woman seem less competent, but appearing too competent makes a woman seem less likeable (Schneider et al. 2010).

In other words, women are taught, in sometimes subtle but nonetheless persistent ways, that they either do not have the necessary authority to express themselves politically or that voicing their opinions will have negative consequences for their social and professional lives.

On the flip side, the relationship between gender and political engagement is notably not fixed. Where women and girls are presented with role models, they become more involved with politics. Research shows, for example, that when women witness other women seeking high-profile political office, they become more politically engaged (Burns, Schlozman, and Verba 2001; Atkeson 2003; Hansen 1997). As Karpowitz and Mendelberg's (2014) work shows, women speak up with greater frequency and communicate more effectively when the interaction between their numbers and the institutional setting's decision rules provide them with opportunity to do so. Put differently, the influence of gender on political expression is a variable (shaped by other influences) rather than a constant.

Unlike this body of research, our analyses do not focus on the conditions that facilitate women's political speech. We focus instead on the content and policy consequences of women's expression once the hurdles to political expression have been overcome[3]. But there is a fundamental link between the conclusions presented in this book and the implications drawn from previous research; all of this work raises the question of how and when women, who are frequently muted in political debates, are able to locate a place for themselves in the public sphere.

Our analyses illustrate that women consistently found ways to make their voices heard on debates over birth control policy, even when underrepresented and in the minority. Women championed the development of hormonal birth control, writing letters about their experiences and opening clinics in defiance of the law. Protesters brought attention to all-male hearings on hormonal birth control in the 1970s—a strategy that would be employed to great effect by birth control advocates four decades later in response to Congressman Darrell Issa's all-male panel. When Sandra Fluke's invitation to appear before Congress was rejected, Minority Leader Nancy Pelosi staged a panel and gave Fluke the opportunity to testify, elevating her status as a spokesperson on the issue. Justices Sonia Sotomayor and Elena Kagan delivered pointed commentary and questioning during oral arguments in *Hobby Lobby*. Justice Ruth Bader Ginsburg's forceful dissent in that case generated considerable press coverage, sending echoes of her arguments around the country. Though they were less frequent authors in amicus briefs, women openly opined on birth control policy and its implications for women's rights and health. Whether they viewed their role through a particularly gendered lens or not, women throughout these debates embodied the words of Shirley Chisholm, herself an outspoken supporter of increased birth control access: "If they don't give you a seat at the table, bring a folding chair."

What Do They Say?

Our findings on the relationship between a speaker's gender and that speaker's framing of the contraception mandate were remarkably consistent across legislatures, courts, the media, and the public. In each one of these domains and across the entire period of our study, women were more likely to emphasize gendered frames while men were more likely to emphasize religious freedom. Specifically, in chapter 4 we showed that in floor debates as well as oversight hearings, women emphasized reproductive rights and gendered frames far more frequently than men. While questions of religious liberty were not raised in the Senate debate, men emphasized religion in the oversight hearing. In chapter 5 we discussed the emphasis placed on gendered frames in Ginsburg's *Hobby Lobby* dissent and demonstrated a strong connection between the gender of an amicus brief authors and the frame of that amicus brief—with briefs authored by a larger proportion of women being significantly more likely to select health, reproductive rights, and gendered frames overall. In chapter 7 we showed that female journalists highlighted gendered themes in their reporting on the contraceptive mandate more than male reporters. Male journalists, by contrast, were far more likely to invoke religious liberty and strategic game considerations. In other words, regardless of time or forum, women consistently speak with a different voice than men when discussing contraception.

Consistency should not be conflated with uniformity, and our data offer many examples of men using gendered frames (e.g., male senators emphasizing women's health in the Senate floor debate) and women using nongendered frames (e.g., female reporters authoring a strategic game frame article). Moreover, while we discuss a number of instances where the gender effects appear stronger than any partisan or ideological influences, in other cases the relationship between these interrelated variables is more difficult to disentangle. That being said, once again the overarching patterns are very clear: in a number of different forums and at a number of different moments, women were, on balance and often controlling for other factors, more likely than men to talk about birth control in terms of their health and rights.

Does It Matter?

Did the combination of who speaks and what was said matter for the timing, tone, and trajectory of debates over birth control? This is perhaps the most complicated question to answer, given that "mattering" can mean so many things in a far-reaching study such as this. Nevertheless, the answer our data provides to this question is a resounding "yes." Who spoke mattered a great deal for media coverage. Female reporters cited more women as sources (chapter 6) and covered birth control debates more substantively (chapter 5) than their male counterparts. What's more, the sourcing decisions made by female reporters exerted their own, independent effect on how stories about the contraceptive mandate were framed—with articles quoting more women being more likely to emphasize gendered themes even after controlling for a reporter's gender.

Who spoke and what they said also mattered a great deal for public opinion. Women were more likely than men to endorse requirements that insurance plans cover contraception (chapter 8), and exposure to news articles employing gendered frames (i.e., the kind of frames female journalists most commonly used) significantly increased support for the ACA's birth control mandate (chapter 9). Furthermore, our experimental results suggest that reading an article written by a woman could play an important role in shaping how news consumers (particularly women) view the news media and the political system more broadly (chapter 9).

Finally, who spoke and what they said mattered for policy adoption. In chapter 3 we demonstrated that states with more women serving as legislators were more likely to enact birth control coverage laws even after controlling for a host of other political, religious, and ideological factors. In chapter 4 we discussed the way that Senator Barbara Mikulski rallied women senators to fight for the inclusion of the statutory language that would ultimately result in the contraceptive mandate. Without those women, it's likely that ACA would never have mandated birth control coverage as part of preventative care. Throughout the book, we have also documented how women's exclusion from the debate has policy consequences as well. We cannot say for sure if more women on the Supreme Court would have changed the outcome of *Hobby Lobby* (certainly that would depend on the ideological orientation and judicial philosophy of those women), but we do know that the outcome of that case hinged largely on the most prominent male framing of the mandate (religious freedom) eclipsing the most prominent female framing of the mandate (health). Given the points raised throughout the volume about the link between access to birth control in terms of women's overall health and equality, our conclusions lead us to support Karpowitz and Mendelberg's (2014) contention:

> Policy can look very different when made by women—the needs of vulnerable populations tend to be placed front and center, and the poor become less destitute. When women are empowered under the right conditions, they are more likely than men to speak for, sponsor and advocate, or vote for policies that assist women, children, families, stigmatized or disadvantaged minorities, and the vulnerable in society, for more generous policies on a number of social service measures, or for policies that serve the common good (20).

This last point gives us the opportunity to highlight an additional plank of our argument about the impact of representation: the question of who speaks and what they say matters in ways that extend far beyond the immediate policy decisions revealed during a single court ruling or vote in the legislature. In the largest possible sense, women are unlikely to be viewed as legitimate and valuable interlocutors in public debate if they are systematically underrepresented in newspapers, legislatures, courts, and executive offices. More narrowly, when representation shapes frames it can have long-term implications for how a particular policy issue is understood, and that understanding can dramatically shape policy outcomes down the road. In this way, who speaks and what they say are sometimes just as consequential in defeat as they are in victory. By emphasizing particular frames, policy actors can keep those arguments viable for the next round of debate. The fact that women promoted health and reproductive rights framing in dissents, congressional hearings, amicus briefs, and news reports, even when those frames were outnumbered by religious discussions, means that future advocates still have those messages to marshal. Nothing illustrates this point better than the fact that the most recent developments on contraceptive coverage emphasize the same arguments that were used in 2011.

We would be remiss if we did not point out the limits to this narrative of women breaking through in terms of which women's voices were actually heard in the debate over contraception. Two observations in particular deserve mention here. First, to the extent that women exerted an influence on the debate over contraception through using their voices, that influence was overwhelmingly concentrated among the small group of women who hold formal leadership positions within government institutions and advocacy organizations. As our data show, female members of Congress, Supreme Court justices, journalists, and interest-group representatives accounted for nearly all of the publicly communicated rhetoric related to the ACA's contraceptive mandate between the HHS ruling and *Zubik*. The nonelite women directly affected by the mandate policy were rarely asked to speak for themselves and frequently appeared in our data only as an undifferentiated aggregate referenced by political leaders on one side of the aisle or another (e.g., "It's important for millions of women around the country," "the decision means that millions of women will have access to affordable birth control," "It just doesn't make sense to take this benefit away from millions of women," "Today's vote is a victory for the millions of American women and families who were in danger of losing access to vital health services," etc.). While nonelite women were slightly more likely to provide quotes for newspaper articles than men, overall, the individual voices of unofficial actors in the American political system are rarely heard. In fact, the same thing that feminist scholars say about supposedly gendered traits such as physiology, athleticism, and driving ability applies to our study's conclusion about political influence in contraception debates: there were "more significant within-group differences than between-group differences" (Lorber 2011, 18).

Our study of the dynamics behind contraception debates does remind us, however, that the boundary between elite and nonelite political actors in the United States is rarely rigid and always porous. There is no better exemplar of this lesson than Sandra Fluke. Prior to February 2012 Fluke was the relatively unknown president of Georgetown Law Students for Reproductive Justice. After her invitation to address Representative Darrell Issa's panel was rejected, however, Fluke was handed a large megaphone to amplify her political views not just on reproductive rights policy but on every aspect of the American political system. In addition to delivering widely covered testimony before the House Democrats' Steering and Policy Committee, Fluke was interviewed by countless news outlets, featured on the cover of *Ms.* magazine, and invited to deliver a special address to the 2012 Democratic National Convention. In 2014 she ran unsuccessfully for a state senate seat in California. Although her particular path to being heard was unconventional, unintentional, and (possibly) unwanted, Fluke's role in bringing attention to the contraception issue and promoting the "war on women" frame that guided the 2012 election campaign was essential. At certain moments in the course of political debates, nonelite actors exert a tremendous influence and, in the process, become elites in their own right.

Second, high-profile discussions of race and ethnicity were, troublingly, nearly nonexistent in the political debates surrounding contraception. As discussed in chapters 5 and 6, there were 191 newspaper articles published on contraception between August 1, 2011, and August 1, 2012. Collectively, these failed to reference a single civil rights organization related to race or ethnicity (such as the National Association for the Advancement of Colored People, the Southern Poverty Law Center, or League of United Latin American Citizens) and quoted only two of 63 total members of the Congressional Black Caucus or Congressional Hispanic Caucus serving in the 112th Congress. Unsurprisingly given these sourcing decisions, a mere three of the 191 reports published in American newspapers on the contraceptive mandate between August 1, 2011, and August 1, 2012, discussed questions of race or ethnicity in any way. Perhaps more importantly, all three of these news reports were framed around strategic game considerations rather than substantive questions. A March 6, 2012, story in the *Washington Times*, for example, reported that "[b]y a margin of nearly 4-to-1, likely Republican primary voters said the GOP should stake out a tough stance, even if it will cost the party Hispanic support" (Dinan 2012). Sounding a similar note, a *Washington Post* story published on February 9, 2012, emphasized that "GOP lawmakers appear to see a political opportunity in the issue with Hispanics, many of whom are Catholics" (Wallsten and Aizenman 2012). In a report on the failed Senate attempt to overturn the mandate, the *Dayton*

(OH) *Daily News* quoted Democratic strategist Mary Anne Marsh saying, "A lot of African-Americans and Latinos are going to vote in this election, and many are culturally conservative. So they may be faced with the dilemma, 'Do I vote for my health care or do I vote for my religion?'" (McCarty 2012).

This is not to say that the racial dimensions of this policy were never raised. On the contrary, advocacy groups including the Black Women's Health Imperative and National Latina Institute for Reproductive Health spoke out forcefully in amicus briefs, public commentary on the rule adoption, and other forums about the unique challenges faced by women of color in accessing birth control. But these messages did not permeate most public deliberation and accounts. Race and ethnicity came up rarely in legislative hearings, oral arguments, administrative announcements, and as we noted above, press coverage. Our findings suggest that this may well be linked to a paucity of women in color in newsrooms and elected office.

This lack of attention to race and ethnicity at the highest levels of these debates is particularly troubling given the relevance of contraceptive policy to communities of color.[4] To take just one example, African American and Latino women have much higher abortion rates and much higher rates of unintended pregnancy than white women. An important part of this disparity is differential access to and use of contraceptives (Cohen 2008). And, as we discuss in chapter 2, the history of contraception policy in communities of color is fraught and often harrowing. The fact that public debates neglected this component of the contraception issue is revealing and strongly suggests the American political system's need for greater intersectional representation.

Broader Political and Policy Implications

During the 1950s and 1960s the Republicans were slightly more supportive of women's rights claims than the Democrats (Wolbrecht 2002). Small differences aside, however, prior to the mid-1970s, both parties strongly supported the so-called women's rights agenda. In 1972 the Democratic and Republican Party platforms endorsed the Equal Rights Amendment, federal child care programs, and a host of other women's rights policies advocated by feminists (Wolbrecht 2002). Over the course of the next eight years, however, this consensus gave way to a polarization around gender issues. By 1980 the parties' platforms bore little resemblance to each other—with Democrats and Republicans splitting on the questions of abortion and ratification of the ERA. This divergence continued through the 1980s, 1990s, and early 2000s. As Wolbrecht argues, "Polarization over women's rights has emerged as one of the most readily identifiable, if not defining, distinctions between the parties" (Wolbrecht 2000, 4).

By the time states were considering contraception mandates, the differences between the parties on women's rights issues at the national level were large and clear. It is somewhat surprising, therefore, that this polarization did not initially subsume legislative behavior or public opinion toward contraception in the same way it did for other issues related to personal sexual behavior. As shown in previous chapters, partisan control did not predict the adoption or content of state-level contraceptive mandates (chapter 3), and early surveys found widespread support for birth control coverage from across the political spectrum (chapter 9).

The consensus was short-lived, and the politics of contraception was quickly enveloped by the nation's rapidly polarizing political divisions. While there is some academic disagreement about the scope of ideological polarization in the United States (Fiorina, Abrams, and Pope 2008; Abramowitz 2010), most research shows that the parties have become more ideologically "sorted" (i.e., liberals are now extremely likely to be Democrats and conservatives are extremely likely to be Republicans) over the last three decades (Levendusky 2009) and that Democrats and Republicans now like each other less than ever before (Iyengar, Sood, and Lelkes, 2012). Political scientists have offered up a nearly endless litany of explanations for this state of affairs—including but not limited to digital media (Epstein and Robertson 2015; Pariser 2012; Sunstein 2017), the collapse of the Soviet Union (Haidt and Abrams 2015), income inequality (Barber et al. 2015; Voorheis, McCarty, and Shor 2016), immigration (McCarty, Poole, and Rosenthal 2006), and Newt Gingrich's changes to the legislative calendar in 1995 (Haidt and Hetherington 2012).

Perhaps most important in understanding polarization (particularly the affective variety of personal dislike) is that the parties now represent different policy approaches *and* different social groups. Democrats are increasingly the party of women, nonwhites, professionals, and residents of urban areas, while Republican voters are disproportionately older white men, evangelical Christians, and residents of rural areas (Iyengar and Krupenkin 2018). The result is that differences in party affiliation today go hand in glove with differences in worldview and individuals' sense of social and cultural identity (Mason 2015). Rejection of one's policy opinions quickly becomes equated with rejection of one's identity. Nearly all differences over policy begin to take on a moral character and the political world quickly becomes a Manichaean struggle between good and evil. In Mason and Wronski's (2018) words, "As social identities are increasingly associated with one party or the other, and as partisans increasingly identify with these party-associated groups, the American political divide grows more intractable."

In the 2012 debate over the contraceptive mandate, an identity-based politics of gender was pitted against an identity-based politics of religion as the two main parties aggressively mobilized to defend the perceived interests of their electoral coalition's most valuable groups. Large "God-based," gender, and partisan gaps in opinion opened up on the question of birth control coverage in 2012 and remain in place today. The rhetoric coming from both sides predictably intensified. A debate over health insurance coverage became a "war on women" or, depending on one's perspective, a "war on religion." Opposing the HHS's rule was, in the words of Senator Mikulski, part of "a systematic war against women" (Pear 2012). Supporting the HHS's rule was, according to chairperson of the board at Franciscan Alliance Inc. Sister Jane Marie Klein, "nothing less than a direct attack on religion and First Amendment rights" (Wetzstein 2012). Supporters of the mandate, according to Rush Limbaugh, were "sluts." When elite debates take place using the vocabulary of "war" (e.g., "assaults," "attacks," and "battles") common ground will be difficult to find. Tellingly, a 2016 Pew survey found that fewer than 30% of Americans said that they could sympathize with the opinion of those who disagree with them on the contraceptive mandate.

The 2012 debate over birth control coverage was simultaneously a symptom and, to a much lesser extent, a cause of the coarsening of American political discourse and the rapid escalation of interparty animosity in the United States. The controversies surrounding contraception left a number of other indelible marks on the nation's politics. The birth control mandate was arguably a central factor in securing President Obama's 2012 reelection and victory for Democratic candidates in a number of key congressional races. As detailed in chapter 9, the "war on women" became a central theme of the 2012 campaign and for Democratic candidates around the country. In the most artistic and memorable illustration of this theme, Planned Parenthood created a giant pack of birth control pills called "Pillamina" to follow Mitt Romney on the campaign trail in the summer of 2012. This campaigning appeared to influence voters. In 2008 the gender gap between Obama and John McCain was 7%. In 2012, however, the gender gap grew to 10%. More importantly, support for the birth control mandate was significantly related to voting for Obama for both women and men voters (Deckman and McTague 2015). As Deckman and McTague conclude, "The birth control mandate was a winning issue for the Democratic Party in 2012" (2015, 19).

Our findings offer important lessons for the 2016 presidential election as well. A number of inquiries into media coverage of that election have noted that press coverage of policies was eclipsed by coverage of horserace dynamics or controversies (Patterson 2016; Faris et al. 2017). In one analysis, policy constituted a mere 10% of reporting, while horserace and controversy accounted for 42% and 17%, respectively (Patterson 2016). These disparities are not new; horserace coverage has dominated election coverage for decades (Patterson 1993). But a few elements of the 2016 election illustrate why it is particularly relevant in the context of our project.

Hillary Clinton, the first woman presidential nominee on a major party ticket, spoke extensively during her campaign about reproductive rights in general, and birth control in particular. Her first major speech after winning the primary was to Planned Parenthood, where she emphasized the importance of birth control to women's health and economic standing. At this event and others, she frequently grounded her positions and policy prescription in women's equality, and highlighted women's personal experiences as relevant and authoritative. In a rebuttal to Trump on abortion in the third presidential debate, for example, she argued, "You should meet with some of the women I've met with, women I've known" (VanSickle-Ward 2016). Indeed, a gendered framing of a range of issues, or "gender mainstreaming," was a hallmark of her campaign (Dittmar 2015). This gendered framing of policy did not fare well in terms of garnering news coverage; Trump received roughly twice as much issue coverage as did Clinton (Faris et al. 2017) and far more press coverage overall (Patterson 2016). Our findings regarding women's more substantive press coverage of the birth control debate compared to men's more strategic game coverage suggest an obvious question: might more women reporting on the 2016 election have led to more substantive coverage of the policy positions of the first women nominee? More broadly, our work invites a serious reflection about the consequences of highlighting strategic elements of policies and elections over substantive ones—of covering politics like a game.

Perhaps most importantly, the mandate had a dramatic policy impact. Contraception coverage under the ACA shifted the economics of contraception in the United States. According to the Kaiser Family Foundation, the percentage of women reporting any out-of-pocket expenses on oral contraceptives dropped from 21% prior to the ACA to only 3% in 2017 (Ranji, Salganicoff, Sobel, and Rosenzweig 2017). In addition, a study by the Perelman School of Medicine at the University of Pennsylvania found that oral contraceptive costs declined by 38% and IUD costs fell by 68% after implementation of the ACA. Interestingly, these declines were not a result of an increase in contraception use (Riddell, Taylor, and Alford 2017). Overall, the mandate was estimated to save women nearly $1.5 billion on birth control pills alone in 2013 (National Women's Law Center Fact Sheet 2017). We have argued throughout the book that women spoke in particular ways about birth control because it affected their lives in tangible ways. These statistics, then, are a powerful reminder that while the political dynamics surrounding the contraceptive debate are fascinating, the consequences of the mandate should also be thought of in the most basic terms: how it changed the health and economic status of the women who rely on birth control.

This reflection on policy implications further serves as an important reminder of the lessons our book offers regarding the necessity of identity politics.

Political discourse of late has frequently framed identity politics in highly negative terms—blaming it for hardening political divisions and balkanizing the population. Certainly the heated rhetoric we described earlier in this section is linked precisely to those concerns. Yet our findings about the ways in which women's voices impacted birth control policy highlights that identities matter for a reason, and that emphasizing identity may shape policies and politics for the better. In other words, the rallying cry of "if you're not at the table, you're on the menu" is more than just a catchy phrase, it encapsulates fundamental links between descriptive and substantive representation, links that were ever present in the case of contraception policy.

Conclusion

This book should eliminate any lingering doubts that women may have about whether their participation in debates about reproductive rights policies matters. The evidence we offer tells both a frustrating and a compelling tale about women's political power. Specifically, it suggests that while women are frequently outnumbered and underrepresented in the legislature, the courts, the bureaucracy, and the media, they can still have a substantial and lasting effect on the issues that directly impact their lives.

The juxtaposition of women's voices persisting despite obstacles and setbacks was brought into sharp relief during the fall of 2018. In November of that year, the Trump administration finalized regulations that significantly expanded which organizations were eligible for conscience clause exemptions from the birth control coverage of the mandate (covered in chapter 4). In other words, pending a response from the courts, a far greater number of employers would be able to opt out of offering the birth control coverage that advocates fought hard to secure under the ACA. And yet the birth control mandate remained quite popular. And while both sides of the debate watched the final regulations carefully, they did not garner anywhere near the press coverage of earlier events in the fight over birth control access. In part this is because the final rules came immediately after the 2018 midterm elections.

The elections resulted in a Democratic majority in the House—a majority generally supportive of the mandate. Perhaps more noteworthy for our purpose, the elections also resulted in record numbers of women taking congressional office, though they remain firmly in the minority (after the 2018 elections women were 25% of the Senate and 23% of the House). One of those women was Deb Haaland (D-NM), who became, along with Sharice Davids (D-KS), the first two Native American women elected to the U.S. Congress. Birth control didn't dominate headlines the way it did in 2012, but Haaland spoke openly during her campaign about her support of reproductive rights and how her positions were born from her experiences:

> I got my health care at Planned Parenthood all through law school because it was affordable and accessible. . . . They offer birth control, they offer check-ups, I mean they did a lot of things for women and you could always get an appointment there. It was very, very accessible. So that helped me when I didn't have a lot of money, when I was a student, as a single mom. And I just look at my own experiences as something I would advocate for young women as well. (Boguhn 2018)

Haaland was not alone in highlighting her lived experience in relationship to her policy stance. Lauren Underwood (D-IL), the youngest black women ever elected to Congress, contextualized her support for reproductive rights in terms of her experience as a nurse: "I've made my career in healthcare. As a nurse, one of my core values is a patient's right to autonomy, to make choices about his or her own body."[5] Candidate (and now representative) Katie Hill (D-CA) not only spoke of "birth control as health care" but released an emotional video during the campaign highlighting her struggle as a teen over how to handle a unplanned pregnancy.[6]

The future of the birth control mandate is uncertain. But whatever happens for birth control access—and reproductive rights, and other policies that affect women more generally—in the coming years, one thing is certain: women's voices will play a significant role. Based on what we've heard and read in writing this book, we expect those voices to come through loud and clear.

APPENDICES

Appendix A: Coding Terms for Frames in Legislative and Judicial Deliberation

Frames

Religion/Religious Freedom: This frame highlights the effect of the policy on religious liberty and frequently focused on the appropriateness and breadth of an exemption of contraceptive coverage for religious entities, particularly those administered by or affiliated with the Catholic Church.

Search Terms:

religion
religions
religious
faith
faiths
Christian
Christians
Jewish
Jew
Jews
Muslim
Muslims
Islam
Catholic
Catholics
Jesuit
Jesuits

God
Church
Churches
Free Exercise
First Amendment
Theological

Health: This frame includes women's health (including the importance of birth control to women's overall health), public health (such as discussions of population control and teen pregnancy), and discussion of how birth control coverage connects to health care reform and preventative care more generally.

Search Terms:

health
physician
physicians
hospital
hospitals
prescription
prescriptions
medication
medications
preventative
healthcare
medical
preventive
doctor
doctors
treatment
treatments
pharmacy
pharmacies
STD
STI
sexually transmitted infection
sexually transmitted disease
sexually transmitted infections
sexually transmitted diseases
STIs
STDs
cancer

cancers
HPV

Reproductive Rights, Women's Rights, and Autonomy: This frame emphasizes the agency of women. Relevant topics include gender equality, women's bodily autonomy and self-determination, reproductive rights, and discussions of inclusion and exclusion of women from the conversation.

Search Terms:

women
woman
female
females
equality
reproductive
reproduction
autonomy
gender
equal
voice
voices
her
she

Economics: Articles using this frame focus on what fees, taxes, and/or externalities would be bestowed upon the public, insurance companies, and employers by the mandated coverage of contraception.

Search Terms:

economic
corporation
corporations
fee
fees
expense
expenses
business
insurance
insurances
tax

taxes
fine
fines
afford
affordable
employment cost
costs

Morality: This category encompasses frames that deal with appropriate moral or sexual behavior, including premarital sex and perceived sexual promiscuity.

Search Terms:

morality
moral
sex
sexuality
premarital
promiscuity
immoral
sin
principles
principle
objectionable

Partisanship/Strategy: The partisanship frame covers discussions of political strategy, the two major parties, their platforms, and the presidential candidates in the 2012 election (Obama and Romney).

Search Terms:

Obama
Romney
election
elections
ideology
Democrat
Democrats
Democratic
Republican
Republicans
partisan

poll
polls
public opinion
public opinions
survey
surveys
strategy
strategies

Appendix B: Amicus Briefs

Amicus Briefs Filed in *Hobby Lobby*

Association of Gospel Rescue Missions
Ovarian Cancer National Alliance
Constitutional Accountability Center
Physicians for Reproductive Health
The states of California, Connecticut, Hawaii, Illinois, Iowa, Maine, Maryland, New York, Oregon, Vermont, and Washington
American Jewish Committee
Pacific Legal Foundation
Azusa Pacific University
Center for Constitutional Jurisprudence
Reproductive Research Audit
National Religious Broadcasters
Senators Orin G. Hatch et al.
Democrats for Life of America and Bart Stupack
Michigan, Ohio, and 18 Other States
Drury Development Corp. et al.
National Association of Evangelicals
American Freedom Law Center
Texas Black Americans for Life
Hon. Daniel H. Branch
Church-State Scholars Frederick Mark Gedicks, et al.
Freedom from Religion Foundation
State of Oklahoma
Liberty, Life, and Law Foundation et al.
Beverly LaHaye Institute and Janice Shaw Crouse, Ph.D.
67 Catholic Theologians and Ethicists
Women Speak for Themselves
United States Conference of Catholic Bishops
Cato Institute
Knights of Columbus
U.S. Women's Chamber of Commerce
Guttmacher Institute and Professor Sara Rosenbaum
American Jewish Committee
Religious Organizations
National Women's Law Center
91 Members of the United States House of Reps.
American College of Obstetricians and Gynecologists et al.

Foreign and Comparative Law Experts Lawrence O. Gostin
Corporate and Criminal Law Professors
California et al.
National League of Cities et al.
Ovarian Cancer National Alliance et al.
Lambda Legal Defense and Education Fund Inc. et al.
Family Research Council
Liberty Institute
Breast Cancer Prevention Institute et al.
9 Academic Institutions et al.
C12 Group, LLC
National Jewish Commission on Law and Public Affairs (COLPA) et al.
Liberty University and Liberty Counsel
Brennan Center for Justice at N.Y.U. School of Law
Constitutional Accountability Center
U.S. Senators Murray et al.
Catholic Medical Association
American Civil Rights Union
Massachusetts Citizens for Life Inc. et al.
Council for Christian Colleges & Universities et al.
Christian Booksellers Association et al.
Eagle Forum Education & Legal Defense Fund Inc. et al.
Foundation for Moral Law
Association of American Physicians and Surgeons Inc. et al.
Rutherford Institute
Ethics and Public Policy Center
U.S. Senators Ted Cruz et al.
Church of the Lukumi Babalu Aye Inc. et al.
Judicial Watch
38 Protestant Theologians et al.
Electric Mirror, LLC, et al.
American Center for Law & Justice et al.
Thomas More Law Center
John A. Ryan Institute for Catholic Social Thought
Judicial Education Project
Constitutional Law Scholars
Westminster Theological Seminary
Jewish Social Policy Action Network
Independent Women's Forum
Historians and Legal Scholars
National Health Law Program et al.
Professor Emeritus of Law Charles E. Rice et al.

Freedom X et al.
J.E. Dunn Construction Group Inc. et al.
The Center for Inquiry et al.
David Boyle
Christian Legal Society et al.
88 Members of Congress
Julian Bond et al.
The International Conference of Evangelical Chaplain Endorsers
Women's Public Policy Groups et al.
Honorable Joseph B. Scarnati III et al.

Amicus Briefs Filed in *Zubik*

Orthodox Jewish Rabbis
United States Conference of Catholic Bishops et al.
CNS International Ministries Inc. and Heartland Christian College
Breast Cancer Prevention Institute
Residents and Families of Residents at Homes of the Little Sisters of the Poor
The School of the Ozarks Inc., d/b/a College of the Ozarks
Justice and Freedom Fund
Ethics and Public Policy Center
Texas et al.
Southern Baptist Theological Seminary et al.
Christian Legal Society et al.
Church of the Lukumi Babalu Aye Inc. et al.
Christian and Missionary Alliance Foundation Inc. et al.
207 Members of Congress
National Jewish Commission on Law and Public Affairs
Eagle Forum Education & Legal Defense Fund Inc.
Former Justice Department Officials
Cato Institute and Independent Women's Forum
National Association of Evangelicals et al.
50 Catholic Theologians and Ethicists
Association of American Physicians and Surgeons et al.
Constitutional Law Scholars
Women Speak for Themselves
Liberty Counsel
Council for Christian Colleges and Universities
The Knights of Columbus
Bart Stupak et al.
Dominican Sisters of Mary, Mother of the Eucharist, et al.
Thomas More Law Center

ACNA Jurisdiction of the Armed Forces and Chaplaincy et al.
Eternal Word Television Network
David Boyle
Thirteen Law Professors
International Conference of Evangelical Chaplain Endorsers
Concerned Women for America
Michael J. New, Ph.D., Associate Scholar at the Charlotte Lozier Institute
American Center for Law and Justice
U.S. Justice Foundation et al.
Carmelite Sisters of the Most Sacred Heart of Los Angeles et al.
The Catholic Benefits Association et al.
Religious Institutions
American Humanist Association
Harvard Law School for Health and Law Policy Innovation et al.
American Civil Liberties Union et al.
Church-State Scholars
The Ovarian Cancer Research Fund Alliance et al. (2 volumes)
Baptist Joint Committee for Religious Liberty
Compassion & Choices
National Women's Law Center and 68 Other Organizations
Norman Dorsen et al.
American Jewish Committee et al.
American College of Obstetricians and Gynecologists et al.
National Latina Institute for Reproductive Health et al.
Catholics for Choice et al.
Former State Attorneys General et al.
Foreign and International Law Experts Lawrence O. Gostin et al.
240 Students, Faculty, and Staff at Religiously Affiliated Universities
American Academy of Pediatrics
Scholars of Religious Liberty Sarah Barringer Gordon et al.
Health Policy Experts
Anti-Defamation League et al.
Black Women's Health Imperative
Guttmacher Institute and Professor Sara Rosenbaum
Lambda Legal Defense and Education Fund Inc. et al.
123 Members of the United States Congress
Military Historians
The National Health Law Program
California, et al.
Honorable Robert C. "Bobby" Scott
The Center for Inquiry, and American Atheists

Appendix C: Sample Treatment Article for Authorship and Sourcing Experiment

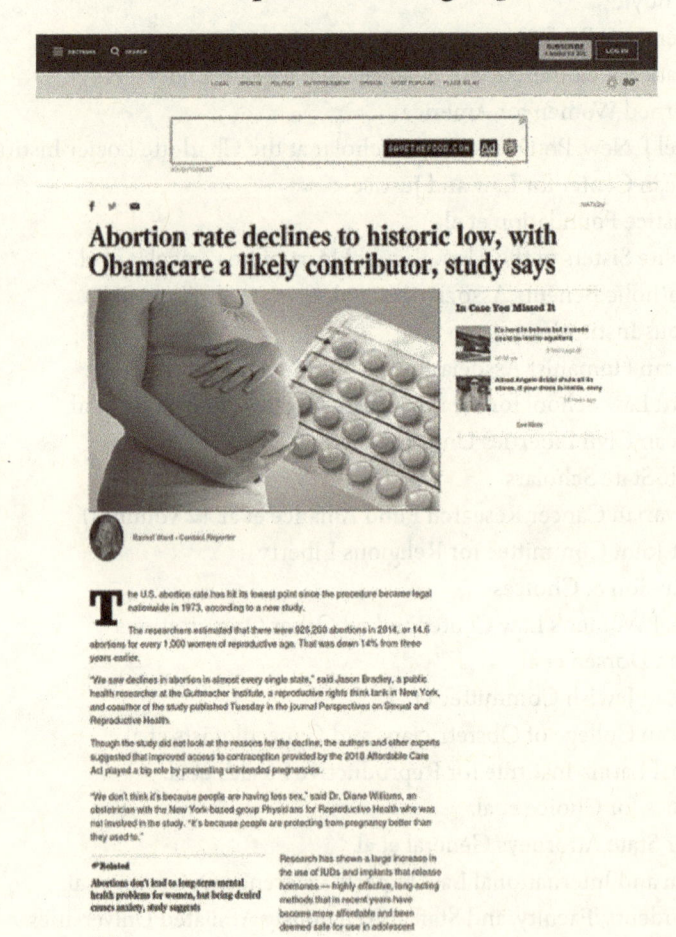

Abortion rate declines to historic low, with Obamacare a likely contributor, study says

Rachel Ward – Contact Reporter

The U.S. abortion rate has hit its lowest point since the procedure became legal nationwide in 1973, according to a new study.

The researchers estimated that there were 926,200 abortions in 2014, or 14.6 abortions for every 1,000 women of reproductive age. That was down 14% from three years earlier.

"We saw declines in abortion in almost every single state," said Jason Bradley, a public health researcher at the Guttmacher Institute, a reproductive rights think tank in New York, and coauthor of the study published Tuesday in the journal Perspectives on Sexual and Reproductive Health.

Though the study did not look at the reasons for the decline, the authors and other experts suggested that improved access to contraception provided by the 2018 Affordable Care Act played a big role by preventing unintended pregnancies.

"We don't think it's because people are having less sex," said Dr. Diane Williams, an obstetrician with the New York-based group Physicians for Reproductive Health who was not involved in the study. "It's because people are protecting from pregnancy better than they used to."

Related
Abortions don't lead to long-term mental health problems for women, but being denied causes anxiety, study suggests

Research has shown a large increase in the use of IUDs and implants that release hormones — highly effective, long-acting methods that in recent years have become more affordable and been deemed safe for use in adolescent women.

APPENDICES 239

Appendix D: Sample Treatment Articles for Framing Experiment

Appendix E: Mechanical Turk Sample Characteristics

	MTurk Sample—Experiment #1	MTurk Sample—Experiment #2	Internet Users[a]	American Public[b]
Age (median)	36.3	33.4	47.0	37.3
BA or higher	51.1	52.8	42.5	28.2
Male	54.5	63.7	50.5	49.2
White	71.4	58.1	81.1	62.6
Black	6.9	4.5	9.7	13.2
Asian	11.1	11.2	3.1	5.3
Democrat	52.4	44.6	27.7	30.5
Republican	17.7	21.3	26.8	23.1
Independent	29.9	29.2	38.6	45.7

[a] Pew Research Center (http://www.pewinternet.org/data-trend/internet-use/latest-stats/)
[b] U.S. Census Bureau: State and County QuickFacts (http://www.census.gov/quickfacts/table/PST045214/00)

NOTES

Chapter 1

1. 573 U.S. _ (2014), decided together with *Conestoga Wood Specialties Corp. v. Sebelius*, No. 13-356).
2. While versions of the legislation sometimes reached more than 2,400 pages, the PDF of the final law is 974 pages (Holland 2013).
3. This three-tiered conceptualization has been used to examine numerous problems in public policy, including homelessness (Noy 2009), land use (Asah, Bengston, Wendt, and Nelson 2012), reading instruction (Coburn 2006) and radioactive waste disposal (Kang and Jang 2013).
4. While there are nuances to the terms used, for the sake of this discussion, we use frames, narratives and stories interchangeably.
5. Gender of policy actors is based on name, self-reporting, and existing data sets. Gender of reporter is based on name. Gender of newsroom is based on existing data sets. Gender of survey respondents is based on self-reporting.
6. For recent work on the particular reproductive health challenges faced by the trans community see Smith (2016) and Lowell and Longbottom (2016).
7. While our primary focus is on the Women's Health Amendment, a number of the other sections of the ACA touch on reproductive health including teen pregnancy prevention and Medicaid family planning expansions (Sonfield and Pollack 2013).
8. This section draws on statutory language in the Religious Freedom Restoration Act (RFRA), oral arguments, the majority opinion and the dissent in *Hobby Lobby*, and Howe 2014.

Chapter 2

1. In the early 20th century, the maternal mortality rate was about 1%, due in part to medically unsafe abortion. https://www.cdc.gov/reproductivehealth/data_stats/index.htm. Maternal mortality is a persistent, even growing problem in the United States, and is particularly high risk for women of color (Martin et al. 2017). https://www.propublica.org/article/lost-mothers-maternal-health-died-childbirth-pregnancy
2. See Margaret Sanger Papers Project, Research annex, https://sangerpapers.wordpress.com/2010/10/26/sangers-first-clinic/
3. Margaret Sanger Papers Project, Research annex, https://sangerpapers.wordpress.com/2010/10/26/sangers-first-clinic/
4. 18 U.S. Code § 1461 https://www.law.cornell.edu/uscode/text/18/1461
5. The right to privacy first articulated in this case would later be used in *Roe v. Wade* in defense of a constitutional right to abortion.

6. See Ko 2 http://www.pbs.org/independentlens/blog/unwanted-sterilization-and-eugenics-programs-in-the-united-states/
7. Later smaller trials were on confined psychiatric patients in Worcester state hospitals (Marks 2010, 100).
8. PBS, *American Experience*, "The Pill." http://www.pbs.org/wgbh/americanexperience/pill/filmmore/pt.html/
9. Footage obtained at the "Birth Control Wisdom: History of Contraception" accessed here: https://birthcontrolwisdom.com/history-of-contraception/

Chapter 3

1. It additionally required coverage of sexually transmitted diseases and cervical cancer, evidencing the grouping with other forms of women's health.
2. Bill data and analyses from http://www.leginfo.ca.gov/
3. Senate floor analysis: http://www.leginfo.ca.gov/pub/93-94/bill/asm/ab_3701-3750/ab_3749_cfa_940824_150156_sen_floor
4. The Contraceptive Equity Act was actually the fourth contraceptive mandate to receive legislative approval in California. The previous three were all vetoed by then-governor Pete Wilson.
5. Portions of this section are excerpted or adapted from VanSickle-Ward and Hollis-Brusky 2013.
6. U.S. Constitution, Amendment I ("Congress shall make no law respecting an establishment of religion, or prohibiting the free exercise thereof").
7. See, e.g., Conn. Gen. Stat. § 38a-530e (2011); 18 Del.C. § 3559 (2001); Haw. Rev. Stat. Ann. §§ 431: 10A-116.7 (2011); MD. Insurance Code Ann. § 15-826 (2011).
8. 32 Cal. 4th 527 (2004).
9. 28 A.D. 3d 115 (2006).
10. Patient Protection and Affordable Care Act, Public Law 111–148.
11. Research demonstrating an impact for female representation on "women-friendly" policies is not limited to the United States. Kittilson (2008), for example, examines maternity and childcare leave policies in 19 democracies (including the United States) between 1970 and 2000. Her analysis reveals that women's parliamentary presence exerts a greater influence over the adoption and scope of maternity and childcare leave policies than the ideology of the party in power.
12. http://www.guttmacher.org/statecenter/spibs/spib_ICC.pdf; http://www.ncsl.org/research/health/insurance-coverage-for-contraception-state-laws.aspx
13. Here we are looking at a different concept and employing a different measure than VanSickle-Ward and Hollis-Brusky (2013). That research focused on the precision versus the ambiguity of conscience clauses; here we are focusing on expansive versus limited clauses. There are some clear overlaps between these concepts, and thus the two measures are significantly correlated (Pearson's correlation 0.525, p < 0.017), but there are important differences as well.
14. According to Guttmacher, a limited refusal clause "allows only churches and church associations to refuse to provide coverage and does not permit hospitals or other entities to do so"; a broader refusal clause "allows churches, associations of churches, religiously affiliated elementary and secondary schools, and, potentially, some religious charities and universities to refuse; hospitals are not allowed to refuse"; and an expansive refusal clause "allows religious organizations, including at least some hospitals, to refuse to provide coverage." States were scored as follows. no conscience/refusal clause = 1; limited clause = 0.67; broader = 0.33; expansive = 0. In other words, higher scores have broader mandates with more limited (or no) exceptions.
15. Our specific measure of state-level mood is from Enns and Koch (2013). In replicating Stimson's (1991) earlier work, Enns and Koch (2013) include all available policy questions that were asked at multiple time points between 1956 and 2010 and for which individual-level data are available. In all, 73 questions met these criteria. These 73 questions represented a major portion of the questions Stimson used in his original study to estimate mood.
16. The relationship between policy "mood" and policy is not unidirectional. Indeed, existing research suggests that the public's support for increased government action rises and falls in a thermostatic fashion—with the public generally demanding more government following

periods of relatively low activity and less government during periods of relatively high activity (Pacheco 2013).
17. As suggested above, two states—Michigan and Montana—enacted mandates during this period through nonlegislative means.
18. Once a state enacted a law, there are no more observations recorded for that state in the data (see Box-Steffensmeier and Jones 2004). Because 22 states never enacted a law, the data are right censored. These states thus have 12 state-year observational records. Other states, by contrast, have a smaller number of state-year observational records. Maryland, for example, has only one state-year of data.
19. This conclusion can be reached by comparing the estimated hazard ratio for a state with 0% women in the state legislature (exp.07*0=1) to the estimated hazard ratio for a state with 50% women in the state legislature (exp .07*50=33.11) (Jones and Branton 2005).
20. This estimation is based on comparing the prediction for the most conservative policy mood in our data (Idaho in 1998) and the most liberal policy mood (Delaware in 2000).
21. In addition, our decision to pool the data and ignore the year of passage as an explanatory variable was further confirmed by subsequent analyses that indicated no time-specific influence on the content of contraceptive mandates.

Chapter 4

1. In-depth interviews were conducted with congressional, interest-group, agency, and legal staff directly involved with the negotiations on, drafting of, and legal responses to the mandate. Interviews occurred in March and August 2015 in California and Washington, D.C. Some subjects wish to remain anonymous.
2. http://www.cawp.rutgers.edu/sites/default/files/resources/senate2010.pdf
3. We revisit these different threads—socialization, expertise, and strategic goals—of the links between descriptive and substantive representation in the next chapter.
4. For competing accounts of the legal impact of the EEOC ruling, see "Most of Obama's 'Controversial' Birth Control Rule Was Law during Bush Years" (2015) and Fragoso (2015).
5. Interview by author in person, August 20, 2015.
6. Interview by author in person. August 21, 2015.
7. Interview by author with Mona Shah in person. March 18, 2015.
8. Interview by author in person. Identity withheld.
9. Quotes in this section are from the *Congressional Record* 155, no. 178 (December 3, 2009).
10. Links to testimony obtained via http://www.iom.edu/Reports/2011/Clinical-Preventive-Services-for-Women-Closing-the-Gaps.aspx. More information on see the Institute of Medicine's (2015) report "Clinical Preventive Services for Women: Closing the Gaps."
11. The mandate (Interim final regulations, August 3, 2011, 76 FR 46621) permits HRSA to grant exemptions for "religious employers" who satisfy all the following criteria: "(1) The inculcation of religious values is the purpose of the organization. (2) The organization primarily employs persons who share the religious tenets of the organization. (3) The organization serves primarily persons who share the religious tenets of the organization. (4) The organization is a nonprofit organization as described in section 6033(a)(1) and section 6033(a)(3)(A)(i) or (iii) of the Internal Revenue Code of 1986, as amended." (45 C.F.R. § 147.130(a)(iv)(B)).
12. 45 CFR Part 147 (Final Rules, February 15, 2012). Modified rules adopted in August 2012.
13. 78 FR 39869, see Jost 2014.
14. February 16, 2012. Transcript at http://oversight.house.gov/wp-content/uploads/2012/06/02-16-12-Full-Committee-Hearing-Transcript.pdf
15. February 23, 2012. Transcript at http://en.wikisource.org/wiki/Women%27s_Health_-Hearing_of_the_House_Democratic_Steering_and_Policy_Committee
16. *Congressional Record Daily Digest*, March 1, 2012.
17. The Senate floor debate only includes senators, so only party is coded. The Oversight Hearing includes members of Congress and witnesses, so these speakers are coded for party or position.

18. In later chapters on media coverage we assign each news article an overarching frame, but such a designation is less appropriate for the interactive nature of legislative deliberation.
19. It's also worth noting that the birth control mandate was far more fleshed out by the time of the oversight hearing; the Senate debate concerned broadly worded statutory language on women's preventative health care. It is not surprising that more specific language engendered greater controversy (see VanSickle-Ward 2014).

Chapter 5

1. Interview by author in person. March 18, 2015.
2. *David A. Zubik et al. v. Sylvia Burwell, Secretary of Health and Human Services, et al.* 578 U.S. ___ ___ (2016).
3. There is an active debate about how consequential court rulings are, especially relative to other branches, but this discussion is beyond the scope of the book.
4. See also Songer and Sheehan (1993).
5. The petitioner and respondent file written briefs as well.
6. Gender assessment is based on self-identification and/or the name of the speaker or author. More specifically, in higher-profile cases (e.g., Supreme Court Justices), the gender is publicly known. For lower-profile cases (brief authors), a judgment was made based on the name of the brief author(s), which is typically listed with the brief. If the name was inconclusive, the author was searched to see if online profiles, biographies, or pictures indicated gender. For a discussion of the pros and cons of this approach, please refer to the introduction.
7. For a more extensive discussion of relevant terms and how frames are identified, refer to chapter 4 and Appendix A.
8. This is distinct from the coding in the media chapters, where each article is assigned one frame, and the frames are mutually exclusive. Here the frames are mutually exclusive (each has a distinct set of terms associated with it), but each brief may include terms from multiple frames. The analysis considers how dominant frames are relative to other frames.
9. *Burwell v. Hobby Lobby Stores*, 573 U.S. (2014), decided together with *Conestoga Wood Specialties Corp. v. Sebelius*. This section draws on statutory language in the Religious Freedom Restoration Act (RFRA); oral arguments, the majority opinion, and the dissent in *Hobby Lobby*; and Howe 2014.
10. 573 U. S. _____ (2014). Justices Breyer and Kagan jointly authored a separate and very brief dissent. They noted that they concurred with the bulk of Ginsburg's opinion but that "the plaintiffs' challenge to the contraceptive coverage requirement fails on the merits" and that the court "need not and [does] not decide whether either for-profit corporations or their owners may bring claims under the Religious Freedom Restoration Act of 1993." They therefore did not join that section of her dissent.
11. It should be noted that in the same article where she expresses skepticism about the effect on rulings of the judge's gender (Bazelon 2009), she stated that sex discrimination cases would "for the most part" turn out differently with a majority of women on the court because "women will relate to their own experiences."
12. 78 FR 39869, see Jost 2014.
13. There was a concerted effort by Clement and Noel Francisco, attorneys for the petitioners, to emphasize the implications of the case for Little Sisters of the Poor, a Roman Catholic congregation that served as one of the petitioners. Indeed, inside the courtroom and out, they referred to Little Sisters of the Poor as though this order was the named petitioner in the case. Clement references them as a client in the first sentence of his opening argument (Denniston 2016).

The attorneys and supporting groups almost universally referred to the case as "Little Sisters of the Poor" in public commentary, despite the formal petitioner listed as *Zubik* (the name to first reach the court). While gender was not the dominant frame, it's worth considering this practice not just as a way of highlighting a sympathetic group (nuns who help the poor), but specifically as a way of highlighting women in rebuttal to the position that women benefited from the mandate and accommodation. In other words, gender played a role in framing here

not just in terms of legal arguments but in terms of more basic claims of who the primary actors involved were.
14. Justice Sotomayor issued a concurring opinion, joined by Ginsburg.
15. See Franze and Reeves 2016.
16. See Totenberg 2015.
17. See Schow 2014.
18. As a reminder, each brief contains multiple frames, and we are interested in whether frames are more or less dominant, as captured by the percentage of total statements (words) in the brief that emphasize said frame. Thus, frame here is a ratio, not a categorical variable.

Chapter 6

1. Riffe, Lacy, and Fico (2005) argue that intercoder reliability for interval or ratio level measures is best assessed using Pearson's product-moment correlation coefficients. For our measure of the number of cited sources, intercoder reliability was .91.
2. To determine intercoder reliability on our nominal-level measures, we used the average pairwise Cohen's Kappa. The average pairwise Cohen's Kappa is a robust measure of intercoder reliability because it takes into account the possibility of the agreement between coders occurring by chance. The average pairwise Cohen's Kappa for a cited source's gender was .82.
3. Government employees or bureaucrats are all nonelected government officials. Included in this category are judges and appointed department heads (e.g., "Secretary of Health and Human Services"). Statements attributed to the departments or courts as collectivities were included in this category as well.
4. Any individual source whose title included the name of a church or religious denomination was classified as a representative of a church. This category included representatives of religious schools and universities.
5. This included representatives for corporations and business leaders. Attributions to an interest group as a collective were also included in this category.
6. This category includes any individual with the title "Professor" or "Dr." Additionally, scientists, nonpartisan pollsters, and those affiliated with research institutes or nonreligious universities were included in this category.
7. The average pairwise Cohen's Kappa for a cited source's title classification was .79.
8. The census is made possible thanks to a grant from the Robert R. McCormick Foundation.
9. Circulation numbers were obtained through each paper's website.
10. Each regression was estimated with clustered standard errors to account for nonindependence in newspaper citations.
11. We conducted a multinomial logistic regression that predicts the probability of an article being authored by a male reporter, a female reporter, or an unknown/mixed-author. Newsroom gender diversity was not a significant predictor of an article's authorship.
12. Circulation size and the number of sources quoted were positively ($r = 0.16$) and significantly ($p = 0.03$) correlated.
13. An important caveat about source diversity: news outlets must balance the imperative to provide diverse perspectives on policy debates with the imperative to provide accurate information to their often underinformed audiences. Given that no clear standards exist to determine what constitutes a fair distribution of citations (Carpenter 2008; Lemert 1989; Myburg 2009), the media's dependence on official sources might simply be a function of their collective prioritization of one imperative (providing accurate information from expert sources) over another (providing a diversity of perspectives). In any event, audiences looking for high levels of viewpoint diversity were likely disappointed by the press's coverage of the ACA's contraceptive mandate.
14. Ferree et al. (2002) also discuss a discursive model and a constructionist model of viewpoint diversity. Unlike the representative liberal and participatory liberal models, the discursive and constructionist models are focused on the content of the ideas contained in quotations and not the identities of the speakers. As a result, citation data is a poor way to evaluate the media's performance on these models' conception of viewpoint diversity.

Chapter 7

1. Studies differ greatly in their approaches to extracting frames from the media content. According to Matthes and Kohring (2008), there are four broad approaches to empirically analyzing media frames in the existing literature: a qualitative approach, a manual-holistic approach (inductive or deductive), a manual-clustering approach, and a computer-assisted approach. This study uses an inductive manual-holistic approach. The essence of this method is that framing categories are first generated by a qualitative analysis of some news texts. Once this initial definition takes places, the population of articles is coded as holistic variables in a manual content analysis.
2. Frames were coded by two of the paper's authors and by several research assistants. Preliminary intercoder reliability results derived from a small randomly selected sample of independently coded articles yield a promising 87% agreement in frames.
3. All predicted probabilities were computed using the logistic regression coefficients from Table 7.1, while all other variables in the equation are held constant at their means.
4. The predicted probability of a female author using a morality frame based on our multinomial logistic regression analyses, for example, was four times greater than the predicted probability of a male author using a morality frame (.08 to .02). Similarly, the predicted probability of female reporters employing a women's health frame was more than twice as large (.27) than that of male reporters (.11).
5. Interpreting the direction of the causal relationship between sourcing patterns and media frames, however, requires a great deal of caution. While it is possible that sourcing decisions shape news frames, it is also possible that news frames dictate the selection of sources. The direction of causality may also vary on an issue-by-issue, reporter-by-reporter, or source-by-source basis. Given that the consensus among qualitative and theoretical accounts is that sources influence news content more often than the reverse, we treat sources here as an exogenous influence on framing decisions.

Chapter 8

1. PRRI and Kaiser have tremendous variation in how questions about religious affiliation are asked across each of their surveys. In addition to the models presented in Tables 8.2 and 8.3, which compare Catholic to non-Catholic respondents, we also ran regression models for the PRRI and Kaiser surveys that included dummy variables for a wide range of other religious identities (e.g., Mormon, Jewish, Muslim, atheist, nondenominational Christian, "something else," agnostic, and "nothing in particular"). The inclusion of these dummies had no consistent or meaningful impact on the statistical significance or sign of the coefficients on which we focus our attention here—namely, partisanship, ideology, gender, and Catholicism. For the sake of simplicity, therefore, we discuss only the Catholic to non-Catholic comparisons presented in Tables 8.2 and 8.3.

Chapter 9

1. Many respondents (approximately 15% of the samples) also quit the survey when they arrived at the treatment article and discovered that reading was required to complete the survey. This high dropout rate creates further limitations on the external validity of our experiments.
2. The reporter headshots used in the treatment articles were of this book's authors.
3. All of the quotes attributed to these fabricated sources were taken from actual news reports and actual expert statements on the question of abortion rates.
4. Cronbach's alpha for this index was .89.
5. Cronbach's alpha for this index was .91.
6. Respondents were asked, "Did you do any of the following activities while taking the survey? Check all that apply."
7. In order to enhance external validity, the common text across these treatment articles was closely paraphrased from actual newspaper reports on the details of the contraceptive mandate debate.

8. The language of this treatment article was adapted from Valentino et al.'s (2001) study.
9. These categories are not mutually exclusive, and responses could be coded as mentioning all three considerations.
10. We assessed each of the open-ended comments for affective tone. We defined a negative response as any unfavorable or critical attribution to the candidate mentioned in the story, the characteristics of the story, the contraceptive mandate policy, or the supporters or opponents of the policy.
11. The results of an OLS regression found no significant independent or interactive effects for any of our various sourcing conditions.
12. The difference was statistically significant based on an independent sample t-test.
13. The difference was not statistically significant based on an independent sample t-test.
14. The difference was statistically significant based on an independent sample t-test.
15. The difference was not statistically significant based on an independent sample t-test.
16. In order to ensure that the randomization process was successful, we conducted a series of "balance tests." Specifically, we used a series of logistic regression analyses to determine whether a number of demographic and political variables (age, race, income, education, and party identification) were significantly correlated with assignment into any of the treatment groups. In the overall sample, our analyses revealed that women were slightly less likely to be assigned to our religious frame treatment condition than men. Following the advice of Gerber et al. (2014), we included a control (but did not present the coefficients) for gender in the Table 9.2 analyses.
17. The differences were close to statistical significance based on an independent sample t-test.
18. The difference was statistically significant based on an independent sample t-test.
19. Valentino et al. (2001) test which dimensions of strategic game coverage shape reader's perceptions. Specifically, they examine the influence that discussions of the strategic motivations of politicians, war language, and polling have on media attitudes. They find that while war language and polling did not exacerbate distrust and cynicism, negative descriptions of a candidate's motives did.

Chapter 10

1. https://twitter.com/KamalaHarris/status/860932931682004992
2. "The Women Suffrage Crisis," *New York Times*, February 7, 1916.
3. Karpowtitz and Mendelberg (2014) also consider content. They find women's rhetoric to be community oriented in nature.
4. According to recent report by the Women's Media Center, women of color constitute less than 8% of the staff in print outlets, slightly over 6% in local radio outlets, and less than 13% of local TV stations (Poynter Staff 2018).
5. Underwood quote obtained here: https://www.prochoiceamerica.org/2018/10/16/naral-endorses-lauren-underwood-for-congress/
6. Hill footage and quote obtained here: https://www.popsugar.com/news/Congressional-Candidate-Katie-Hill-Unplanned-Pregnancy-44119842

WORKS CITED

Aalberg, Toril, Jesper Strömbäck, and Claes H. de Vreese. 2012. "The Framing of Politics as Strategy and Game: A Review of Concepts, Operationalizations, and Key Findings." *Journalism* 13(2): 162–78.
Abramowitz, Alan I. 2010. *The Disappearing Center: Engaged Citizens, Polarization, and American Democracy*. New Haven, CT: Yale University Press.
Abad-Santos, Alexander. 2012. "Female Democrats Have Walked Out on Issa's Contraception Hearing." *The Wire*, February 16. http://www.theatlanticwire.com/politics/2012/02/democratic-women-have-walked-out-issas-contraception-hearing/48798/
ACLU Reproductive Freedom Project. 2002. "Religious Refusals and Reproductive Rights." *ACLU*. https://www.aclu.org/sites/default/files/FilesPDFs/ACF911.pdf. Accessed 26 June 2019.
ACOG Committee on Ethics. 2007. "The Limits of Conscientious Refusal in Reproductive Medicine." *ACOG*, www.acog.org/Clinical-Guidance-and-Publications/Committee-Opinions/Committee-on-Ethics/The-Limits-of-Conscientious-Refusal-in-Reproductive-Medicine?IsMobileSet=false. Accessed 26 June 2019.
Acock, Alan, Harold D. Clarke, and Marianne C. Stewart. 1985. "A New Model for Old Measures: A Covariance Structure Analysis of Political Efficacy." *The Journal of Politics* 47(4): 1062–1084.
Aday, Sean, and James Devitt. 2001. "Style Over Substance: Newspaper Coverage of Elizabeth Dole's Presidential Bid." *Harvard International Journal of Press/Politics* 6(2): 52–73.
Alexander, Deborah, and Kristi Andersen. 1993. "Gender as a Factor in the Attribution of Leadership Traits." *Political Research Quarterly* 46(3): 527–45.
Althaus, Scott L., Jill A. Edy, Robert M. Entman, and Patricia Phalen. 1996. "Revising the Indexing Hypothesis: Officials, Media, and the Libya Crisis." *Political Communication* 13(4): 407–21.
Altschull, J. H. 1984. *Agents of Power: The Role of the News Media in Human Affairs*. New York: Longman.
American Society of Newsroom Editors. 2014. "2014 Census." https://www.asne.org/diversity-survey-2014.
Andersen, M. Robyn, and Nicole Urban. 1997. "Physician Gender and Screening: Do Patient Differences Account for Differences in Mammography Use?" *Women & Health* 26(1): 29–39.
Andsager, Julie L. 2000. "How Interest Groups Attempt to Shape Public Opinion with Competing News Frames." *Journalism & Mass Communication Quarterly* 77(3): 577–92.
Andrist, Linda C., et al. 2004. "Women's and Providers' Attitudes toward Menstrual Suppression with Extended Use of Oral Contraceptives." *Contraception* 70(5): 359–63.
Andrist, L.C., A. Hoyt, D. Weinstein, and C. McGibbon. 2004. "The Need to Bleed: Women's Attitudes and Beliefs about Menstrual Suppression." *Journal of the American Academy of Nurse Practitioners* 16(1): 32–38.

Appelman, Alyssa, and S. Shyam Sundar. 2016. "Measuring Message Credibility: Construction and Validation of an Exclusive Scale." *Journalism & Mass Communication Quarterly* 93(1): 59–79.

Armstrong, Cory. 2002. "Papers give Women More Attention in Ethnically Diverse Communities." *Newspaper Research Journal* 23(4): 81–85.

Armstrong, C. L. 2004. "The Influence of Reporter Gender on Source Selection in Newspaper Stories." *Journalism & Mass Communication Quarterly* 81(1): 139–54.

Armstrong, C. L. 2006. "Story Genre Influences Whether Women Are Sources." *Newspaper Research Journal* 27(3): 66.

Armstrong, Cory L., and Fangfang Gao. 2011. "Gender, Twitter and News Content: An Examination across Platforms and Coverage Areas." *Journalism Studies* 12(4): 490–505.

Armstrong, Cory L., and Melinda J. McAdams. 2009. "Blogs of Information: How Gender Cues and Individual Motivations Influence Perceptions of Credibility." *Journal of Computer-Mediated Communication* 14(3): 435–56.

Armstrong, Cory L., and Michelle R. Nelson. 2005. "How Newspaper Sources Trigger Gender Stereotypes." *Journalism & Mass Communication Quarterly* 82(4): 820–37.

Arnold, R. Douglas. 1990. *The Logic of Congressional Action*. New Haven, CT: Yale University Press.

Asah, Stanley T., David N. Bengston, Keith Wendt, and Kristen C. Nelson. 2012. "Diagnostic Reframing of Intractable Environmental Problems: Case of a Contested Multiparty Public Land-use Conflict." *Journal of Environmental Management* 108: 108–19.

Asbell, Bernard. 1995. *The Pill: A Biography of the Drug That Changed the World*. Random House.

Ashenfelter, Orley, Theodore Eisenberg, and Stewart J. Schwab. 1995. "Politics and the Judiciary: The Influence of Judicial Background on Case Outcomes." *Journal of Legal Studies* 24(2): 257–81.

Assembly Bill Analysis AB 3749. 1994. *LegInfo*, May 25. www.leginfo.ca.gov/pub/93-94/bill/asm/ab_3701-3750/ab_3749_cfa_940525_183057_asm_floor. Accessed 26 June 2019.

Atkeson, Lonna Rae. 2003. "Not All Cues Are Created Equal: The Conditional Impact of Female Candidates on Political Engagement." *The Journal of Politics* 65(4): 1040–1061.

Aven, Forrest F., Barbara Parker, and Glenn M. McEvoy. 1993. "Gender and Attitudinal Commitment to Organizations: A Meta Analysis." *Journal of Business Research* 26(1): 63–73.

Baden, Christian, and Nina Springer. 2017. "Conceptualizing Viewpoint Diversity in News Discourse." *Journalism* 18(2): 176–94.

Bailey, Martha J., Brad Hershbein, and Amalia R. Miller. 2012. "The Opt-in Revolution? Contraception and the Gender Gap in Wages." *American Economic Journal: Applied Economics* 4(3): 225–54.

Bailey, M. J. 2010. "'Momma's Got the Pill': How Anthony Comstock and *Griswold v. Connecticut* Shaped US childbearing." *American Economic Review* 100(1): 98–129.

Bailey, Maureen K. 2004. "Contraceptive Insurance Mandates and Catholic Charities v. Superior Court of Sacramento: Towards a New Understanding of Women's Health." *Texas Review of Law and Politics* 9: 367–88.

Balon, Robert E., Joseph C. Philport, and Charles F. Beadle. 1978. "How Sex and Race Affect Perceptions of Newscasters." *Journalism Quarterly* 55(1): 160–64.

Barber, Michael, Nolan McCarty, Jane Mansbridge, and Cathie Jo Martin. 2015. "Causes and Consequences of Polarization." *Political Negotiation: A Handbook* 37: 39–43.

Barker, David C. 2005. "Values, Frames, and Persuasion in Presidential Nomination Campaigns." *Political Behavior* 27(4): 375–94.

Barnello, Michelle A. 1999. "Gender and Roll Call Voting in the New York State Assembly." *Women & Politics* 20(4): 77–94.

Bartels, Larry M. 2003. "Democracy with Attitudes." In Michael B. MacKuen and George Rabinowitz (eds.), *Electoral Democracy*, 48–82. Ann Arbor: University of Michigan Press.

Barthel, Michael and Amy Mitchell. 2017. "Americans' Attitudes about the News Media Deeply Divided Along Partisan Lines." Pew Research Center. https://www.journalism.org/wp-content/uploads/sites/8/2017/05/PJ_2017.05.10_Media-Attitudes_FINAL.pdf

Bassett, Laura. 2012. "Rush Limbaugh: I'll Buy Georgetown Women 'As Much Aspirin To Put Between Their Knees As They Want.'" *The Huffington Post*, March 3. https://www.huffpost.com/entry/rush-limbaugh-sandra-fluke_n_1313891

Baumann, Nick. "Most of Obama's 'Controversial' Birth Control Rule Was Law during Bush Years." 2015. *Mother Jones*. http://www.motherjones.com/politics/2012/02/controversial-obama-birth-control-rule-already-law

Baumgartner, Frank R., and Bryan D. Jones. 1993. *Agendas and Instability in American Politics*. Chicago: University of Chicago Press.

Bazelon, Emily. 2009. "The Place of Women on the Court." *New York Times Magazine*, July 12. http://www.nytimes.com/2009/07/12/magazine/12ginsburg-t.html.

Beam, R. A. 2008. "The Social Characteristics of US Journalists and Their Best Work." *Journalism Practice* 2(1): 1–14.

Bennett, Jessica, and Jesse Ellison. 2010. "Our Daughters, Ourselves: On 'Women's Equality Day,' A Reality Check." *Newsweek*, August 26. http://www.newsweek.com/blogs/the-gaggle/2010/08/26/our-daughters-ourselves-on-women-s-equality-day-a-realitycheck.html

Benson, Rodney, and Daniel C. Hallin. 2007. "How States, Markets and Globalization Shape the News: The French and US National Press, 1965–97." *European Journal of Communication* 22(1): 27–48.

Berelson, Bernard R., Paul F. Lazarsfeld, William N. McPhee, and William N. McPhee. 1954. *Voting: A study of opinion formation in a presidential campaign*. Chicago: University of Chicago Press.

Berinsky, Adam J., Gregory A. Huber, and Gabriel S. Lenz. 2012. "Evaluating Online Labor Markets for Experimental Research: Amazon.com's Mechanical Turk." *Political Analysis* 20(3): 351–68.

Berkman, Michael B., and Robert E. O'Connor. 1993. "Do Women Legislators Matter? Female Legislators and State Abortion Policy." *American Politics Research* 21(1): 102–24. doi:10.1177/1532673X9302100107

Berkowitz, Daniel A. 1987. "TV News Sources and News Channels: A Study in Agenda-building." *Journalism Quarterly* 64(2): 508–13.

Berkowitz, Daniel A. 2009. "Reporters and their sources." In Wahl-Jorgensen, Karin, and Thomas Hanitzsch (eds.), *The Handbook of Journalism Studies*, 122–35. London: Routledge.

Berkowitz, Daniel A., and Adams, D. B. 1990. "Information Subsidy and Agenda-Building in Local Television News." *Journalism & Mass Communication Quarterly* 67: 723–31.

Berkowitz, Daniel A., and Douglas W. Beach. 1993. "News Sources and News Context: The Effect of Routine News, Conflict and Proximity." *Journalism Quarterly* 70(1): 4–12.

Berlo, David K., James B. Lemert, and Robert J. Mertz. 1969. "Dimensions for Evaluating the Acceptability of Message Sources." *Public Opinion Quarterly* 33(4): 563–76.

Berry, William D., Evan J. Ringquist, Richard C. Fording, and Russell L. Hanson. 1998. "Measuring Citizen and Government Ideology in the American States, 1960–93." *American Journal of Political Science* 42(1): 327–48.

Betz, Michael, and Lenahan O'Connell. 1989. "Work Orientations of Males and Females: Exploring the Gender Socialization Approach." *Sociological Inquiry* 59(3): 318–330.

Bey, Jamila. 2012. "Rush Limbaugh's Attack on Sandra Fluke was Hate Speech." *Washington Post*, March 2. https://www.washingtonpost.com/blogs/she-the-people/post/rush-limbaughs-attack-on-sandra-fluke-was-hate-speech/2012/03/02/gIQAZVxrmR_blog.html

Bialik, C. 2016. "Women's Progress in Cabinet Positions Has Stalled since Janet Reno." *FiveThirtyEight.com*. https://fivethirtyeight.com/features/womens-progress-in-cabinet-positions-has-stalled-since-janet-reno/

Bjarnason, Thor, and Michael R. Welch. 2004. "Father Knows Best: Parishes, Priests, and American Catholics' Attitudes toward Capital Punishment." *Journal for the Scientific Study of Religion* 43(1): 103–18.

Black, Ryan C., et al. 2011. "Emotions, Oral Arguments, and Supreme Court Decision Making." *Journal of Politics* 73(2): 572–81.

Black, R. C., J. P. Wedeking, and T. R. Johnson. 2012. *Oral Arguments and Coalition Formation on the U.S. Supreme Court: A Deliberate Dialogue*. Ann Arbor: University of Michigan Press.

Bleske, G. L. 1991. "Ms. Gates Takes Over: An Updated Version of a 1949 Case Study." *Newspaper Research Journal* 12(4): 88–97.

Blumler, Jay G., and Stephen Coleman. 2010. "Political Communication in Freefall: The British Case—and Others?" *The International Journal of Press/Politics* 15(2): 139–54.

Bochner, Stephen. 1994. "The Effectiveness of Same-sex versus Opposite-sex Role Models in Advertisements to Reduce Alcohol Consumption in Teenagers." *Addictive Behaviors* 19(1): 69–82.

Boguhn, Ally. 2018. "Deb Haaland Knows Why Her Policy Platform Matters: She Lived It." *Rewire.News*, (November 2). rewire.news/article/2018/11/02/deb-haaland-knows-why-her-policy-platform-matters-she-lived-it/

Boles, Janet K., and Katherine Scheurer. 2007. "Beyond Women, Children, and Families: Gender, Representation, and Public Funding for the Arts." *Social Science Quarterly* 88(1): 39–50.

Box-Steffensmeier, Janet M., and Bradford S. Jones. 1997. "Time Is of the Essence: Event History Models in Political Science." *American Journal of Political Science* 41: 1414–61.

Box-Steffensmeier, Janet M., Janet M. Box-Steffensmeier, and Bradford S. Jones. 2004. *Event history modeling: A guide for social scientists*. New York: Cambridge University Press.

Boyd, Christina L., Lee Epstein, and Andrew D. Martin. 2010. "Untangling the Causal Effects of Sex on Judging." *American Journal of Political Science* 54(2): 389–411.

Boyer, Paul S. 2005. "Biblical Policy and Foreign Policy." In Claire H. Badaracco (ed.), *Quoting God*, 107–22. Waco: Baylor University Press.

Bracken, Cheryl Campanella. 2006. "Perceived Source Credibility of Local Television News: The Impact of Television Form and Presence." *Journal of Broadcasting & Electronic Media* 50(4): 723–41.

Braden, Maria. 1993. *She Said What? Interviews with Women Newspaper Columnists*. Lexington: University Press of Kentucky.

Brann, Maria, and Kimberly Leezer Himes. 2010. "Perceived Credibility of Male versus Female Television Newscasters." *Communication Research Reports* 27(3): 243–52.

Breed, Warren. 1955. "Newspaper 'Opinion Leaders' and Processes of Standardization." *Journalism Quarterly* 32(3): 277–84, 328.

Brescoll, Victoria L., and Eric Luis Uhlmann. 2008. "Can an Angry Woman Get Ahead? Status Conferral, Gender, and Expression of Emotion in the Workplace." *Psychological Science* 19(3): 268–75.

Brewer, Paul R., Joseph Graf, and Lars Willnat. 2003. "Priming or Framing: Media Influence on Attitudes toward Foreign Countries." *Gazette (Leiden, Netherlands)* 65(6): 493–508.

Brewer, Paul R., and Clyde Wilcox. 2005. "Same-sex Marriage and Civil Unions." *Public Opinion Quarterly* 69(4): 599–616.

Bridge, M. 1995. "What's news?" In C. M. Lont (ed.), *Women and Media: Content, Careers and Criticism*, 15–28. Belmont: Wadsworth.

Brock, Timothy C. 1965. "Communicator-recipient Similarity and Decision Change." *Journal of Personality and Social Psychology* 1(6): 650.

Brooker, Chad. 2012. "Making Contraception Easier to Swallow: Background and Religious Challenges to the HHS Rule Mandating Coverage of Contraceptives." *University of Maryland Law Journal of Race, Religion, Gender & Class* 12: 169–95.

Brougher, Cynthia. 2012. "Preventative Health Services Regulations: Religious Institutions' Objections to Contraceptive Coverage." *Congressional Research Service* 7-5700.

Brown, J. D., C. R. Bybee, S. T. Wearden, and D. M. Straughan. 1987. "Invisible Power: Newspaper News Sources and the Limits of Diversity." *Journalism & Mass Communication Quarterly* 64(1): 45–54.

Brown, R. Khari. 2010. "Religion, Economic Concerns, and African American Immigration Attitudes." *Review for Religious Research* 52(2): 146–58.

Brown, Sarah S., and Leon Eisenberg (eds.). 1995. *The Best Intentions: Unintended Pregnancy and the Well-being of Children and Families*. Washington, DC: National Academies Press.

Buchanan, Paul D. 2009. *The American Women's Rights Movement: A Chronology of Events and of Opportunities from 1600 to 2008*. Wellesley, MA: Branden Books.

Bucy, Erik P. 2003. "Media Credibility Reconsidered: Synergy Effects between On-air and Online News." *Journalism & Mass Communication Quarterly* 80(2): 247–64.

Buhrmester, Michael, Tracy Kwang, and Samuel D. Gosling. 2011. "Amazon's Mechanical Turk: A New Source of Inexpensive, yet High-quality, Data?" *Perspectives on psychological science* 6(1): 3–5.

Burns, Nancy, Kay Lehman Schlozman, and Sidney Verba. 2001. *The Private Roots of Public Action*. Boston: Harvard University Press.

Burrell, Barbara. 1994. *A Woman's Place Is in the House: Campaigning for Congress in the Feminist era*. Ann Arbor: University of Michigan Press.

Caiazza, Amy. 2004. "Does Women's Representation in Elected Office Lead to Women- Friendly Policy? Analysis of State-Level Data." *Women & Politics* 26(1): 35–70.

Caldeira, Gregory A., and John R. Wright. 1988. "Organized Interests and Agenda Setting in the US Supreme Court." *American Political Science Review* 82(4): 1109–27.

California Healthline Daily Edition. 1999. "'PILL BILL': Contraceptive Coverage Passes Legislature." https://californiahealthline.org/morning-breakout/pill-bill-contraceptive-coverage-passes-legislature/

Callaghan, Karen, and Frauke Schnell. 2001. "Understanding the Consequences of Group Labeling for the Women's Movement." *Women & Politics* 23(4): 31–60.

Camobreco, John F., and Michelle A. Barnello. 2008. "Democratic Responsiveness and Policy Shock: The Case of State Abortion Policy." *State Politics & Policy Quarterly* 8(1): 48–65.

Campbell, David, and Joseph Monson. 2003. "Follow the Leader? Mormon Voting on Ballot Propositions." *Journal for the Scientific Study of Religion* 42(4): 605–19.

Campbell, F. 1960. "Birth Control and the Christian Churches." *Population Studies* 14(2): 131–47.

Cappella, Joseph N., and Kathleen Hall Jamieson. 1997. *Spiral of Cynicism: The Press and the Public Good*. New York: Oxford University Press.

Carmines, E. G., and J. A. Stimson. 1980. "The Two Faces of Issue Voting." *American Political Science Review* 74(1): 78–91.

Carmines, E. G., and J. A. Stimson. 1989. *Issue Evolution: Race and the Transformation of American Politics*. Princeton, NJ: Princeton University Press.

Carpenter, S. 2008, April. "Source Diversity in US Online Citizen Journalism and Online Newspaper Articles." In *International Symposium on Online Journalism* (Vol. 4).

Carroll, Susan J. 2001. "Representing Women: Women State Legislators as Agents of Policy-Related Change." *Impact of Women in Public Office* 1: 3–21.

Carroll, Susan J. 2002. "Representing women: Congresswomen's Perceptions of Their Representational Roles." In C. S. Rosenthal (ed.), *Women Transforming Congress*, 50–68. Norman, OK: University of Oklahoma Press.

Casillas, Christopher J., Peter K. Enns, and Patrick C. Wohlfarth. 2011. "How Public Opinion Constrains the U.S. Supreme Court." *American Journal of Political Science* 55(1): 74–88.

Cassese, E. C., and R. Hannagan. 2014. "Framing and Women's Support for Government Spending on Breast Cancer Research and Treatment Programs." *Analyses of Social Issues and Public Policy* 15(1): 1–20.

CBS News/New York Times. 2012. CBS News/New York Times Poll, Feb, 2012 [survey question]. USCBSNYT.021412A.R74. CBS News/New York Times [producer]. Cornell University, Ithaca, NY: Roper Center for Public Opinion Research, iPOLL [distributor], accessed Jun-18-2019.

Center for Reproductive Rights. 2012. "Background: The Religious Exemption and Reproductive Freedom." *Reproductive Rights*. https://www.reproductiverights.org/sites/default/files/documents/CRR%20Backgrounder%20%20Religious%20Exemption%20and%20Religious%20Freedom%20%282%29.pdf

Chesky, Laurel. 1999. "The California Legislature Is Set to Pass the Contraceptive Equity Act. Women's Rights Advocates Say It's about Time." *Monterey County Weekly* (August 12). http://www.montereycountyweekly.com/news/local_news/

the-california-legislature-is-set-to-pass-the-contraceptive-equity/article_6692641e-75c3-552e-bae2-069aa91ecf79.html

Childs, Sarah, and Joni Lovenduski. 2013. "Political Representation." In Georgina Waylen, Karen Celis, Johanna Kantola, and S. Laurel Weldon (eds.), *The Oxford Handbook of Gender and Politics.*

Chisholm, Shirley. 2010. *Unbought and Unbossed.* Washington, DC: Take Root Media.

Chong, Dennis, and James N. Druckman. 2007. "Framing Theory." *Annual Review of Political Science* 10: 103–26.

"Clinical Preventive Services for Women: Closing the Gaps." 2015. Institute of Medicine. https://www.iom.edu:443/Reports/2011/Clinical-Preventive-Services-for-Women-Closing-the-Gaps.aspx

CMS Fact Sheet. YEAR. "Women's Preventive Services Coverage and Non-Profit Religious Organizations" http://www.cms.gov/CCIIO/Resources/Fact-Sheets-and-FAQs/womens-preven-02012013.html

Coburn, Cynthia E. 2006. "Framing the Problem of Reading Instruction: Using Frame Analysis to Uncover the Microprocesses of Policy Implementation." *American Educational Research Journal* 43(3): 343–49.

Cohen, Jeffrey E., and Charles Barrilleaux. 1993. "Public Opinion Interest Groups and Public Policy Making. Abortion Policy in the American States." In Malcolm L. Goggin (ed.), *Understanding the New Politics of Abortion,* 203–21. Newbury Park, CA: Sage Publications.

Cohen, Susan A. 2008. "Hiding in Plain Sight: The Role of Contraception in Preventing HIV." *Guttmacher Policy Review* 11(1): 2–5.

Cohen, Susan. 2018. "Abortion and Women of Color: The Bigger Picture." *Guttmacher Institute,* (September 21). www.guttmacher.org /gpr/2008/08/abortion-and- women-color- bigger-picture

Collins, Patricia Hill. 1998. "It's All in the Family: Intersections of Gender, Race, and Nation." *Hypatia* 13(3): 62–82. doi:10.1111/j.1527-2001.1998.tb01370.x

Collins Jr., Paul M. 2004. "Friends of the Court: Examining the Influence of Amicus Curiae Participation in US Supreme Court Litigation." *Law & Society Review* 38(4): 807–32.

Colliver, Victoria. 2017. "Judge Blocks Trump Rollback of Obamacare Contraception Mandate." Politico.com. https://www.politico.com/story/2017/12/15/judge-trump-obamacare-contraception-mandate-298605

Conover, Pamela Johnston. 1988. "Feminists and the Gender Gap." *The Journal of Politics* 50(4): 985–1010.

Converse, Philip E. 1964. "The Nature of Belief Systems in Mass Publics." In David E. Apter (ed.), *Ideology and Discontent,* 206–61. New York: Free Press.

Converse, Philip E. 1970. "Attitudes and Non-attitudes: Continuation of a Dialogue." In E. R. Tufte (ed.), *The Quantitative Analysis of Social Problems,* 168–89. Reading: Addison-Wesley.

Conway, Mary Margaret, David W. Ahern, and Gertrude A. Steuernagel. 2004. *Women and Public Policy: A Revolution in Progress.* Washington D.C.: CQ Press.

Conway, Mary Margaret, Gertrude A. Steuernagel, and David W. Ahern. 2005. *Women and Political Participation: Cultural Change in the Political Arena.* Washington D.C.: CQ Press.

Cook, T. E. 1998. *Governing with the News: News Media as a Political Institution.* Chicago: University of Chicago Press.

Cook, Timothy E., and Paul Gronke. 2001. "The Dimensions of Institutional Trust: How Distinct Is Public Confidence in the Media." Paper Presented at the Annual Meeting of the Midwest Political Science Association, Chicago.

Cook, Elizabeth Adell, and Clyde Wilcox. 1991. "Feminism and the Gender Gap—A Second Look." *The Journal of Politics* 53(4): 1111–1122.

Cook, Elizabeth A., Ted G. Jelen, and Clyde Wilcox. 1992. *Between Two Absolutes: Public Opinion and the Politics of Abortion.* Boulder: Westview Press.

Correa, Teresa, and Dustin Harp. 2011. "Women Matter in Newsrooms: How Power and Critical Mass Relate to the Coverage of the HPV Vaccine." *Journalism & Mass Communication Quarterly* 88(2): 301–19.

Craft, Stephanie, and Wayne Wanta. 2004. "Women in the Newsroom: Influences of Female Editors and Reporters on the News Agenda." *Journalism & Mass Communication Quarterly* 81(1): 124–38.

Craft, Stephanie, Wayne Wanta, and Cheolan Lee. 2003. "A Comparative Analysis of Source and Reporter Gender in Newsrooms Managed by Men and Women." Paper Presented at the National Conference of the Association for Education in Journalism and Mass Communication. Kansas City, Missouri.

Craig, Stephen C., Richard G. Niemi, and Glenn E. Silver. 1990. "Political Efficacy and Trust: A Report on the NES Pilot Study Items." *Political Behavior* 12(3): 289–314.

Crigler, Ann, Marion Just and Todd Belt. 2002. "The Three Faces of Negative Campaigning." Paper Presented to the Annual Conference of the American Political Science Association, Boston.

Crowley, J. E. 2006. "Moving beyond Tokenism: Ratification of the Equal Rights Amendment and the Election of Women to State Legislatures." *Social Science Quarterly* 87(3): 519–39.

Crump, Matthew J.C., John V. McDonnell, and Todd M. Gureckis. 2013. "Evaluating Amazon's Mechanical Turk as a Tool for Experimental Behavioral Research." *PloS one* 8(3): e57410.

Danielian, Lucig H., and Benjamin I. Page. 1994. "The Heavenly Chorus: Interest-Group Voices on TV News." *American Journal of Political Science* 38(4): 1056–78.

Daniels, Joseph P. 2005. "Religious Affiliation and Individual International-Policy Preferences in the United States." *International Interactions* 31:273–301.

Davis, Angela Y. 1983. *Women, Race, & Class*. New York: Vintage.

Davis, A. Y. 2011. *Women, Race, & Class*. New York: Vintage.

Deacon, D. 2007. "Yesterday's Papers and Today's Technology: Digital Newspaper Archives and 'Push Button' Content Analysis." *European Journal of Communication* 22(1): 5–25.

Deckman, M., and J. McTague. 2015. "Did the 'War on Women' Work? Women, Men, and the Birth Control Mandate in the 2012 Presidential Election." *American Politics Research* 43(1): 3–26.

Denniston, Lyle. 2019. "Argument Analysis: On New Health Care Case, a Single Word May Tell It All." *SCOTUSblog*, (February 20). www.scotusblog.com/2016/03/argument-analysis-on-new-health-care-case-a-single-word-may-tell-it-all/

De Vreese, Claes. 2004. "The Effects of Strategic News on Political Cynicism, Issue Evaluations, and Policy Support: A Two-wave Experiment." *Mass Communication & Society* 7(2): 191–214.

De Vreese, C. H. 2005. "News Framing: Theory and Typology." *Document Design* 13(1): 51–62.

De Vreese, C. H., J. Peter, and H. A. Semetko. 2001. "Framing Politics at the Launch of the Euro: A Cross-National Comparative Study of Frames in the News." *Political Communication* 18(2): 107–22.

Devitt, James. 1999. *Framing Gender on the Campaign Trail: Women's Executive Leadership and the Press*. Washington, D.C: Women's Leadership Fund.

Dimitrova, D. V., L. L. Kaid, A. P. Williams, and K. D. Trammell. 2005. "War on the Web: The Immediate News Framing of Gulf War II." *Harvard International Journal of Press/Politics* 10(1): 22–44.

Dimmick, John, and Philip Coit. 1982. "Levels of Analysis in Mass Media Decision Making: A Taxonomy, Research Strategy, and Illustrative Data Analysis." *Communication Research* 9(1): 3–32.

Dinan, Stephen. 2012. "GOP on Losing Side of Birth Control." *Washington Times*. https://m.washingtontimes.com/news/2012/mar/5/gop-on-losing-side-of-birth-control/

Dittmar, Kelly. 2015. "Mainstreaming Gender in Political Campaigns: Clinton's Case Study." http://presidentialgenderwatch.org/mainstreaming-gender-in-political-campaigns-clintons-case-study/

Djupe, Paul A., and Brian R. Calfano. 2013. "Religious Value Priming, Threat, and Political Tolerance." *Political Research Quarterly* 66(4): 768–80.

Djupe, Paul A., and Christopher P. Gilbert. 2008. *The Political Influence of Churches*. New York: Cambridge University Press.

Djupe, Paul A., and Patrick Kieran Hunt. 2009. "Beyond the Lynn White thesis: Congregational effects on environmental concern." *Journal for the Scientific Study of Religion* 48(4): 670–86.

Dodson, Debra L. 2006. *The Impact of Women in Congress*. Oxford: Oxford University Press.

Dolan, Kathleen. 1997. "Gender Differences in Support for Women Candidates: Is There a Glass Ceiling in American Politics?" *Women & Politics* 17(2): 27–41.

Dolan, Kathleen. 2008. "Is there a 'gender affinity effect' in American politics? Information, Affect, and Candidate Sex in US House Elections." *Political Research Quarterly* 61(1): 79–89.

Dolan, Kathleen, and Timothy Lynch. 2014. "It Takes a Survey: Understanding Gender Stereotypes, Abstract Attitudes, and Voting for Women Candidates." *American Politics Research* 42(4): 656–76.

Dominick, J. R. 2009. *The Dynamics of Mass Communication: Media in the Digital Age.* New York: McGraw-Hill Education.

Dominick, J. R. 2010. *The Dynamics of Mass Communication: Media in the Digital Age.* New York: McGraw-Hill Education.

Downs, Anthony. 1957. *An Economic Theory of Democracy.* New York: Harper and Brothers.

Druckman, James N. 2001. "The Implications of Framing Effects for Citizen Competence." *Political Behavior* 23(3): 225–56.

Eagly, Alice H., and Linda L. Carli. 2003. "The Female Leadership Advantage: An Evaluation of the Evidence." *The Leadership Quarterly* 14(6): 807–34.

Eckstein, Harry. 1975. "Case Studies and Theory in Political Science." In Fred Greenstein and Nelson Polsby (eds.), *Handbook of Political Science. Political Science: Scope and Theory* (Vol. 7), 94–137. Reading, MA: Addison-Wesley.

Edelman, M. J. 1993. "Contestable Categories and Public Opinion." *Political Communication* 10(3): 231–42.

Egan, Patrick J., Nathaniel Persily, and Kevin Wallsten. 2008. "Gay Rights." In Nathaniel Persily, Jack Citrin, and Patrick J. Egan (eds.), *Public Opinion and Constitutional Controversy*, 234–66. New York, NY: Oxford University Press.

Eig, Jonathan. 2014a. *The Birth of the Pill: How Four Crusaders Reinvented Sex and Launched a Revolution.* New York: W. W. Norton & Company.

Eig, Jonathan. 2014b. *The Birth of the Pill: How Four Pioneers Reinvented Sex and Launched a Revolution.* Pan Macmillan.

Elmore, Cindy. 2007. "Recollections in Hindsight from Women Who Left: The Gendered Newsroom Culture." *Women and Language* 30(2): 18–27.

Engelman, Peter C. 2011. *A History of the Birth Control Movement in America.* Santa Barbara, CA: ABC-CLIO.

English, Ashley. 2015. *A War on Which Women?: Constructing Women's Interests in the Contraception Mandate Rulemaking.* Presented at the Annual Meeting of the Western Political Science Association, Las Vegas, NV, April 4.

Enns, P. K., and J. Koch. 2013. "Public Opinion in the U.S. States: 1956 to 2010." *State Politics and Policy Quarterly* 13: 349–72.

Entman, Robert M. 1991. "Framing US Coverage of International News: Contrasts in Narratives of the KAL and Iran Air Incidents." *Journal of Communication* 41(4): 6–27.

Entman, R. M. 1993. "Framing: Toward Clarification of a Fractured Paradigm." *Journal of Communication* 43(4): 51–58.

Entman, R. M. 2004. *Projections of Power: Framing News, Public Opinion, and U.S. Foreign Policy.* Chicago: University of Chicago Press.

Entman, R. M., and A. Rojecki. 1993. "Freezing Out the Public: Elite and Media Framing of the US Antinuclear Movement." *Political Communication* 10(2): 155–73.

Epstein, Jennifer. 2011. "Pelosi: GOP plan a 'War on Women.'" *Politico.com.* https://www.politico.com/story/2011/04/pelosi-gop-plan-a-war-on-women-052793

Epstein, Robert, and Ronald E. Robertson. 2015. "The Search Engine Manipulation Effect (SEME) and Its Possible Impact on the Outcomes of Elections." *Proceedings of the National Academy of Sciences* 112(33): E4512–21.

Ericson, R. 1999. "How Journalists Visualize Fact." *Annals of the American Academy of Political and Social Science* 560(1): 83–95.

Ericson, Richard, Patricia Baranek, and Janet Chan. 1989. *Negotiating Control: A Study of News Sources*. Toronto: Open University Press.
Erikson, Robert S., Gerald C. Wright, and John P. McIver. 1993. *Statehouse Democracy: Public Opinion and Democracy in American States*. New York: Cambridge University Press.
Everbach, T. 2005. "The 'Masculine' Content of a Female-Managed Newspaper." *Media Report to Women* 33(4): 14–22.
Everbach, T. 2006. "The Culture of a Women-Led Newspaper: An Ethnographic Study of the *Sarasota Herald-Tribune*." *Journalism and Mass Communication Quarterly* 83 (fall): 477–93.
Everbach, Tracy, and Craig Flournoy. 2007. "Women Leave Journalism for Better Pay, Work Conditions." *Newspaper Research Journal* 28(3): 52–64.
"Exclusive: Ruth Bader Ginsburg on Hobby Lobby Dissent." 2015. Yahoo News. http://news.yahoo.com/katie-couric-interviews-ruth-bader-ginsburg-185027624.html
Falk, Erika. 2008. *Women for President: Media Bias in Eight Campaigns*. Chicago, IL: University of Illinois Press.
Fallows, James M. 1997. *Breaking the news: How the media undermine American democracy*. New York: Vintage.
Farhang, Sean, and Gregory Wawro. 2004. "Institutional Dynamics on the US Court of Appeals: Minority Representation under Panel Decision Making." *Journal of Law, Economics, and Organization* 20(2): 299–330.
Faris, Robert M., Hal Roberts, Bruce Etling, Nikki Bourassa, Ethan Zuckerman, and Yochai Benkler. 2017. "Partisanship, Propaganda, and Disinformation: Online Media and the 2016 U.S. Presidential Election." Berkman Klein Center for Internet & Society Research Paper, August 24, 2017. https://cyber.harvard.edu/publications/2017/08/mediacloud
Farnsworth, Stephen J., and S. Robert Lichter. 2003. "The 2000 New Hampshire Democratic Primary and Network News." *American Behavioral Scientist* 46(5): 588–99.
Farnsworth, Stephen J., and S. Robert Lichter. 2011. *The Nightly News Nightmare: Media Coverage of US Presidential Elections, 1988–2008*. Washington DC: Rowman & Littlefield.
Ferree, Myra Marx, et al. 2002. *Shaping Abortion Discourse: Democracy and the Public Sphere in Germany and the United States*. Cambridge: Cambridge University Press.
Ferree, Myra Marx, William A. Gamson, Jürgen Gerhards, and Dieter Rucht. 2002. "Four Models of the Public Sphere in Modern Democracies." *Theory and Society* 31(3): 289–324.
Fetzer, Joel S. 2001. "Shaping Pacifism: The Role of the Local Anabaptist Pastor." In S. E. S. Crawford and L. R. Olson (eds.), *Christian Clergy in American Politics*, 177–86. Baltimore: Johns Hopkins University Press.
Fico, Frederick, and Eric Freedman. 2008. "Biasing influences on Balance in Election News Coverage: An Assessment of Newspaper Coverage of the 2006 US Senate Elections." *Journalism & Mass Communication Quarterly* 85(3): 499–514.
Fico, Frederick, Eric Freedman, and Brad Love. 2006. "Partisan and Structural Balance in Newspaper Coverage of US Senate Races in 2004 with Female Nominees." *Journalism & Mass Communication Quarterly* 83(1): 43–57.
Fico, Frederick, John D. Richardson, and Steven M. Edwards. 2004. "Influence of Story Structure on Perceived Story Bias and News Organization Credibility." *Mass Communication & Society* 7(3): 301–18.
Finer, Lawrence B., and Mia R. Zolna. 2011. "Unintended Pregnancy in the United States: Incidence and Disparities, 2006." *Contraception* 84(5): 478–85. doi:10.1016/j.contraception.2011.07.013
Fiorina, Morris P., Samuel A. Abrams, and Jeremy C. Pope. 2008. "Polarization in the American Public: Misconceptions and Misreadings." *The Journal of Politics* 70(2): 556–60.
Flanagin, Andrew J., and Miriam J. Metzger. 2000. "Perceptions of Internet Information Credibility." *Journalism & Mass Communication Quarterly* 77(3): 515–40.
Flock, Elizabeth. 2012. "Birth Control Hearing on Capitol Hill Had Mostly Male Panel of Witnesses" [photo]. *Washington Post*. Blogs. February 16. http://www.washingtonpost.com/blogs/

worldviews/post/birth-control-hearing-on-capitol-hill- had-all-male-panel-of-witnesses/ 2012/02/16/gIQA6BM5HR_blog.html

Ford, Dana. 2010. "Bus Driver Says He Was Fired Over Planned Parenthood Dispute." *CNN*, July 21. www.cnn.com/2010/CRIME/07/21/texas.bus.abortion.suit/index.html. Accessed 26 June 2019.

Fox, Richard L., and Zoe M. Oxley. 2003. "Gender Stereotyping in State Executive Elections: Candidate Selection and Success." *The Journal of Politics* 65(3): 833–50.

Fragoso, Michael A. 2012. "The EEOC and Federal Contraceptive Regulation." *National Review*, March 23. https://www.nationalreview.com/bench-memos/eeoc-and-federal-contraceptive-regulation-michael-fragoso/

Franklin, Bob, Justin Lewis, and Andrew Williams. 2010. "Journalism, News Sources and Public Relations." In Stuart Allan (ed.), The *Routledge Companion to News and Journalism*, 202–12. New York: Routledge.

Franze, Anthony and R. Reeves Anderson. 2016. "In Unusual Term, Big Year for Amicus Curiae Briefs at the Supreme Court." *The National Law Journal*, September 21. https://www.arnoldporter.com/~/media/files/perspectives/publications/2016/09/in-unusual-term-big-year-for-amicus-curiae-at-the-supreme-court.pdf

Frederick, Brian. 2009. "Are Female House Members Still More Liberal in a Polarized Era? The Conditional Nature of the Relationship between Descriptive and Substantive Representation." *Congress and the Presidency* (January). http://vc.bridgew.edu/polisci_fac/51

Frederick, Brian. 2010. "Gender and Patterns of Roll Call Voting in the US Senate." *Congress & the Presidency* 37(2): 103–24.

Frederick, Brian. 2011. "Gender Turnover and Roll Call Voting in the US Senate." *Journal of Women, Politics & Policy* 32(3): 193–210.

Freedman, Eric, Frederick Fico, and Megan Durisin. 2010. "Gender Diversity Absent in Expert Sources for Elections." *Newspaper Research Journal* 31(2): 20–33.

Freedman, Eric, Frederick Fico, and Brad Love. 2007. "Male and Female Sources in Newspaper Coverage of Male and Female Candidates in US Senate Races in 2004." *Journal of Women, Politics & Policy* 29(1): 57–76.

Frost, Jennifer J., Lori F. Frohwirth and Mia R. Zolna. 2016. "Contraceptive Needs and Services, 2015 Update." *Guttmacher*. www.guttmacher.org/report/contraceptive-needs-and-services-2014-update. Accessed 26 June 2019.

Frum, David. 2012. "Are we being fair to Rush Limbaugh?" *CNN.com*, March 5. https://www.cnn.com/2012/03/05/opinion/frum-rush-limbaugh-fairness/index.html

Gallagher, Margaret. 2001. "Reporting on Gender in Journalism." *Nieman Reports* 55(4): 63–65.

Gallup Organization. 1939. Gallup Poll (AIPO), Dec, 1939 [survey question]. USGALLUP.180A. QA10. Gallup Organization [producer]. Cornell University, Ithaca, NY: Roper Center for Public Opinion Research, iPOLL [distributor], accessed Jun-17-2019.

Gallup Organization. 1961. Gallup Poll (AIPO), Mar, 1961 [survey question]. USGALLUP.61-642.R028. Gallup Organization [producer]. Cornell University, Ithaca, NY: Roper Center for Public Opinion Research, iPOLL [distributor], accessed Jun-17-2019.

Gallup Organization. 1964. Gallup Poll (AIPO), Nov, 1964 [survey question]. USGALLUP.702. Q013. Gallup Organization [producer]. Cornell University, Ithaca, NY: Roper Center for Public Opinion Research, iPOLL [distributor], accessed Jun-17-2019.

Gallup Organization. 2016. Gallup Poll, May, 2016 [survey question]. USGALLUP.052616. R21R. Gallup Organization [producer]. Cornell University, Ithaca, NY: Roper Center for Public Opinion Research, iPOLL [distributor], accessed Jun-18-2019.

Galtung, Johan. 2006. "Peace Journalism as an Ethical Challenge." *Global Media Journal: Mediterranean Edition* 1(2): 1–5.

Gamble, Vanessa, and J. Houck. 1994. "A High Voltage Sensitivity: A History of African-Americans and Birth Control." Committee on Unintended Pregnancy, Institute of Medicine. Washington, DC.

Gamson, W. 1992. *Talking Politics*. Cambridge: Cambridge University Press.
Gamson, William. A., & Modigliani, Andre. 1987. "The Changing Culture of Affirmative Action". In R. A. Braumgart (ed.), *Research in political sociology*, Vol. 3, 137–77. Greenwich, CT: JAI.
Gamson, W. A., and A. Modigliani. 1989. "Media Discourse and Public Opinion on Nuclear Power: A Constructionist Approach." *American Journal of Sociology* 95(1): 1–37.
Gandy, Imani. 2015. "How False Narratives of Margaret Sanger Are Being Used to Shame Black Women." *Rewire*, August 20. www.rewire.news/article/2015/08/20/false-narratives-margaret-sanger-used-shame-black-women/. Accessed 26 June 2019.
Gandy, Oscar H. 1982. *Beyond Agenda Setting: Information Subsidies and Public Policy*. Norwood, NJ: Ablex.
Gans, Herbert. 1979. *Deciding What's News*. New York: Vintage.
Gaziano, Cecilie, and Kristin McGrath. 1986. "Measuring the Concept of Credibility." *Journalism Quarterly* 63(3): 451–62.
Geiger, Kim, and Michael A. Memoli. 2012. "Rush Limbaugh: Obama Calls Sandra Fluke to Express 'Support.'" *Los Angeles Times*, March 2. http://www.latimes.com/news/politics/la-pn-rush-limbaugh-obama-calls-sandra-fluke-to-express-support-20120302,0,6050153.story
Gerber, Alan, Kevin Arceneaux, Cheryl Boudreau, Conor Dowling, Sunshine Hillygus, Thomas Palfrey, Daniel Biggers, and D. J. Henry. 2014. "Reporting Guidelines for Experimental Research: A Report from the Experimental Research Standards Committee." *Journal of Experimental Political Science* 1: 81–98.
Gibson, Megan. 2015. "The Long, Strange History of Birth Control. Time." (February 2). www.time.com/3692001/birth-control-history-djerassi/. Accessed 26 June 2019.
Gieber, Walter. 1956. "Across the Desk: A Study of 16 Telegraph Editors." *Journalism Quarterly* 33(4): 423–32.
Gilbert, Christopher P. 1993. *The Impact of Churches on Political Behavior: An Empirical Study*. Westport, CT: Greenwood.
Gilbert, Jacqueline. 2006. "When Rights Collide: In a Battle between Pharmacists' Right of Free Exercise and Patients' Right to Access Contraception, Who Wins? A Possible Solution for Nevada." w 7: 212.
Gilens, Martin. 1996. "'Race Coding' and White Opposition to Welfare." *American Political Science Review* 90(3): 593–604.
Gillibrand, K. 2012. "Women Are the Key to Holding On to the Senate." https://www.dailykos.com/stories/2012/09/27/1137167/-Women-Are-The-Key-To-Holding-Onto-The-Senate
Ginsburg, Ruth Bader. *Dissenting Opinion. Burwell v. Hobby Lobby Stores*, Inc., 134 S. Ct. 2751.
Gladstone, Brooke and Bob Garfield. 2004. "Rolodex Journalism." *On the Media* (December 24).
Gladwell, M., 2000. "John Rock's Error. What the Co-Inventor of the Pill Didn't Know: Menstruation Can Endanger Women's Health." *New Yorker* (March 13), 52–63.
Goldberg, Michelle. 2012. "The War on Women Backfires." *Newsweek*. https://www.newsweek.com/war-women-backfires-63761
Goldin, Claudia, and Lawrence F. Katz. 2002. "The Power of the Pill: Oral Contraceptives and Women's Career and Marriage Decisions." *Journal of Political Economy* 110(4): 730–70.
Golshan, Tara. 2017. "3 GOP Women Were Left out of the Senate's Obamacare Repeal Effort. They Just Tanked It." *Vox*, (July 18). www.vox.com/policy-and-politics/2017/7/18/15991020/3-gop-women-tank-obamacare-repeal
Goodman, Joseph K., Cynthia E. Cryder, and Amar Cheema. 2013. "Data Collection in a Flat World: The Strengths and Weaknesses of Mechanical Turk Samples." *Journal of Behavioral Decision Making* 26(3): 213–24.
Grabe, Maria Elizabeth, Lelia Samson, Asta Zelenkauskaite, and Narine S. Yegiyan. 2011. "Covering Presidential Election Campaigns: Does Reporter Gender Affect the Work Lives of Correspondents and Their Reportage?" *Journal of Broadcasting & Electronic Media* 55(3): 285–306.
Graber, Doris. 2006. *Mass Media and American Politics*. Seventh edition. Washington, D.C.: CQ Press.

Graber, Doris. 2008. *Mass Media and American Politics*. Eight edition. Washington, D.C.: CQ Press.

Grant, Jan. 1988. "Women As Managers: What They Can Offer to Organizations." *Organizational Dynamics* 16(3): 56–63.

Grant, J. Tobin, and Thomas J. Rudolph. 2003. "Value Conflict, Group Affect, and the Issue of Campaign Finance." *American Journal of Political Science* 47(3): 453–69.

Greenlee, Jill. 2014. *The Political Consequences of Motherhood*. Ann Arbor: University of Michigan Press.

Greer, Jennifer D. 2003. "Evaluating the Credibility of Online Information: A Test of Source and Advertising Influence." *Mass Communication and Society* 6(1): 11–28.

Griffin, Anna. 2014. "Where Are the Women?" *Nieman Reports*. http://niemanreports.org/articles/where-are-the-women/

Grimes, David A. (ed.). 2000. "History and Future of Contraception: Developments over Time." *The Contraception Report* 10(6): 15–25.

Grogan, Colleen M. 1994. "Political-economic Factors Influencing State Medicaid Policy." *Political Research Quarterly* 47(3): 589–622.

Gronke, Paul, and Timothy E. Cook. 2007. "Disdaining the media: The American Public's Changing Attitudes toward the News." *Political Communication* 24(3): 259–81.

Grose, Christian R., Neil Malhotra, and Robert Parks Van Houweling. 2015. "Explaining Explanations: How Legislators Explain their Policy Positions and How Citizens React." *American Journal of Political Science* 59(3): 724–43.

"Guaranteeing Coverage of Contraceptives: Past and Present." 2012, August 1. National Women's Law Center. http://www.nwlc.org/resource/guaranteeing-coverage-contraceptives-past-and-present

Guth, James L., John C. Green, Lyman A. Kellstedt, Corwin E. Smidt, and Margaret M. Poloma. 1997. *The Bully Pulpit: The Politics of Protestant Clergy*. Lawrence: University Press of Kansas.

Guth, James L., John C. Green, Lyman A. Kellstedt, and Corwin E. Smidt. 2005. "Faith and Foreign Policy: A View from the Pews." *The Review of Faith and International Affairs* 3 (Fall): 3–9.

Guttmacher Institute. 2012. State Policies in Brief: Insurance Coverage of Contraceptives. http://www.guttmacher.org/statecenter/spibs/spib_ICC.pdf

Guttmacher Institute. 2014. Facts on Contraceptive Use in the United States. http://www.guttmacher.org/pubs/fb_contr_use.html

Guttmacher Institute. 2018a. Fact Sheet: Contraceptive Use in the United States. July. https://www.guttmacher.org/fact-sheet/contraceptive-use-united-states.

Guttmacher Institute. 2018b. State Laws and Policies: Insurance Coverage of Contraceptives. http://www.guttmacher.org/statecenter/spibs/spib_ICC.pdf

Haider-Markel, Donald P., and Mark R. Joslyn. 2001. "Gun Policy, Opinion, Tragedy, and Blame Attribution: The Conditional Influence of Issue Frames." *Journal of Politics* 63(2): 520–43.

Haidt, Jonathan, and Marc J. Hetherington. 2012. "Look How Far We've Come Apart." *The New York Times*. https://campaignstops.blogs.nytimes.com/2012/09/17/look-how-far-weve-come-apart/

Haidt, Jonathan, and Sam Abrams. 2015. "The Top 10 Reasons American Politics Are so Broken." *Washington Post Wonkblog*. http://www.washingtonpost.com/news/wonkblog/wp/2015/01/07/the-top-10-reasons-american-politicsare-worse-than-ever

Hamilton, Alexander and James Madison. 1788. "Federalist No. 63." *Congress*, www.congress.gov/resources/display/content/The+Federalist+Papers#TheFederalistPapers-63. Accessed June 26, 2019.

Hancock, Ange-Marie. 2004. *The Politics of Disgust: The Public Identity of the Welfare Queen*. New York: New York University Press.

Hancock, Ange-Marie. 2007. "When Multiplication Doesn't Equal Quick Addition: Examining Intersectionality as a Research Paradigm." *Perspectives on Politics* 5 (1): 63–79.

Hansen, Anders. 1991. "The Media and the Social Construction of the Environment." *Media, Culture & Society* 13(4): 443–58.

Hansen, Susan B. 1993. "Differences in Public Policies toward Abortion. Electoral and Policy Context." In Malcolm L. Goggin (ed.), Understanding the New Politics of Abortion, 222–48. Newbury Park, CA: Sage Publications.

Hansen, Susan B. 1997. "Talking about Politics: Gender and Contextual Effects on Political Proselytizing." *The Journal of Politics* 59(1): 73–103.

Hansen, Susan B. 2014. *The Politics of Sex: Public Opinion, Parties, and Presidential Elections*. London: Routledge.

Hardin, Marie, Scott Simpson, Erin Whiteside, and Kim Garris. 2007. "The Gender War in US Sport: Winners and Losers in News Coverage of Title IX." *Mass Communication & Society* 10(2): 211–33.

Harnois, Catherine. 2015. "Race, Ethnicity, Sexuality, and Women's Political Consciousness of Gender." *Social Psychology Quarterly* 78: 365–86.

Harting, Donald, et al. 1969. "Family Planning Policies and Activities of State Health and Welfare Departments." *Public Health Reports* 84(2): 127.

Hartley, John. 1982. *Understanding News*. London: Routledge.

Haugen, Marit S., and Berit Brandth. 1994. "Gender Differences in Modern Agriculture: The Case of Female Farmers in Norway." *Gender & Society* 8(2): 206–29.

Haussman, Melissa. 2013. *Reproductive Rights and the State: Getting the Birth Control, RU-486, and Morning-After Pills and the Gardasil Vaccine to the U.S. Market*. Santa Barbara, CA: Praeger.

Haynes, Chris, Jennifer Merolla, and S. Karthick Ramakrishnan. 2016. *Framing Immigrants: News Coverage, Public Opinion, and Policy*. New York: Russell Sage Foundation.

"HHS Mandate Information Central." 2015. Becket Fund. http://www.becketfund.org/hhsinformationcentral/

Hock, Heinrich. 2007. "The Pill and the College Attainment of American Women and Men." Working Papers wp2007_10_01, Department of Economics, Florida State University..

Holland, Justin. 2013. "Is 'Obamacare' really that long?" *Texas State Financial*. https://txstatefinancial.com/2013/07/27/obamacare-long/

Hollis-Brusky, Amanda. 2015. *Ideas with Consequences: The Federalist Society and the Conservative Counterrevolution*. Studies in Postwar American Political Development. New York, NY: Oxford University Press.

Holman, Mirya R. 2014. *Women in Politics in the American City*. Philadelphia: Temple University Press.

Howe, Amy. 2014. Court Rules in Favor of For-profit Corporations, But How Broadly? In Plain English. *SCOTUS Blog*, 30 June 2014. www.scotusblog.com/2014/06/court-rules-in-favor-of-for-profit-corporations-but-how-broadly-in-plain-english/. Accessed 26 June 2019.

Huber, John D., and Charles R. Shipan. 2002. *Deliberate Discretion?: The Institutional Foundations of Bureaucratic Autonomy*. Cambridge: Cambridge University Press.

Huckfeldt, Robert, Eric Plutzer, and John Sprague. 1993. "Alternative Contexts of Political Behavior: Churches, Neighborhoods, and Individuals." Journal of Politics 55(2): 365–81.

Huckfeldt, Robert, and John Sprague. 1995. *Citizens, Politics, and Social Communication: Information and Influence in an Election Campaign*. New York: Cambridge University Press.

Huddy, Leonie, and Nayda Terkildsen. 1993. "Gender Stereotypes and the Perception of Male and Female Candidates." *American Journal of Political Science* 37(1): 119–47.

Huddy, Leonie, Erin Cassese, and Mary-Kate Lizotte. 2008. "Gender, Public Opinion, and Political Reasoning." In Christina Wolbrecht, Karen Beckwith, and Lisa Baldez (eds.), *Political Women and American Democracy*, 31–49. Cambridge, MA: Cambridge University Press.

Hunter, James Davison. 1991. *Culture Wars*. New York: Basic Books.

Institute of Medicine. 2011. "Clinical Preventive Services for Women: Closing the Gaps." https://www.nap.edu/catalog/13181/clinical-preventive-services-for-women-closing-the-gaps

Institute of Medicine (US) Committee on Unintended Pregnancy. 1995. "The Best Intentions: Unintended Pregnancy and the Well-Being of Children and Families." Edited by S. S. Brown and L. Eisenberg. Washington, DC: National Academies Press.

Institute of Politics at Harvard University. 2012. Attitudes toward Politics and Public Service Survey, Sep, 2012 [survey question]. USIOPHU.12POLPS.R48. Institute of Politics at Harvard University [producer]. Cornell University, Ithaca, NY: Roper Center for Public Opinion Research, iPOLL [distributor], accessed Jun-18-2019.

Iyengar, Shanto. 1991. *Is Anyone Responsible?: How Television Frames Political Issues.* Chicago: University of Chicago Press.

Iyengar, Shanto, and Masha Krupenkin. 2018. "The Strengthening of Partisan Affect." *Political Psychology* 39(1): 201–18.

Iyengar, Shanto, and Adam Simon. 1993. "News Coverage of the Gulf Crisis and Public Opinion: A Study of Agenda-setting, Priming, and Framing." *Communication Research* 20(3): 365–83.

Iyengar, Shanto, Gaurav Sood, and Yphtach Lelkes. 2012. "Affect, Not Ideology: A Social Identity Perspective on Polarization." *Public Opinion Quarterly* 76(3): 405–31.

Iyengar, S., H. Norpoth, and K. S. Hahn. 2004. "Consumer Demand for Election News: The Horserace Sells." *Journal of Politics* 66(1): 157–75.

Jacoby, William G. 2000. "Issue Framing and Public Opinion on Government Spending." *American Journal of Political Science* 44(4): 750–67.

Jamieson, Kathleen Hall. 1993. *Dirty Politics: Deception, Distraction, and Democracy.* Oxford: Oxford University Press.

Jasperson, Amy E., Dhavan V. Shah, Mark Watts, Ronald J. Faber, and David P. Fan. 1998. "Framing and the Public Agenda: Media Effects on the Importance of the Federal Budget Deficit." *Political Communication* 15(2): 205–24.

Jeffres, L. W., C. Cutietta, L. Jae-won, and L. Sekerka. 1999. "Differences of Community Newspaper Goals and Functions in Large Urban Areas." *Newspaper Research Journal* 20(3): 86–98.

Jelen, Ted G. 2009. "Religion and American public Opinion: Social Issues." In C. E. Smidt, L. A. Kellstedt, & J. L. Guth (eds.), *The Oxford Handbook of Religion and American Politics*, 217–42. New York: Oxford University Press.

Jelen, Ted G., and Clyde Wilcox. 1997. "Conscientious Objectors in the Culture War?: A Typology of Attitudes toward Church-state Relations." *Sociology of Religion* 58(3): 277–87.

Jelen, Ted G., and Clyde Wilcox. 2003. "Causes and Consequences of Public Attitudes toward Abortion: A Review and Research Agenda." *Political Research Quarterly* 56(4): 489–500.

Johnson, Thomas J., and Barbara K. Kaye. 1998. "Cruising Is Believing?: Comparing Internet and Traditional Sources on Media Credibility Measures." *Journalism & Mass Communication Quarterly* 75(2): 325–40.

Johnson, Timothy R., Paul J. Wahlbeck, and James F. Spriggs. 2006. "The Influence of Oral Arguments on the US Supreme Court." *American Political Science Review* 100(1): 99–113.

Johnson, Timothy R., et al. 2009. "Inquiring Minds Want to Know: Do Justices Tip Their Hands with Questions at Oral Argument in the US Supreme Court." *Washington University Journal of Law & Policy* 29: 241.

Johnston, Richard. 2006. "Party Identification: Unmoved Mover or Sum of References?" *Annual Review of Political Science* 9: 329–51.

Jones, Bradford S., and Regina P. Branton. 2005. "Beyond Logit and Probit: Cox Duration Models of Single, Repeating, and Competing Events for State Policy Adoption." *State Politics and Policy Quarterly* 5(4): 420–43.

Jon Stewart's Eye on the Ladies. 2015. Comedy Central. http://thedailyshow.cc.com/videos/ktzh26/jon-stewart-s-eye-on-the-ladies

Jost, Timothy. 2014. "Implementing Health Reform: New Accommodations for Employers on Contraceptive Coverage." *Health Affairs*, August 22. https://www.healthaffairs.org/do/10.1377/hblog20140822.040980/full/. Accessed 1 July 2019.

Kahn, Kim Fridkin. 1994. "Does Gender Make a Difference? An Experimental Examination of Sex Stereotypes and Press Patterns in Statewide Campaigns." *American Journal of Political Science* 38(1): 162–95.

Kahn, Kim Fridkin. 1996. *The Political Consequences of Being a Woman: How Stereotypes Influence the Conduct and Consequences of Political Campaigns.* New York: Columbia University Press.

Kalb M. 1998. *The Rise of the New News: A Case Study of Two Root Causes of the Modern Scandal Coverage.* Washington, DC: John F. Kennedy School of Government.

Kamins, Michael A., Meribeth J. Brand, Stuart A. Hoeke, and John C. Moe. 1989. "Two-sided versus One-sided Celebrity Endorsements: The Impact on Advertising Effectiveness and Credibility." *Journal of Advertising* 18(2): 4–10.

Kang, Minah, and Jiho Jang. 2013. "NIMBY or NIABY? Who Defines a Policy Problem and Why: Analysis of Framing in Radioactive Waste Disposal Facility Placement in South Korea." *Asia Pacific Viewpoint* 54(1): 49–60.

Karpowitz, Christopher F., and Tali Mendelberg. 2014. *The Silent Sex: Gender, Deliberation, and Institutions.* Princeton, NJ: Princeton University Press.

Kaufmann, Karen M. 2002. "Culture Wars, Secular Realignment, and the Gender Gap in Party Identification." *Political Behavior* 24(3): 283–307.

Kaufmann Karen M. 2006. "The Gender Gap." *PS: Political Science and Politics.* 39(3):447–53.

Kaufmann, Karen M., and John R. Petrocik. 1999. "The Changing Politics of American Men: Understanding the Sources of the Gender Gap." *American Journal of Political Science* 43(3): 864–87.

Kearney Joseph, D., and W. Merrill Thomas. 2000. "The Influence of Amicus Curiae Briefs on the Supreme Court." *University of Pennsylvania Law Review* 148: 743–855.

Keiser, Lael R., Vicky M. Wilkins, Kenneth J. Meier, and Catherine A. Holland. 2002. "Lipstick and Logarithms: Gender, Institutional Context, and Representative Bureaucracy." *American Political Science Review* 96(3): 553–64.

Kelly, Nathan J., and Christopher Witko. 2014. "Government Ideology and Unemployment in the U.S. States." *State Politics and Policy Quarterly* 14(4): 389–413.

Kenney, Sally J. 2012. *Gender and Justice: Why Women in the Judiciary Really Matter.* New York: Routledge.

Kenton, Sherron B. 1989. "Speaker Credibility in Persuasive Business Communication: A Model Which Explains Gender Differences." *The Journal of Business Communication* 26(2): 143–57.

Kertz, Consuelo Lauda, and Roobina Ohanian. 1992. "Source Credibility, Legal Liability, and the Law of Endorsements." *Journal of Public Policy & Marketing* 11(1): 12–23.

Kilborn, Peter T. 1998. "Pressure Growing to Cover the Cost of Birth Control." *New York Times*, August 2. http://www.nytimes.com/1998/08/02/us/pressure-growing-to-cover-the-cost-of-birth-control.html

Kim, S. T., and D. H. Weaver. 2003. "Reporting on Globalization: A Comparative Analysis of Sourcing Patterns in Five Countries' Newspapers." *Gazette: The International Journal for Communication Studies* 65(2): 121–44.

Kinder, Donald R., and Thomas R. Palfrey (eds.). 1993. *Experimental Foundations of Political Science.* Ann Arbor: University of Michigan Press.

Kinder, Donald R., and Lynn M. Sanders. 1990. "Mimicking Political Debate with Survey Questions: The Case of White Opinion on Affirmative Action for Blacks." *Social Cognition* 8(1): 73–103.

Kinder, Donald R., and Lynn M. Sanders. 1996. *Divided by Color: Racial Politics and Democratic Ideals.* Chicago: University of Chicago Press.

King, Leslie, and Madonna Harrington Meyer. 1997. "The Politics of Reproductive Benefits: US Insurance Coverage of Contraceptive and Infertility Treatments." *Gender and Society: Official Publication of Sociologists for Women in Society* 11(1): 8–30. doi:10.1177/089124397011001002

Kiousis, Spiro. 2001. "Public Trust or Mistrust? Perceptions of Media Credibility in the Information Age." *Mass Communication & Society* 4(4): 381–403.

Kittilson, Miki Caul. 2008. "Representing Women: The Adoption of Family Leave in Comparative Perspective." *Journal of Politics* 70(2): 323–34.

Klarner, Carl. 2013. "State Partisan Balance Data, 1937–2011." *Harvard Dataverse V1.* https://doi.org/10.7910/DVN/LZHMG3

Knoll, Benjamin R. 2009. "And Who Is My Neighbor? Religion and Immigration Policy Attitudes." *Journal for the Scientific Study of Religion* 48(2): 313–31.

Ko, Lisa. 2016. "Unwanted Sterilization and Eugenics Programs in the United States." *PBS*, January 29. www.pbs.org/independentlens/blog/unwanted-sterilization-and-eugenics-programs-in-the-united-states/. Accessed 26 June 2019.

Koch, Jeffrey W. 1999. "Candidate Gender and Assessments of Senate Candidates." *Social Science Quarterly* 80(1): 84–96.

Kohut, Andrew, John C. Green, Robert C. Toth, and Scott Keeter. 2000. *The Diminishing Divide: Religion's Changing Role in American Politics*. Washington DC: Brookings Institution Press.

Koppelman, Alex. 2012. "On Contraception and Liberty." February 16. https://www.newyorker.com/news/news-desk/on-contraception-and-liberty. Accessed 26 June 2019.

Kousser, Thad. 2002. "The Politics of Discretionary Medicaid Spending, 1980–1993." *Journal of Health Politics, Policy and Law* 27(4): 639–72.

Kreitzer, Rebecca J. 2015. "Politics and Morality in State Abortion Policy." *State Politics and Policy Quarterly* 15(1): 41–66.

Kronebusch, Karl. 1997. *Medicaid politics: Policymaking Contexts and the Politics of Group Differences in the American States*. Dissertation Harvard University.

Kubasek, Nancy K., Daniel C. Tagliarina, and Corinne Staggs. 2007. "The Questionable Constitutionality of Conscientious Objection Clauses for Pharmacists." *Journal of Law and Public Policy* 16: 225–64.

Kulik, Carol T., Elissa L. Perry, and Molly B. Pepper. 2003. "Here Comes the Judge: The Influence of Judge Personal Characteristics on Federal Sexual Harassment Case Outcomes." *Law and Human Behavior* 27(1): 69–86.

Kurpius, D. D. 2002. "Sources and Civic Journalism: Changing Patterns of Reporting?" *Journalism and Mass Communication Quarterly* 79(4): 853–66.

Lacy, Stephen, Frederick Fico, and Todd Simon. 1989. "The Relationship among Economic, Newsroom and Content Variables: A Path Analysis." *Journal of Media Economics* 2(2): 51–66.

Ladd, Jonathan. 2009. "The Neglected Power of Elite Opinion Leadership to Produce Antipathy toward the News Media: Evidence from a Survey Experiment." *Political Behavior* 32(1): 29–50.

Ladd, Jonathan McDonald. 2010. "The Neglected Power of Elite Opinion Leadership to Produce Antipathy toward the News Media: Evidence from a Survey Experiment." *Political Behavior* 32(1): 29–50.

Ladd, Jonathan. 2011. *Why Americans Hate the Media and How It Matters*. Princeton, NJ: Princeton University.

Lasorsa, Dominic, and Stephen Reese. 1990. "News Source Use in the Crash of 1987: A Study of Four National Media." *Journalism Quarterly* 67: 60–71.

Lau, Richard R., and Mark Schlesinger. 2005. "Policy Frames, Metaphorical Reasoning, and Support for Public Policies." *Political Psychology* 26(1): 77–114.

Lawless, Jennifer L. 2004. "Women, War, and Winning Elections: Gender Stereotyping in the Post-September 11th era." *Political Research Quarterly* 57(3): 479–90.

Lawless, Jennifer L., and Richard L. Fox. 2010. *It Still Takes a Candidate: Why Women Don't Run for Office*. New York: Cambridge University Press.

Lawrence, R. G. 2000. "Game-Framing the Issues: Tracking the Strategy Frame in Public Policy News." *Political Communication* 17(2): 93–114.

Lax, Jeffrey R., and Justin Phillips. 2012. "The Democratic Deficit in the States." *American Journal of Political Science* 56: 148–66.

Layman, Geoffrey. 2001. *The Great Divide: Religious and Cultural Conflict in American Party Politics*. New York: Columbia University Press.

Layton, Alexi, and Alicia Shepard. 2013. "Lack of Female Sources in NY Times Front-Page Stories Highlights Need for Change," Poynter, July 16. http://www.poynter.org/latest-news/top-stories/217828/lack-of-female-sources-in-new-york-times-stories-spotlights-need-for-change/

Lea, Martin, and Russell Spears. 1992. "Paralanguage and Social Perception in Computer-mediated Communication." *Journal of Organizational Computing and Electronic Commerce* 2(3): 321–41.

Lee, Taeku. 2002. *Mobilizing Public Opinion: Black Insurgency and the Civil Rights Movement.* Chicago: University of Chicago Press.

Lee, Y. 2007. "Effects of Market Competition on Taiwan Newspaper Diversity." *Journal of Media Economics* 20(2): 139–56.

Lee, Taeku, and Mark Schlesinger. 2001. "Signaling in Context: Elite Influence and the Dynamics of Public Support for Clinton's Health Security Act." KSG Faculty Research Working Paper No. RWP01-029. https://papers.ssrn.com/sol3/papers.cfm?abstract_id=284023

Leege, David C., Kenneth D. Wald, Brian S. Krueger, and Paul D. Mueller. 2002. *The Politics of Cultural Differences.* Princeton, NJ: Princeton University Press.

Leeper, Mark Stephen. 1991. "The Impact of Prejudice on Female Candidates: An Experimental Look at Voter Inference." *American Politics Quarterly* 19(2): 248–61.

Lemert, J. B. 1989. *Criticizing the Media: Empirical Approaches.* Newbury Park, CA: Sage.

Len-Ríos, Maria, Amanda Hinnant, and Ji Yeon Jeong. 2012. "Reporters' Gender Affects Views on Health Reporting." *Newspaper Research Journal* 33(3): 76–88.

Len-Ríos, M. E., S. A. Park, G. T. Cameron, D. L. Duke, and M. Kreuter. 2008. "Study Asks If Reporter's Gender or Audience Predict Paper's Cancer Coverage." *Newspaper Research Journal*, 29(2): 91–99.

Len-Ríos, M. E., S. Rodgers, E. Thorson, and D. Yoon. 2005. "Representation of Women in News and Photos: Comparing Content to Perceptions." *Journal of Communication* 55(1): 152–68.

Levendusky, Matthew S. 2009. "The Microfoundations of Mass Polarization." *Political Analysis* 17(2): 162–76.

Lewin, Tamar. 1991. "A Plan to Pay Welfare Mothers for Birth Control." *New York Times on the Web* Feb 9: 9.

Lichter, S. Robert, and Richard Noyes. 1996. Good Intentions Make Bad News: Why Americans Hate Campaign Journalism. Washington DC: Rowman & Littlefield.

Liebler, Carol M., and Susan J. Smith. 1997. "Tracking Gender Differences: A Comparative Analysis of Network Correspondents and Their Sources." Journal of Broadcasting & Electronic Media 41(1): 58–68.

Lillis, M. 2012, March 21. "Pelosi Accuses the GOP of Waging a War on Women in Fundraising Pitch." The Hill. https://thehill.com/homenews/house/217319-pelosi-fundraising-for-democrats-accuses-gop-of-waging-war-on-women

"Lines Crossed: Separation of Church and State. Has the Obama Administration Trampled on Freedom of Religion and Freedom of Conscience?" 2015. U.S. House of Representatives Committee on Oversight and Government Reform, February 16. http://oversight.house.gov/hearing/lines-crossed-separation-of-church-and-state-has-the-obama-administration-trampled-on-freedom-of-religion-and-freedom-of-conscience/

Lipka, Michael. 2013. Majority of U.S. Catholics' Opinions Run Counter to Church on Contraception, Homosexuality. https://www.pewresearch.org/fact-tank/2013/09/19/majority-of-u-s-catholics-opinions-run-counter-to-church-on-contraception-homosexuality/

Liptak, Adam. 2014. Birth Control Order Deepens Divide Among Justices. *NY Times*, July 3. https://www.nytimes.com/2014/07/04/us/politics/supreme-court-order-suspends-contraception-rule-for-christian-college.html. Accessed 26 June 2019.

Lipton-Lubet, Sarah. 2013. "Contraceptive Coverage under the Affordable Care Act: Dueling Narratives and Their Policy Implications." *Journal of Gender Social Policy & the Law* 22(2): 343–385.

Lorber, Judith. 2011. *Gender Inequality: Feminist Theories and Politics.* Oxford: Oxford University Press.

Louis Harris & Associates. 1964. Harris Survey, Feb, 1964 [survey question]. USHARRIS.021064.R1. Louis Harris & Associates [producer]. Cornell University, Ithaca, NY: Roper Center for Public Opinion Research, iPOLL [distributor], accessed Jun-17-2019.

Lowell, Caitlin and Erin Longbottom. 2016. Trans & Non-Binary Folks on Why Birth Control Isn't Just for Cis Women. *NWLC*, November 16. www.nwlc.org/blog/trans-non-binary-folks-on-why-birth-control-isnt-just-for-cis-women/. Accessed 26 June 2019.

Lowell, Staci D. 2004. "Striking a Balance: Finding a Place for Religious Conscience Clauses in Contraceptive Equity Legislation." *The Cleveland State Law Review* 52: 441.

Lowrey, Wilson, Lee B. Becker, and Aswin Punathambekar. 2003. "Determinants of Newsroom Use of Staff Expertise: The Case of International News." *Gazette (Leiden, Netherlands)* 65(1): 41–63.

Luker, Kristin. 1985. *Abortion and the Politics of Motherhood*. Vol. 759. Berkeley: University of California Press.

Lynch, Holly Fernandez. 2010. *Conflicts of Conscience in Health Care: An Institutional Compromise*. Cambridge, MA: MIT Press.

Manning, P. 2001. *News and News Sources: A Critical Introduction*. London: Sage.

Mansbridge, Jane. 1999. "Should Blacks Represent Blacks and Women Represent Women? A Contingent 'Yes.'" *The Journal of Politics* 61(3): 628–57.

Marinucci, C., and J. Garofoli. 2012. "Birth Control Issue Rankles Women of Both Parties." Associated Press, December 27. http://www.sfgate.com/politics/article/Birth-control-issue-rankles-women-of-both-parties-3362577.php

Marist Poll. 2012. Knights of Columbus/Marist Poll, May, 2012 [survey question]. USMARIST.052212KN.R03. Marist College Institute for Public Opinion [producer]. Cornell University, Ithaca, NY: Roper Center for Public Opinion Research, iPOLL [distributor], accessed Jun-18-2019.

Markham, David. 1969. "The Dimensions of Source Credibility of Television Newscasters." *Journal of Communication* 18(1): 57–64.

Marks, Lara. 2010. *Sexual Chemistry: A History of the Contraceptive Pill*. New Haven, CT: Yale University Press.

Martin-Kratzer, Renee, and Esther Thorson. 2007. "Use of Anonymous Sources Declines in U.S. Newspapers." *Newspaper Research Journal* 28: 56–70.

Martin, Nina. 2019. "Lost Mothers." *ProPublica*, (March 9). www.propublica.org/article/lost-mothers-maternal-health-died-childbirth-pregnancy

Mason, Lilliana. 2015. "'I Disrespectfully Agree': The Differential Effects of Partisan Sorting on Social and Issue Polarization." *American Journal of Political Science* 59(1): 128–45.

Mason, Lilliana. 2018. "Ideologues without Issues: The Polarizing Consequences of Ideological Identities." *Public Opinion Quarterly* 82(S1): 280–301.

Mason, Lilliana, and Julie Wronski. 2018. "One Tribe to Bind Them All: How Our Social Group Attachments Strengthen Partisanship." *Political Psychology* 39: 257–77.

Matthes, Jörg. 2009. "What's in a Frame? A Content Analysis of Media Framing Studies in the World's Leading Communication Journals, 1990–2005." *Journalism & Mass Communication Quarterly* 86(2): 349–67.

Matthes, J., and M. Kohring. 2008. "The Content Analysis of Media Frames: Toward Improving Reliability and Validity." *Journal of Communication* 58(2): 258–79.

May, Elaine Tyler. 2011. *America and the Pill: A History of Promise, Peril, and Liberation*. New York: Basic Books.

Mayer, Jeremy. 2004. "Christian Fundamentalists and Public Opinion toward the Middle East." *Social Science Quarterly* 85: 694–712.

McCann, Carole R. 1999. *Birth Control Politics in the United States, 1916–1945*. Ithaca, NY: Cornell University Press.

McCarty, Mary. 2012. "Senate Vote Revives Birth Control Debate; 51–48 Vote Rejects Bill to Overturn Federal Mandate of Contraceptive Coverage." *Dayton Daily News* (March 2).

McCarty, Nolan, Keith Poole, and Howard Rosenthal. 2006. *Polarized America: The Dance of Political Ideology and Unequal Riches*. Cambridge, MA: MIT Press.

McCroskey, James C., and Jason J. Teven. 1999. "Goodwill: A Reexamination of the Construct and Its Measurement." *Communications Monographs* 66(1): 90–103.

McFarlane, Deborah R., and Kenneth J. Meier. 2000. *The Politics of Fertility Control: Family Planning and Abortion Policies in the American States*. New York: Chatham House Publishers.

McFarlane, Deborah R., and Kenneth J. Meier. 2001. *The Politics of Fertility Control: Family Planning and Abortion Policies in the American States*. London: Chatham House Publishers.

McGuire, Kevin T. 1990. "Obscenity, Libertarian Values, and Decision Making in the Supreme Court." *American Politics Quarterly* 18(1): 47–67.

McGuire, Kevin T. 1995. "Repeat Players in the Supreme Court: The Role of Experienced Lawyers in Litigation Success." *The Journal of Politics* 57(1): 187–96.

McGuire, Kevin T., and James A. Stimson. 2004. "The Least Dangerous Branch Revisited: New Evidence on Supreme Court Responsiveness to Public Preferences." *Journal of Politics* 66(4): 1018–35.

McLeod, Douglas M., and Benjamin H. Detenber. 1999. "Framing Effects of Television News Coverage of Social Protest." *Journal of Communication* 49(3): 3–23.

McLeod, Douglas M., Gerald M. Kosicki, and Jack M. McLeod. 1994. "The Expanding Boundaries of Political Communication Effects." In J. Bryant & D. Zillman (eds.), *Media Effects, Advances in Theory and Research*, 123–62. Hillsdale, NJ: Lawrence Erlbaum.

McQuail, Denis. 2000. "Some Reflections on the Western Bias of Media Theory." Asian *Journal of Communication* 10(2): 1–13.

Meier, Kenneth J., and Deborah R. McFarlane. 1993. "The Politics of Funding Abortion: State Responses to the Political Environment." *American Politics Quarterly* 21(1): 81–101.

Meier, Kenneth J., and Jill Nicholson-Crotty. 2006. "Gender, Representative Bureaucracy, and Law Enforcement: The Case of Sexual Assault." *Public Administration Review* 66(6): 850–60.

Merolla, Jennifer L., and Elizabeth J. Zechmeister. 2009. *Democracy at Risk: How Terrorist Threats Affect the Public*. Chicago: University of Chicago Press.

Meyer, P. 1988. "Defining and Measuring Credibility of Newspapers: Developing an Index." *Journalism Quarterly* 65(3): 567–74.

Mezey, Susan Gluck. 1994. "Increasing the Number of Women in Office: Does It Matter?" In Elizabeth Adell Cook, Sue Thomas, and Clyde Wilcox (eds.), *The Year of the Woman: Myths and Realities*, 255–70. Boulder: Westview.

Mikulski, Barbara. 2009. "S.Amdt.2791 to S.Amdt.2786 to H.R.3590—111th Congress (2009–2010)—Actions." December 3. https://www.congress.gov/amendment/111th-congress/senate-amendment/2791/actions

Mikulski Calls for Continued Action to Protect Women's Health Following Dangerous Supreme Court Decision. 2014. *Insurance News Net*, July 16 www.insurancenewsnet.com/oarticle/mikulski-calls-for-continued-action-to-protect-womens-health-following-dangerou-a-530558. Accessed 26 June 2019.

Miller, Jed. 2006. "The Unconscionability of Conscience Clauses: Pharmacists' Consciences and Women's Access to Contraception." *Health Matrix* 16: 237–78.

Miller, Joanne M., and Jon A. Krosnick. 2000. "News Media Impact on the Ingredients of Presidential Evaluations: Politically Knowledgeable Citizens Are Guided by a Trusted Source." *American Journal of Political Science* 44(2): 301–15.

Mills, Kay. 1997. "What Difference Do Women Journalists Make." In Pipa Norris (ed.), *Women, Media and Politics*. Oxford: Oxford University Press.

Mitchell, Amy and Jesse Holcomb. 2016. "State of the News Media 2016." https://www.journalism.org/2016/06/15/state-of-the-news-media-2016/2010/

Moniz, Michelle H., Matthew M. Davis, and Tammy Chang. 2014. "Attitudes about Mandated Coverage of Birth Control Medication and Other Health Benefits in a US National Sample." *JAMA* 311(24): 2539–41.

Mooney, Christopher Z., and Mei-Hsien Lee. 1995. "Legislative Morality in the American states: The Case of Pre-Roe Abortion Regulation Reform." *American Journal of Political Science* 39(3): 599–627.

Morrison, Joseph L. 1965. "Illegitimacy, Sterilization, and Racism a North Carolina Case History." *Social Service Review* 39(1): 1–10.

Mulac, Anthony, James J. Bradac, and Pamela Gibbons. 2001. "Empirical Support for the Gender-as-culture Hypothesis: An Intercultural Analysis of Male/female Language Differences." *Human Communication Research* 27(1): 121–52.

Murray, Patty. 2017. "If You're Not at the Table, You're on the Menu—Senator Patty Murray." *Medium*, (May 23). medium.com/@PattyMurray/if-youre-not-at-the-table-you-re-on-the-menu-932c0f76550a

Myburg, M. 2009. "More Public and Less Experts: A Normative Framework for Reconnecting the Work of Journalists with the Work of Citizens." *Global Media Journal: African Edition* 3(1): 1–14.

National Conference of State Legislatures. 2012. Insurance Coverage for Contraception Laws. http://www.ncsl.org/research/health/insurance-coverage-for-contraception-state-laws.aspx, accessed September 2018.

National Opinion Research Center, University of Chicago. 1974. General Social Survey 1974, Feb, 1974 [survey question]. USNORC.GSS74.R64A. National Opinion Research Center, University of Chicago [producer]. Cornell University, Ithaca, NY: Roper Center for Public Opinion Research, iPOLL [distributor], accessed Jun 17, 2019.

National Opinion Research Center, University of Chicago. 1975. General Social Survey 1975, Feb, 1975 [survey question]. USNORC.GSS75.R58A. National Opinion Research Center, University of Chicago [producer]. Cornell University, Ithaca, NY: Roper Center for Public Opinion Research, iPOLL [distributor], accessed Jun 17, 2019.

National Opinion Research Center, University of Chicago. 1977. General Social Survey 1977, Feb, 1977 [survey question]. USNORC.GSS77.R099A. National Opinion Research Center, University of Chicago [producer]. Cornell University, Ithaca, NY: Roper Center for Public Opinion Research, iPOLL [distributor], accessed Jun 17, 2019.

National Opinion Research Center, University of Chicago. 1982. General Social Survey 1982, Feb, 1982 [survey question]. USNORC.GSS82.R170A. National Opinion Research Center, University of Chicago [producer]. Cornell University, Ithaca, NY: Roper Center for Public Opinion Research, iPOLL [distributor], accessed Jun 17, 2019.

National Opinion Research Center, University of Chicago. 1983. General Social Survey 1983, Feb, 1983 [survey question]. USNORC.GSS83.R203A. National Opinion Research Center, University of Chicago [producer]. Cornell University, Ithaca, NY: Roper Center for Public Opinion Research, iPOLL [distributor], accessed Jun 17, 2019.

National Women's Law Center. 2017. "Fact Sheet: May 2017." https://nwlc.org/wp-content/uploads/2017/05/BC-Benefit-Whats-At-Stake.pdf

Nedelman, Michael, Tami Luhby, Laura Jarrett and MJ Lee. 2017. "Trump Administration Deals Major Blow to Obamacare Birth Control Mandate." *CNN.com*. https://www.cnn.com/2017/10/06/health/trump-birth-control-mandate/index.html

Nelson, Jennifer. 2003. *Women of Color and the Reproductive Rights Movement*. New York: New York University Press.

Nelson, Thomas E., and Donald R. Kinder. 1996. "Issue Frames and Group-centrism in American Public Opinion." *The Journal of Politics* 58(4): 1055–78.

Nelson, Thomas E., and Zoe M. Oxley. 1999. "Issue Framing Effects on Belief Importance and Opinion." *The Journal of Politics* 61(4): 1040–67.

Nelson, David E., and Nancy Signorielli. 2007. "Reporter Sex and Newspaper Coverage of the Adverse Health Effects of Hormone Therapy." *Women & Health* 45(1): 1–15.

Nelson, Thomas E., Rosalee A. Clawson, and Zoe M. Oxley. 1997. "Media Framing of a Civil Liberties Conflict and Its Effect on Tolerance." *American Political Science Review* 91(3): 567–83.

Newport, Frank. 2009. "This Christmas, 78% of Americans Identify as Christian." https://news.gallup.com/poll/124793/this-christmas-78-americans-identify-christian.aspx

Nicholson, Stephen P., and Robert M. Howard. 2003. "Framing Support for the Supreme Court in the Aftermath of Bush v. Gore." *The Journal of Politics* 65(3): 676–95.

Niemi, Richard G., and Jane Junn. 1993. "Civics Courses and the Political Knowledge of High School Seniors." Paper Presented at the Annual Meeting of the American Political Science Association. Washington D.C.

Nikolchev, Alexandra. 2010. "A Brief History of the Birth Control Pill." *PBS*, May 7. www.pbs.org/wnet/need-to-know/health/a-brief-history-of-the-birth-control-pill/480/. Accessed 26 June 2019.

No Más Bebés, Rene Tajima-Peña (dir.). 2015. *GOOD DOCS*.

Norrander, Barbara. 1999. "The Evolution of the Gender Gap." *Public Opinion Quarterly* 63(4): 566–76.

Norrander, Barbara, and Clyde Wilcox. 2008. "The Gender Gap in Ideology." *Political Behavior* 30(4): 503–23.

Noy, Darren. 2009. "When Framing Fails: Ideas, Influence, and Resources in San Francisco's Homeless Policy Field." *Social Problems* 56(2): 223–42.

Nteta, T. M., and K. J. Wallsten. 2012. "Preaching to the Choir? Religious Leaders and American Opinion on Immigration Reform." *Social Science Quarterly* 93(4): 891–910.

Ohanian, Roobina. 1990. "Construction and Validation of a Scale to Measure Celebrity Endorsers' Perceived Expertise, Trustworthiness, and Attractiveness." *Journal of Advertising* 19(3): 39–52.

O'Keefe, D. 1990. *Persuasion*. Newbury Park, CA: Sage Publications.

Olson, Laura R., Wendy Cadge, and James T. Harrison. 2006. "Religion and Public Opinion about Same-sex Marriage." *Social Science Quarterly* 87(2): 340–60.

Olson, L. R., and J. C. Green. 2006. "The Religion Gap." *PS: Political Science & Politics* 39(3): 455–59.

Osborn, Tracy L. 2012. *How Women Represent Women: Political Parties, Gender, and Representation in the State Legislatures*. New York: Oxford University Press.

Pacheco, Julianna. 2013. "The Thermostatic Model of Responsiveness in the American States." *State Politics and Policy Quarterly* 13: 306–32.

Paolacci, Gabriele, Jesse Chandler, and Panagiotis G. Ipeirotis. 2010. "Running Experiments on Amazon Mechanical Turk." *Judgment and Decision Making* 5(5): 411–19.

Pariser, Eli. 2012. *The Filter Bubble: How the New Personalized Web Is Changing What We Read and How We Think*. New York: Penguin Books.

Parkinson, John. 2012. "Women's Health vs. Religious Freedom: House Leaders Debate Birth Control Mandate." ABC News, March 1. http://abcnews.go.com/blogs/politics/2012/03/womens-health-vs-religious-freedom-house-leaders-debate-birth-control-mandate/

Patterson, Thomas. 1993. *Out of Order*. New York: Knopf.

Patterson, Thomas. 2016. "News Coverage of the 2016 General Election: How the Press Failed Voters." https://shorensteincenter.org/news-coverage-2016-general-election/

Pear, Robert. 2012. "Senate Rejects Step Targeting Coverage of Contraception." *New York Times*. https://www.nytimes.com/2012/03/02/us/politics/senate-kills-gop-bill-opposing-contraception-policy.html

Pear, Robert. 2013. "Birth Control Rule Altered to Allay Religious Objections." *New York Times*, February 1. http://www.nytimes.com/2013/02/02/us/politics/white-house-proposes-compromise-on-contraception-coverage.html

Pear, Robert. 2017. "13 Men, and No Women, Are Writing New G.O.P. Health Bill in Senate." *The New York Times*, May 8. www.nytimes.com/2017/05/08/us/politics/women-health-care-senate.html

Pearson, Kathryn, and Logan Dancey. 2011a. "Speaking for the Underrepresented in the House of Representatives: Voicing Women's Interests in a Partisan Era." *Politics & Gender* 7(4): 493–519. doi:10.1017/S1743923X1100033X

Pearson, Kathryn, and Logan Dancey. 2011b. "Elevating Women's Voices in Congress: Speech Participation in the House of Representatives." *Political Research Quarterly* 64(4): 910–23. doi:10.1177/1065912910388190

Pease, T. 1990. "Ducking the Diversity Issue." *Newspaper Research Journal* 11(3): 24–37.

Peresie, Jennifer L. 2005. "Female Judges Matter: Gender and Collegial Decisionmaking in the Federal Appellate Courts." *Yale Law Journal* 114(7): 1759–90.

Perry, Barbara Ann. 1991. *A Representative Supreme Court?: The Impact of Race, Religion, and Gender on Appointments*. Vol. 66. Westport, CT: Greenwood Press.

Pew Research Center. 2015. "Today's Washington Press Corps More Digital, Specialized." http://www.journalism.org/2015/12/03/the-role-of-wire-services/

Pew Research Center. 2016. "Very Few Americans See Contraception as Morally Wrong." https://www.pewforum.org/2016/09/28/4-very-few-americans-see-contraception-as-morally-wrong/

Phillips, Kevin. 2006. *American Theocracy: The Peril and Politics of Radical Religion, Oil and Borrowed Money in the 21st Century.* New York: Viking.

Piper-Aiken, Kimberly. 1999. "Journalists and Gender: An Analysis of the New York Times Coverage of the 1996 US Presidential Election." Annual Meeting of the Association for Education in Journalism and Mass Communication, New Orleans.

Pitkin, Hanna F. 1967. *The Concept of Representation.* Berkeley: University of California Press.

Pitkin, Hanna F. 1972. *The Concept of Representation.* Berkeley: University of California Press.

Poggione, Sarah. 2004. "Exploring Gender Differences in State Legislators' Policy Preferences." *Political Research Quarterly* 57(2): 305–14.

Poindexter, P. M., L. Smith, and D. Heider. 2003. "Race and Ethnicity in Local Television News: Framing, Story Assignments, and Source Selections." *Journal of Broadcasting & Electronic Media* 47(4): 524–36.

Politifact. 2012, August 8. "Barack Obama Says Mitt Romney Opposes Contraception Mandate and Would Cut Planned Parenthood Funding." https://www.politifact.com/truth-o-meter/statements/2012/aug/08/barack-obama/obama-slams-romney-on-contraception-and-planned-pa/

Porto, Mauro P. 2007. "Frame Diversity and Citizen Competence: Towards a Critical Approach to News Quality." *Critical Studies in Media Communication* 24(4): 303–21.

Postlethwaite, Debbie, James Trussell, Anthony Zoolakis, Ruth Shabear, and Diana Petitti. 2007. "A Comparison of Contraceptive Procurement Pre- and Post-Benefit Change." *Contraception* 76(5): 360–65.

Postmes, Tom, Russell Spears, and Martin Lea. 1998. "Breaching or Building Social Boundaries? SIDE-effects of Computer-mediated Communication." *Communication Research* 25(6): 689–715.

Potter, W. J. 1985. "Gender Representation in Elite Newspapers." *Journalism & Mass Communication Quarterly* 62(3): 636–40.

Powers, A., and F. Fico. 1994. "Influences on Use of Sources at Large US Newspapers." *Newspaper Research Journal* 15(4): 87–97.

Poynter Staff. 2018. "New Report Shows Lack of Progress for Women of Color in the Media." https://www.poynter.org/business-work/2018/new-report-shows-lack-of-progress-for-women-of-color-in-the-media/

Price, Kimala. 2010. "What Is Reproductive Justice?: How Women of Color Activists Are Redefining the Pro-choice Paradigm." *Meridians: Feminism, Race, Transnationalism* 10(2): 42–65.

Price, Vincent, David Tewksbury, and Elizabeth Powers. 1997. "Switching Trains of Thought: The Impact of News Frames on Readers' Cognitive Responses." *Communication Research* 24(5): 481–506.

Puro, Steven. 1971. "The Role of the Amicus Curiae in the United States Supreme Court: 1920–1966." PhD thesis, State University of New York, Buffalo.

Quinnipiac University Polling Institute. 2012. Quinnipiac University Poll, Feb, 2012 [survey question]. USQUINN.022312.R54. Quinnipiac University Polling Institute [producer]. Cornell University, Ithaca, NY: Roper Center for Public Opinion Research, iPOLL [distributor], accessed Jun-18-2019.

Rand, David G. 2012. "The Promise of Mechanical Turk: How Online Labor Markets Can Help Theorists Run Behavioral Experiments." *Journal of Theoretical Biology* 299: 172–79.

Ranji, Usha, A. Salganicoff, L. Sobel, and C. Rosenzweig. 2017. "Ten Ways That the House American Health Care Act could affect women." *Kaiser Family Foundation.* http://kff.org/womens-health-policy/issue-brief/ten-ways-that-the-house-american-health-care-act-could-affect-women

Rasmussen, Amy Cabrera. 2011. "Contraception as Health? The Framing of Issue Categories in Contemporary Policy Making." *Administration & Society* 43(8): 930–53.

Rassbach, Eric C. 2013. "The Affordable Care Act Employer Mandate Cases: Regulation versus Conscience on Its Way to the United States Supreme Court." *Oxford Journal of Law and Religion* (February): rwt004. doi:10.1093/ojlr/rwt004

Reed, James. 2014. *The Birth Control Movement and American Society: From Private Vice to Public Virtue*. Princeton, NJ: Princeton University Press.

Reeves, Richard V., and Joanna Venator. 2015. "Sex, Contraception, or Abortion? Explaining Class Gaps in Unintended Childbearing." Brookings Institution. http://www.brookings.edu/research/papers/2015/02/26-class-gaps-in-unintended-childbearing-reeves

Rein, Martin, and Donald Schön. 1994. *Frame Reflection: Toward the Resolution of Intractable Policy Controversies*. New York: Basic Book.

Reingold, Beth. 2000. *Representing Women: Sex, Gender, and Legislative Behavior in Arizona and California*. Chapel Hill: University of North Carolina Press.

Reingold, Beth. 2008. "Women as Office Holders: Linking Descriptive and Substantive Representation." In *Political Women and American Democracy*, edited by Christina Wolbrecht, Karen Beckwith, and Lisa Baldez, 128–47. New York: Cambridge University Press.

Reingold, Beth, and Adrienne R. Smith. 2012. "Welfare Policymaking and Intersections of Race, Ethnicity, and Gender in US State Legislatures." *American Journal of Political Science* 56(1): 131–47.

Rhee, June Woong. 1997. "Strategy and Issue Frames in Election Campaign Coverage: A Social Cognitive Account of Framing Effects." *Journal of Communication* 47(3): 26–48.

Rhode, Deborah L. 2014. *What Women Want: An Agenda for the Women's Movement*. Oxford: Oxford University Press.

Riffe, Dan, Stephen Lacy, and Frederick Fico. 2005. *Analyzing Media Messages: Using Quantitative Content Analysis in Research*. Mahwah, NJ: Lawrence Erlbaum Associates.

Roberts, Dorothy E. 1997. *Killing the Black Body: Race, Reproduction, and the Meaning of Liberty*. New York: Pantheon Books.

Roberts, Dorothy E. 1999. *Killing the Black Body: Race, Reproduction, and the Meaning of Liberty*. New York: Vintage Books.

Roberts Jr., John G. 2005. "Oral Advocacy and the Re-emergence of a Supreme Court Bar." *Journal of Supreme Court History* 30(1): 68–81.

Roberts, Marilyn, and Maxwell McCombs. 1994. "Agenda Setting and Political Advertising: Origins of the News Agenda." *Political Communication* 11(3): 249–62.

Rochefort, David A., and Roger W. Cobb. 1994. *The Politics of Problem Definition: Shaping the Policy Agenda*. Lawrence, Kansas: University Press of Kansas.

Rodgers, S., and E. Thorson. 2000. "'Fixing' Stereotypes in News Photos: A Synergistic Approach with the *Los Angeles Times*." *Visual Communication Quarterly* 7(3): 8–17.

Rodgers, Shelly, and Esther Thorson. 2003. "A Socialization Perspective on Male and Female Reporting." *Journal of Communication* 53(4): 658–75.

Rodgers, Shelly, Esther Thorson, and Michael Antecol. 2000. "'Reality' in the St. Louis Post-Dispatch." *Newspaper Research Journal* 21(3): 51–68.

Rodrique, Jessie M. 1991. "The Afro-American Community and the Birth Control Movement, 1918–1942." Doctoral Dissertations 1896–February 2014. 1173. https://scholarworks.umass.edu/dissertations_1/1173

Rosenfield A., et al. 1991. "Long-term Contraceptives and the Threat of Coercion." Paper presented at Dimensions of New Contraceptive Technologies: Norplant and Low-Income Women. New York, NY: Kaiser Family Foundation.

Rosenkrantz, H. G. 1992. "Welcome to the Gay '90s." *Washington Journalism Review* (December). https://www.questia.com/read/1G1-13401948/welcome-to-the-gay-90s

Rosenthal, Cindy Simon. 2008. "Sports Talk: How Gender Shapes Discursive Framing of Title IX." *Politics & Gender* 4(1): 65–92.

Ross, K. 2007. "The Journalist, the Housewife, the Citizen, and the Press." *Journalism* 8(4): 440–73.

Ross, Loretta J. 1992. "African-American Women and Abortion: A Neglected History." *Journal of Health Care for the Poor and Underserved* 3(2): 274–84.

Ross, Karen, and Cynthia Carter. 2011. "Women and News: A Long and Winding Road." *Media, Culture & Society* 33(8): 1148–65.

Saad, Lydia. 2010. "The New Normal on Abortion: Americans More Pro-Life." Gallup, May 14. https://news.gallup.com/poll/128036/new-normal-abortion-americans-pro-life.aspx

Saad, Lydia. 2012. "Contraception Debate Divides Americans, Including Women." https://news.gallup.com/poll/152963/contraception-debate-divides-americans-including-women.aspLx

Saidel, Judith R., and Karyn Loscocco. 2005. "Agency Leaders, Gendered Institutions, and Representative Bureaucracy." *Public Administration Review* 65(2): 158–70.

Sandstrom, A. 2016. "Women Relatively Rare in Top Positions of Religious Leadership." Pew Research Center. http://www.pewresearch.org/fact-tank/2016/03/02/women-relatively-rare-in-top-positions-of-religious-leadership/

Schattschneider, Elmer Eric. 1975. *The Semisovereign People: A Realist's View of Democracy in America*. Belmont, CA: Wadsworth Publishing Company.

Scheufele, D. A. 1999. "Framing as a Theory of Media Effects." *Journal of Communication* 49(4): 103–22.

Scheufele, D. A. 2000. "Agenda-Setting, Priming, and Framing Revisited: Another Look at Cognitive Effects of Political Communication." *Mass Communication & Society* 3(2): 297–316.

Schneider, Andrea Kupfer, Catherine H. Tinsley, Sandra Cheldelin, and Emily T. Amanatullah. 2010. "Likeability v. Competence: The Impossible Choice Faced by Female Politicians, Attenuated by Lawyers." 17 *Duke Journal of Gender Law & Policy* 17(2): 363–384.

Schoen, Johanna. 2005. *Choice & Coercion: Birth Control, Sterilization, and Abortion in Public Health and Welfare*. Chapel Hill: University of North Carolina Press.

Schow, Ashe, and Danny Johnston. 2014. "Two-Thirds of Briefs Filed with Supreme Court in Hobby Lobby Case Support the Company." *Washington Examiner*, January 29. www.washingtonexaminer.com/two-thirds-of-briefs-filed-with-supreme-court-in-hobby-lobby-case-support-the-company

Schroedel, J. R. 2000. *Is the Fetus a Person? A Comparison of Policies across the Fifty States*. Ithaca, NY: Cornell University Press.

Schudson, Michael. 2003. *The Sociology of News*. San Diego: University of California.

Sears, David O. 1986. "College Sophomores in the Laboratory: Influences of a Narrow Data Base on Social Psychology's View of Human Nature." *Journal of Personality and Social Psychology* 51(3): 515.

Segal, Jeffrey A., and Harold J. Spaeth. *The Supreme Court and the Attitudinal Model Revisited*. New York: Cambridge University Press, 2002.

Segal, Jennifer A. 2000. "Representative Decision Making on the Federal Bench: Clinton's District Court Appointees." *Political Research Quarterly* 53(1): 137–50.

Semetko, Holli A., and Claes H. de Vreese. 2004. *Political Campaigning in Referendums: Framing the Referendum Issue*. London: Routledge.

Semetko, H. A., and P. M. Valkenburg. 2000. "Framing European Politics: A Content Analysis of Press and Television News." *Journal of Communication* 50(2): 93–109.

Senate Bill Analysis AB 3749. 1994. *LegInfo*, August 24. www.leginfo.ca.gov/pub/93-94/bill/asm/ab_3701-3750/ab_3749_cfa_940824_150156_sen_floor. Accessed 26 June 2019.

Shah, Dhavan V., Mark D. Watts, David Domke, and David P. Fan. 2002. "News Framing and Cueing of Issue Regimes: Explaining Clinton's Public Approval in Spite of Scandal." *Public Opinion Quarterly* 66(3): 339–70.

Shapiro, Robert Y., and Harpreet Mahajan. "Gender Differences in Policy Preferences: A Summary of Trends from the 1960s to the 1980s." *Public Opinion Quarterly* 50(1): 42–61.

Shaw, Donald L., Lynda P. Cole, Roy L. Moore, and Richard R. Cole. 1981. "Men versus Women in Bylines." *Journalism Quarterly* 58(1): 103–06.

Shaw, Eugene F. 1973. "Media Credibility: Taking the Measure of a Measure." *Journalism Quarterly* 50(2): 306–11.

Shen, Fuyuan, and Heidi Hatfield Edwards. 2005. "Economic Individualism, Humanitarianism, and Welfare Reform: A Value-based Account of Framing Effects." *Journal of Communication* 55(4): 795–809.

Shepherd, Jack. 1964. "Birth Control and the Poor: A Solution." *Look* 28: 63–67.

Shoemaker, Pamela, and Stephen Reese. 1996. *Mediating the Message: Theories of Influences on Mass Media Content.* New York: Longman.

Shullman, Sarah Levien. 2004. "The Illusion of Devil's Advocacy: How the Justices of the Supreme Court Foreshadow Their Decisions during Oral Argument." *The Journal of Appellate Practice and Process* 6(2): 271.

Sigal, L. V. 1973. *Reporters and Officials: The Organization and Politics of Newsmaking.* Lexington, MA: D. C. Heath.

Silverstein, Gordon. 2009. *Law's Allure: How Law Shapes, Constrains, Saves, and Kills Politics.* Cambridge: Cambridge University Press.

Simien, Evelyn M., and Rosalee A. Clawson. 2004. "The Intersection of Race and Gender: An Examination of Black Feminist Consciousness, Race Consciousness, and Policy Attitudes." *Social Science Quarterly* 85(3): 793–810. doi:10.1111/j.0038-4941.2004.00245.x

Singletary, Michael W. 1976. "Components of Credibility of a Favorable News Source." *Journalism Quarterly* 53(2): 316–19.

Sisk, Gregory C., Michael Heise, and Andrew P. Morriss. 1998. "Charting the Influences on the Judicial Mind: An Empirical Study of Judicial Reasoning." *New York University Law Review* 73(5). http://papers.ssrn.com/sol3/papers.cfm?abstract_id=2447727

Slothuus, Rune. 2005. "Political Taste as a Marker of Class: A Bourdieu Approach to the Study of Public Opinion Formation." *World Political Science* 1(2): 73–98.

Smidt, Corwin. 2005. "Religion and American Attitudes Towards Islam and an Invasion of Iraq." *Sociology of Religion* 66:243–61.

Smith, s.e. 2016. Trans? Good luck accessing Reproductive Health Care. *Rewire News*, May 17. https://rewire.news/article/2016/05/17/trans-reproductive-health-care/. Accessed 30 June 2019.

Smith, Adrienne R., Beth Reingold, and Michael Leo Owens. 2012. "The Political Determinants of Women's Descriptive Representation in Cities." *Political Research Quarterly* 65(2): 315–29.

Smith, Conrad. 1993. "News Sources and Power Elites in News Coverage of the Exxon Valdez Oil Spill." *Journalism Quarterly* 70: 393–403.

Smith, Gregory Allen. 2008. *Politics in the parish: The political influence of catholic priests.* Washington, DC: Georgetown University Press.

Snider, Susannah. 2019. "How Much Birth Control Costs Will Depend on the Method You Use and Your Insurance Coverage." *U.S. News and World Report*, May 2. https://money.usnews.com/money/personal-finance/family-finance/articles/the-cost-of-birth-contro

Sniderman, Paul M., and Sean M. Theriault. 2004. "The Structure of Political Argument and the Logic of Issue Framing." In Willem E. Saris and Paul M. Sniderman (eds.), *Studies in Public Opinion: Attitudes, Nonattitudes, Measurement Error, and Change*, 133–65. Princeton, NJ: Princeton University Press.

Snow, David A., and Robert D. Benford. 1988. "Ideology, Frame Resonance, and Participant Mobilization." *International Social Movement Research* 1(1): 197–217.

Snow, D. A., R. Vliegenthart, and C. Corrigall-Brown. 2007. "Framing the French 'Riots': A Comparative Study of Frame Variation." *Social Forces* 86(2): 385–415.

Soley, Lawrence C. 1989. *The news shapers: The individuals who explain the news.* School of Journalism and Mass Communication: University of Minnesota.

Solinger, Rickie. 1992. *Wake Up Little Susie: Single Pregnancy and Race before Roe v. Wade.* New York: Routledge.

Solinger, Rickie. 2013. *Wake Up Little Susie: Single Pregnancy and Race Before Roe v. Wade.* New York: Routledge.

Soloski, J. 1989. "Sources and Channels of Local News." *Journalism Quarterly* 66: 864–70.

Sonfield, A., and H. A. Pollack. 2013. "The Affordable Care Act and Reproductive Health: Potential Gains and Serious Challenges." *Journal of Health Politics, Policy and Law* 38(2): 373–91. doi:10.1215/03616878-1966342

Songer, Donald R., and Reginald S. Sheehan. 1993. "Interest Group Success in the Courts: Amicus Participation in the Supreme Court." *Political Research Quarterly* 46(2): 339–54.

Speroff, L., and P. Darney. 1996. "Clinical Guidelines for Contraception at Different Ages." *A Clinical Guide for Contraception* 2: 295–321.

Splichal, Sigman L., and Bruce Garrison. 1995. "Gender As a Factor in Newsroom Managers' Views on Covering The Private Lives of Politicians." *Mass Communication Review* 22: 101–08.

Stabile, Susan J. 2004. "State Attempts to Define Religion: The Ramifications of Applying Mandatory Prescription Contraceptive Coverage Statutes to Religious Employers." *Harvard Journal of Law and Public Policy* 28(3): 741–780.

Steele, Janet E. 1995. "Experts and the Operational Bias of Television News: The Case of the Persian Gulf War." *Journalism & Mass Communication Quarterly* 72(4): 799–812.

Sternadori, Miglena Mantcheva, and Esther Thorson. 2009. "Anonymous Sources Harm Credibility of All Stories." *Newspaper Research Journal* 30(4): 54–66.

Stimson, James A. 1991. *Public Opinion in America: Moods, Cycles, and Swings*. Boulder, CO: Westview Press.

Stimson, James A., Michael B. MacKuen, and Robert S. Erikson. 1995. "Dynamic Representation." *American Political Science Review* 89(3): 543–65.

Stone, Deborah A. 1997. *Policy Paradox: The Art of Political Decision Making* (Vol. 13). New York: WW Norton.

Stout, Christopher T., Kelsy Kretschmer, and Leah Ruppanner. 2017. "Gender Linked Fate, Race/ethnicity, and the Marriage Gap in American Politics." *Political Research Quarterly* 70(3): 509–22.

Sullivan, Emily. 2018. "Women of Color Are Severely Underrepresented In Newsrooms, Study Says." *NPR*, March 7. www.npr.org/sections/thetwo-way/2018/03/07/591513558/women-of-color-are-severely-underrepresented-in-newsrooms-study-says. Accessed 26 June 2019.

Sundar, S. Shyam, and Clifford Nass. 2001. "Conceptualizing Sources in Online News." *Journal of Communication* 51(1): 52–72.

Sunstein, Cass R. 2017. "A prison of Our Own Design: Divided Democracy in the Age of Social Media." Democratic Audit UK.

Swers, Michele L. 2002. *The Difference Women Make: The Policy Impact of Women in Congress*. Chicago, IL: University of Chicago Press.

Swers, Michele L. 2013. *Women in the Club: Gender and Policy Making in the Senate*. Chicago, IL: University of Chicago Press.

Tajfel, Henri. 1979. "Individuals and Groups in Social Psychology." *British Journal of Social and Clinical Psychology* 18(2): 183–90.

Tajfel, Henri, and John C. Turner. 1986. "An integrative theory of intergroup conflict." In W. G. Austin & S. Worschel (eds.), *The Social Psychology of Intergroup Relations*, 33–47. Pacific Grove, CA: Brooks/Cole Publishing.

Tankard, J., L. Hendrickson, J. Silberman, K. Bliss, and S. Ghanem. 1991. "Media frames: Approaches to conceptualization and measurement." Paper presented to the Association for Education in Journalism and Mass Communication. Boston, MA.

Tatalovitch, Raymond, and David Schier. 1993. "The Persistence of Ideological Cleavage in Voting on Abortion Legislation in the House of Representatives, 1973–1988." *American Politics Quarterly* 21(1): 125–39.

Tedesco, J. C. 2002. "Network news coverage of campaign 2000: The public voice in context". In Denton, R. E. (ed.), *The 2000 presidential campaign: A communication perspective*, 199–224. Westport, CT: Praeger.

Tedesco, J. C. 2005. "Issue and strategy agenda setting in the 2004 presidential election: Exploring the candidate–journalist relationship." *Journalism Studies* 6(2): 187–201.
Terkel, Amanda. 2017. "Room Full of Men Decides Fate of Women's Health Care." *HuffPost*, March 23. www.huffpost.com/entry/room-men-maternity-coverage_n_58d416e6e4b02d33b749b713
Tewksbury, David, Jennifer Jones, Matthew W. Peske, Ashlea Raymond, and William Vig. 2000. "The Interaction of News and Advocate Frames: Manipulating Audience Perceptions of a Local Public Policy Issue." *Journalism & Mass Communication Quarterly* 77(4): 804–29.
The Center for Consumer Information & Insurance Oversight. Women's Preventive Services Coverage and Non-Profit Religious Organizations. *CMS*, www.cms.gov/CCIIO/Resources/Fact-Sheets-and-FAQs/womens-preven-02012013.html. Accessed June 26, 2019.
Thompson, Kirsten M.J. 2013. "A Brief History of Birth Control in the US." *Our Bodies Ourselves*, (December 14). www.ourbodiesourselves.org/book-excerpts/health-article/a-brief-history-of-birth-control/. Accessed 26 June 2019.
Thorp, Frank, Luke Russert, and Michael O'Brien. 2012. "Boehner calls Limbaugh remarks 'inappropriate.'" *First Read on MSNBC.com*, March 2. http://firstread.msnbc.msn.com/_news/2012/03/02/10561783-boehner-calls-limbaugh-remarks-inappropriate
Tolbert, Caroline J., and Gertrude A. Steuernagel. 2001. "Women Lawmakers, State Mandates and Women's Health." *Women & Politics* 22(2): 1–39.
Totenberg, Nina. 2015. "Record Number of Amicus Briefs Filed In Same-Sex-Marriage Cases." *NPR*, April 28. www.npr.org/sections/itsallpolitics/2015/04/28/402628280/record-number-of-amicus-briefs-filed-in-same-sex-marriage-cases
Tuchman, Gaye. 1977. "The Exception Proves the Rule: The Study of Routine News Practice." *Strategies for Communication Research* 6(1): 43–62.
Tuchman, G. 1978. "Making News: A Study in the Construction of Reality." In Tuchman, G., A. K. Daniels, and J. W. Benét (eds.), *Hearth and Home: Images of Women in the Mass Media*, 3–38. New York: Oxford University Press.
Turk, Judy VanSlyke. 1986. "Information Subsidies and Media Content: A Study of Public Relations Influence on the News." *Journalism and Communication Monographs* 100(1): 1–29.
Turk, Judy VanSlyke. 1987. "Sex-role Stereotyping in Writing the News." *Journalism Quarterly* 64(2): 613–17.
Turk, Judy VanSlyke, and Bob Franklin. 1987. "Information Subsidies: Agenda-setting Traditions." *Public Relations Review* 13(4): 29–41.
USA Today. 2012. Gallup/USA Today Poll, Mar, 2012 [survey question]. USGALLUP.2012TR0325. Q03. Gallup Organization [producer]. Cornell University, Ithaca, NY: Roper Center for Public Opinion Research, iPOLL [distributor], accessed Jun-19-2019.
Valentino, Nicholas A., Matthew N. Beckmann, and Thomas A. Buhr. 2001a. "A Spiral of Cynicism for Some: The Contingent Effects of Campaign News Frames on Participation and Confidence in Government." *Political Communication* 18(4): 347–67.
Valentino, Nicholas A., Thomas A. Buhr, and Matthew N. Beckmann. 2001b. "When the Frame Is the Game: Revisiting the Impact of "Strategic" Campaign Coverage on Citizens' Information Retention." *Journalism & Mass Communication Quarterly* 78(1): 93–112.
Valkenburg, Patti M., Holli A. Semetko, and Claes H. De Vreese. 1999. "The Effects of News Frames on Readers' Thoughts and Recall." *Communication Research* 26(5): 550–69.
VanSickle-Ward, Rachel. 2014. "'Narrow' Hobby Lobby Ruling Dangerously Affirms That Women's Health Is Separate." Talking Points Memo, July 3. http://talkingpointsmemo.com/cafe/narrow-hobby-lobby-ruling-dangerously-affirms-that-women-s-health-is-separate
VanSickle-Ward, Rachel. 2016. "Clinton's Third and Final Debate Performance in the General Election Powerfully Married Policy Expertise with a Validation of Women's Lived Experiences." Presidential Gender Watch 2016. http://presidentialgenderwatch.org/gender-dynamics-final-presidential-debate/

VanSickle-Ward, R., and A. Hollis-Brusky. 2013. "An (Un)Clear Conscience Clause: The Causes and Consequences of Statutory Ambiguity in State Contraceptive Mandates." *Journal of Health Politics, Policy and Law* 38(4): 683–708.

Van Zoonen, L. 1998. "One of the Girls? The Changing Gender of Journalism." In C. Carter, G. Branston, and S. Allan (eds.), *News, Gender, and Power*, 33–46. London: Routledge.

Villegas, Andrew. 2017. "These States Are Moving to Protect Birth Control Access as Congress Debates ACA Repeal." *Rewire*, July 12. www.rewire.news/article/2017/07/12/states-moving-protect-birth-control-access-congress-debates-aca-repeal/. Accessed 26 June 2019.

Vliegenthart, Rens, and Liesbet Van Zoonen. 2011. "Power to the Frame: Bringing Sociology Back to Frame Analysis." *European Journal of Communication* 26(2): 101–15.

Voakes, P. S., J. Kapfer, D. Kurpius, and D. S. Y. Chern. 1996. "Diversity in the News: A Conceptual and Methodological Framework." *Journalism & Mass Communication Quarterly* 73(3): 582–93.

Volden, Craig. 2002. "The Politics of Competitive Federalism: A Race to the Bottom in Welfare Benefits?" *American Journal of Political Science* 46(2): 352–63.

Voorheis, John, Nolan McCarty, and Boris Shor. 2015. "Unequal Incomes, Ideology and Gridlock: How Rising Inequality Increases Political Polarization." Unpublished Working Paper.

Vos, Tim P., and J. David Wolfgang. 2018. "Journalists' Normative Constructions of Political Viewpoint Diversity." *Journalism Studies* 19(6): 764–81.

Wald, Kenneth D., and Graham B. Glover. 2007. "Theological Perspectives on Gay Unions." In Craig Rimmerman and Clyde Wilcox (eds.), *The Politics of Same-Sex Marriage*, 105–30. Chicago: University of Chicago Press.

Wald, Kenneth D., Dennis E. Owen, and Samuel S. Hill. 1988. "Churches as Political Communities." *American Political Science Review* 82(2): 531–48.

Walden, Rachel. 2008. "Countdown to Conscience Clause Regulation." *Our Bodies Ourselves*, September 22. www.ourbodiesourselves.org/2008/09/countdown-to-conscience-clause-regulation/. Accessed 26 June 2019.

Walker, Thomas G., and Deborah J. Barrow. 1985. "The Diversification of the Federal Bench: Policy and Process Ramifications." *Journal of Politics* 47(2): 596–617.

Wallsten, K., and T. M. Nteta. 2016. "For You Were Strangers in the Land of Egypt: Clergy, Religiosity, and Public Opinion toward Immigration Reform in the United States." *Politics and Religion* 9(3): 566–604.

Wallsten, Kevin, and Melinda Tarsi. 2016. "Persuasion from Below? An Experimental Assessment of the Impact of Anonymous Comments Sections." *Journalism Practice* 10(8): 1019–40.

Wallsten, Peter and Aizenman, N.C. 2012. "Boehner Vows Action to Overturn Obama Administration Rule on Birth Control." *Washington Post*. https://www.washingtonpost.com/politics/boehner.../gIQAfFRczQ_story.html

Watkins, Elizabeth Siegel. 2001. *On the Pill: A Social History of Oral Contraceptives, 1950–1970*. Baltimore, MD: Johns Hopkins University Press.

Weaver, D., R. Beam, B. Brownlee, P. Voakes, and G. Wilhoit. 2007. *The American Journalist in the 21st Century: U.S. News People at the Dawn of a New Millennium*. Mahwah, NJ: Erlbaum.

Weaver, D., and S. N. Elliott. 1985. "Who Sets the Agenda for the Media? A Study of Local Agenda-Building." *Journalism Quarterly* 62: 87–94.

Weaver, David Hugh, and G. Cleveland Wilhoit. 1992. "The American Journalist in the 1990s: Preliminary Report." In *Freedom Forum*.

Weaver, D., and G. C. Wilhoit. 1996. *The American Journalist in the 1990s: US News People at the End of an Era*. Mahwah, NJ: Erlbaum.

Weibel, David, Bartholomäus Wissmath, and Rudolf Groner. 2008. "How Gender and Age Affect Newscasters' Credibility—An investigation in Switzerland." *Journal of Broadcasting & Electronic Media* 52(3): 466–84.

Weinberg, Jill D., Jeremy Freese, and David McElhattan. 2014. "Comparing Data Characteristics and Results of an Online Factorial Survey between a Population-Based and a Crowdsource-Recruited Sample." *Sociological Science* 1: 292–310.

Weissert, Carol S., ed. 2000. *Learning from Leaders: Welfare Reform, Politics and Policy in Five Midwestern States.* New York: SUNY Press.

Weissert, Carol S. 2004. "Promise and Perils of State-Based Road to Universal Health Insurance in the United States." *The Journal of Health Care Law and Policy* 7(1): 42–69.

Weissert, Carol S., and Susan Silberman. 2002. "Legislative Demands for Bureaucratic Policymaking: The Case of State Medical Boards." *Legislative Studies Quarterly* 27(1): 123–39.

Wetzstein, Cheryl. 2012. "HHS Mandate on Birth Control Cheered, Jeered." *Washington Times.* https://www.washingtontimes.com/news/2012/jan/22/hhs-mandate-on-birth-control-cheered-jeered/

Wetstein, Matthew E. 1996. *Abortion Rates in the United States: The Influence of Opinion and Policy.* New York: SUNY Press.

Wetstein, Matthew E., and Robert B. Albritton. 1995. "Effects of Public Opinion on Abortion Policies and Use in the American States." *Publius: The Journal of Federalism* 25(4): 91–105.

White, D. M. 1950. "The Gatekeeper: A Case Study in the Selection of News." *Journalism Quarterly* 27(4): 383–90.

White, H. Allen, and Julie L. Andsager. 1991. "Newspaper Column Readers' Gender Bias: Perceived Interest and Credibility." *Journalism Quarterly* 68(4): 709–18.

White House Fact Sheet. 2018. "President Donald J. Trump Stands Up for Religious Freedom in The United States." https://www.whitehouse.gov/briefings-statements/president-donald-j-trump-stands-religious-freedom-united-states/

Wilcox, Clyde. 1989. "Popular Support for the New Christian Right." *The Social Science Journal* 26(1): 55–63.

Wilcox, Clyde, and Barbara Norrander. 2001. "Of Mood and Morals: The Dynamics of Opinion on Abortion and Gay Rights." *Understanding Public Opinion,* 2nd ed. Washington, DC: CQ Press.

Wilkins, Vicky M. 2007. "Exploring the Causal Story: Gender, Active Representation, and Bureaucratic Priorities." *Journal of Public Administration Research and Theory* 17(1): 77–94.

Wilson, Joshua C. 2013. *The Street Politics of Abortion: Speech, Violence, and America's Culture Wars.* Stanford, CA: Stanford University Press.

Winston, Pamela. 2002. *Welfare Policymaking in the States: The Devil in Devolution.* Washington, DC: Georgetown University Press.

Wlezien, Christopher B., and Malcolm L. Goggin. 1993. "The Courts, Interest Groups, and Public Opinion about Abortion." *Political Behavior* 15(4): 381–405.

Wolbrecht, Christina. 2000. "Of Presidents and Platforms." In *The Politics of Women's Rights: Parties. Positions, and Change,* 23–72. Princeton, NJ: Princeton University.

Wolbrecht, Christina. 2002. "Female Legislators and the Women's Rights Agenda: From Feminine Mystique to Feminist Era." In C. S. Rosenthal (ed.), *Women Transforming Congress,* 170–239. Norman, OK: University of Oklahoma Press.

Women's Media Center. 2014. "The Status of Women in the US Media." http://www.womensmediacenter.com/bsdimg/2014-Status-Women-Report.pdf?p=page/-/2014-Status-Women-Report.pdf

Woodrum, Eric, and Thomas Hoban. 1992. "Support for Prayer in School and Creationism." *Sociological Analysis* 53(3): 309–21.

Wolbrecht, Christina. 2002. "Explaining Women's Rights Realignment: Convention Delegates, 1972–1992." *Political Behavior* 24(3): 237–82.

Wolbrecht, Christina, Karen Beckwith, and Lisa Baldez (eds.). 2008. *Political Women and American Democracy.* New York: Cambridge University Press.

"Women's Health and Contraception." 2015. C-SPAN.org. http://www.c-span.org/video/?304550-1/womens-health-contraception

Women's Media Center. 2014. "The Status of Women in the US Media." http://www.womensmediacenter.com/bsdimg/2014-Status-Women-Report.pdf?p=page/-/2014-Status-Women-Report.pdf

Yamaguchi, Kazuo. 1991. *Event History Analysis*. Vol. 28. Newbury Park, CA: Sage.

Yarnold, David. 2002. "Why Diversity." *The Quill* 90 (September): 55.

Yin, Robert, K. 1989. *Case Study Research: Design and Methods*. Newbury Park, CA: Sage.

Zaller, John. 1992. *The Nature and Origins of Mass Opinion*. Cambridge: Cambridge University Press.

Zaller, John, and Dennis Chiu. 1996. "Government's Little Helper: US Press Coverage of Foreign Policy Crises, 1945–1991." *Political Communication* 13(4): 385–405.

Zaller, John, and Stanley Feldman. 1992. "A Simple Theory of the Survey Response: Answering Questions versus Revealing Preferences." *American Journal of Political Science* 36(3): 579–616.

Zeldes, G., and F. Fico. 2005. "Race and Gender: An Analysis of Sources and Reporters in the Networks' Coverage of the 2000 Presidential Campaign." *Mass Communication & Society* 8(4): 373–85.

Zeldes, G. A., F. Fico, and A. Diddi. 2007. "Race and Gender: An Analysis of the Sources and Reporters in Local Television Coverage of the 2002 Michigan Gubernatorial Campaign." *Mass Communication & Society* 10(3): 345–63.

INDEX

Note: Tables and figures are indicated by t and f following the page number

For the benefit of digital users, indexed terms that span two pages (e.g., 52–53) may, on occasion, appear on only one of those pages.

abortion
    access to, 45–46
    conscience clause exemptions, 73
    insurance coverage, 40
    legislating, 30
    poverty and, 41
    public opinion on, 154–55
    race, ethnicity, and, 222
abortion policy, 69–70
ACA (Affordable Care Act) contraception mandate, 1–2
accommodation cases, 94–95
"An Act to Discourage Immorality of Unmarried Females by Providing for Sterilization of the Unwed Mother Under Conditions of the Act; and for Related Purposes," 33
Aday, Sean, 132–33
Affordable Care Act (ACA) contraception mandate. *See also* public opinion on ACA contraception mandate; Women's Health Amendment
    conscience clauses, 72, 73–74
    contraceptive coverage prior to, 65–66, 65t
    contraceptive coverage through the, 66–67
    dismantling the, 214–19
    framing the, 12–13, 14
    future of, 45, 215, 227
    identity-based politics in the debate, 223–24
    implementation controversy, 70–73
    legislative support of the, 226–27
    media coverage, 105–7, 106f, 129–31
    policy impact, 225
    precedent preceding, 40, 58–59
    presidential elections and the, 224–25
    public support, 150
    racial dimensions, 222
    repeal, possibility of, 45
    state mandates influence on, 39
    support by news frame, 203f
    women's influence, 219, 220–21
Affordable Care Act (ACA) contraception mandate, conflicts
    Catholic Church, 150, 152, 179–80
    partisanship, 150, 153–54
Affordable Care Act (ACA) contraception mandate, congressional hearings
    media coverage, 105–7, 106f, 129–31
    women's voices, excluding, 74–77, 105–6
Affordable Care Act (ACA) contraception mandate, frames
    analysis of, 78–83, 79f, 81f, 82f
    economic, 79f
    gender effect, 80–83, 81f, 82f
    health, 79f
    morality, 79f
    partisan/strategic, 79f, 80
    religion/religious liberty, 78, 79f
    women's/reproductive rights, 79f, 81–82
Affordable Care Act (ACA), proposal to repeal and replace, 213–17
African Americans, 153
Alito, Samuel, 91, 92, 93–95
Altschull, J. H., 114
Andsager, Julie L., 185

Bartels, Larry M., 168
Beckman, Matthew N., 186–87
Beetlestone, Wendy, 214
Benet, J. W., 108–9
Benford, Robert D., 10

INDEX

Berelson, Bernard R., 172
birth control. *See also* contraception
  costs, 5–6, 105, 225
  delivery methods, 36
  insurance coverage for, 5–6, 105, 155, 156–68, 214
  politicization of, 66–67
  poverty and, 41
  risks, 35, 37
  significance of, 5–7
  term, 27
birth control, history of
  activists role, 37
  advocacy, 26–29
  legal context, 29–32
  race, role of, 32–34
  scientific context, 34–38
birth control information, legislating, 5, 30–31
birth control pill
  FDA approval, 36
  gendered patterns of risk, 35
  prescription coverage policy, 39
  scientific context, 34–37
  user statistics, 36
Bjarnason, Thor, 179
Bleske, G. L., 135
Blithe, Diana, 122
Blunt, Roy, 77
Boehner, John, 105–6
Borchelt, Gretchen, 66
Boxer, Barbara, 122
Braun, Carol Moseley, 63
Brown, Haywood L., 214–15
Buerkle, Ann Marie, 76
Buhr, Thomas A., 186–87
bureaucracy, women in the, 9
Burwell v. Hobby Lobby Stores Inc.
  accommodations, 94–95
  amicus curiae briefs, 96–97, 98, 98*t*, 99*t*
  conscience clause exemption, 88
  gender polarization, 175–77
  insurance coverage ruling, 2, 72
  introduction, 84
  male framing of, 219
  mentioned, 40
  opinion and dissent, 91–94
  oral arguments, 89–91
  public view on ruling, 155–56
  women justice's influence, 217–18, 219
Burwell v. Hobby Lobby Stores Inc., frames
  economic, 98*t*
  gender effect, 98*t*, 99*t*, 100
  health, 98*t*, 99*t*
  morality, 98*t*
  partisan, 98*t*
  religion/religious liberty, 98*t*, 99*t*
  women's/reproductive rights, 98*t*, 99*t*

Burwell v. Hobby Lobby Stores Inc., opinion and dissent frames
  economic, 91, 92*f*, 93–94
  health, 95
  health care, 92*f*
  morality, 92*f*
  partisan, 92*f*
  religion/religious liberty, 91, 92*f*, 93–94
  women's/reproductive rights, 92*f*, 92–93, 95
Burwell v. Hobby Lobby Stores Inc., oral argument frames
  economic, 89–90, 90*f*
  health care, 90*f*, 91
  morality, 90*f*
  partisan, 90*f*
  religion/religious liberty, 89–91, 90*f*
  women's/reproductive rights, 90*f*, 90–91
Byssard, Paul, 29

California, state mandated birth control policy, 40–42
Campbell, David, 179
Campbell, Flann, 28
Capito, Shelley Moore, 214
Cappella, Joseph, 186–87
Carmines, E. G., 154–55
Casey, Bob Jr., 69–70
Catholic Charities of Sacramento v. California, 44
Catholic Charities of the Diocese of Albany v. Serio, 44
Catholic Church, 28–29, 44, 45–46, 150, 152, 179–80
Catholic populations
  on conscience clauses, 48
  public opinion on ACA contraception mandate, 152
  state mandated birth control policy, research, factors influencing scope of, 53–54, 54*t*, 58, 59
  state mandated birth control policy, research, independent variables, 48, 51*t*, 53–54, 54*t*
Chang, Min Chueh, 34
Chang, Tammy, 171
Chern, S. S. Y., 107–8
Chisholm, Shirley, 33–34, 217
Chong, Dennis, 186, 201
Clawson, Rosalee A., 185–86, 188–89
Clement, Paul D., 89
Clinton, Bill, 136
Clinton, Hillary, 225
Collins, Susan, 70, 214
Comstock, Anthony, 30
Comstock Act, 30–31
Comstock laws, 5
condoms, 26
Conestoga Wood Specialties, 88
Congress

federal contraceptive coverage policy, 62–65, 65t, 67
  Senate demographics, 63
  women in, 39–40, 226–27
Conscience and Religious Freedom Division (HHS), 214
conscience clauses
  abortion policy and, 45–46
  ACA (Affordable Care Act) contraception mandate, 73–74
  birth control mandates, 7
  Catholic populations, 48
  expanding the, 226
  factors influencing adoption of, 57–58
  female governors and, 48
  mandated coverage and, 47
  political party affiliation and, 48, 49
  public policy mood, 49
  state mandated birth control policy, 7, 43–44
  states adopting, 50, 53f
  variation in, 46
  women legislators and, 47
contraception. *See also* birth control
  costs, 40–41
  insurance coverage for, 2, 40–41
  legislating, 5, 6
  women's health and, 5–7
contraception debate
  frames in the, 12–15
  framing, male vs. female, 218
  identity-based politics in the, 223–24
  importance of gender in the, 218–22
  partisanship in the, 222–23, 224
  presidential elections and the, 224
  race and ethnicity in the, 221–22
  understanding, importance of, 39
  women's voices, excluding, 215–17, 219, 220
  women's voices, importance of, 226–27
contraceptive devices, legislating the sale of, 5
Contraceptive Equity Act, 41, 42
contraceptives, defined, 43–44
contraceptive users, statistics, 5, 29
Converse, Philip E., 201–2
Correa, Teresa, 134–35
Corrigall-Brown, C., 133–34
Couric, Katie, 2, 94
courts, contraception coverage in the. *See also specific cases*
  analysis, gender and frames, 97–100
  conclusion, 100–1
  literature review, 84–87
  methodology, 87–88
  outcomes, women's impact on, 84–85
courts, contraception coverage in the, amicus curiae briefs
  gender effect, 86, 96–100, 97t, 98t, 99t
  impact of, 86
  women's impact on, 86–87
courts, contraception coverage in the, frames
  economic, 89–90, 90f, 91, 92f, 93–94, 98t
  gendered, 84–85
  gender effect, 98t, 99t
  health, 90f, 91, 92f, 93–94, 95, 98t, 99t
  importance of, 85
  literature review, 84–87
  morality, 90f, 92f, 98t
  partisan, 90f, 92f, 98t
  religion/religious liberty, 89–91, 90f, 95, 96, 98t, 99t
  women's/reproductive rights, 90f, 90–91, 92f, 92–94, 95, 98t, 99–100, 99t
Craft, Stephanie, 113, 134–35
Cummings, Elijah, 75
cynicism, political, 206t, 207

Dancey, Logan, 64–65
Daniels, A. K., 108–9
Davids, Sharice, 226–27
Davis, Angela, 32–33, 171
Debs, Eugene, 27
Deckman, M., 171, 224
DeFelice, Pasquale, 29
Devitt, James, 132–33
de Vreese, C. H., 136, 137, 186–87
diaphragms, 26
Dictionary Act, 91
Djerassi, Carl, 34
Djupe, Paul A., 179
Dole, Elizabeth, 132–33
Domke, David, 136
Downs, Anthony, 172
Druckman, James N., 186, 201
Du Bois, W. E. B., 32–33
Durisin, Megan, 113, 133–34

economic frame
  ACA mandate, 79f
  Burwell v. Hobby Lobby Stores Inc., 89–90, 90f, 91, 92f, 93–94, 98t
  courts, contraception coverage in the, 89–90, 90f, 91, 92f, 93–94, 98t
  defined, 13
  Zubik v. Burwell, 98t
Eig, Jonathan, 25, 29
Eisenstadt v. Baird, 5, 31–32, 151
elite opinion theory, 172–73
Entman, R. M., 10, 131, 133–34, 137
Equal Rights Amendment (ERA), 222
Equity in Prescription Insurance and Contraception Act, 65–66
ethnicity. *See* race and ethnicity
eugenics, 32
Everbach, T., 135
expert witnesses, 11

Faber, Ronald J., 136
Fallows, James M., 139
family planning clinics, 29–30
Fan, David P., 136
federal contraceptive coverage policy. *See also* Affordable Care Act (ACA) contraception mandate
    factors influencing adoption of, 62–65, 67
    introduction, 62–63
    literature review, 63–65
    timeline of events, 65t
Federal Health Benefits Plan, 42
Feingold, Russ, 70
Feree, Mayra Marx, 6
Fico, Frederick, 113, 115–16, 133–35
First Amendment, 43–44, 155–56
Flanagin, Andrew J., 200
Fluke, Sandra, 1–2, 40, 75–76, 77, 105, 175, 217, 221
Fram, Alan, 214
frames
    episodic, 185–86
    individual, 131 (see also *specific frames*)
framing
    the contraception debate, 12–15
    defined, 10
    diagnostic, 10–12
    motivational, 10, 12
    policymaking and, 9–12
    prognostic, 10–12
Franklin, Bob, 107–8
Freedman, Eric, 113, 115–16, 133–35
Frum, David, 105–6

Gamson, W. A., 6
Gans, Herbert, 133
Garfield, Bob, 122
Garrison, Bruce, 135
gay sex, 154–55
gender, operationalizing, 15–16
genocide, racial, 153
Gerhards, Jürgen, 6
Gilbert, Chris, 178, 179
Ginsburg, Ruth Bader, 2, 3, 87, 92–94, 95, 96, 217–18
Gladstone, M., 122
Glass, David H., 33
Goldberg, Michelle, 175
Goldman, Emma, 27
governors, women
    conscience clauses and, 36
    state mandated birth control policy, research, 48, 51t, 53, 54t, 56–57
Greene, J. C., 177–78
Gregoire, Christine, 56–57
Griswold v. Connecticut, 5, 31–32, 151

Haaland, Deb, 226–27
Hahn, K. S., 135, 139–40
Harp, Dustin, 134–35
Harris, Kamala, 213
Hartley, John, 125–26
#WhereAreTheWomen? 2, 75
Haynes, Chris, 12
health care
    preventive, 68, 69–70
    for women, disparities in, 68–69
health frame
    Burwell v. Hobby Lobby Stores Inc., 90f, 91, 92f, 95, 98t, 99t
    contraception and, 5–7
    courts, contraception coverage in the, 90f, 91, 92f, 93–94, 95, 98t, 99t
    defined, 13
Hefner, Paul, 41
Hertzberg, Robert, 41
Hill, Katie, 227
Hill, Samuel S., 178
Hirono, Mazie, 63
Hollis-Brusky, A., 7
hormonal birth control. *See* birth control
Hull, Jane Dee, 56–57
Humanae Vitae (Paul VI), 28

identity politics, 223–24, 225–26
The Impact of Churches on Political Behavior (Gilbert), 178
insurance coverage
    abortion, 40
    birth control, 105
    for birth control, 155, 156–68
    birth control, 214
    preventive contraceptive care, 40–41
    state mandated birth control, groups supporting, 41–42
    state mandated birth control, opposition to, 42
    sterilization, 40
    for Viagra, 41–42
Issa, Darrell, 1–2, 74, 75–76, 105, 129, 217, 221
Iyengar, S., 135, 136, 139–40, 185–86

Jackson, Hannah Beth, 42
Jamieson, Kathleen Hall, 186–87
Jasperson, Amy E., 136
Johnson, Nancy L., 42
journalism studies, 107–8
judiciary, research on women in the, 8–9

Kagan, Elena, 89, 217
Kapfer, J., 107–8
Karpowitz, Christopher, 37–38, 216–17, 219
Kennedy, John F., 29
Kennedy, Justice, 94–95
King, Leslie, 6

Klein, Jane Marie, 223–24
Kurpius, D., 107–8

Lawrence, R. G., 139, 140–41
Lazarsfeld, Paul F., 172
Lee, Taeku, 172
legislators, women
  conscience clauses and, 47
  research on, 8
  state mandated birth control policy, research, 47–48
  state mandated birth control policy and, 39–40, 45, 46–47
  state mandated birth control policy research on, 51t, 52–53, 54t, 56, 58–59
Lewinsky, Monica, 136
Lewis, Justin, 107–8
Limbaugh, Rush, 105–6, 223–24
Lipton-Lubet, Sarah, 12–13
Loscocco, Karyn, 9
Love, Brad, 113, 115–16, 134–35
Lungren, Dan, 76

MacFarlane, Deborah R., 11
Madison, James, 63
Maloney, Carolyn, 2–3, 75
Marker, Russell, 34
Marks, Lara, 35, 36
Marsh, Mary Anne, 221–22
Maryland, 42
Mason, Lilliana, 223
May, Elaine, 27
McCain, John, 105–6, 224
McConnell, Mitch, 213
McCormick, Katherine, 34, 37
McFarlane, Deb, 45–46
McPhee, William N., 172
McTague, J., 171, 224
Mechanical Turk (MTurk) (Amazon), 190–92
media, women in, impact of underrepresentation
  conclusion, 211–12
  consequences, 182–83
  credibility, 182–83
  discussion, 207–11
  frames, 185–86
media, women in, impact of underrepresentation, frames
  credibility, 183–85
  strategic game
    effects, 186–87
    literature review, 186–87
    methodology, experiment #2, 194–98
    results, experiment #2, 201–7
  substantive, effects
    literature review, 185–86
    methodology, experiment #2, 194–98
    results, experiment #2, 201–7
media, women in, impact of underrepresentation, hypotheses
  credibility, 187–88
  framing effects, 188–90
media, women in, impact of underrepresentation, methodology
  MTurk, using, 190–92
  reporter and source gender (experiment #1), 190–94
  substantive and strategic game frames (experiment #2), 194–98
media, women in, impact of underrepresentation, results
  reporter and source gender (experiment #1), 199f, 199–200, 201f
  substantive and strategic game frames (experiment #2), 201–7
media coverage
  ACA congressional hearings, 105–7, 106f
  conclusion, 127–28
  discussion, 124–27
  gender effect, 108–9, 111, 113, 114, 117–19, 218–19
  hypotheses, 114–16
  literature review, 107–14
  presidential election (2016), 224–25
  results, 119–24
media coverage, methodology
  dependent variables, 116–18
  independent variables, 118–19
media coverage, source diversity
  failure of, 125–27
  by gender, 120–22, 121f, 123t
  gender effect, 120–24, 125–27
  importance of, 107–10
  literature review, 107–14
  by type, 120f, 121f, 123t
media coverage, source diversity, influences on
  external pressures, 114
  organizational influences, 113
  personal attributes, 110–11
  professional routines, 112
media credibility, 109–10, 183–85, 187–88, 201f, 209–10
media frames
  defined, 131
  dependent variable, 131–32, 136–37
  economic, 140f, 144f
  elections and partisanship, 140f, 144f
  factors influencing, 143t
  gender, 141–44, 146
  gendered frame, 137–39
  generic, 136
  hypotheses, 137–39
  influence of, 208–9
  influences on, 144–45
  introduction, 130–31

media frames (cont.)
  issue-specific, 136
  literature review, 131–32
  methodology, 136–37
  morality, 140f, 144f
  religious freedom, 140f, 141, 144f, 145–46
  reproductive rights, 140f, 141, 144f
  results, 139–46, 143t, 144f
  strategic game frame, 135, 137, 140–41
  by type, 140f
  women's health, 140f, 144f
media frames, literature review, variables influencing
  external pressures, 135–36
  gender, 132–35
  organizational influences, 134–35
  personal attributes, 132–33
  professional routines, 133–34
Meier, Kenneth, 11, 45–46
Mendelberg, Tali, 37–38, 216–17, 219
Merolla, Jennifer L., 12
Metzger, 200
Meyer, Madonna Harrington, 6
midterm elections (2018), 226–27
Mikulski, Barbara, 62–63, 66, 67–68, 69, 70–71, 219, 223–24
Miller, John, 194–95
Moniz, Michelle H., 171
Monson, Joseph, 179
morality frame
  ACA mandate, 79f
  birth control access and the, 30
  Burwell v. Hobby Lobby Stores Inc., 90f, 92f, 98t
  courts, contraception coverage in the, 90f, 92f, 98t
  defined, 14
  state mandated birth control, 45–46
  women, effect on, 30
  Zubik v. Burwell, 98t
morality politics, 59–60
motherhood
  involuntary, 26–27
  voluntary, 27
  womanhood vs., 28
Murkowski, Lisa, 69–70, 214
Murray, Patty, 68, 213

Negro Project, 32–33
Nelson, Ben, 69–70
Nelson, David E., 132–33
Nelson, Gaylord, 37
Nelson, Thomas E., 185–86, 188–89
Nelson Pill Hearings, 37
news sources, defined, 107–8, 133
Norpoth, H., 135, 139–40
Nteta, T. M., 179

Obama, Barack, and administration, 1–2, 6–7, 72, 94–95, 105–6, 153–54, 155, 175, 224
O'Connor, Sandra Day, 5
Olson, L. R., 177–78
Owen, Dennis E., 178
Oxley, Zoe M., 185–86, 188–89

partisanship
  ACA mandate and, 150, 153–54
  contraception debate and, 222–23, 224
  elections and, 140f, 144f
  women's rights and, 222–23
partisan/strategic game frame
  ACA mandate, 79f, 80
  Burwell v. Hobby Lobby Stores Inc., 90f, 92f, 98t
  courts, contraception coverage in the, 90f, 92f, 98t
  defined, 14
  public opinion on ACA mandate, 172–75, 177f
  Zubik v. Burwell, 98t
Paul VI, 28, 152
Pearson, Kathryn, 64–65
Pelosi, Nancy, 76, 105–6, 153–54, 217
Pence, Mike, 213
Peterson, Steven, 194–95
Pincus, Gregory, 26, 34, 35
Pitkin, Hannah, 7–8, 9
Planned Parenthood, 27
Planned Parenthood of Southeastern Pa. v. Casey, 5
political engagement, gender and, 216–17
pornography, 30
poverty
  abortion and, 41
  birth control and, 41, 45–46
  sterilization, forced, 153
pregnancy, unintentional, 5–6
Pregnancy Discrimination Act, 65–66
pregnancy prevention, historically, 26–27
premarital sex, 154–55
presidential election (2012), 224
presidential election (2016), 224–25
privacy rights, 31–32
Public Health Service Act, 66
public opinion on ACA contraception mandate
  on access to birth control, 151–55, 152f, 207–8
  on access to birth control information, 151–52
  Catholic populations, 152
  conclusion, 180–81
  fluctuations in, 207–8
  introduction, 150
  on paying for birth control, 155–71
  race and ethnicity, 153
  surveys, 157t
public opinion on ACA mandate, structure
  determinants of support, 173t, 174t
  gender, 175–77, 176f, 219
  partisan, 172–75, 177f

religious affiliation/religiosity, 177–80
    studies, 171–72
Putting Prevention First Act, 65–66

race and ethnicity
    ACA mandate, 222
    contraception debate and, 221–22
    public opinion on ACA mandate, 153
    reproduction and, 32–34, 153
    state mandated birth control policy, research, 49–50, 54*t*, 55–56
Ramakrishnan, S. Karthick, 12
Rasmussen, Amy, 12–13
Reese, Stephen, 107–8, 110, 112, 113, 114, 125, 131–32, 133
Reid, Harry, 67
Reingold, Beth, 7–8
Relf v. Weinberger, 153
religion, establishment of, 46
religion and contraception, 28–29
religion/religious freedom frame
    ACA mandate, 78, 79*f*
    Burwell v. Hobby Lobby Stores Inc., 89–91, 90*f*, 92*f*, 93–94, 98*t*, 99*t*
    courts, contraception coverage in the, 89–91, 90*f*, 95, 96, 98*t*, 99*t*
    defined, 13
    establishment of religion vs., 46
    public opinion on ACA mandate, 177–80
    Zubik v. Burwell, 98*t*, 99*t*
Religious Freedom Restoration Act (RFRA), 88, 89–90, 92, 94–95
religious liberty, 215
representation
    descriptive, 7–8, 39–40
    research on, 7–9
    substantive, 7–8, 39–40
reproductive rights, 218
Rice-Wray, Edris, 35
Richards, Cecile, 175, 213, 214–15
Roberts, Dorothy, 32
Roberts, John G. Jr., 88
Rock, John, 29, 34, 35
Rodgers, S., 114, 126–27, 132–33
Roe v. Wade, 73
Rojecki, A., 133–34
Rolodex journalism, 122
Romney, Mitt, 224
Rosenstock, Linda, 70–73
Rosenthal, Cindy Simon, 12
Rucht, Dieter, 6

Saidel, Judith R., 9
Sanger, Margaret, 26, 27–28, 29, 30–31, 32–33, 34, 37
Satterthwaite, Adaline, 35
Scalia, Antonin, 95

Scheufele, D. A., 148–49
Schlesinger, Mark, 172
Sears, David O., 191
Sebelius, Kathleen, 122
Segal, Jeffrey A., 86–87
Semetko, H. A., 136–37, 185–86
Sessions, Jeff, 214–15
Seventeenth Amendment, 63
sex for pleasure, 27, 28
sexuality, regulating, 30
Shah, Dhavan, 136
Shah, Mona, 84
Shaheen, Jeanne, 56–57
Shoemaker, Pamela, 107–8, 110, 112, 113, 114, 125, 131–32, 133
Signorielli, Nancy, 132–33
The Silent Sex (Karpowitz & Mendelberg), 216
Smith, Gregory Allen, 179
Snow, D. A., 10, 133–34
Snowe, D. A., 131–32
Snowe, Olympia J., 42, 70
social identity theory, 188
socioeconomics of unplanned pregnancies, 5–6
Sotomayor, Sonia, 92, 95, 217
Spaeth, Harold J., 86–87
Speier, Jackie, 41
Splichal, Sigman L., 135
Stabenow, Debbie, 68
state mandated birth control policy
    conscience clauses, 7, 43–44
    equity across states, 42–43
    evolution of contraceptive coverage law, 40–42
    exemptions, religious, 40
    factors shaping passage and content, 39–40
    importance of, 45–46
    independent variables, 46–47
    insurance coverage for, 40–42
    legislation, comparing, 42–44
    politics shaping, 44–45
    states adopting, 40–42, 50, 52*f*, 53*f*
    understanding, importance of, 39
    variation in, 46
    women legislators and, 39–40, 45, 46–47
state mandated birth control policy, research
    discussion, 58–61
    literature review, 44–47
state mandated birth control policy, research data and methods, 47–50
    female governor, 48
    independent variables, 51*t*
    women legislators, 47–48
state mandated birth control policy, research, factors influencing scope of
    Catholic populations, 53–54, 54*t*, 58, 59
    Democratic unified government, 54*t*
    discussion, 58–61
    female governor, 53, 54*t*, 56–57

state mandated birth control policy, research, factors influencing scope of (*cont.*)
   morality politics, 59–60
   partisan control of government, 55–56
   public ideology, 54*t*
   public party identification, 53, 54*t*
   public policy mood, 54–55, 54*t*
   public political predisposition, 57–58
   race and ethnicity, 54*t*, 55
   Republican unified government, 54*t*
   women legislators, 52–53, 54*t*, 56, 58–59
state mandated birth control policy, research, independent variables
   Catholic populations, 48, 51*t*, 53–54, 54*t*
   Democratic unified government, 48, 51*t*, 54*t*, 55–56
   female governor, 51*t*, 53, 54*t*, 56–57
   public ideology, 48, 51*t*, 54*t*
   public party identification, 48–49, 51*t*, 54*t*
   public policy mood, 49, 51*t*, 54–55, 54*t*
   race and ethnicity, 49–50, 55–56
   Republican unified government, 48, 51*t*, 54*t*, 55–56
   women legislators, 51*t*, 52–53, 54*t*, 56
state mandated birth control policy, research, results
   adoption of contraceptive mandates, 50–56, 52*f*, 53*f*, 54*t*
   overall, 50
   scope of enacted mandates, 56–58, 57*t*
sterilization
   forced, 32, 33, 153
   insurance coverage for, 40
Steuernagel, Gertrude A., 46
Stimson, J. A., 154–55
Stone, Deborah, 10–11
Stuart, David, 195
Swers, Michele, 63, 64
Swift, Jane, 56–57

Thorson, E., 114, 126–27, 132–33
Tolbert, Caroline J., 46
Trump, Donald, 213, 214–19, 225, 226
Tuchman, G., 108–9

Underwood, Lauren, 227
United States v. One Package of Japanese Pessaries, 31

Valentino, Nicholas A., 186–87, 194–95
Valkenburg, P. M., 136, 185–86
VanSickle-Ward, Rachel, 7
Verrilli, Donald B., 96
Viagra, 41–42
Vliegenhart, R., 133–34
Voakes, P. S., 107–8, 128
Vos, Tim P., 110, 210

Wald, Kenneth D., 178
Wallsten, K., 179
Wanta, Wayne, 113, 134–35
Watkins, Becca, 76
Watts, Mark, 136
wealth gap, 45–46
Welch, Michael R., 179
Welsh, Michelle, 42
Wheaton College, 72
White, H. Allen, 185
white supremacy, 32
Williams, Andres, 107–8
Windham, Lori, 97
Wolbrecht, Christina, 222
Wolfgang, J. David, 110, 210
Wolfson, Alice, 37–38
The Woman Rebel (Sanger), 9, 28
women. *See also* media, women in the
   in the judiciary, research on, 8–9
   morality frame, effect on, 30
   political engagement of, 216–17
Women in the Club (Swers), 63
women of color
   abortion and, 222
   feminist, 33–34
Women's Health Amendment, 62–63, 66, 67–70, 93, 100–1. *See also* Affordable Care Act (ACA) contraception mandate
women's liberation, 27
women's/reproductive rights frame
   ACA mandate, 79*f*, 81–82
   Burwell v. Hobby Lobby Stores Inc., 90–91, 92*f*, 92–93, 95, 98*t*, 99*t*
   courts, contraception coverage in the, 90*f*, 90–91, 92*f*, 92–94, 95, 98*t*, 99–100, 99*t*
   defined, 13
   Zubik v. Burwell, 98*t*, 99*t*
women's rights, partisanship and, 222–23
women's voices, excluding
   congressional oversight hearings, 74–77, 105–6
   contraception debate, 215–17, 219, 220
Wronski, Julie, 223

Yarnold, David, 110

Zaller, John, 168, 172–73, 179
Zubik v. Burwell
   amicus curiae briefs, 96–97, 98, 98*t*, 99*t*
   introduction, 2–3, 84
   mentioned, 220–21
Zubik v. Burwell, frames
   economic, 98*t*
   gender effect, 98*t*, 99*t*, 100
   health, 98*t*, 99*t*
   partisan, 98*t*
   religion, 98*t*, 99*t*
   women's/reproductive rights, 98*t*, 99*t*